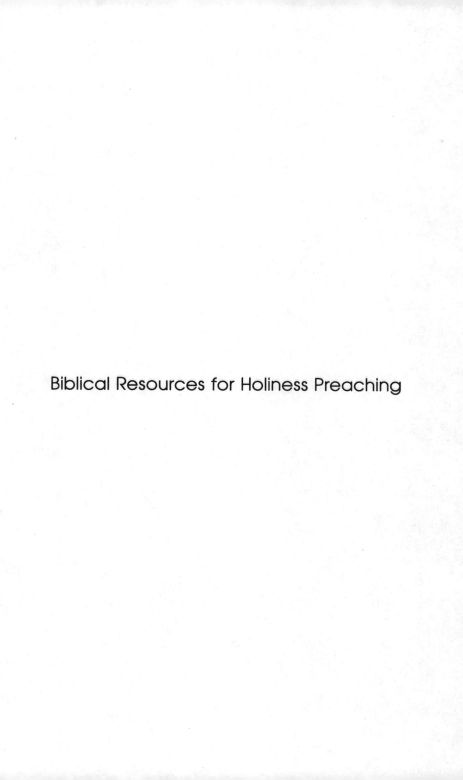

Biblical Resources for Holiness Preaching

Biblical Resources
for Holiness Preaching
From Text to Sermon

Edited

by

H. Ray Dunning and Neil B. Wiseman

Beacon Hill Press of Kansas City
Kansas City, Missouri

Contents

Dedicated to M. A. "Bud" Lunn

Foreword

Biblical Resources for Holiness Preaching—from Text to Sermon provides a rich biblical resource developed by scholars and preachers in the Wesleyan tradition. The volume offers many models of the holiness preaching process. Each chapter opens with a contemporary focus that seeks to highlight the relevance of the text to present concerns. This is followed by an exegesis of the passage and closes with suggestions for application, preaching ideas, and in most cases a partially developed sermon.

The book contains only representative examples of the many scriptural passages bearing on this biblical doctrine. Many central holiness texts have not been included. The editors and publisher believe the book is both comprehensive and thorough enough to help every preaching son of Wesley proclaim the old story to modern folks. The choice of the texts and planning of the volume was done by a representative committee composed of H. Ray Dunning, William M. Greathouse, M. A. Lunn, William Miller, T. Crichton Mitchell, John M. Nielson, Richard S. Taylor, Wesley Tracy, and Neil B. Wiseman.

The contributors are of diverse age, education, interest, experience, and geography. In these pages, veteran theologians and practicing pastors meet with the reader to study, write, and preach the doctrine of Christian holiness. This volume vigorously illustrates G. B. Williamson's premise: "Since the teaching of holiness is so vitally related to all the doctrines that are held fundamental and central by the Church of Jesus Christ, the scriptural and logical preaching of any doctrine will lead to the proclamation of the [doctrine] of holiness."[1] Authentic holiness preaching stands at the heart of the Christian gospel. Two more wide-ranging essays are included in order to provide broad, biblical context for the individual exegeses.

Often while working with these powerful scriptural passages and these gifted contributors, I have felt like I handled electric wires of spiritual vitality as I stood on holy ground in the presence of past and present spiritual giants. Magnificent inspirations for every minister's preaching can be found in these pages. And the process will intensify as the book gets used.

The idea for this book started in the fertile mind and warm heart of M. A. "Bud" Lunn, who was on the staff of Nazarene Publishing House for about 40 years. He served as manager for 27 years, and his father led the House for many years before him as Bud was growing up. This father-and-son team have influenced the literature of the modern holiness movement more than any other two men in recent history. How fitting, then, that the planning for this book took place just a few weeks before Mr. Lunn's retirement from the managerial leadership of Nazarene Publishing House and that it is dedicated to him. This book is the completion of another of his unnumbered publishing dreams.

My heart is filled with an increased eagerness to be more like Christ because of my associations with those who had a part in making this book possible.

—NEIL B. WISEMAN

1. G. B. Williamson, *Preaching Scriptural Holiness* (Kansas City: Beacon Hill Press, 1953), 12.

Note to the Reader

If the reader will look at the topics under which the various essays are grouped, it should become apparent that holiness in human experience can be seen scripturally from a variety of perspectives. That is a fact that can be quite confusing to persons who require simple, stereotyped formulations of doctrine. But the fact is that this great variety provides a richness that enables the preacher to proclaim the truth of full salvation without monotony or sterile repetition.

Another point needs to be stressed. This is NOT a book to be read but a resource to be studied. It does not lend itself to being perused from cover to cover as a theology or history book. It contains studies that can best be appropriated by careful and intensive study with Bible in hand to check out all references and their implications.

In most cases there is a Key Text quoted at the beginning of each chapter. Scripture references from this key text are set in boldface type.

Introduction

One central adage of modern communication theory goes like this: "Words don't have meanings, people do." Someone else has suggested the same idea in a somewhat humorous but more round-about fashion: "I know that you believe you understand what you think I said, but I am not sure you realize that what you heard is not what I meant."

Preaching is not exempt from this problem of communication. In fact, such problems may be intensified in this medium, since there is such a diversity of perceptions in the area of religious language. The term "holiness" is subject to this wide range of meanings. There are few terms that conjure up so many divergent ideas in the minds of those who hear it.

Not only is this the case, but even within the compass of the Bible, "holiness" and its cognate term, "sanctification," have a variety of meanings and applications. This is partly due to the fact that the Bible was produced over a lengthy historical period with its documents growing out of particular historical settings; thus it is dynamic rather than static in nature.

But this diversity also results from the fact that the language is called upon to carry a lot of freight. If the communicator of the word fixes on one denotation of the terms and attempts to apply that to every occurrence, he will inevitably pervert the Scripture.

In part, it is in the light of this broad and variegated use of language and the importance of maintaining the integrity of Scripture that this book is proposed. Its purpose is twofold: (1) to assist the working pastor in his week-to-week commitment to faithfully proclaim the biblical Word including the holiness message, and (2) to expose the pervasiveness of this message in the Bible when its holistic implications are exposed. Many holiness preachers are not aware of the riches of truth that may be mined from the Word of God. In looking for a specific structure of experience or a certain narrow vocabulary, they find themselves in a serious dilemma and resort either to topical preaching, which carries little authority, or to wresting Scripture in a way that does not handle the Word with integrity.

Thus the primary presupposition of this book concerns the importance of biblical preaching, the authority of Scripture, and the necessity for properly interpreting the biblical texts.

Holiness Texts

Perhaps it will be helpful at the outset to attempt a clarification of what is intended by "holiness texts." The ambiguity, as well as the presuppositions present in such a designation, bristles on every side. We have already indicated the variety of denotations of the terms in question.

The term "holiness" is essentially ascribed to God. He alone is holy in a nonderivative sense. It designates Him as in a class by himself. The term itself originally implied "otherness." Because God is holy and there is no reality equal to Him, He has the right to demand undivided loyalty and love with no rivals.

It is this aspect of holiness that defines the essence of sin. It may be defined as "unbelief" (putting one's trust in someone or something other than God), "egocentricity" (the elevation of self to the position of lordship), "idolatry" (giving first place to the creation rather than to the Creator), or "sensuality" (living for self-gratification rather than the glory of God). These various classic proposals avoid a moralistic understanding of sin characteristic of much folk theology that identifies it with certain behaviors. Indeed, certain behaviors may in fact manifest the essence of sin, but they cannot be equated with it without remainder. It is the holiness of God and His right to exclusive love and obedience that alone defines the essence of sin.

Holiness in mankind is always derived. Mankind (or things) is "set apart," thereby belonging to God, by an act of consecration and thus becomes holy. It is the character of God that gives content to this "derived holiness." Hence we can find references that imply no ethical content (at least from a Christian perspective), such as "holy prostitute," one dedicated to the service of the fertility gods of Canaan.

In the OT it early became apparent that God's holiness involved certain ethical qualities: justice, righteousness (concern for the needy), love, faithfulness to promises, and so on. Hence the great prophets, in particular, exhorted the people who belonged to the Lord to demonstrate *His* character in *theirs*. It is on this basis that Amos and Hosea, for instance, cried out against social injustice and covenant faithlessness. As Amos put it, "Let justice roll down like waters, and righteousness like a perennial stream" (5:24, Smith-Goodspeed).

"Sanctification" was originally a ceremonial term that referred to the act or process by which a person or thing became God's property or possession. As such, there was high risk that the ritual that effected this change of ownership could become a ritualism that resulted in no moral transformation. Careful reading of the prophets will reveal how pervasive was the actualization of this risk.

In the OT there eventually emerged the realization that ritual sanctification was inadequate. Out of the recognition that the old covenant made explicit provision for only this kind of sanctification, there arose the longing for a new covenant with new provisions that would make available a *real* sanctification (Jer. 31:31 ff.; Ezek. 36:25 ff.).

In the NT the claim is made that this hope has become a reality (see Hebrews 10). While the ceremonial use of the "holiness vocabulary" persists (see Matt. 23:17), the normative understanding involves the prophetic view of holiness that entails ethical transformation and behavior. Even when the ceremonial character of the language is most clearly present (as in Hebrews), it is always informed by the ethical concern. It is never merely ceremonialism.

The really new revelation in the NT concerns the character of God. There is not a discontinuity of understanding but a deepening. In the light of this new understanding, the ethical holiness of God is defined by the person and work of Christ. On the principle noted above, sanctification becomes the work of the Holy Spirit by which the person (things now tend to drop out of the picture) is really transformed into the character of God as perceived in Jesus Christ. It is seen as the production of Christlikeness in both the individual and the community of faith into which he is incorporated by baptism. Even where the technical vocabulary is not present, if these ideas are present we are dealing with holiness passages.

A further implication of the NT understanding is crucial. Since Jesus Christ not only represents God to man but also embodies the perfect actualization of ideal manhood, He defines what it means for man to be in the image of God. This calls our attention to another strand of holiness teaching in the NT. Every passage that refers explicitly or implicitly to the divine purpose of bringing man into conformity to the image of God (Christ) centrally expresses the holiness message.

John Wesley, the father of the modern holiness movement, insightfully grasped the movement of biblical thought that we have briefly traced, along with the central NT perception of the image of God as defining the goal of God's saving work and thus defining sanctification as a "real" change (justification is a *relative* change), and as to its content it is the "renewal of man in the image of God." When these two definitions are put together, we have a message that

> breathes in the prophecy, thunders in the law, murmurs in the narrative, whispers in the promises, supplicates in the prayers, resounds in the songs, sparkles in the poetry, shines in the types, glows in the imagery, voices in the language, and burns in the spirit of the whole scheme, from its alpha to its omega—its beginning to its end. Holiness! Holiness needed! Holiness required! Holiness offered! Holiness attainable! Holiness a present duty, a present privilege, a present enjoyment, is the progress and completeness of its wondrous theme! It is the truth glowing all over and voicing all through revelation; singing and shouting in all its history, and biography, and poetry, and prophecy, and precept, and promise, and prayer; the great central truth of the system. . . . The wonder is, that all do not see, that any rise up to question, a truth so conspicuous, so glorious, so full of comfort.[1]

Here we have discovered the mother lode of sanctification/holiness truth. What we propose to do in this book is to mine some of the precious ore from this rich vein and make some suggestions toward refining it into the reality that will adorn the people of God so that they may serve and "worship the Lord in the beauty of holiness" (1 Chron. 16:29; Pss. 29:2; 96:9, all KJV).

It should be observed here that we have defined "holiness texts" in terms of content. This is because the Bible gives its attention to this aspect of the truth. It does not address itself in much of a direct way to the structure of religious experience. This is largely derived by inference from biblical passages and experience (see John Wesley's *Plain Account of Christian Perfection*). W. T. Purkiser called attention to this in his small volume titled *Interpreting Christian Holiness:*

> It must be remembered that the letters of the New Testament are all addressed to Christians. They were written from within the context of faith, and directed to those who had been converted.
>
> For this reason, there is no effort on the part of the writers to identify sanctification as a work of grace following conversion or the new birth.[2]

In earlier days many identified the message with the structure and sought to find evidence for it in the biblical material. This resulted in much proof-texting that was less than adequate. When we recognize the fact that the Bible speaks essentially and holistically about the content, we may be relieved from this quest that seems to drive holiness preaching to topical treatments that avoid exposition of Scripture. John Wesley had a firm grasp of this fact and hence manifested great flexibility regarding the structure of experience. He insisted that we may speak of how God normally works but not of how He must work. Early holiness apologist Daniel Steele likewise warned against the imposition of a rigid pattern upon the work of the Spirit in the light of, in William James's famous phrase, "the varieties of religious experience."

> We learn from books and from the lectures of some theological professors that both regeneration and entire sanctification are states of grace sharply defined, entered upon instantaneously after certain definite steps, and followed by certain very marked results. But the young preacher soon learns that there are eminently spiritual members of his church whose experiences have not been in accordance with this regulation manner. They have passed through no marked and memorable crises. Hence they have no spiritual anniversaries. The young pastor is puzzled by these anomalies. At last, if he is wise he will conclude that the books describe normal experiences to which the Holy Spirit does not limit itself, and that an abnormal method of gaining a spiritual change or elevation is by no means to be discounted.[3]

However, in spite of his flexibility concerning the way God, in His sovereignty, works in human life, Wesley insisted that at some point in the divine activity there was a moment—an instantaneous moment—in which perfect love became a reality.

In his sermon "The Repentance of Believers," Wesley makes this point very plain:

> Though we watch and pray ever so much, we cannot wholly cleanse either our hearts or hands. Most sure we cannot, till it shall please our Lord to speak to our hearts again, to speak the second time, "Be clean"; and then only the leprosy is cleansed. Then only, the evil root, the carnal mind, is destroyed; and inbred sin subsists no more. But if there be no such second change, if there be no instantaneous deliverance after justification, if there be *none but* a gradual work of God (that there is a gradual work none denies), then we must be content, as well as we can, to remain full of sin till death; and, if so, we must remain guilty till death, continually *deserving* punishment.[4]

When the message of biblical holiness was transplanted to American soil, it underwent some significant transformations. These changes were not unanticipated among certain of Wesley's followers, such as John Fletcher and Joseph Benson, but they became the central expression of Christian perfection in the pre- and post-Civil War holiness revival. For purposes of this book, it is important to recognize that this change involved the appropriation of scriptural resources upon which Wesley was reticent to draw, particularly the Book of Acts. For Wesley, sanctification was interpreted in Christological terms, whereas the new interpretation spoke in pneumatological (Spirit language) terms. The latter arose chiefly out of a Calvinistic context and emphasized power.[5]

The union of the Wesleyan message with this strand of biblical teaching is classically illustrated in the title of A. M. Hills' book *Holiness and Power.* Arising in America out of revivalism, this interpretation of holiness saw the experience of sanctification to be the dynamic needed to revitalize the church and empower it to carry out its evangelistic mission in the world. This particular way of interpreting holiness became part of the heritage of the holiness denominations that arose out of this revival and finds expression in the exegetical pieces in this volume under the last heading, "The Holy Spirit—Agent of Sanctification," as well as throughout many of the other sections.

It is clear that the holiness movement reads the Scripture with two sets of glasses, and it is fair to allow both to come to expression in a work like this. It is also fair to recognize the divergences between these positions and hope for a legitimate interface between them.

Vocabulary for Biblical Interpretation

This brings us to the functional purpose of this volume: to provide models of biblical interpretation that lay the foundation for preaching the Word of God with integrity. In order to facilitate this discussion, we wish to introduce some vocabulary that is used in the field of biblical study.

Biblical interpretation used to be generally referred to as *hermeneutics.* This big word has fallen into considerable disuse. However, it has been revived in the scholarly community with a somewhat different emphasis. Generally it implies "to bring to understanding." This suggests that a text in an ancient document (like the Bible) comes from an era so far removed from the contemporary world that a considerable chasm exists between the understanding of what the writer meant and what the present-day reader might hear. The task of hermeneutics is to bridge the chasm between these two horizons and bring the original message in its integrity to understanding in the present situation. This involves the whole process of moving "from text to sermon."

A second term still enjoys widespread currency and must be understood. This is the term *exegesis.* Literally it means to "lead out" or "read out" and refers to all those procedures necessary to identify the true meaning of a passage of Scripture. It is often set in contrast to *eisegesis,* which means to "read in." The exegete is the one who attempts to bring the passage to expression in its original significance. Donald Miller has this in mind when he defines *exegesis* as "right listening."

Exegesis is both an art and a science. It requires both special skills that may be learned and a measure of insight that is a native endowment, a gift of God. This latter is certainly one of the "gifts and graces" for which the church should look in validating persons to enter the ministry, since it is the minister's primary responsibility to "preach the Word" (2 Tim. 4:2).

Early exegetes operated on the premise that every passage had multiple meanings. Modern exegetes have long since abandoned this belief, which prevailed from the second century to the Reformation. Biblical scholarship is committed to the premise that a given passage has only one meaning, and no matter who or how many exegetes work on that passage, if they do their work properly, they will come to the same conclusion. If this premise is not true, the logical outcome is that the Bible has no meaning at all. If it means what each of us thinks it means, and there is no *objective* meaning existing apart from our subjective perceptions, then the Bible has no meaning, but there are only meanings that *we* impose on a collection of words.

A legitimate question arises here. Why, then, is there disagreement among interpreters? First, it should be noted that there is a significant unanimity among exegetes on many passages. The diversity among competent biblical scholars is not as extensive as one might at first think. A major threat to this consensus is the multiplicity of idiosyncratic persons and groups who propagate renegade and irresponsible interpretations. In addition, most people tend to think that they are competent interpreters, even though they may have no specialized training. Our Protestant heritage *seems* to encourage this presupposition. But if properly understood, it does not. While putting the Bible in the hands (and language) of the common people is sound, Protestantism provides a corrective to rampant individualism in interpretation by insisting that certain persons in the community should be set aside for a special task, that of being trained in specialized skills and understandings so that they can be the resident "interpreters" in biblical studies and theology. This is the Protestant concept of the ministry. The ministry is a functional office, and lack of training in exegesis is incomprehensible.

However, beyond this there are scriptures that are quite difficult to interpret, and hence a certain tentativeness is appropriate in declaring what they mean. Martin Luther insisted that while the central core of the gospel is clear for even the most simpleminded to grasp, there are some passages that we shall never fully understand because we cannot recover the historical situation that is essential to properly interpret them. These are oftentimes the passages out of which the cults make hay.

This insight reminds us that we are in a more privileged position than Luther or even the last generation for that matter. Why? Because we are the recipients of an explosion of biblical studies that has uncovered great vistas of biblical backgrounds (including the Dead Sea Scrolls) that enhance our capacity to recover what passages mean. Still, there are some ancient passages that have yet to be brought to light. It must be added quickly that none of these affect fundamental doctrines.

No doubt the reader is uneasy over the claim that a passage of Scripture has only one meaning. Many have expressed this concern. It thus should be noted that while there is only one meaning, there are many applications. This provides a significant insight into the difference between *exegesis* and *exposition.* The first involves a high degree of uniformity, but the second allows considerable diversity, depending on the situation addressed and the personality of the communicator of the Word. Preaching, then, is not a stereotyped activity but is the expression of "truth through personality" (Phillips Brooks).

For this reason, in this volume we seek to provide extensive exegetical help (not to be identified with authoritative exegesis) and also some homiletical suggestions as well as full-length sermons, even though these will inevitably reflect the expositor's personality. Preaching someone else's sermon is David fighting in Saul's armor, and in that case Goliath probably wins.

All this suggests that approaching the task of exegesis requires a measure of objectivity. One writer in a fishing magazine observed of springtime fishing that "crappie are caught by tradition," meaning that the angler looks in the same spots every year during the spawning season. He contended, however, that the better fish are found at a deeper level. The same principle is often at work in biblical interpretation. Texts are often interpreted by tradition. Sometimes this blinds the reader to the possibility of deeper and even different meanings. It is traumatic to discover that a traditional passage does not support the interpretation long ascribed to it. But it is the concern of the planning committee of this volume that we maintain the integrity of the Scripture and that the wresting or misusing of texts be stoutly resisted. The result may be a whole reorientation in some cases; but if the authority of the Word is thereby maintained, so be it. Otherwise it is the authority of the person who imposes his views upon the passage that is being respected and not the Scripture itself. Subscribers to the Roman Catholic Council of Trent (1545-63) may allow tradition to sit in judgment upon Scripture, but those of us in the Wesleyan-Arminian segment of the Protestant church are committed to the priority of Scripture in both theory and practice. Tradition must always submit to the authority of the Bible—rightly interpreted.

One more preliminary concern of the planning committee, and others, needs to be aired. This pertains to the matter of proof-texting, which all desire to avoid. Almost everyone today who understands the nature of faithful biblical interpretation recognizes that proof-texting is a bad word, but it turns out to be difficult to define. Let us make a few suggestions here toward defining it and pointing out some of the deficiencies of the method.

Proof-texting generally begins elsewhere than with the biblical material. Older systematic theologies often used this approach to support their theses. Doctrinal statements were set forth and a collection of scriptural references appended to support these ideas. On the surface this does not appear to be a problem. However, the fallacy occurs when the theses were derived deductively from other grounds and then verses cited that had only verbal or artificial connection with the theological proposition deduced from other sources. That is, the biblical support comes in at the tail end of the process, much like the sermon that is prepared and then a text sought to lend some credibility to it.

Perhaps the greatest difficulty lies in the fact that few texts (meaning one or two verses) are able to stand alone. In a very real sense, no text does. It is part of a larger whole. The division of our Bible into chapters and verses often obscures this fact. Hence, if a verse adequately brings to expression the valid message of the larger context, and that message logically supports the theses in question, citing that text is not considered proof-texting in the wrong sense. This implies that the appropriate order of movement in biblical interpretation is from the whole to the part and only then to such doctrinal statements that may be the legitimate formulation of the biblical truth seen in its interconnection with the whole of Scripture. In a word, it means that biblical theology must be done before systematic theology can be done.[6]

W. T. Purkiser seconds this understanding in terms of the way the message of holiness comes to expression in the Scripture:

The doctrine of Christian holiness is based upon the total thrust of the Scriptures. It is not merely a thread or line of truth running through the Word of God. It is rather a network of teaching which is an essential part of the fabric of the whole.

Holiness has its proof texts—although it would be more correct to call them data—evidences which support the conviction that sanctifying grace is real in human life. They should not be ignored. But even more important is the message of the whole. Behind clichés and stereotypes based on a few isolated passages is the rich and varied teaching of the Bible itself.[7]

Steps from Text to Sermon

We are now in a position to address the basic procedure that leads one from text to sermon. It would seem unnecessary to say that generally speaking the first step in sermon preparation is the choice of a text or a biblical theme (in which case the approach is different from what is about to be described). This understands biblical preaching to be "the exposition of a biblical text or of some segment of the Bible's teaching, and the proclamation of that as normative for Christian faith and practice."[8]

From this point, we would suggest that there are two major steps in "exegeting" the text as a preparation for translating its message into preaching or homiletical form.

Step 1. Scholars refer to this step as *grammatico-historical exegesis.* It involves attempting to determine what the text meant in its original setting logically, linguistically, literarily, culturally, socially, and historically.

This procedure should begin with the largest possible context and move logically to the focal point of the passage under investigation. Here, the exegete whose training has included a broad background of biblical studies is at a distinct advantage, since he has more than likely become aware, almost by second nature, that the Bible itself is a distinctive kind of book that reflects a particular character and has a dynamic unity. Hence he can place the section of scripture in which the text is found in the context of this dynamic unity without recourse to extensive background study in every instance. The truth of Eccles. 10:10 is so appropriate here: "If the ax is dull, and one does not sharpen the edge, then he must use more strength" (NKJV). It argues for the necessity of both strong preparation for ministry by intensive Bible study and an ongoing program of continuing education. The following textual treatments will usually illustrate such a background and show how it can be drawn upon to illuminate the text.

Our special concern in this volume is "holiness passages." In the light of this first step in the exegetical method we are looking at those points at which the holistic biblical message of God's purpose to restore man to his lost destiny (image of God) comes significantly to expression, or passages that bear on this theme.

Words are vehicles of communication, hence the way a writer uses terms is also important in bringing his message to understanding. Here a word of caution is necessary. Word usage is the clue to the author's intention, and this is most often derived from the term's logical connection with context. While word studies, so popular in some sectors, have some value as semantic exercises, they do not have the crucial significance they were once thought to have.

The semantic derivation of a word is not nearly as important as the way it is used in a given context. This is especially the case with the NT, where the language is Greek. Tracing a term to its semantic origin may place it in a foreign setting. Hellenistic philosophy is usually the seedbed of the Greek terms used in the NT, but when a NT writer uses them, he is not buying into the content provided from Hellenism. Normally his thinking and language is influenced by Hebrew or OT thought.[9]

Knowledge of Greek and Hebrew provides the exegete with important tools for in-depth biblical study, but the average person without these skills can usually grasp what the writer is attempting to say by paying attention to the logical development of ideas in the flow of the writer's thought. Maybe this is the reason John Wesley's directives for ministerial preparation put study of the Bible and logic at the top of the list of subjects to be mastered.

Step 2. The second stage in determining the meaning of a text is termed *theological exegesis.* In a word, this involves laying bare the theology that informs the text. This step probably calls for more explanation than the first, since it is not quite as familiar but is equally as critical in preparation of preaching.

In this step, the movement from whole to part is even more significant and perhaps more wide-ranging. It involves beginning with the broad background of biblical theology. We are assuming that there is a biblical theology and furthermore that there is an OT and an NT theology that has coherence and may be identified with some certainty. These theologies have a structure that comes to expression in every text with varying degrees of completeness. In some passages it is minimally present, in others with greater fullness. But there are no nontheological passages in the Bible. It also appears to be the case that larger blocks of material are usually required in the OT to give expression to a theological point. Maybe it takes the whole Book of Esther, for example, to give voice to a single theological truth.

It should also be noted that various segments of Scripture have their own unique theological vocabulary and insights. For instance, it is legitimate to speak of a Johannine theology, a Pauline theology, and so on. This means that we cannot uncritically take for granted that the same language means the same thing when used in the Synoptic Gospels and in Hebrews. Each biblical writer retains his own distinctive characteristics while giving expression to the overarching theological truth of the Bible.

The second implication of this point is that it is the theological element that is the authoritative aspect of the passage. Sometimes the literal meaning of the passage is so culturally conditioned as to have applicability only to that historical situation. For instance, Paul's exhortations to slaves and masters in Eph. 6:5-9 and Col. 3:22—4:1 have merely antiquarian interest to the 20-century citizen of democratic society. But the theological truth to which he is giving expression in these time-conditioned terms has enduring significance and binding authority.

The exegetical work has not been completed until the student can summarize the key theological meaning of the passage in a terse proposition.

Lest the reader think we are preoccupied with only a scholar's concern, hear the words of Fred B. Craddock on preaching when he says, "One cannot arrive with any confidence at an interpretation of a text until that interpretation has been illuminated by the theology of the writer from whom the text was taken."[10]

One additional substep is required when exegeting an OT passage. It is a B.C. word in its original meaning but must become an A.D. word in order to be proclaimed in a Christian congregation. This raises the whole question of the Christian use of the OT, an issue debated for centuries. We cannot address that matter in this brief introduction but can only point out that the Christian significance of the OT is seen by looking at it through the spectacles of the person and work of the Lord Jesus Christ, who "filled full" all the OT: Law, Prophets, and Psalms (Writings) (see Luke 24:44).

A Christian preacher would not, for instance, preach as normative the sacrifices of Leviticus 1—7; but he could identify the theology that comes to expression in these rituals, see how this theology is filled full of new content by the sacrifice of Jesus, and proclaim the significance of the Atonement as enriched by the insights of these ancient rites.

Having done this work carefully, the preacher is now in a position to begin to put his research into preachable form. This is the homiletical task. It involves "exegeting" his congregation, since the nature, composition, and situation of his audience will have some input into how the message is to be focused. There is a clear difference between an audience in a prison chapel setting and the congregation of a middle-class church composed almost entirely of mature believers. It is here that the preacher's creativity comes into the picture. He does not create his message, but he looks for effective means to communicate that message that bears the marks of his own personality, thought patterns, and so on. He may be adept at unforced alliteration; he may have a repertoire of significant illustrations that will serve to highlight the truth without becoming ends in themselves; he may choose any number of approaches discussed in standard homiletics texts as the vehicle to proclaim the biblical message that he has unearthed or, as in the case of this volume, had provided for him by others.

One further question needs to be addressed to prepare the reader to plunge into the treasure house that follows. Is there a special method of deriving the message of holiness from the Bible? The answer is both yes and no. There is certainly not a secret key that gives meanings to texts that others cannot see. But it is the case that everyone reads the Bible with a set of theological presuppositions. No sincere seeker after truth will reject a straightforward, clear-cut statement, but inferences from Scripture are a different matter. They are the result of perspective. This claim is explicitly taught in Scripture in 2 Corinthians 3. The Jewish rabbi, says Paul, reads his Bible (OT) with a veil over his mind and thus does not understand it. But when his mind or heart turns to the Lord Jesus, the veil is removed, and his Scripture becomes a new book. Does he see different words? Is there some invisible writing that now becomes visible? No, but his perspective is changed, and he sees implications that he never could see before in the light of his faith in Jesus the Christ.

The distinctive of the Wesleyan position, as Mr. Wesley himself saw, was the claim of the possibility of perfection or freedom from sin *in this life*. This, he argued, was the watershed between the views of the Wesleyan revival and its opponents (often Calvinists). What made the difference between these two positions? To a great extent it was Wesley's "optimism of grace" (Colin Williams' term).

Mr. Wesley built his faith in the possibility of entire sanctification on four foundation stones: (1) promises of perfection, (2) prayers for perfection, (3) commands to perfection, and (4) examples of perfection in Scripture. The premise that informed the Wesleyan revival was that whatever God promises, He provides. The promises are explicit, and the other three are implicit (Wesley's word was "covered") promises. Some would look at human frailties and the pervasiveness of sin and deny the reality of present sanctification, but Wesley looked at the possibilities of grace and affirmed that God could indeed "cut short [His] work . . . in righteousness" (Rom. 9:28, KJV), break "the power of canceled sin," and set "the prisoner free" (Charles Wesley). In the light of this, he saw the "holiness message" in the very warp and woof of Scripture. And so may we!

—H. RAY DUNNING

Endnotes

1. R. S. Foster, *Christian Purity* (New York: Eaton and Mains, 1897), 80.
2. W. T. Purkiser, *Interpreting Christian Holiness* (Kansas City: Beacon Hill Press of Kansas City, 1971), 15.
3. Daniel Steele, *Steele's Answers* (Chicago: Christian Witness Co., 1912), 128.
4. *The Standard Sermons of John Wesley,* ed. Edward H. Sugden (London: Epworth Press, 1961), 2:390-91.
5. See Melvin Dieter, *The Holiness Revival of the Nineteenth Century* (Metuchen, N.J.: Scarecrow Press, 1980); Donald W. Dayton, "The Doctrine of the Baptism with the Holy Spirit: Its Emergence and Significance," *Wesleyan Theological Journal* 13 (Spring 1978): 114-26; Timothy L. Smith, "The Doctrine of the Sanctifying Spirit: Charles G. Finney's Synthesis of Wesleyan and Covenant Theology," ibid., 92-113.
6. See Krister Stendall, "Biblical Theology," in *Interpreter's Dictionary of the Bible,* ed. George A. Buttrick (New York: Abingdon Press, 1962), 1:418-32.

7. Purkiser, *Interpreting,* 9-10.

8. John Bright, *The Authority of the Old Testament* (Grand Rapids: Baker Book House, Twin Books Series, 1975), 163.

9. David Hill, *Greek Words and Hebrew Meanings* (Cambridge: University Press, 1967).

10. Fred B. Craddock, *Preaching* (Nashville: Abingdon Press, 1985), 115.

WILLIAM M. GREATHOUSE

A Pauline Theology of Sanctification

Romans 5—8 constitutes the only thematic treatment of the doctrine of sanctification in the Bible. An understanding of this section is therefore mandatory for the holiness exponent.

The technical treatment of the subject begins at 5:12, but 5:1-11 introduces the theme. The introduction is significant not only in showing the relation of sanctification to God's prior work of justification but also in making it clear that sanctification begins at justification and embraces the total process of salvation.

Paul's text for the Epistle to the Romans is Hab. 2:4, quoted in 1:17, which F. F. Bruce thinks should be literally rendered, "The just by faith/shall live." On this view the RSV translation ("He who through faith is righteous shall live") reflects how Paul employs the text in developing his argument. "He who through faith is righteous" summarizes the apostle's treatment of justification concluding with 4:25. "Shall live" indicates that justification through faith in Christ brings the *life* of salvation (his thesis beginning at 5:1).

Although John Wesley adopts the traditional rendering of 1:17, his analysis of Romans 1—8 accords with Bruce's. "Concerning faith and justification" is Wesley's caption of 1:18—4:25 and "Concerning salvation" his heading for 5:1—8:39. More specifically, in his notes on 5:1 he writes, *"Being justified by faith . . .* is the sum of the preceding chapters." "The fruits of justifying faith" we enjoy through Christ and the gift of the Spirit. He identifies these as "peace, hope, love, and power over sin," and identifies them as "the sum of the fifth, sixth, seventh, and eighth chapters."[1]

Rom. 5:1 is therefore the hinge between the apostle's doctrines of justification and sanctification, the latter being understood negatively as freedom from sin (chaps. 6—7) and positively as renewal in the forfeited image (or "glory") of God by the eschatological gift of the Spirit (see 3:23; 8:17-24, 28-30; cf. 1 Cor. 3:16-18). Initiated at justification and consummated at glorification, the process demands a second crisis of total consecration to God (6:13, 19).

We now turn to Paul's specific treatment of the subject.

Christ and Adam (5:12-21)

While Paul refers first to Adam and then to Christ in spelling out the Fall and our restoration, the section should properly be titled "Christ and Adam." Adam is but **a type** *[typos]* **of the one who was to come** (5:14, RSV). The reality is in Christ, through whom Paul's existence has been recreated (2 Cor. 5:17). Adam is the shadow; Christ is the substance. The emphasis throughout this section is placed upon the "much more" grace that comes through Christ. The Fall in Adam is but the backdrop of our redemption in Christ. The good news is: "A second Adam to the fight / And to the rescue came!"[2]

For Paul, Christ and Adam are more than historical individuals; they are *the heads of two contrasting, yet overlapping, orders of existence.* This is the key to our present passage.

H. Wheeler Robinson coined the term "corporate personality" to express the biblical concept of solidarity. In contrast to modern man influenced by the Enlightenment, who thinks of mankind as an aggregate of discrete individuals, the Hebrews thought in terms of the group—the family, clan, nation, or race. Their thought, about Israel for example, could oscillate freely between the individual and the group. Israel could be either their father or the nation. On this view Paul can think of Adam as either the first man or as mankind (see Gen. 5:1, KJV). Adam as a "corporate personality" is both the first man and "the old man" (Adam—and ourselves in Adam). Christ, on the other hand, is both the Redeemer and "the new man" (Christ—and ourselves in Him). Adam and those in him are the old, fallen humanity; Christ and those in Him are the new, redeemed humanity—His Body, the Church.

Other interpreters prefer to think in terms of representation. When the head of a nation, for example, declares war, he does so as its representative. Thus, in his sin Adam represented us badly. In

Adam's fall **all sinned** (5:12, Wesley, RSV, NIV). By the same token, in Christ all are redeemed. "We are convinced that one has died for all; therefore all have died," Paul writes in a complementary passage. "And he died for all, that those who live might live no longer for themselves but for him who for their sake died and was raised" (2 Cor. 5:14-15, RSV). In Adam all died *in* sin; in Christ all died *to* sin. Each acted as our representative, *for our sake.* Thinking this way, many modern interpreters speak of Adam and Christ as "fields of force." From each radiate forces that touch us profoundly, either for death or life. When Adam disobeyed, **sin entered into the world, and death by sin** (Rom. 5:12, KJV); sin as an enslaving power took possession of the race. But when Christ obeyed the Father, grace as a liberating power became available, so that **where sin abounded, grace did much more abound** (v. 20, KJV).

Whether we think realistically or representatively, or combine the two views as Wesley did, Paul teaches that the crucifixion of Jesus was the crucifixion of **our old man** (cf. 6:6) and His resurrection the creation of "the new man . . . after God . . . in righteousness and true holiness" (Eph. 4:24, KJV).

With this background in mind we can say:

1. Adam and Christ are the heads of two contrasting, overlapping orders of human existence. The old—initiated by Adam's defection—is an order where sin reigns in death (see chap. 7). The new—initiated by Christ's redemption—is an order where grace reigns in righteousness (see chaps. 6 and 8).

2. By nature we are in Adam, through whom we have inherited indwelling sin. "Sin is a racial fact before it is an individual act." Guilt as culpability, however, does not attach to the inborn propensity to self-sovereignty, which is the essence of original sin. But spiritual death does take effect when this propensity provokes us to personal transgression (see 7:9; cf. 4:15).

3. By grace we are in Christ, through whom we receive **the free gift** that **came upon all men unto justification of life** (5:18, KJV). This "free gift" of God's grace is twofold: (1) universal unconditional justification and (2) prevenient grace counteracting original sin. **One man's act of righteousness leads to acquittal and life for all men** (5:18, RSV). Every human being born on earth is covered by the Atonement—until original sin provokes to personal transgression. Furthermore, along with the propensity to self-sovereign-

ty, which is our inheritance in Adam, we receive free grace from Christ in sufficient measure to respond to the gospel and be saved.

4. When as sinners we appropriate God's grace by a personal act of saving faith in Christ, we are recreated and incorporated into the order of Christ where grace reigns in righteousness. **If, because of one man's trespass, death reigned through that one man, much more will those who receive the abundance of grace and the free gift of righteousness** *reign in life* **through the one man Jesus Christ** (5:17, RSV, italics added). Through Christ we may **live [our] lives victoriously** (Phillips). This abounding grace is ours in Christ "not only in the remission of that sin which Adam brought on us . . . but infusion of holiness."[3]

5. The grand announcement of this passage is therefore vv. 20-21. Paul's pessimism of nature is more than matched by his optimism of grace. C. H. Dodd concludes: "Salvation is more than a device of freeing an individual from his guilt: it must cut at the root of that corporate wrongness which underlies individual transgression. That is, according to Paul, what has been effected by the work of Christ. In Him men are lifted into a new order in which goodness is as powerful and dominant as was sin in the order represented by Adam; or, rather, is far more powerful and dominant."[4] In Christ we have freedom from both the reign and root of sin!

Sanctification Through Union with Christ (6:1-23)

Paul's thesis in Romans 6 is that the person who is righteous before God by faith is a person who has been sanctified by God. A Christian's sanctification is a matter of experiential knowledge (vv. 1-11). This knowledge includes with it, however, the imperative to realize the power and fullness of sanctification by entire consecration to God (vv. 12-13, 19). When we have obeyed this imperative, it can be said of us, **But now that you have been set free from sin and have become slaves of God, the return** [literally, "fruit"] **you get is sanctification and its end, eternal life** (v. 22, RSV). Sanctification in its entirety is the fruit of our union with Christ.

The exegetical key to Romans 6 is Paul's distinction between the indicative and imperative moods. The indicative describes what *was, is,* or *shall be;* the imperative, what *must be.* In Paul's gospel of grace the imperative *arises out of* the indicative; both are parts of one divine working (see Phil. 2:12-13). Because God is at work in us, we *can* work; because He is at work in us, we *must* work.[5] It is all of God's grace, from first to last (cf. Phil. 1:6; Rom. 1:17). Not to see and maintain the organic wholeness of the divine-human working in our salvation leads to a false dichotomy between justification and sanctification, making justification God's work and sanctification our human endeavor, with the result that beginning in the Spirit, we end in the flesh (cf. Gal. 3:1-3). Although demanding our total consecration, entire sanctification is entirely by grace. "Without God, we cannot; without us, God will not" (Augustine).

In 6:1-10 Paul employs the indicative. As those who have identified with Christ in faith and baptism, the Roman believers have thereby **died to sin,** been **buried . . . with him by baptism into death,** and **raised from the dead by the glory of the Father** to **walk in newness of life.** Their **old self was crucified with him** (all RSV), so that they were now free from the service of sin. These aorist indicatives point back to the critical and completed action of God in their conversion. They culminate in Paul's first imperative. In view of this, he says, **you also must consider yourselves dead to sin and alive to God in Christ Jesus** (v. 11, RSV)—*because in fact you actually are so.* This is the force of the Greek imperative *logidzesthe,* an accounting term.[6] On the basis of your union with Christ, Paul urges, *"become what you are."* Freedom from sin is found **in Christ Jesus,** whom God has made for us our sanctification as well as our righteousness (cf. 1 Cor. 1:30).

The imperatives that immediately follow call for our entire consecration to God as the proper expression of our faith and of our freedom in Christ. Do not abuse your freedom, Paul warns, or sin will reestablish its reign in your body (v. 12). **Do not go on presenting the members of your body to sin as instruments of unrighteousness; but present yourselves to God as those alive from the dead, and your members as instruments of righteousness to God** (v. 13, NASB). In v. 19 Paul repeats this call for entire consecration. **For just as you presented your members as slaves to impurity and to lawlessness, resulting in further lawlessness, so now present your members as slaves to righteousness,** *resulting in sanctification* (NASB, italics added). The aorist tense makes it clear that this consecration is to be a decisive and completed act. And it is **for sanctification** (6:19, RSV).[7]

Here in Paul's definitive treatment of sanctification through Christ we find the two crises of conversion and full sanctification clearly indicated. Because God is sovereign love and Jesus Christ is Lord, the initial crisis creates a situation that demands a second. The question is simply, will I "let God be God"?

The sin that remains is what Millard Reed speaks of as "the delusion of self-sovereignty" or what Oswald Chambers defines as "my claim to my right to myself." As long as I claim any part of my life for myself, *Adamic sin remains.* Until I acknowledge and yield utterly to God's claims upon my total existence, sin continues *in* me. But when I yield, "all Christ wrought *for* me on the Cross is wrought *in* me by the Holy Spirit." But that is to anticipate chap. 8.

We are surely justified to assume that Paul's gospel of sanctification, so carefully worked out here in Romans 6, is the structure of his theology that informs all he says elsewhere on the subject. It surely illuminates 1 Cor. 2:14—3:4. It makes sense of his call for "perfecting holiness" in 2 Cor. 6:14—7:1. The very structure of Romans 6, with its interplay of indicatives and imperatives, is reproduced in Col. 2:8—3:15. And it is certainly the gospel logic behind Paul's appeal for the Thessalonians' entire sanctification (1 Thess. 5:23, NASB). Wesley's claim that God justifies us in order to sanctify us goes to the very heart of Paul's gospel, indeed in his insistence that sanctification may be *entire.*

The Inability of the Law to Sanctify (7:1-25)

In this chapter Paul is **speaking to those who know the law** (v. 1, RSV), that is, to the significant element in the Roman church who were Jewish believers in danger of not grasping the fact that Christ has brought an end to the Mosaic system, thereby making possible a freedom from sin the law could never provide.

The apostle has already introduced the theme in 6:14, where he says, **For sin shall not be master over you, for you are not under law, but under grace** (NASB). The clear implication is that to be under law is to be under sin's mastery. Freedom from sin also means freedom from the law.

But this does not mean lawlessness. **Are we to sin** [aorist, "commit one act of sin"] **because we are not under law but under grace? By no means!** (6:15, RSV). The force of the aorist is, "Shall we make provision for a single act of disobedience?" (cf. 13:14). The reminder that we are **not under law, but under grace** points forward to 7:4 where Paul explains that under grace we are joined to Christ in covenant love. For us, then, sin is not simply transgressing the law, it is breaking covenant—an act that severs us from Christ and puts us back under servitude to sin and death (6:16, 23).

Chapter 7 is therefore not an interruption of Paul's thought but its further development and enrichment. Here he is exploring a truth that lies at the very heart of his gospel, that to be under law is to be under the mastery of sin, but to be under grace is to be liberated from sin.

Freedom from the Law (7:1-6)

The chapter opens with an illustration. **A married woman,** Paul says, **is bound by law to her husband as long as he lives; but if her husband dies she is discharged from the law** that binds her to him and is free to marry another man (vv. 2-3, RSV).

If we keep in mind the interrelatedness of law and sin and of grace and freedom in the thought of the apostle, the analogy makes perfect sense.

1. The woman is the true "self" capable of living either under law or under grace.

2. The law is the Mosaic system viewed primarily as "commandment" (see vv. 9, 10, 11, 12, 13).

3. The first husband is "our old man" (our unregenerate self in Adam); as long as he is alive, we are under law.

4. The new husband is the risen Christ, to whom under grace we are united by faith in covenant love.

The key to the analogy is v. 4: **Likewise, my brethren, you have died to the law through the body of Christ** [offered up on the Cross], **so that you may belong to another, to him who has been raised from the dead in order that we may bear fruit for God** (RSV).

Verse 4 corresponds precisely with 6:6. **Our old man** (KJV—Adam, and we in him) was crucified with Christ (historically at Calvary and personally at conversion). Therefore the law that bound us to him is dissolved. *So we must consider ourselves dead not only to sin but also to the law* (cf. 6:11).

The further application of the analogy in vv. 5 and 6 clinches Paul's thought. **While we *were* living in the flesh** (v. 5, RSV, italics added) points back to our pre-Christian state. In that state **our sinful passions, aroused by the law, were at work in our members to bear fruit for death** (a preview of 7:14-25; cf. Gal. 5:18-21).

But now [as those united to Christ under grace] **we are discharged from the law,** *dead to that which held us captive,* **so that we serve not under the old written code but in the new life of the Spirit** (v. 6, RSV, italics added; anticipatory of 8:1-4; cf. Gal. 5:22-23).

The Function of the Law (7:7-13)

Paul realizes his argument has raised a serious question: If life under the law is life in sin, does that mean **the law is sin? By no means!** he rejoins (v. 7a, RSV).

To understand this section, we must distinguish between the original intention of the law (to disclose God's will for human life, v. 7b) from the actual function of the law (turning sin into transgression, vv. 8-9). "The law is not as such and originally sinful, but in fact it leads to the experience of sin."[8]

In itself, **the law is holy, and the commandment is holy and just and good** (v. 12, RSV). Obviously this is a reference to the Decalogue, which speaks to us with the authority of the holy God and commands us to be perfect in love as He is perfect (cf. Matt. 22:34-40). But when this holy law confronted me as a member of Adam's fallen race, **sin sprang to life and I died; the very commandment that promised life proved death to me** (vv. 9-10, paraphrase). Such is the dialectical understanding of the law demanded by 7:12 and 5:20.

What is it that the law brings to life? It is *pasan epithumian,* "all desire"—"the passion to assert oneself against God and neighbor," as Kasemann describes it. As such it can come to expression *religiously* in the striving for achievement before God; *morally* it is covetousness or lust. The latent egoism of my fallen humanity is activated by the divine commandment, and when this occurs, the death that followed Adam's transgression takes effect in me (cf. 5:12). Indwelling sin provides the law its **opportunity** to deceive me and kill me (v. 11, RSV).

This is the understanding of the law Paul gained from the perspective of his new existence in Christ (cf. 5:12-21). The fact that a pious Pharisee would never understand the law in this way simply shows that when he reads the law, a veil is over his face—a veil that only faith in Christ can remove (see 2 Cor. 3:12-16).

The Powerlessness of the Law (7:14-25)

Paul's use of the present tense in this new section has led many scholars to the false conclusion that he is now describing present Christian experience.

The fallacy of this position is that it treats this section as an isolated problem, as though it were not a part of Paul's larger argument in these chapters. If we accept what he has already said in chap. 6 (that as Christians we have died to sin) and what he is about to show in chap. 8 (that the law of the Spirit of life in Christ Jesus has set us free from the law of sin and death), then this chapter cannot possibly be construed as the picture of normal Christian existence. In this very chapter the apostle has already made the point that we have died to the law by our faith in Christ crucified (7:1-6). How can a person who has died to the law be described as being dominated by the law, and therefore by sin (vv. 23, 25)?

The use of the present tense here becomes clear if we understand Paul's main point. Although a case can be made for seeing this section as his continuing defense of the law, it is hard to contest the point that the apostle's real purpose here is to show *the controlling power of indwelling sin.* The transition to the present tense can easily be made from this perspective. After the opening sentence the Torah recedes into the background, and everything focuses on our plight as the victims of indwelling sin. *The sin that came to life in its encounter with the law now rules our human existence apart from Christ.*

Let Paul now speak for himself: **We know that the law is spiritual; but I am carnal, sold under sin** (v. 14, RSV). The law has its origin in the Spirit of God and derives its character from that Spirit; "but I am unspiritual." This free rendering catches Paul's exact meaning. Apart from the Spirit living in me and revealing Christ in and through me, I *am* "flesh." By "flesh" Paul means the total person alienated from the life of God and therefore under the control of sin.

As a consequence of the Fall and my participation in it by personal transgression, **I am carnal, sold under sin.** The sin that came to life in my encounter with God's holy law now *lives* in me and *takes me captive.* The result is, I do not determine my own actions—*sin does.* Verses 15-25 picture human existence under the domination of indwelling sin (just as chap. 8 will picture human existence indwelt and controlled by the Holy Spirit).

The bondage of sin may be understood in two ways. One way to view it is as the *moral* dilemma of a person endeavoring to do God's will by relying only on his own resources. In recent years some scholars have come to see the problem as the *religious* dilemma of a pious person who in his endeavor to do the will of God as he sees it in the law, ends up doing just the opposite. Blinded by self-righteousness, the legalist uses the law to assert his own sinful self.

1. Traditionally, the bondage described in this section has been understood as a *moral* dilemma, "the ethical cleavage between will and act or wish and reality" (Kasemann). Certainly in this passage we are reminded of a universally experienced conflict between the ideal of obedience to the law of God and the actual reality of human nature under the pressure of an occupying power, indwelling sin.

"The passion to assert oneself against God and neighbor" that was **wrought in me** by the law (7:8) is unquestionably the quintessence of sin; but this pride inevitably gives birth to sensuality (see 1:18-31; cf. Gal. 5:19-21). If pride is the root, concupiscence is the fruit of sin. The passage here bears witness to the moral depravity that results from indwelling sin.

Even Gentiles who know God's law only in the form of conscience (see Rom. 2:14-16) understand this dilemma. Ovid is often quoted in this connection:

> *My reason this, my passion that, persuades;*
> *I see the right, and approve it too;*
> *I hate the wrong, and yet the wrong pursue.*

Epictetus' words are closer to Paul's: "What he wants he does not do, and what he does not want he does." This tradition was prevalent among the Jews of the Diaspora and was surely known by Paul. Understood as an ethical dilemma, these verses portray "the paradox of moralism."

The indwelling Spirit is the only answer to this dilemma. **Those who are in the flesh cannot please God. But you are not in the flesh, you are in the Spirit, if in fact the Spirit of God dwells in you** (8:8-9, RSV). By giving us the Spirit, the Father transfers us from the realm of the flesh to the realm of Christ.

2. But a deeper application of this passage opens up Paul's radical Christian critique of the law as creating a dilemma in the *religious* realm.

I do not understand my own actions, Paul confesses. **For I do not do what I want, but I do the very thing I hate** (v. 15, RSV). If the word *ginōskein* is taken in its biblical sense as meaning "to choose" (see Amos 3:2), Paul is saying, "I do not determine my own actions." "A person thinks he knows what he is doing and what he can expect," Kasemann explains. "But he lives under an illusion, since the will of God becomes the basis of one's own pious self-assertion and thus leads to one's own destruction."[9]

"The hour is coming," Jesus warned the apostles, "when whoever kills you will think he is offering service to God" (John 16:2, RSV). This was exactly the case with Paul's persecution of the church.

> Paul's good intentions—to do the will of God as he understood it from the law—led him to oppose Christ, and so to do the opposite of what he wanted. Zealous for the law, Paul the Pharisee sought to do God's will, yet in that zeal opposed God and did the very evil he sought to eradicate through his persecuting activity. Seeking God's will in the law (and hence blameless; Phil. 3:6), Paul the Pharisee had been led to oppose Christ, and hence to do the opposite of God's will. So had sin taken control of the law, and so it led him astray.[10]

"The crucifixion of Christ is the logical consequence of self-righteousness," says Emil Brunner. This is the danger of any religion that centers on God's law rather than on Christ. In reflecting on his deliverance from such Pharisaical self-righteousness, Paul could only say, **Thanks be to God through Jesus Christ our Lord!** (Rom. 7:25, RSV). Only as the Spirit brings us into the orbit of God's love in Christ can we be saved from the deadly sin of self-righteousness.

The Conclusion of the Matter

It is significant that in vv. 14-25 Paul has avoided, with evident design, any specifically Christian reference—the term *pneuma* (Spirit) in particular—and used only terms denoting natural personality functions, like *nous* (mind). The contrast in this respect to 8:1-11 is striking, where the special Christian terms referring to Christ and the Spirit abound. We can only conclude that the apostle intends his readers to understand that in 7:14-25 he is not describing promised *Christian* experience.

If this is so, why have so many excellent commentators, beginning with the great Augustine, seen these verses as the analogy of Christian experience? The answer must be the conclusion we reached in the analysis of chap. 6, that while the *reign* of sin is broken in conversion to Christ, its *root* still remains to trouble the believer. In chap. 6 the imperative was: Become what you are—"dead to sin" and "alive to God in Christ Jesus" (v. 11). In chap. 7 it is: Become what you are—"dead to the *law*" and alive to God in Christ Jesus (see v. 4).

Paul's single point in this chapter is *the powerlessness of the law to sanctify,* as his conclusion in v. 25 makes clear: **So then, *I of myself* serve the law of God with my mind, but with my flesh I serve the law of sin** (RSV, italics added). "I of myself"—*autos egō* means "I, left to myself" (Moffatt), "I relying on my own resources" (A. M. Hunter). The final manifestation of the "flesh" *(sarx)* is the illusion that "I of myself" can fulfill God's holy law. In chap. 6 remaining sin was seen as "my claim to my right to myself," which calls for *entire consecration.* Here it is seen as spiritual pride (with resulting depravity), which calls for *entire sanctification.* As long as the Adamic "I" lives within me, I am still "under law" (6:15), where sin perverts God's holy law into "the law of sin and death" (8:2). This is why Godet can say, "Paul speaks of the unregenerate man without concerning himself with the question how far the unregenerate heart still remains in the regenerate believer."[11] Under the law I am not only depraved but also religiously deceived. "The heart is deceitful above all things, and desperately wicked" (Jer. 17:9a, KJV). The remaining Adamic "I" so easily becomes the legalistic Pharisee who would use the very law of God to promote its own pride! "Who can know it?" (Jer. 17:9b). Only the Christian whose eyes have been opened through his faith in Christ (cf. 2 Cor. 3:4-18).

Wretched man that I am! Who will deliver me from this body of death? Thanks be to God through Jesus Christ our Lord! (Rom. 7:24-25, RSV). Paul is now ready to declare his doctrine of true sanctification through the indwelling Spirit of Christ.

Sanctification by the Spirit (8:1-39)

The grand announcement of this chapter is that **what the law**

could not do (v. 3, KJV) for fallen humanity, *God* has done in Christ. **There is therefore now no condemnation** [neither legal nor personal] **for those who are in Christ Jesus** (v. 1, RSV); for to be in Christ is to be saved from both the *guilt* and *power* of sin.[12]

The first section of this chapter can be divided into two parts: (1) Sanctification by the Spirit *through* Christ (vv. 1-8) and (2) Sanctification by the Spirit *of* Christ (vv. 9-11).

Sanctification by the Spirit Through Christ (8:1-8)

What the law, weakened by the flesh, could not do (v. 3) God has done for us—in Christ and the gift of the Spirit through Him. **For the law of the Spirit of life in Christ Jesus has set me free from the law of sin and death** (v. 2, both RSV).[13] From Christ, and Christ alone, flows the Spirit of real life and holiness.

1. *The Spirit fulfills the law* (vv. 1-4). "The law of the Spirit is nothing more than the Spirit himself in his ruling function in the sphere of Christ," says Kasemann. "He creates life and separates not only from sin and death but also from their instrument, the perverted law of Moses."[14] But observe, He separates us from that perverted law in order that He may establish and fulfill in us **the just requirement** (v. 4, RSV) of God's original Torah.

What was not possible to the law in its perverted form because of indwelling sin, God has made possible by **sending his own Son in the likeness of sinful flesh and for sin** (v. 3, RSV), that is, to *meet* sin in the place where it dwells and rules, and there to condemn, judge, and remove it.[15] As a Denizen of the flesh, the Son of God "'condemned' that 'sin' which was 'in' our 'flesh,'" says Wesley; "gave sentence, that sin should be destroyed, and the believer wholly delivered from it."[16] On the very ground where sin had established itself—that is, in human personality—the Son of God has vanquished sin and potentially sanctified our human existence!

The first Adam disobeyed God and died; the last Adam died rather than disobey God, becoming "obedient unto death, even death on a cross" (Phil. 2:8). "Therefore God has highly exalted him" (v. 9). And "being . . . exalted at the right hand of God, and having received from the Father the promise of the Holy Spirit, he has poured out" (Acts 2:33, all RSV) the sanctifying Spirit, *reproducing in the yielded believer the holiness He himself won by His perfect obedience to the Father!*[17] Thus the glorified Christ, through the gift of the Pentecostal Spirit, inaugurated the new covenant promised in Jer. 31:31-34 (cf. Ezek. 36:25-27).

Through the Spirit from Christ we are enabled to fulfill **the just requirement of the law** (Rom. 8:4, RSV). And what is that requirement? "Owe no one anything except to love one another, for he who loves another has fulfilled the law" (13:8, NKJV; see 13:8-10). "God's love has been poured into our hearts through the Holy Spirit which has been given to us" (5:5, RSV).

2. *The Spirit Deposes the Flesh* (vv. 5-9). Furthermore, by dethroning sin and establishing the reign of grace in us, the Holy Spirit brings an end to the flesh. **You are not in the flesh, you are in the Spirit, if in fact the Spirit of God dwells in you** (8:9, RSV). This is not addressed to the saints in heaven but to the saints in Rome!

For Paul "flesh" and "Spirit" are two conflicting forces, and every person is controlled by the one or the other. To **walk . . . according to the flesh** is to be under the control of indwelling sin; to **walk . . . according to the Spirit** is to be under the control of the indwelling Spirit (v. 4, RSV).

In v. 5 Paul shows the relation of the believer's "walk" to his essential "being" (a point not clear in either NIV or RSV, but demanded by the Greek). **For those who *are* [ontes] according to the flesh set their minds on the things of the flesh, but those who are according to the Spirit, the things of the Spirit** (NASB). "This is literally an ontological statement," says Wood, "for the Greek participle *ontes* from which that philosophical term is derived appears here in the text."[18] If we *are* of the flesh we have the mind-set of the flesh; if we *are* of the Spirit, that of the Spirit. The Greek noun for "mind" *(phronēma),* the aspiration of which this verse speaks, proceeds from the *einai* or "being," and produces the *peripatein,* the "walking" of v. 4. "The *I, ego,* is distinct from both tendencies; but it yields itself without fail to the use of the one or the other—to the former, as the *I* of the natural man; to the latter, as the *I* of the regenerate man." As our state, so our tendency; as our tendency, so our conduct.[19]

The mind-set *(phronēma)* of the flesh is that of the autonomous self, "the life of the *I* for itself."[20] This is "death" to the essential self—separation from God and the personal disintegration and corruption that inevitably follow. The mind-set of the Spirit, on the other hand, is a "mind . . . set . . . on things . . . above, . . . where

Christ is, seated at the right hand of God," a life "hid with Christ in God" (see Col. 3:1-4). This is a life that draws its sustenance, direction, and satisfaction from God in Christ. **To set the mind on the Spirit is life and peace** (Rom. 8:6)—God's *shalom,* "which passes all understanding" (Phil. 4:7, all RSV).

For the mind that is set on the flesh is hostile to God; it does not submit to God's law, indeed it cannot; and those who are in the flesh cannot please God (Rom. 8:7-8, RSV). "Fallen man's fierce hostility to God," says Cranfield, "is the response of his egotism (which is the essence of his fallenness) to God's claim to his allegiance. Determined to assert himself, to assert his independence, to be the centre of his own life, to be his own god, he cannot help but hate the real God whose very existence gives the lie to all his self-assertion."[21]

But you are not in the flesh, you are in the Spirit, Paul triumphantly announces, **if in fact the Spirit of God dwells in you** (v. 9*a,* RSV). Although still in the "body" *(sōma),* we may be free from the "flesh" *(sarx)!* "For the Christian, the flesh is dead and deposed (Rom. 8:2ff); it is excluded from participation in the Reign of God (1 Cor. 15:50), while the *sōma*— transformed, i.e., released from the dominion of the flesh—is the vehicle of the resurrection life. The *sōma* is man himself, while *sarx* is a power that lays claim to him and determines him."[22] So, Paul writes, **you are not in the flesh, you are in the Spirit, if in fact the Spirit of God dwells in you.** It really *(eiper)* is a call for the Romans—and us!—to be *sure* that the Spirit has the same determinative influence in our life that sin formerly exerted. "The use of *oikein en* (dwells in) denotes a settled permanent penetrative influence,"[23] possession by a power superior to self. "If the indwelling of the Spirit is spoken of here as that of sin in 7:17ff, in both cases radical possession is indicated which also affects our will according to v. 5."[24]

Any one who does not have the Spirit of Christ does not belong to him (v. 9*b*). "This amounts to saying that all Christians 'have the Spirit' *in greater or less degree.*"[25] Here is a clearly implied distinction between being really indwelt by the sanctifying Spirit and only "having the Spirit" through faith. "The man who does not have the Spirit (whose life bears no evidence of the Spirit's sanctifying work) is no Christian, however much he may claim to be one."[26]

What Paul means here by being really indwelt by the Spirit is what he elsewhere refers to by being "filled" with the Spirit (Eph. 5:18; 3:14-21). The degree of indwelling is dependent upon the degree of yieldedness to God, as we saw in Romans 6 (see comments on 6:12-14, 19). "The Spirit-filled life, or Spirit-possessed life," Myron Augsburger points out, "is not one in which we have a certain amount of the Spirit, but rather one in which He possesses all of us. The Spirit-filled life is one in which the Spirit expresses Himself within an individual as a controlling and overflowing force. The condition is one of yieldedness on our part. We are as filled with the Spirit as we are emptied of self."[27] *It is one thing to "have" the Spirit; it is quite another thing for Him to have us.* In the Spirit-filled life the Holy Spirit is the exact counterpart to the **sin that dwells in me** as a person of the "flesh" (7:17, 20, NKJV).

Sanctification by the Spirit of Christ (8:9-11)

The most significant claim Paul makes in Romans 8 now becomes clear: The Spirit who comes *through* Christ is the Spirit *of* Christ. So he now can write, **But if *Christ* is in you** (v. 10). Verses 9 through 11 treat "the Spirit," "the Spirit of God," "the Spirit of Christ," "Christ," and "his Spirit" as *experientially* synonymous. C. H. Dodd observes here: *"In Christ, in the Spirit, the Spirit within, Christ within* were in effect only different ways of describing one experience, from slightly different points of view. This is not to say that Paul, in a strict theological sense, identified Christ with the Spirit. But his virtual identification of the experience of the Spirit with the experience of the indwelling Christ is of utmost value. It saves Christians from falling into a non-moral, half-magical conception of the supernatural in human experience, and it brought spiritual experience to the test of the historical revelation of God in Christ."[28]

The final proof that I am truly indwelt by the Holy Spirit is that I can confess with Paul, "I have been crucified with Christ; it is no longer I who live, but Christ who lives in me" (Gal. 2:20, RSV), meaning that Jesus Christ lives in me and occupies in me precisely the space that was once occupied by my sinful *ego.*[29]

We must not, however, overlook the fact that Paul still recognizes the limitations imposed by our "mortal bodies." The full manifestation of Christ awaits the resurrection, when our mortal bodies will be finally redeemed (vv. 11, 23).

Standing in the Spirit (8:12-17)

Kasemann introduces this section by observing: "The christological relation of the Spirit finds expression in the new section in the fact that Christ as prototype, as in Heb. 2:1ff, creates new sons of God, i.e. bearers of the Spirit. The antithetical parallelisms of vv. 12-13 take up those of vv. 5-8 at the hortatory level and form a transition to the new theme. . . . The Christian necessarily stands in conflict with the power of the flesh if he is not to fall under the doom of death which this brings. . . . What is at issue is . . . the maintaining of the new life against temptation."[30]

1. *Sarx and Sōma*

So then, brethren, we are debtors, not to the flesh [sarx], **to live according to the flesh—for if you live according to the flesh you will** [peraphrastic future, meaning necessary and certain] **die, but if by the Spirit you put to death the deeds** ["misdeeds," NIV] **of the body** [sōma] **you will live** (vv. 12-13, RSV).

Like sin and the law, the flesh constitutes a threat to the Spirit-filled Christian. These powers remain as a part of the old order to be overcome. The *sōma,* with its appetites, urges, and mechanisms, offers *sarx* a point of attack. Our task as Christians is to **put to death** these **instinctive actions** (Phillips) of the body that, if yielded to, would cause us to disobey God (cf. 1 Cor. 9:27).

The Christian has **no obligations** (TLB) to the flesh—that is, to the self as an autonomous entity. There is a proper self-regard, which Christ enhances; but there is also an improper self-love. "If anyone wishes to be a follower of mine," Jesus said, "he must leave self behind" (Luke 9:23, NEB). False self-love must be utterly repudiated, despite all the siren voices of our narcissistic age. "For whoever would save his life will lose it" (Luke 9:24, RSV). "But if by the Spirit you put to death the deeds of the body you will live." "By the power of the Spirit" is what Paul means. As the body strives to reassert its autonomy, we have the gracious assistance of the promised Comforter who will strengthen us to overcome (John 14:15-17). This is the biblical doctrine of "counteraction"—not of sin but of the body's strivings (cf. 6:12).

2. *Sonship and Holiness*

Verses 14-17 make it clear that the discipline of the holy life is the discipline of filial *love.* Christians are the obedient children of the Heavenly Father, not slaves to an impersonal legal system.

The danger of overemphasizing discipline is that of causing believers who have found the joy of divine adoption to **fall back into [slavish] fear** (v. 15). Having begun in the Spirit, we are also perfected in the Spirit (see Gal. 3:1-3). Thank God, **There is therefore now no condemnation for those who are in Christ Jesus**—*even for remaining sin*—provided they **walk not according to the flesh but according to the Spirit** (Rom. 8:1, 4, all RSV).[31]

In clarifying the nature of Christian discipline, Paul makes two points. First, we are **sons of God ... *led* by the Spirit** (v. 14, italics added). The verb translated **led** suggests the *power* of the Spirit to make us overcomers. Second, as believers we enjoy the *witness* of the Spirit (v. 16, RSV, italics added), enabling us to cry out, **Abba! dear Father!** (cf. v. 15, Barclay). "The joy of the Lord is [our] strength" (Neh. 8:10) as His children, joy arising from the inward assurance that He loves us and accepts us in Christ. Assured by the Spirit He loves us, we love Him in return—and do His will in joyful gratitude. This is the holy life—the joyous and free obedience (perfect love) of God's "adult" children (Wesley).

> *If our love were but more simple,*
> *We should take Him at His word;*
> *And our lives would be all sunshine*
> *In the sweetness of our Lord.*
> —F. W. FABER

Cranfield comments beautifully on this passage:

> It is in the believers' calling God "Father" that God's holy law is established and its "righteous requirement" (v. 4) fulfilled. ... [T]he whole Christian obedience is included in this calling God "Father." The verse, in fact, states in principle everything that there is to say in the way of Christian ethics; for there is nothing more required of us than that we should do just this— with full understanding of what it means, with full seriousness and with full sincerity. For to address the true God by the name of Father with full sincerity and seriousness will involve seeking wholeheartedly to be and think and say and do that which is pleasing to Him and to avoid everything which displeases Him.[32]

Holiness as Hope in the Spirit (8:18-30)

The last verse of the previous section (v. 17) by its movement of thought from sonship to heirship **(and if children, then heirs)** makes the transition to the subject of Christian hope. The immediate link in the preceding section is v. 15, where Paul speaks of **the Spirit of adoption** (both KJV). He realizes our adoption is incomplete.

> It is assured the believer, but it is not yet apparent to the world. It is a concealed sonship . . . obscured by the body of our humiliation. But at the end of the age, when the Lord returns for His own, that sonship will be revealed. All will see that the adoption is a fact. The Spirit is the firstfruits of that disclosure. "Beloved, we are God's children now; it does not yet appear what we shall be, but we know that when he shall appear we shall be like him, for we shall see him as he is" (1 John 3:2).[33]

Relating this to holiness, we must understand that our existence as Spirit-filled Christians is one of **the sufferings of this present time** (v. 18, KJV)—the time between Pentecost and the Parousia. "As to the *spirit,* we are in *the age to come;* as to the *body,* in *the present age.*"[34] Our bodies are no longer the instruments of sin, but they are still not fully redeemed (v. 23).

This present age is a time when **the whole creation has been groaning in travail** (v. 22) of childbirth, awaiting **with eager longing . . . the revealing of the sons of God** at the Second Advent (v. 19). **And not only the creation, but we ourselves, who have the first fruits of the Spirit, groan inwardly as we wait for adoption as sons, the redemption of our bodies** (v. 23, all RSV). Although (if we are really indwelt by the Spirit) the *tyranny* of the flesh is past, the **weakness** (v. 26; **infirmities,** KJV) of the flesh remains. These **infirmities** include, of course, the bodily weakness and pain that eventuate in physical death with the anguish of spirit implied by what we call human suffering. But Paul surely means more than this. The **groanings** (v. 26, KJV) of the Spirit are the birth pangs of our bodily redemption, just as the groanings of **the whole creation** are the travail of nature's redemption (v. 22). As the creation is frustrated, or subject to **futility** (v. 20), so our **infirmities** frustrate the Spirit within us and cause Him to *groan* **with sighs too deep for words** (v. 26, RSV refs.).

Our infirmities surely encompass the whole array of human frailties: the racial effects of sin in our bodies and minds, the scars from past sinful living, emotional damage from traumatic childhood experiences, our prejudices, our neuroses that create emotional depression and cause us to act "out of character," our temperamental idiosyncrasies, our human weakness and fretfulness, and a thousand faults to which our flesh is heir. We may add to this our "involuntary transgressions" of God's perfect law.[35] A full-orbed doctrine of Christian perfection must therefore put the truth within the framework of **this present time** of human frailty.

But if we believe the gospel, **this present time** is also pregnant with hope—a joyful expectation of the Parousia and final glory (vv. 23-24). "If Christianity be not altogether thoroughgoing eschatology," Barth says incisively, "there remains in it no relationship whatever to Christ."[36]

The indwelling Spirit is not only the witness to our adoption but also the "first fruits"—the "foretaste" (Weymouth et al.) and "guarantee" (Eph. 1:14)—of the glory that shall be ours when Christ appears (cf. 2 Cor. 1:21-22; Eph. 1:13-14). "Beloved, now are we the sons of God, and it doth not yet appear what we shall be: but we know that, when he shall appear, we shall be like him; for we shall see him as he is" (1 John 3:2, KJV). *In this hope we were saved* (Rom. 8:24, RSV)! Such hope is not wistful longing; it is confident expectation based on the Resurrection (1 Cor. 15:20-23, 51-58) and confirmed by God's love now shed abroad in our hearts by the Holy Spirit (Rom. 5:1-5).

Superficially, **the sufferings of this present time** seem to hinder God's purpose for us, but in fact everything that seems to frustrate that purpose serves finally only to further it (v. 28). The **good** that God all the while is working in those who love Him is His purpose finally to conform us to the Son, **that he might be the firstborn among many brethren** (v. 29, KJV). *God's ultimate concern is not our happiness but our holiness: the restoration of the divine image lost in the Fall.* "We all"—when we love God with disinterested love—"with unveiled face, reflecting the glory of the Lord, are being changed into his likeness from one degree of glory to another; for this comes from the Lord who is the Spirit" (2 Cor. 3:18, RSV margin; cf. 1 Cor. 15:45).

Security in Christ (8:31-39)

This final majestic paragraph is Paul's inspired peroration, celebrating the glorious truth that we are "superconquerors" through Christ. Chapter 8, which begins with "no condemnation," climaxes with "no separation"! *Sola gloria Deo.*

Endnotes

1. John Wesley, *Explanatory Notes upon the New Testament,* 2 vols. (London: Wesleyan Methodist Book Room, n.d.; reprint, Kansas City: Beacon Hill Press of Kansas City, 1981), vol. 2.

2. J. H. Whale, *Christian Doctrine* (London: Fontana Books, 1960), 50.

3. Wesley, *Notes,* on Rom. 5:20.

4. C. H. Dodd, *The Epistle to the Romans,* in *The Moffatt New Testament Commentary* (New York: Harper and Brothers, 1932), 82.

5. John Wesley, "On Working Out Our Own Salvation," in *The Works of John Wesley,* 3rd ed., 14 vols. (London: Wesleyan Methodist Book Room, 1872; reprint, Kansas City: Beacon Hill Press of Kansas City, 1978), 6:508-13.

6. "The verb *logidzesthai,* as used here, denotes not a pretending ('as if'), nor a mere ideal, but a deliberate and sober judgment on the basis of the gospel, a reasoning which is subject to the discipline of the gospel in that it accepts as its norm what God has done in Christ" (C. E. B. Cranfield, *The Epistle to the Romans,* in *The International Critical Commentary* (Edinburgh: T. and T. Clark, 1975), 1:315.

7. Godet sees *hagiosmos* here (in distinction from *hagiotēs,* "an abstract idea," and *hagiōsunē,* "a personal quality, an inward disposition") to mean "a work which has reached the state of complete realization in the person and life, the result of the divine act expressed by *hagiadzein.*" Frederic Godet, *The Epistle to the Romans,* trans. A. Cusin (New York: Funk and Wagnalls, 1883).

8. Ernst Kasemann, *Commentary on Romans,* trans. Geoffrey W. Bromiley (Grand Rapids: Wm. B. Eerdmans Publishing Co., 1980), 193.

9. Ibid., 203.

10. Paul J. Achtemeier, "Some Things Hard to Understand," *Interpretation* 38 (July 1984): 267.

11. Godet, *Romans,* 282-83.

12. Some ancient MSS add here the conditional clause of v. 4b, "who walk not after the flesh, but after the Spirit," to show that saving faith is a *maintained* relationship of trustful obedience. While not textually defensible, this qualification of what it means to be "in Christ Jesus" is in harmony with Paul's soteriology (cf. 6:15-16, 23; 8:13, 17) and therefore an appropriate reminder to the reader.

13. Strong MS evidence supports *se* (you) instead of *me* (me). This, however, is inadmissible, since *se* is second person singular and the letter is addressed to the collective body of believers. *Se* is more likely a scribal error, reproducing the "se" from the final syllable of the preceding verb *eleutherōsen.* Disregarding the slightly stronger MS evidence for *se,* most versions (except, e.g., NASB, NBV, NEB) follow the contextual evidence for *me.*

14. Kasemann, *Romans,* 215-16.

15. Karl Barth, *A Shorter Commentary on Romans* (Richmond, Va.: John Knox Press, 1959), 90.

16. *Notes,* vol. 2. "He 'pronounced the Doom of Sin.' Sin was thenceforth deposed from its autocratic power." C. Anderson Scott, *Abingdon Bible Commentary* (New York: Abingdon-Cokesbury Press, 1929), 1153.

17. Godet, *Romans,* 300-301.

18. A. Skevington Wood, *Life by the Spirit* (Grand Rapids: Zondervan Publishing House, 1963), 11.

19. Godet, *Romans,* 302.

20. Ibid., 303.

21. Cranfield, *Romans* 1:386-87.

22. Rudolph Bultmann, *Theology of the New Testament*, trans. Kendrick Grobel (New York: Charles Scribner's Sons, 1951), 1:201.

23. W. Sanday and H. C. Headlam, *The Epistle to the Romans*, in *The International Critical Commentary* (New York: Charles Scribner's Sons, 1929), 196.

24. Kasemann, *Romans*, 223.

25. Sanday and Headlam, *Romans*, 197 (emphasis added).

26. Cranfield, *Romans*, 388.

27. Myron S. Augsburger, *Quench Not the Spirit* (Scottdale, Pa.: Herald Press, 1961), 39-40.

28. Dodd, *Romans*, 124.

29. For a graphic putting of Paul's thesis see Dietrich Bonhoeffer, *Ethics*, ed. Eberhard Bethge (New York: Macmillan Co., 1965), 41.

30. Kasemann, *Romans*, 225.

31. See John Wesley's sermon "Satan's Devices," in *Works* 6:32-43, for a powerful sermon on this truth.

32. Cranfield, *Romans*, 393.

33. Wood, *Life by the Spirit*, 106.

34. Godet, *Romans*, 313.

35. See John Wesley, *Works* 11:395-96.

36. Karl Barth, *Epistle to the Romans*, trans. Edwyn C. Hoskyns (London: Oxford University Press, 1960), 314.

— 1 —

HOLINESS
AS RENEWAL
IN THE
IMAGE OF GOD

T. C. MITCHELL

Holiness—Bearing the Family Likeness

And now, dear children, continue in him, so that when he appears we may be confident and unashamed before him at his coming. If you know that he is righteous, you know that everyone who does what is right has been born of him. How great is the love the Father has lavished on us, that we should be called children of God! And that is what we are! The reason the world does not know us is that it did not know him. Dear friends, now we are children of God, and what we will be has not yet been made known. But we know that when he appears, we shall be like him, for we shall see him as he is. Everyone who has this hope in him purifies himself, just as he is pure. Everyone who sins breaks the law; in fact, sin is lawlessness. But you know that he appeared so that he might take away our sins. And in him is no sin. No one who lives in him keeps on sinning. No one who continues to sin has either seen him or known him. Dear children, do not let anyone lead you astray. He who does what is right is righteous, just as he is righteous. He who does what is sinful is of the devil, because the devil has been sinning from the beginning. The reason the Son of God appeared was to destroy the devil's work. No one who is born of God will continue to sin, because God's seed remains in him; he cannot go on sinning, because he has been born of God. This is how we know who the children of God are and who the children of the devil are: Anyone who does not do what is right is not a child of God: nor is anyone who does not love his brother (1 John 2:28—3:10).

Ever since the advent of *Roots,* people have been interested in searching out their family ancestry. The General Registry Office in

London receives scores of inquiries annually concerning "family trees," and that is duplicated throughout the United States. Sometimes there is a serendipity, but occasionally there is an embarrassing discovery. Conversely, no doubt certain early members of a family would be chagrined over the way their descendants turned out.

In our scripture text, John raises the question of the family characteristics of the children of God. This is a matter that is given widespread attention in the Bible. It makes it clear that God our holy Father has set His heart on having a family in which every member will be as like himself as is possible for creatures to be like their Creator. With this profound objective He began. Gen. 1:26 is absolutely clear on that: "Let us make man in our image, in our likeness."

Exegetical Section

Scholarly opinion is divided over whether 2:28-29 belongs with the previous passage or opens a new section. The weight seems to us to swing toward its being a transition to a new thought, though not unrelated to the preceding section. Marshall says: "'And now' is simply a way of marking a new section. . . . In the previous verse John had counselled them to remain in Christ, and now he achieves an easy transition to his next line of thought by a repetition of this phrase which serves to underline and emphasize its importance."[1] F. F. Bruce concurs.[2]

In the previous passage (2:18-27) John had argued that the Antichrist was already present in the world in the persons of those who denied that Jesus was the Christ or had "come in the flesh" (4:2). In the face of this threat to the apostolic teaching, he exhorts his readers to let the truth abide in them (2:24). Now, in the light of the certain appearing (though uncertain as to time)[3] of Jesus at the Second Advent, he exhorts them to **continue in him** (v. 28). Just as following the first admonition is the antidote to false teaching, so following the second one is the ground of confidence (absence of shame) at Christ's appearing.

It seems clear that John is seeking to combat a teaching that could be called "antinomian" (against law). As F. F. Bruce puts it, "The new teaching [against the Incarnation] thus combined a new theology with a new morality."[4] Such persons will be embarrassed at the Second Advent because they do not **continue in him,** neither do they practice righteousness.

On the surface it may appear that John is supporting the idea of works righteousness by suggesting that practicing righteousness is the basis of confidence at Jesus' parousia,[5] it is the doing what is right that makes one acceptable at that event. But even though he brings it in at the end, John is really saying that the practicing of righteousness is the outflow of being **born of him.**

I. H. Marshall expresses the significance of this point clearly:

> What John is trying to stress is that doing what is right is the consequence of spiritual birth; hence if a person does what is right, this is a sign of spiritual birth. Naturally, this does not mean that any morally upright person is a child of God, even though he makes no religious profession; when John says that "everyone who loves has been born of God" (4:8), he does not mean that atheists who love are really Christians. John is quite clear that being a Christian is dependent on believing in Jesus Christ and loving one another (3:23), and his other remarks must be understood in this context. Here he has in mind the problem of testing the truth of claims to be true Christian within the church, and he asserts that true righteousness (the kind shown by Jesus) is possible only on the basis of spiritual birth. So the readers themselves can take comfort that, if they do what is righteous, this is a sign that they are born of God, and hence that they can have confidence for the day of judgment.[6]

There is an ambiguity in trying to identify the antecedents to the pronouns in these verses. **Continue in him, when he appears, unashamed before him,** and **he is righteous** apparently refer to Jesus Christ, whereas **born of him** refers to God the Father (so I. H. Marshall, Raymond Brown, etc.).

There is theological significance in this ambiguity, however. John has been insisting on the centrality of the Incarnation and its indispensable role in both understanding who God is and coming into right relation with Him (as children to a Father). Hence the attributes of God that provide the basis for fellowship with God (light, love, life, and righteousness) are embodied, illustrated, and clarified in Jesus. To come to Christ, in these terms, is to come to God. In substance, it makes little difference whether the reference is to the Father or the Son because the children relate to the Father through the Son.

Being **born of him** makes one a child of God; and as Bruce puts it, "John makes it clear that membership in the family of God is to be recognized by the family likeness. . . . If anyone claims to belong to His family and does not practice righteousness, his claim cannot be admitted."[7]

Everyone who does what is right *(dikaiosunē),* that is, "righteousness" or "justice." This phrase (used three times in this passage) is set in contrast to doing sin. But, as Raymond Brown says:

> It means more than not sinning; for justice involves holiness (Rev. 22:11 puts doing justice in parallelism with being holy, and contrasts this with acting unjustly and being unclean). One can do justice only if one is acting according to a holiness that dwells within, even as "to do truth" [cf. 1:6] means to act according to the truth internal to the Christian, for whom Jesus is the truth. Christ is just by his very nature as the Son of God and automatically [?] he does God's will because he and the Father are one. If human beings do what is just [are holy], it is because they are children of God begotten in Christ's likeness.[8]

Unfortunately, the chapter division interrupts the flow of thought, since the idea introduced in 2:28-29 is continued and more fully elaborated in 3:1-15. All the themes germinally implied in the first two verses are there repeated and amplified. Actually 3:1-3 restates in fuller form the abstract principle first articulated in compact form in 2:28-29; 3:4-10 then details it even further by providing a series of sharp contrasts between the **children of God** and the **children of the devil** (v. 10).

3:1-3. Whereas in the Gospel, chap. 3, John's thought moves from the new birth (v. 5) to God's love (v. 16), here the thought moves in the reverse order. The possibility of being **children of God** via the new birth is grounded in God's amazing love (see Charles Wesley's hymn, "And Can It Be?").

How great is the love the Father has lavished on us (3:1). E. M. Blaiklock has beautifully interpreted this well-loved verse: "See what unearthly love God has given us that we should be called (as indeed we are) the children of God." He continues: "The interrogative pronoun here employed means literally 'of what country.' 'Of what country is this love . . . ?' asks John. Matthew uses the same word in Matt. 8:27; 'and they were astonished, saying, of what country is this man that the winds and the waves obey him . . . ?' In other words, what unearthly personage is this man?"[9]

And that is what we are. This phrase, omitted from the KJV because not found in later manuscripts, reminds us that "people and things are what [God] calls them."[10] This refers to a rite of legitimation in which by naming the child as his son, the father acknowledges that it is indeed his child. So as Marshall says, "There is no legal fiction in this."[11]

The reason the world does not know us. Like the Son who was not recognized by those to whom He came (or the Father in the Son; the basic meaning is the same, although there is the ambiguity that is common to John), so those who are His will not be recognized as such either. Thus, this point strengthens the assurance of John's readers, since they are under persecution (see Rom. 8:35-36).

3:2-3. **Now we are**—underline the word **now.** In this present situation, the reality of being children of God is vouchsafed, but there is a glorious hope of a more perfect conformity to the "family likeness." Here we have the tension between the already and the not yet that characterizes all NT theology. Even as we now are children of God (and by implication like the Father [and Son] in a partial sense), we are also being prepared for what we shall be. This is the blessed hope and faith of the believer and becomes the incentive for pursuing that "holiness, without which no man shall see the Lord" (Heb. 12:14, KJV).

The Jerusalem Bible renders it: "Surely everyone who entertains this hope must purify himself, must try to be as pure as Christ." This is a reinforcement of John's standard of Christian living that is seen to be living "like Jesus" (cf. 2:6; 3:16).

3:4-10. In the remaining verses of our text John spells out the antitheses between the **children of God** and the **children of the devil** (see v. 10) by arguing that the former are characterized by practicing righteousness while the latter practice sin (unrighteousness).

Sin is the complete antithesis of life in Christ, for the work of Christ was to atone for sin and completely take it away. He is the sinless One, and "with this sinless person we are one. . . . Between abiding in Christ and sinning there is such an absolute incompatibility, that whosoever sinneth is . . . not merely in the position of not abiding in him . . . he is in the very same case with the man who has never either seen him or known him."[12]

Sin is lawlessness (v. 4). The KJV, following the Geneva Bible, has an unusually unfortunate rendering of this phrase as "sin is the transgression of the law." This fails sharply to capture the meaning.

John is quickly nipping in the bud any objection to his point on the part of any who would quibble over the definition of sin by broadening the concept to include *any* lack of conformity to the law of God. In a word, it is rebellion against God; and as F. F. Bruce points out, it is possible to logically convert this proposition to read "lawlessness is sin," because the two are identical in meaning. This immediately aborts any claims to "sinless perfection" in the absolute sense (this is what is usually meant by "perfectionism"), a distinction John Wesley was always careful to maintain.

The reason the Son of God appeared was to destroy the devil's work (v. 8). John is telling us that to love without sin not only is God's intention for the believer but also has been provided for in the work of Christ. This was one of John Wesley's favorite proof texts for his teaching about the present availability of entire sanctification. **The devil's work** is sin in the human heart, but the grace of Christ is more than sufficient to purify or cleanse the heart, since the Blood goes "deeper than the stain has gone" (Raymond Browning). Notice the word **destroy** is used here, much stronger than any term implying "suppress."

God's seed remains in him; he cannot go on sinning, because he has been born of God (v. 9). This phrase has given scholars trouble. This quote is an interpretation rather than a translation, since the original has "his seed." The pronoun could refer to either Jesus Christ himself (Gal. 3:16; 1 John 5:13) or to the Holy Spirit (2:20-27) or most likely, in the light of the context, to the divine life principle inseminated in us to effect the new birth, making us members of the family of God. Thus this interpretation is probably correct.

The *NIV Study Bible* note is helpful at this point: "The picture is of human reproduction, in which the sperm . . . bears the life principle and transfers the paternal characteristics."

"Cannot sin" (KJV) has created even more problems. Properly understood it refers not to the impossibility but to the incompatibility of sin in the lives of God's children. Daniel Steele renders it: "He cannot sin. Rather 'be sinning.' A course of willful sin is incompatible with continued sonship or likeness to God. Moral contradictions cannot co-exist in one person. He cannot be a thief and an honest man at the same time; neither can he be sinning and a true child of God at the same instant. Persistence in sinning extinguishes sonship or similarity to God, loving what He loves and hating what He hates. So long as love to God is the undiminished motive there can be no career of sin."[13]

Bishop Westcott wrote: "The idea of divine sonship and sin are mutually exclusive. As long as the relationship with God is real, sinful acts are but accidents."[14] That is, it is an isolated act contrary to the tenor of a holy life, springing from some weakness or defect in a person whose whole life-style is rooted in love to God.

"If we could keep our minds constantly on the thought of v. 3," says Yeager, "the ideal of sinless perfection in this life might possibly be realized. This is why Paul tells us that we can be 'transformed by the renewing of the mind' (Rom. 12:1-2)."[15] Or as Boice says, "The sin which the Christian cannot do is willful or deliberate sin."[16] John Wesley had the same line of thought when he wrote:

> Even Christians, therefore, are not *so* perfect as to be free either from ignorance or error: . . . nor from infirmities. Only let us take care to understand this word aright: only let us not give that soft title to known sins, as the manner of some is. . . . I mean hereby, not only those which are properly termed *bodily infirmities,* but all those inward or outward imperfections which are not of a moral nature.[17]

Theological Exegesis

The holiness theology that informs this great passage stems from God's intention stated in Gen. 1:26: "Let us make man in our image." Man's destiny is to reflect the image or likeness of his Creator. In the state of integrity in the Garden, Adam and Eve initially lived out this destiny as they existed in proper relation to God, each other, the earth over which they were given dominion, and themselves as long as they acknowledged their creaturely dependence.[18]

This true created likeness, however, was not sufficient for man; the first pair grasped at a false likeness offered by Satan ("you will be like God," Gen. 3:5), and a dreadful unlikeness to the holy Father appeared in humanity: The Bible calls it "sin." This loss of the image was passed along to Adam's posterity in some mysterious way. "By one man's disobedience many were made sinners" (Rom. 5:19, KJV).

The profound purpose of the holy Father appeared to have been thwarted, but in "the fulness of the time" (Gal. 4:4, KJV) the true image and likeness reappeared in the "second man [who] is the Lord from heaven" (1 Cor. 15:47, KJV), for "the Word became flesh and made his dwelling among us" (John 1:14). He was the express image of the holy Father, and in Him men saw the true likeness as God had intended it; He was the light, the life, and the love of God (v. 4). His own world and His own folk did not know Him, but Scripture makes clear the purpose of His coming: It was **to destroy the devil's work** (1 John 3:8), and to make possible the fulfillment of the purpose of the holy Father to have a family in which each member will be as like the holy Father as Jesus Christ was in the days of His flesh (2:6). "For those God foreknew he also predestined to be conformed to the likeness of his Son, that he might be the firstborn among many brothers" (Rom. 8:29).

This glorious end could not have been achieved by any means other than the incarnation, death, and resurrection of "the Holy One of God" (Mark 1:24); "for what the law was powerless to do in that it was weakened by the sinful nature, God did by sending his own Son in the likeness of sinful man to be a sin offering . . . in order that the righteous requirements of the law might be fully met in us, who do not live according to the sinful nature but according to the Spirit" (Rom. 8:3-4). And now there are two humanities in the world, two families each bearing the likeness of their father: There are **the children of God** and there are **the children of the devil** (1 John 3:10).

The motive and purpose of the incarnation of the Word dominates this section (see also John 1:1-12), but the second coming of Him who was incarnate is presented in such a way as to indicate that that coming and appearing is both an encouragement to and a test of personal holiness (2:28; 3:2-3). The "life" and "likeness" of the holy Father that once manifested itself in the world both as Savior and Pattern will once again appear. This is not speculation, it is promise; for although some texts render it "if He appears" (Weymouth; cf. ASV, Williams), to John there is no uncertainty about it: The life once manifested and given to destroy the works of the devil will be manifested the second time "apart from sin" (Heb. 9:28, ASV, NKJV) to achieve the final family gathering. By his statements in 2:28 and 3:2-3 the apostle is pulling the carpet out from under the feet of any person—heretic or hypocrite—who may be falsely hoping to be accepted by Christ at His appearing but who remains unlike Him now. Unlikeness will cause a shrinking away from Him, but the sincere belief, expectation, and hope of being like Him by seeing Him as He is becomes the strongest of motivations toward heart purity here and now. Seeing Him now with the eyes of the heart (Matt. 5:8), we see Him as in a dark glass (1 Cor. 13:12, KJV); but we do see Him, and seeing Him, we are being "transformed into his likeness" (2 Cor. 3:18); yet we will ultimately **see him as he is** (1 John 3:2) and be made as like Him as grace can make us. What that likeness will finally be has not yet been made clear, but the certainty is that we shall certainly become as He is. In the meantime, by His cleansing blood (1:8-9), by His intercession (2:1-2), and by the constant indwelling of the Holy Spirit (1:26; 3:24; 4:4, 12-13) His children will be made holy, be kept holy, and be presented blameless before Him (Jude 24-25). In this way will be brought to pass all that the holy Father had in mind with regard to a holy family.

Sermon Suggestions

Topic: **Holiness and the Second Coming**

Text: 1 John 3:2-3

Introduction: You could get into this message by taking some extra time to elaborate on the OT's future-oriented hope for a sanctifying relation to God (illus. with Jeremiah 31 and Ezekiel 36) and how some forms of later rabbinic theology gave up on the possibility, coming to hold that righteousness (holiness) could only become a possiblity in the age to come. Then point out how the NT announces that the age to come has broken into the present age, thus making holiness possible as a *present* reality. But just as the kingdom of God is both present and future, so is holiness. Thus the believer looks forward to the Second Advent as the time of the consummation of the kingdom of God and the perfection of his holiness.

A. The certainty of the Second Advent in contrast to the uncertainty of the time (cf. 2 Pet. 3:3-9).
B. This uncertainty is the occasion for our daily pursuit of greater conformity to God's design for our lives (Christlikeness).
    1. It is the pursuit, rather than perfect attainment, that God expects out of us.

    2. The full embodiment of spiritual adulthood in Jesus is always beyond us, calling us to greater heights.

    3. Failure to "go on" in this pursuit (Heb. 6:1) will result in shame at His appearing.

    4. Constant, designed spiritual growth gives us a sense of confidence at the thought of His coming.

C. The comfort of realizing that all those marks of finitude that keep us from realizing perfect holiness in this life will be removed at the Second Coming. But "until then . . ."

Topic: **Holiness, the Antithesis of Sin**

Text: 1 John 2:29; 3:4-10

Introduction: A good entry into this message would be to develop the background of the Epistle, highlighting the false teaching of antinomianism that John is seeking to counteract by pointing out the inconsistency of claiming to be **children of God** while continuing in sin. This is the same outcome as Paul opposes in Romans 6 but results from a different line of reasoning (see any good standard commentary for the background to 1 John).

A. What is sin? **Lawlessness!**

B. Jesus' work was designed to **destroy** sin both as an act and as an inward bent.

C. Our behavior betrays our heritage: either a child of God (shown by doing righteousness) or a child of the devil (shown by doing sin).

Conclusion: Let us respond to the provision of the Atonement for full salvation by allowing His grace to purify us and, with His help, doing **what is right,** thus showing that we have been born again and are **children of God.**

Sermon on the Text

Topic: **Holy Children of the Holy Father**

Introduction: Our modern teenagers have an expression in which they try to express the inexpressible. They say, "That's unreal!" They may at that very moment be looking at, feeling, hearing, or touching whatever it is. It's "real," all right, but it is nevertheless utterly incredible!

The apostle John is in much the same frame of mind. Perhaps I can plug into this teenage exuberance of expression and suggest a homespun rendering of the apostle's sentence and sentiment:

> Man alive! This whole affair is unreal! It's way out! It's unearthly! It's fantastic! See the kind of love that the Father has not only shown to us but given to us! That the likes of us should not only be called, but actually be, the family of God.

It is obvious that the translators have struck the impossible task, that of capturing and capitalizing amazement: "What manner of love" (KJV); "How great is the love" (NEB, NIV); "Consider the incredible love" (Phillips); "See what love" (RSV, Weymouth); "See how much the Father has loved us!" (TEV); "See what unearthly love" (Laidlaw).

A Christian is, by definition, "a man amazed." The child of God is amazed at God, amazed at the love of God, amazed at the grace of God. The child of God is amazed at himself, at what he has become despite what he was; amazed at the revolution God's love produces in his character and conduct. John's emphasis falls on the words "and such we are" (ASV, NASB). There ought to be a way of lining up a regiment of exclamation marks, like the flag bearers at the Olympics, to lead in for public display the unspeakable marvel of the love of God! Certainly the apostle John is a man amazed, a child of wonder! His mind boggles in utter astonishment, incredulity, amazement, and wordless wonder at the unbelievable situation into which God's love has led Him and us! "Behold what love, what boundless love, the Father has bestowed on sinners lost, that we should be now called the sons of God!" And that not merely in name, it "really is what we are!"

A. *The Source of Our Belonging to the Holy Family: The Love of the Father*

An adopted child fell into a mood of despondency when he first learned that he had not been brought into the family through the normal processes of procreation. But his parents knew how to handle the situation. "With your brother and sister," said they, "we took what came, but you we chose!" Such parental assurance the Heavenly Father gives His children. "God has sent the Spirit of his Son into our hearts, crying, 'Abba! Father!' " (Gal. 4:6, RSV; cf. Rom. 8:15). But John's statement is much stronger. He says, "And such we are." Adopted? Yes! Called God's children? Yes! The figure is strong and beautiful, but not strong enough. "God's call is effectual; people and things *are* what He calls them."

From before time began, God determined to have a family. He set His heart on that. A family that would share His nature; be holy as He, loving as He, righteous as He. This intention of God, announced in the words "Let us make man in our image, after our likeness" (Gen. 1:26, KJV), was temporarily frustrated through the rebellion of the first creatures created in His image; but His intention continues to echo and reecho through the corridors of revelation and history. At times it sounded like a voice calling in the night, "This my son is dead!" At other times glorious affirmations ring out, and the intention of God "in bringing many sons to glory" (Heb. 2:10) develops in His own way until He cries, "This my son was dead, and is alive again; he was lost, and is found" (Luke 15:24, KJV).

For, in the process of time, and when the right moment arrived, "God sent forth His Son . . . the Son of His love" (Gal. 4:4; Col. 1:13, both NKJV) unsullied, unflecked by sin, unlimited in love, blameless in righteousness. And in Jesus all the love, light, and life of God were not only shown but also given. To a willful and rebellious humanity God in Christ declared that His intention and purpose was not merely an ideal but also a reality. He showed us visibly what it is to belong to the holy family, and He declared it to be intelligible, desirable, and possible. For "as many as received Him" (i.e., God's Word incarnate, His dream demonstrated, His stated purpose right here in flesh and blood among us), "to them He gave the right to become children of God" (John 1:12, NKJV), "begotten not by human descent, nor through an impulse of the flesh, nor through the will of a human father, but from God" (v. 13, Weymouth). Love found a way!

"For if, by the trespass of the one man, death reigned through that one man, how much more will those who receive God's abundant provision of grace and of the gift of righteousness reign in life through the one man, Jesus Christ" (Rom. 5:17).

That kind of love is unearthly! It is from another country; it is God's love invading time and history, creating a new humanity, and bringing into His royal family those who really want to be there, and will "bear the family likeness of his Son, that he might be the eldest of a family of many brothers" (Rom. 8:29, Phillips). These He chose long ago, these He called when His time came, these He made right with himself, and these He lifted to the honor, privilege, and splendor of life in His own family! (Cf. v. 30, Phillips.) God's love has done it. Love unearthly, incredible, incomprehensible, and absolutely divine. *There* is the Source of our belonging to the family. And now take another step and think about:

B. *The Force of Our Belonging to the Holy Family: The Love of the Family*

On the gates of the Wesley Chapel in City Road, London, there hangs Wesley's Christian "coat of arms," a cross with the words "God is love." That really is the emblem of the holy family. We are His only "because He first loved us." But the truth stretches in two directions. "We love because he first loved us. . . . God is love. Whoever lives in love lives in God, and God in him. In this way, love is made complete among us" (1 John 4:19, 16-17). Whoever loves God must also (i.e., of dispositional necessity) love his brother. The family likeness is chiefly divine love, poured "into our hearts by the Holy Spirit, whom he has given us" (Rom. 5:5).

It can emphatically be declared, the apostle says, that this is the whole of Christian life in the family of God. The holy family has been authenticated from its very beginnings by one great and non-counterfeitable element: family love. "This is the message you heard from the beginning: We should love one another" (1 John 3:11). "By this all men will know that you are my disciples" (John 13:35). The apostle enforces this fact through a contrast and an example. The contrast: "Do not be like Cain" (1 John 3:12). The example: Be like Jesus Christ (see v. 16).

Divine love is the lifeblood of the holy family. A broken family is one in which the so-called members have nothing to talk about, no common interest or concern or purpose for being together. The force behind and within the family of God is the life and love of God in the soul of each member. It is a matter not merely of feeling "for" but of feeling "with" each other. That may seem idealistic and utopian, a life-style far removed from reality and possibility; and certainly it would be so, and would remain so, but for the Spirit of love poured into our hearts. He is the Force of our family life and living; He alone is the Force "that binds / Our hearts in Christian love."

We have all heard repeatedly of the small boy who, carrying his brother who was almost as big as himself, was asked by a passerby, "Isn't he far too heavy for you?" The child is reported to have responded, "He's not heavy—he's my brother!" The truth, however, is that sometimes he is heavy, but he is still my brother to be loved, helped, and carried if necessary. Probably I weigh as heavily on him at times.

The force of our belonging to the holy family is love of the family. Charles Wesley expressed it winsomely in his prayer:

> *Help us to help each other, Lord,*
> *Each other's cross to bear;*
> *Let each his friendly aid afford,*
> *And feel his brother's care.*
>
> *Help us to build each other up,*
> *Our little stock improve;*
> *Increase our faith, confirm our hope,*
> *And perfect us in love.*

The apostle, all through his letter, keeps ever before us this characteristic distinctive of love in the holy family. But there is another that is the twin of this. That is:

C. *The Course of Our Belonging to the Holy Family: The Love of Holy Living*

1. The Blessed Heredity. **No one who is born of God will continue to sin** (v. 9). **No one who lives in him keeps on sinning** (v. 6). The union of sin and Christ in the same heart is not possible. The man or woman in Christ inhabits a holy household, is a member of the family of the holy Father, and is called to live habitually and closely in touch with the holy Father, in touch with the holy Father's "holy child Jesus" (Acts 4:27, 30, KJV).

The course of life in the holy family, the principle that animates that life and underlies all belonging and awareness in that family is holiness and righteousness. It cannot be other than that in this family. It is the law of heavenly heredity. The "seed" of God is the life principle of every family member. Their pedigree is in v. 1, and this being so, "Because you are sons, God sent the Spirit of his Son into our hearts, the Spirit who calls out, *'Abba,* Father'" (Gal. 4:6). "The Spirit calls out"—note that! The family witness is not merely human profession but the Holy Spirit's inward and outward witness. By the inward witness family members know that they belong; by the outward witness everyone else knows that they belong.

> *His Spirit to us He gave,*
> *And dwells in us, we know!*
> *The witness in ourselves we have,*
> *And all its fruits we show!*

The life of God in the souls of His children is outwardly certified by its effects. The tree is known by its fruits. Since God is righteous and holy, divine life is righteous and holy.

a. Because God is love, divine life is shown in love.

b. Because God is light, the life of His children is demonstrated by love of truth and truthful living. As John would put it, it is infinitely more reasonable that black be a shade of white than that God's sons and daughters have the characteristics of the devil (cf. John 8:44, 47).

(1) The origin of sin—the devil (1 John 3:8, 10*a*)

(2) The essence of sin—lawlessness (v. 4)

(3) The inconsistency of sin with godliness (vv. 6-7)

(4) The purpose of the incarnation and passion of the Son of God (v. 8*b*)

Each and all of these, singly and cumulatively, spell out the truth. No one who is a child of the holy Father can continue a life of sinning: **Do not let anyone lead you astray** on that (v. 7).

When a child of God falls into an act of sin, it is a grievous experience; it quenches his joy, breaks his peace, disturbs his relationship with the holy Father, and causes him to mourn in his deepest soul. But thanks be to God, "If any man sin, we have an advocate with the Father" (2:1, KJV), none other than "the Holy One of God," our Elder Brother who alone puts away sin.

> *Five bleeding wounds He bears, Received on Calvary.*
> *They pour effectual prayers; They strongly plead for me!*
> . . . .
> *The Father hears Him pray, His dear Anointed One;*
> *He cannot turn away The presence of His Son.*
> —CHARLES WESLEY

Hence it is written, "If we confess our sins, he is faithful and just and will forgive us our sins and purify us from all unrighteousness" (1:9).

The course of life in the holy family is to live righteously and unblamably before God all the days of our lives, allowing Him to work on us day by day, making us daily a little more like Jesus.

2. The Blessed Hope (vv. 2-3). All that we have read and said refers to the "now." **Now we are children of God** (3:2). Let us attend to the present moment and to our present condition. Let us continue in Him, doing **what is right** (2:29); simply trusting every day; loving God with all our heart, soul, mind, and strength; receiving from the Spirit inward grace and power to love because He first loved us, to bear each other's burdens, and to help our Lord lift the load of the world's great woes. Our priority and concern is *now,* living up to the privileges and responsibilities of our presently belonging to the holy family. It is God's work *now* that is the basis of all our blessed hope for the future. His love will last without diminishing. His purposes will ripen fast; we shall know Jesus then and there if we walk with Him here and now. We know so very little of that life that is to come when the family of God is finally and fully gathered into the Father's house of many mansions. But what we do know is very blessed. **We shall be like him, for we shall see him** [even and exactly and actually] **as he is** (3:2). Our hope is set on Him. He is our Life now and forever, and a hope set, and resting, and centering on Him cannot but control life now.

John finds it impossible to punctuate his rhapsody. That unearthly love has unearthly intentions. What these are we do not yet fully see or grasp, but the ultimate is splendor beyond earthly knowledge and expression: **We shall be like him**! In some ways we are called to be like Him *now* (2:6; 3:16), and we *are now* being changed, thank God, from those ways in which we are not like Him (2 Cor. 3:18). But when He reappears, that likeness will be made complete. Thus, because I have, hold, and cherish such a blessed hope, I continue to walk with Him, abide in Him, pressing ever more closely to His unseen presence. I desire not to be ashamed before Him then, so I keep near Him now. This life-style may make me a bit of a mystery to people now, but then—so was He! (3:1; cf. John 3:10). This is the course of life in the holy family, and its glorious objective! The holy family will be gathered home to the house of the Father:

Some from earth; from glory some;
Served only "Till He come!"

I'm so glad I belong to the holy family. With grateful love I sing with Methodism's songster:

> *O that all with us might prove,*
> *The fellowship of saints!*
> *Find supplied, in Jesus' love,*
> *What every member wants:*
> *Grasp we our high calling's prize,*
> *Feel on earth our sins forgiven,*
> *Rise, in His whole image rise,*
> *And meet our Head in heaven!*

Endnotes

1. I. Howard Marshall, *The Epistles of John,* in *The New International Commentary on the New Testament,* ed. F. F. Bruce (Grand Rapids: Wm. B. Eerdmans Publishing Co., 1978), 165.

2. F. F. Bruce, *The Epistles of John* (Grand Rapids: Wm. B. Eerdmans Publishing Co., 1970), 78.

3. Raymond Brown says that "in this period of Greek *ean* [if] often means 'whenever, when.' . . . [It] does not indicate uncertainty about eventuality but about the exact time." *The Epistles of John,* in *The Anchor Bible,* ed. W. F. Albright and D. N. Freedman (Garden City, N.Y.: Doubleday and Co., 1982), 379.

4. *Epistles of John,* 26.

5. This term for the Second Advent is used 24 times in the NT, but this is its only occurrence in the Johannine literature. It has become transliterated as a technical term.

6. *Epistles of John,* 169.

7. *Epistles of John,* 79. Bruce identifies the pronoun in "He is righteous" with God, but see discussion above.

8. *Epistles of John,* 384-85.

9. E. M. Blaiklock, *Faith Is the Victory: Studies in the First Epistle of John* (London: Paternoster Press, 1957).

10. Bruce, *Epistles of John,* 85. This phrase has strong manuscript support.

11. *Epistles of John,* 170.

12. Robert Candlish, *First Epistle of John* (Grand Rapids: Kregel Publications, 1979), 258.

13. *Half-Hours with St. John* (Chicago: Hodder and Stoughton, 1909), 74-75.

14. B. F. Westcott, *The Epistles of John* (Grand Rapids: Wm. B. Eerdmans Publishing Co., 1960), 108.

15. *The Renaissance New Testament* 17:351.

16. James Montgomery Boice, *Epistles of John* (Grand Rapids: Zondervan Publishing Co., 1979), 109.

17. *The Standard Sermons of John Wesley,* ed. Edward H. Sugden (London: Epworth Press, 1961), 2:155.

18. See H. Ray Dunning, *Grace, Faith, and Holiness: A Wesleyan Systematic Theology* (Kansas City: Beacon Hill Press of Kansas City, 1988), chap. 15.

HENRY W. SPAULDING II

Holiness— God's Predestined Purpose for His People

And we know that in all things God works for the good of those who love him, who have been called according to his purpose. For those God foreknew he also predestined to be conformed to the likeness of his Son, that he might be the firstborn among many brothers (Rom. 8:28-29).

Contemporary Focus

My grandmother embodied the truth of our text. She never commanded attention when walking down the street. No one would have been impressed by her clothes or her house. Still she knew a great deal about what it meant to live for Christ. Part of her discipleship was to raise a family through the terror of the depression. She lost her oldest son during World War II to a kamikaze pilot. Arthritis plagued her for the last 20 years of her life. Living was not easy. Yet in the midst of this sometimes difficult life, she maintained a growing relationship with Christ.

The attitude of her life seemed very close to Paul's affirmation, **In all things God works for the good of those who love him.** She seemed to be aware of God's redeeming love in the various circumstances of life. Even during those times of remembering how her eldest son had died, she felt a deep sense of God's goodness. She had doubts, but through it all she believed God.

A new gospel is emerging in our time. Everything from a promotion at work to a new house is promised to those who believe. This kind of gospel is popular in good times but quickly passes when the going is difficult. Paul is giving witness in our text to another kind of gospel—the gospel of the crucified and resurrected Christ. He does not promise an easy time, or even apparent success, but he does give witness to the goodness of God. He affirms that the sustaining grace of God is sufficient for the trials and failures of life. Paul chooses to focus attention upon the God who works through every circumstance, and he calls attention to God's intention for His people: Christlikeness. If holiness is real, it must work in the crucible of life. Paul knew it, and my grandmother knew it. Holiness is for living!

Exegetical Section

Our text is one of the best-known passages in the Scripture. Unfortunately, v. 28 is usually quoted in isolation from its context and thus is easily turned into a "security blanket" that interprets God's goal for our lives in egocentric ways. But in context with v. 29, which is necessary to complete the thought, it becomes a tremendous challenge to cooperate with God in His intentions for us.

It comes near the end of a remarkable chapter that begins, "Therefore, there is now no condemnation for those who are in Christ Jesus." This redeeming grace is also an enabling grace, as Paul so clearly says in vv. 28-29. This affirmation fits well with what has preceded it in the total sweep of the message of Romans.

Paul begins Romans by painting a dismal picture of humanity. Both the Gentile, who violates the knowledge of the truth given by general revelation (1:19-20), and the Jew, who has received the revealed truth through the law, stand guilty before God (3:23). Neither have an excuse for their sin, since God has not left himself without a witness to any person. The faithfulness of God makes the sinfulness of humanity all the more intolerable. But a vision of God's intention for humankind breaks through this black cloud when Paul announces the "righteousness from God, apart from [the] law [that] has been made known, to which the Law and the Prophets testify. This righteousness from God comes through faith in Jesus Christ to all who believe" (3:21-22). He then illustrates this righteousness through faith by the life of Abraham.

From this point, he explores the full provisions of God's redemptive plan that offer a full and free pardon to those who believe. But our appropriation of these provisions by faith does not relieve us of the necessity of living a holy life. It implies a responsibility to live like a person who has "been brought from death to life" (6:13). It also implies a freedom from the law as a vehicle of sanctification, a freedom that points to a righteousness that transcends the law (7:6). Chapter 7 reinforces this truth by a dramatic portrayal of the existential struggle of one who unsuccessfully attempts to be sanctified through the law. It culminates with the realization of the necessity of divine enablement (vv. 24-25). It is, in fact, only through this enabling grace that Christian liberty can be found. Chapter 8 is a celebration of this liberty and a manifesto of the privileges and responsibilities of those who are "in Christ" (v. 1) and in whom Christ lives (v. 11). Thus the apostle covers the whole sweep of God's redeeming activity in human history. *As a climax to this great movement of grace, our text stands as a brilliant summary of God's intentions for His people.*

And we know. There is little doubt that Paul has presented a powerful argument to this point. Romans is a carefully worked out statement of his vision of grace. In chap. 8 he is beginning to pull together the various themes presented in the book and boldly affirms that what will follow, as well as what has preceded our text, is grounded in this God of grace. This is the basis for his sure knowledge.

Beyond the logic of his theological argument, the truth is attested by experience. God's grace works in day-to-day life as well as in theory. The few verses following the text (31-36) can be best understood as an affirmation arising out of the experience of a man who has suffered for the gospel (2 Cor. 6:4-10). What follows (vv. 37-39) is the foundation upon which Paul is able to affirm the sustaining and sanctifying grace of God.

In all things God works. Essentially, Paul is saying that God is active in the world. A good deal of theological discussion surrounds the precise meaning of this phrase. Some believe Paul is saying that God causes everything. This finally makes God responsible for both good and evil. A more Wesleyan view does not attempt to decide whether God caused or even allowed what appears to be an evil situation. What it does affirm is that God is active in all circumstances, not as a cause but as a Redeemer, one who intervenes in the events that occur in a believer's life to accomplish His full redemptive intentions for them.

For the good of those who love him. This clarifies the good of God's activity. He is at work to bring good out of every experience in life. The meaning of this promise hangs on the term **good,** which is a purpose word. That is good that fulfills the purpose for which it was designed or that functions according to its nature. A watch is "good" if it keeps time, because that was the purpose that the maker had in mind. This assumes that there is a purpose for which man was created. Such an assumption is antithetical to the atheistic existentialism of Jean-Paul Sartre, who denies there is a human nature and thus no value (good) except that which man creates for himself. The biblical view is that God made humankind in such a fashion that there is a predestined "good," and it is this that He desires to actualize in human life.

The condition of this promise is that it is made to **those who love him.** This suggests not only confidence in God's purpose for us but also a willing submission to His sovereign will in working it out. John Wesley speaks of our love for God (and others) as the only religion worthy of the God who gave it, and comments: "This love we believe to be the medicine of life, the never-failing remedy for all the evils of a disordered world, for all the miseries and vices of men. Wherever this is, there are virtue and happiness going hand in hand. There is humbleness of mind, gentleness, long-suffering, the whole image of God; and at the same time a peace that passeth all understanding, and joy unspeakable and full of glory."[1]

Who have been called according to his purpose. This appears to complete the argument of the verse. Paul has asserted that (1) God is active in the world, and (2) God is about the task of bringing good out of every situation. But he has not yet explained what the **purpose** is to which God has called His people. This, of course, pertains only to those who seek God's will in their lives, that is, those who were "effectively called." The "effectively called" are "those whose hearts and minds were so thoroughly influenced by the Holy Spirit that they became aware of their sinfulness, began to understand their need of Christ, and embraced him as their Lord and Savior."[2]

For those God foreknew. The thought expressed here is meant as a continuation of what Paul was saying in v. 28. Those **who have been called according to his purpose** are the people whom God knows. The content of this knowledge is related to God's care for His children (Ps. 1:6). There are examples in Scripture where God (or Jesus) "knew beforehand" what was to happen: the response of the Pharaoh to Moses (Exodus 6—12), the betrayal of Jesus by Judas (Matt. 26:14-16), and the denial of Peter (vv. 69-75) are examples of events known beforehand. Yet, every promise in the Scripture, whether it is for the righteous remnant (Isa. 35:1-2), the benefits of wisdom (Prov. 2:12), or the meaning of discipleship (Matt. 5:3-12), is in some sense related to the foreknowledge of God. It is in this latter sense that Paul intends to express himself. It should not be understood as involving some kind of determination that destroys the possibility of free personal relations between man and God.

He also predestined. This means that "God has a purpose and a plan and a design and a task for man."[3] This phrase further qualifies what Paul means by the foreknowledge of God. Predestination is a term with a rich and rather diverse theological heritage. Some define predestination as the sovereign act of God that declares that certain people will be saved and others condemned. Those who hold this view feel that God foreknows because He has predestined everything.

Another interpretation of predestination is to say that God predestines in the sense that He predetermines how we will be saved. He sets the bounds of salvation ahead of time (Eph. 1:4). There is nothing here that suggests that God decides who will be saved and who will be condemned. In fact, the natural reading of this text would indicate that God elects all who will believe. God calls everyone; those who believe are elected through His grace.

In this particular passage, predestination refers to the character that God purposes to produce in those who love Him.

To be conformed to the likeness of his Son. The holiness dimension of our text is clearly expressed here. All of life, including that which appears to be evil, is intended by God to make His children more like Christ. The content of this **likeness** cannot be derived exegetically from this text but may be seen throughout the NT Epistles as well as by implication from the Gospels. From these sources we learn, among other things, that this **likeness of his Son**

is expressed in a moral freedom from the law (Gal. 5:1, 6), which is an even deeper level of obedience to God (Phil. 1:27; 2:10-11). Christlikeness includes sexual purity (Eph. 5:3) but extends beyond that to the kind of attitude that seeks to please the Lord in every aspect of life (6:10). Christlikeness changes every relationship: wives/husbands (5:22-33), children/parents (6:1-4), and even employee/employer (6:5-9). This same attitude enables those who are conformed to His likeness to be compassionate, kind, humble, gentle, patient, forbearing, forgiving, and most of all, loving (Col. 3:12-14).

God watches over His children with a purpose in mind, that they be like Christ. This grand purpose is evident in creation (Gen. 1:26-27) and continues through all of God's dealing with His people. It is the reason that God **works in all things** for His people. This little phrase also summarizes the argument Paul started in Rom. 5:9, "Since we have now been justified by his blood, how much more shall we be saved from God's wrath through him!" It is as if the entire intent of a good God comes dramatically into focus. The process of sanctification is the pattern of God's relationship with His children.

That he might be the firstborn among many brothers. Here, Paul envisions a new race, or more appropriately, a new family with Christ as the Head and all who stand in line with Him bearing the family likeness.

Theological Exegesis

All preaching in one way or the other is about God. Whether the theme is creation, justice, salvation, or heart holiness, the subject is always the God who stands at the center of the Christian faith. The text clearly presents a picture of God and His purpose for us. According to William Greathouse, "Our redemption is . . . not the working out of our fickle human purposes or of our self-initiated choices; rather it represents the outworking of God's eternal plan."[4] Paul affirms that God is active. He is not a stone image oblivious to the struggles of His people. He is actively involved in their lives. It may not always be evident to the natural eye, but faith perceives that God is at work.

It is not enough to say that God is active in the world. We must know what He is doing. Paul addresses this issue by suggesting that what God does is good. In this text the good that God is working to produce relates to the redemption of His people. This redemption involves both an initial action and an ongoing process in the lives of those who follow Jesus. Mildred Bangs Wynkoop talks about God's dealing with us as "the process of ripening of Christian character. It begins in the genesis of Christian life and continues so long as integrity is essential to love."[5]

Another affirmation in the passage is that for the Christian, life is a sanctifying experience. According to John Wesley, "the apostle declares who those are whom he foreknew and predestinated to glory; namely, those who are *conformable to the image of his Son.*"[6] It is clear that this text refers to all who seek to obey God. Life has many turns, but with God each individual can be more like Christ each day of the journey. The picture here is of that person who has allowed life's troubles to make him better and purer. This does not deny instantaneous sanctification; it rather points to a holistic work that continually goes on in the life of the believer. Both aspects of the NT truth of sanctification are expressed rather well by Wesley: "I believe this perfection is always wrought in the soul by a simple act of faith; consequently, in an instant. But I believe a gradual work, both preceding and following that instant."[7] Now Paul is suggesting that this life of grace ultimately enables a person to overcome every obstacle. He even proclaims that God has so fashioned the world and humankind that through His Spirit everyone can be **conformed to the likeness of his Son.**

There is one more step, "Those he justified, he also glorified" (8:30). This is the final consummation of God's redeeming activity.

Preaching Ideas

Holiness viewed in its broadest meaning is the process of becoming more like Christ. The experience of God's grace is evident in justification, entire sanctification, and the courage to live in every moment. This text offers a great opportunity to integrate holiness into the various challenges of life. It is a great text for looking at the life of holiness on a large scale. It is just possible that preaching holiness from this text will help people see that holiness really is relevant to their own Christian pilgrimage. The following paragraphs suggest how it is possible to do this.

Suggestion One

"Holiness: God's Intentions and Man's Response." The basic point of this sermon would be that holiness is born out of man's response to the good intentions of God. *First,* God's intentions are good: *(a)* Seen in the Creation (Gen. 2:7). God created humankind for fellowship, glory, and obedient service. *(b)* Manifested in the Exodus (Exod. 12:31-42 and Hos. 11:1-4). This event contains the seed of the entire gospel story of deliverance from sin. God has not called His children to live in bondage. *(c)* In the Final Resurrection (Rom. 6:5). The ultimate victory over death and sin comes from being identified with Jesus Christ. *Second,* man's response to God is equally clear. *(a)* We ought to live as God created us (Rom. 8:22-23). The path of our life ought to show the world our divine origin. *(b)* We ought to live in freedom (1 Cor. 10:23 and Rom. 6:18). The Christian has the privilege of living free of the bondage brought by sin. *(c)* We ought to live with a sense of victory (Rom. 6:14). God gives the ability to live above the frustrations of the moment.

Suggestion Two

"Conformed by the Grace of God." The central idea of this sermon relates to the promise of God to make us more like His Son. *First,* the great purpose of God is that all be conformed. "God works for the good." *(a)* God's purpose goes to the very beginning of the world (Gen. 3:15). *(b)* God's purpose goes to the very end of history (Rev. 22:17). *Second,* the great provision of God is that all be conformed: "those God foreknew he also predestined." *(a)* God has provided through the life of Jesus (John 1:17). *(b)* God has provided through the death and resurrection of Jesus (1 Cor. 15:21-22). *Third,* God extends a great privilege to those who are conformed to His image: "that he might be the firstborn among many brothers." *(a)* We can enjoy the privilege of adoption (Rom. 8:15-17 and Gal. 4:4-7, KJV). *(b)* We can enjoy the privilege of a pure heart (Matt. 5:8 and 2 Cor. 1:12).

Suggestion Three

"These Things We Know." The fundamental premise of this sermon would be that holiness is grounded in a God who offers assurance in our changing world. *First,* God is at work in our world. *(a)* He seeks to bring good out of every situation (Mic. 2:12-13). *(b)* A merging of purpose with God is essential to a meaningful life

(Amos 5:4-6). *Second,* God knows His children. *(a)* He has created us (Isa. 43:1). *(b)* He watches over us (Pss. 23:1-6 and 59:17). *Third,* God seeks to make us more like Him. *(a)* Salvation is the intent of God's redeeming activity on our behalf (Lev. 19:2 and Ps. 107: 13-16). *(b)* The final aim of God is for me to be like Christ—conformed to His image (Eph. 4:20-24).

Suggestion Four

"A Changed Perspective." The basic idea of this sermon would be to interpret holiness in terms of a distinctive perspective on life. *First,* a growing relationship to God changes our relationship to the world. *(a)* We begin to see God as the Cause of everything good (Acts 17:24-25). *(b)* We sense a purpose in life (Eph. 5:1-2 and Phil. 3:12). *Second,* a growing relationship with God changes self-understanding. *(a)* Our only hope of fulfillment is in God (1 John 2:5-6). *(b)* A deep sense of purpose pervades life (Matt. 13:45-46). *Third,* a growing relationship with God changes our relationship to people. *(a)* We see people as God's creation (Luke 19:8-9). *(b)* We see people as objects of redemption (1 Cor. 9:19-23).

A Sermon on the Text
Holiness Is for Living

A central point of this text is the livability of holiness. It takes the holiness message beyond temper tantrums, discord, or hatred. Here Paul is dealing with a larger struggle that goes on when life is unkind. He is affirming that the grace he has been talking about works in all circumstances. This message could well apply to a lady whom it was my privilege to pastor. Her husband died suddenly in his late 30s, leaving her with a young family. She had never worked outside of the home. Now she was forced by circumstances to learn a job from the ground up. Life was not easy for her. After her children had grown up, she took a trip to the Northwest. While on the trip, she developed an aneurysm, which made brain surgery necessary. During the last several years she has lost her sight almost completely. She could have given up or grown bitter. Yet her life has always radiated with a witness to heart holiness. It is important that people understand that holiness is for situations like this as well as for the victory over bad temper or the like. This text brings a message of hope to all those who suffer.

An illustration that I have used at this point comes from a simple event in the life of my oldest child. It all goes back to the day she skinned her knee while learning to ride a bicycle. As I attempted to console her, it struck me that this little incident was a parable that helps explain how God deals with us in the life of holiness.

Riding a bicycle is similar to life because it takes effort to maintain one's balance. This thing called living can be a challenge. Existence is a gift of God; living is a choice we must make. God does not call us to be bicycle racers, but He does expect us to keep pedaling. It is only in this way that we incarnate holiness into life.

There is another way in which bicycle riding is associated with life—sometimes it hurts. I sit beside my little girl and feel helpless. She is crying because of a skinned knee. I would, if it were possible, bear the pain for her. I can't. Each of us must bear the pain of our own attempt to live. You see, none of us can learn to ride a bicycle without enduring a few skinned knees. We can all be sure that it will hurt to live, at least occasionally. Therefore, the key is not whether we will hurt, but what will we do in response to pain? If we quit, it will have more disastrous effects than not riding a bicycle. Quitting is too expensive, not to pedal pushing but to living. We must learn to live, in spite of the pain that accompanies it.

Another sense in which bicycle riding is a parable of life is related to purpose. My wife and I were helping Shelly stay straight. As we let go, Shelly took over; yet in merely six feet, she was down. Was it my purpose? Was it avoidable? If it was neither my purpose nor unavoidable, why did it happen? In one form or another this question plagues us all. It is especially problematic when we think of God. Why doesn't God stop us from skinning our knees so much? The plain truth seems to be that life implies certain risks. Whether it is holiness or character, the possibility of a "skinned knee" is unavoidable. Holiness is by faith through grace, but it is also worked out in the hard knocks of life.

Parables have their limits. Bicycle riding is like living, but only sort of like it. God calls us to be more than conquerors and provides His love and strength for the battle. Whether we ever learn to ride a bicycle, we must live. It is only in this way that the fullness of God's power is known. Living is the gift of God's power and our choice. Holiness is the ability and the will to serve God, skinned knees and all.

The basis for this possibility is the positive affirmation of the text: **And we know that in all things God works for the good of those who love him.** On the hope that this brings to us, we find the strength to overcome.

No matter how black the sin or desperate the situation, God always brings hope. He makes all the difference in the world. God is the rainbow that runs through both the pain and the joy of life. A line from a country and western song comes close to making this point: "If we're ever going to see a rainbow, / We are going to have to stand a little pain." Paul knew what it meant to suffer for Christ, and he knew that Christ was able to deliver.

But Paul is not here talking about a stoic acceptance of hardship or remorse. He declares that God has a purpose for each life. Our life is not merely a collection of unattached events. Each person can know the hand of God in his life. We should be very careful to say that this purpose arises out of God's dealing with us in the midst of our dilemmas. He brings a purpose because He can weave a good and redemptive pattern into our lives in the face of all circumstances.

The final purpose of life is to be Christlike (1 Pet. 4:13). The design of life is that God will make us all like Christ. The Scripture is full of examples of what it means to be like Christ: pure, gentle, loving, kind, reconciling, and so on. Nothing in life is able to separate us from the purpose of God to make us more like Christ. In fact, the great promise of God is that in each and every circumstance we can be more like our Lord and Savior.

When I think of this truth, my own mother comes to mind. She is a school administrator with impressive credentials. About 1970 her parents got sick, and the illness lasted 10 years. She along with other members of the family elected to keep their parents at home. This meant that each person had to stay in the home with their parents two nights a week. These were rough nights with very little sleep. My mother had other responsibilities as well—her own family and a very demanding job. The nights were long, and she saw her parents waste away as she looked on helplessly. It was painful for her, and there were many dark days. This could have made her bitter. Yet through it all she became more compassionate, more like the Christ who sustained her through those difficult days. This is what this great biblical promise is all about.

Endnotes

1. John Wesley, "An Earnest Appeal to Men of Reason and Religion," in *The Works of John Wesley,* 3rd ed. (Kansas City: Beacon Hill Press of Kansas City, 1978), 8:3.

2. William Hendriksen, "Romans, Chapters 1—8," in *New Testament Commentary* (Grand Rapids: Baker Book House, 1980), 12:281.

3. William Barclay, *The Letter to the Romans,* in *The Daily Study Bible Series* (Philadelphia: Westminster Press, 1957), 120.

4. William M. Greathouse, "The Epistle to the Romans," in *Beacon Bible Commentary,* ed. A. F. Harper (Kansas City: Beacon Hill Press of Kansas City, 1968), 8:190.

5. Mildred Bangs Wynkoop, *A Theology of Love: The Dynamic of Wesleyanism* (Kansas City: Beacon Hill Press of Kansas City, 1972), 301.

6. John Wesley, *Explanatory Notes upon the New Testament,* 2 vols. (Kansas City: Beacon Hill Press of Kansas City, 1981).

7. John Wesley, "Brief Thoughts on Christian Perfection," in *Wesley's Works* 11:446.

C. NEIL STRAIT

The New Life in Christ

Since you died with Christ to the basic principles of this world, why, as though you still belonged to it, do you submit to its rules: "Do not handle! Do not taste! Do not touch!"? These are all destined to perish with use, because they are based on human commands and teachings. Such regulations indeed have an appearance of wisdom, with their self-imposed worship, their false humility and their harsh treatment of the body, but they lack any value in restraining sensual indulgence. Since, then, you have been raised with Christ, set your hearts on things above, where Christ is seated at the right hand of God. Set your minds on things above, not on earthly things. For you died, and your life is now hidden with Christ in God. When Christ, who is your life, appears, then you also will appear with him in glory. Put to death, therefore, whatever belongs to your earthly nature: sexual immorality, impurity, lust, evil desires and greed, which is idolatry. Because of these, the wrath of God is coming. You used to walk in these ways, in the life you once lived. But now you must rid yourselves of all such things as these: anger, rage, malice, slander, and filthy language from your lips. Do not lie to each other, since you have taken off your old self with its practices and have put on the new self, which is being renewed in knowledge in the image of its Creator. Here there is no Greek or Jew, circumcised or uncircumcised, barbarian, Scythian, slave or free, but Christ is all, and is in all. Therefore, as God's chosen people, holy and dearly loved, clothe yourselves with compassion, kindness, humility, gentleness and patience. Bear with each other and forgive whatever grievances you may have against one another. Forgive as the Lord forgave you. And over all these virtues put on love, which binds them all together in perfect unity. Let the peace of Christ rule in your hearts, since as members of one body you were called to peace. And be thankful. Let the word of Christ dwell in you richly as you teach and admonish one another with all wisdom, and as you sing psalms, hymns and spiritual songs with gratitude in your hearts to God. And whatever you do, whether in word or deed, do it all in the name of the Lord Jesus, giving thanks to God the Father through him (Col. 2:20—3:17).

Martin Marty of the University of Chicago once made a devastating criticism of the "born again" movement. Sports figures, movie stars, and celebrities from all areas of public life professed to have experienced a new birth. It was the "in" thing. Dr. Marty, noted for his keen analysis of American Christianity, observed that this movement was not accompanied by any change in life-style. From his point of view, this apparently invalidated much of this religious phenomenon. Paul would agree. What was going on was what Dietrich Bonhoeffer referred to as "cheap grace," forgiveness of sins without the transformation of the sinner. In traditional theological language, it was justification without sanctification.

While the contours of the situation at Colosse were significantly different because of the historical circumstances, the principles were much the same. And the apostle was calling for the transformation in the life of the Colossian believers that their conversion entailed.

Exegetical Section

The language of this section flows from decision to discipleship. Paul leaves no gray areas in his call to live out the implications of having **died with Christ**. The pattern or structure of the whole passage revolves around the concept of **the old self** (man, nature) and **the new self** (man, nature). The appeal is to put off the old and put on the new. The marks of the old life are the manifestations of "worldliness" in the Colossian situation. The marks of the new life are manifestations of the "image of God" as modeled by the character of Christ. Hence we have here a central passage that depicts holiness or sanctification as "the renewal of man in the image of God." Thus holiness is in essence a new life in Christ.

Since you died with Christ (i.e., in baptism) is an assumption of a completed, crisis act. Francis W. Beare puts it this way: "Knowing that you died with Christ."[1] Adam Clarke, commenting on a parallel passage, Rom. 6:3, wrote: "That, as Jesus Christ in His crucifixion died completely, so that no spark of the natural or animal life remained in His body, so those who profess His religion should be so completely separated and saved from sin that they have no more connection with it, not any more influence from it, than a dead man has with or from his departed spirit."[2]

To what, then, has the believer died? **To the basic principles** [rudiments, KJV] **of this world.** The NASB uses "elementary principles." John B. Nielson interprets these as "the lesser spiritual opposing powers."[3] Lightfoot states, "All mundane (worldly) relations have ceased for you."[4] Some have suggested that it refers to astral deities, but most scholars find this unacceptable. It simply refers to the "principles" on which the world operates, its presuppositions.

Do not handle! Do not taste! Do not touch! These are three examples of the worldly principles that the one who has **died with Christ** is to reject. They are assumptions that certain foods are inherently evil and therefore to be avoided. Paul's awareness of the biblical (OT) meaning of creation causes him to reject this faulty point of view. As Barclay translates v. 23, "They have no kind of value in remedying the indulgences of sinful human nature."[5] This provides the rationale for the negative side of Paul's exhortation. "Dying with Christ" entails "putting off" the old life based on faulty presuppositions. He returns to further practical implications of this truth in 3:5 ff.

Since, then, you have been raised with Christ. Now he turns to the positive side of God's provisions. The believer is raised to Resurrection life in Christ. What are the implications of this "raised life"? The first is embodied in the exhortation to **set your hearts on things above . . . Set your minds on things above** (3:1-2). John Wesley translates **minds** as "affections."[6] This aspect of the person encompasses "mind, will, spirit," the basic ingredients of decision making. The word *phroneite* **(set your minds)** means "to be mindful of, think of."[7] "It involves both thought and disposition"; Lightfoot speaks of both a heavenly-mindedness and a heavenly attitude. Some have seen it to involve "thinking about heaven," but in context this exhortation appeals to the believer to live by heavenly values or values consistent with the character of Christ, who now dwells in heaven.

On this admonition, John A. Knight comments: "Clearly one's priorities are to be arranged with spiritual values first and Christ at the pinnacle."[8]

For you died. Wesley has it, *"For ye are dead*—To the things on earth. *And your* real, spiritual *life is hid* from the world, and laid up *in God, with Christ."*[9] This is a death to sin and the world, and the life from such a death seeks Christ.

Your life is now hidden with Christ in God. In physical death/burial, the body is hidden in the earth. In spiritual death symbolized by baptism, one is hidden with Christ. Barclay states, "It was the experience of the early Christians that the very act of baptism wrapped a man round with Christ."[10] Hence, all the hidden resources of Christ are at his disposal, and such are "hidden from the understanding of the world."

Up to this point in the passage, Paul has been working with his concept of dying and rising with Christ as the basis of the new life. It now becomes the basis for a series of imperatives in vv. 5-10.

Put to death is a radical way of calling for a decisive break with the old life. It uses the Greek word *nekrōsate,* which means "to deprive of power, destroy the strength of."[11] Wesley comments, "Slay with a continued stroke." The NASB translates it, "Consider the members of your earthly body as dead." A. T. Robertson suggests, "Treat as dead."[12] John B. Nielson interprets it as "turning of the will away from self to God."[13] Francis W. Beare suggests that its meaning is to "dig it out by the roots and destroy it altogether, so that the new life may have full dominion."[14]

What is to be put to death is **whatever belongs to your earthly nature,** translated in the KJV as "your members which are upon the earth." They are here viewed as members of the "old self" or "old man" (v. 9, KJV).

"Old man" has been used by some as a synonym for original sin. This can only be done when taken out of context. J. Kenneth Grider's interpretation is far sounder in the light of Paul's use of the metaphor both here and in the two other instances (Rom. 6:6; Eph. 4:19-25). He argues that the metaphor refers to "pre-regenerate life." He comments on the Colossian passage:

> Let it be noted especially here that both carnal affections and acts of sin are connected with the "old man," which again suggests that the phrase refers to the unregenerate life instead of

simply to original sin. Paul speaks of putting off carnal affections such as "anger, wrath, malice" (3:8), and also of sin acts such as "filthy communication out of your mouth" (3:8). Then he says, "Lie not one to another, seeing that ye have put off the old man with his deeds" (3:9). If "old man" here were a reference to original sin, Paul would be saying, "You can tell lies all you please while you are regenerate, but not after you are cleansed of original sin. Therefore, since original sin has now been put off, in a second work of grace, quit your lying to one another." On the basis that "old man" refers to the unregenerate life, Paul is saying, "You people now have new hearts. You are newborn, and are not what you used to be. Old things have passed away, and all things are new. Live therefore as regenerate persons, and 'lie not one to another,' seeing that you have put off the old life 'with its sinful deeds.'"[15]

The characteristics that belong to the **earthly nature** then are marks of the old, unregenerate life and must be put aside since they are antithetical to the new life in Christ. We list these marks briefly:

Sexual immorality. From *porneian,* which is best translated "fornication" (KJV), from which is derived our word *pornography* (see 1 Cor. 5:10; 6:9, 18; 2 Cor. 12:21; 1 Thess. 4:3; 1 Tim. 1:9-10).[16]

Impurity. Manifestations of a sin-infested spirit (see Gal. 5:19-21; Eph. 5:3-5).

Lust ("passion," ASV). As Wesley comments, "Every passion which does not flow from and lead to the love of God."[17]

Evil desires. Strong and intense desires out of control, overly influenced by evil.

Greed, which is idolatry ("covetousness," KJV). Here used to mean the desire to have more, and the desire is evil because what he desires has become his god. "If what he covets, loves, and therefore worships is less than God, he is a practical idolater."[18]

Taken off your old self refers to a disarming or disrobing and involves a decision of the will/mind/spirit to **put to death** the things of sin and the sinful nature. This is to be balanced on the positive side by being clothed with **the new self, which is being renewed in knowledge in the image of its Creator.**

Scattered throughout this passage are several indications of the nature of this new life-style, but the overarching description is found in the phrase **being renewed in knowledge in the image of its Creator.** Here is God's comprehensive desire for His people, that they be renewed in the image of God, John Wesley's most comprehensive definition of sanctification. Since Jesus Christ is the embodiment of this image, it entails becoming more and more Christlike in our character, motives, attitudes, and behavior.

As to specifics, it involves a new way of looking at people that knows no distinctions concerning race, color, social status, or any other merely human distinction (3:11). It involves living in relation to others on the basis of truth (v. 9) and forgiveness (v. 13). In a word, it is living a life of undivided love for God and unselfish love of neighbor (v. 14).

As God's chosen people, holy and dearly loved, clothe yourselves with compassion, kindness, humility, gentleness and patience. Here is another indicative followed by an imperative. You *are* holy, so act as a holy person; you *are* loved, so act as one so loved. Relationship begets responsibility that in turn begets response.

The qualities listed in this verse fit into a holy ethic and lifestyle. They uplift and honor God, and as such they are vehicles through which love can flow—the fulfillment of v. 14: **Put on love, which binds them all together in perfect unity.**

Let the peace of Christ rule in your hearts. The word **rule** can be translated "keep on acting as umpire" (Williams; cf. Amp.). As such, when disputes or crises arise, "the decision of Christ will keep us in the way of love."[19]

Let the word of Christ dwell in you richly. Dwell implies that the **word of Christ** is to "take up its stated residence,"[20] or "to make one's home, to be at home."[21] Phillips translates this, "Let the full richness of Christ's teaching find its home among you."

Richly qualifies the indwelling to be "in the largest measure, and with the greatest efficacy; so as to fill and govern the whole soul."[22] The truth of v. 15 is only possible where the truth of v. 16 becomes a reality.

Theological Exegesis

Underlying this whole passage and informing it is Paul's baptismal theology. His argument is the same as in Rom. 6:1ff. The clue to appropriating it is to be aware that the meaning of conversion is derived from the meaning of baptism, which was not considered optional in the Early Church. There were no unbaptized believers.

Believers' baptism was considered by Paul (and the Early Church) to be an identification with Christ's baptism. Thus the meaning of His baptism is transferred to theirs. We must therefore investigate the significance of Jesus' baptism at the hands of John.

The primary significance of the event at the Jordan is seen in the words from heaven. "This is my beloved Son, with whom I am well pleased" (Matt. 3:17, RSV) is a combination of ordination formulae from the OT. One, derived from Ps. 2:7, is a Messianic word; and the other, from Isa. 42:1, is from one of the "Servant Songs." Thus the baptism was Jesus' induction into the vocation of the Servant Messiah, a vocation that implied suffering and death. In a word, His baptism was a declaration of intent to die. It was the Cross enacted beforehand, a proleptic event. From that moment on Jesus' face was set toward the consummation of His mission at the Cross.

In like manner, when Christian baptism was entered into, it carried with it a declaration of intent to die. Symbolically it signaled the death of the old man and the coming into being of the new man, represented by emerging from the baptismal waters. Put in theological terms, God justifies us with a view to sanctification.

In Romans 6, Paul appeals to this meaning to point out how ridiculous it is to consider the possibility of continuing in sin after baptism. To be buried with Christ in baptism was a declaration to put an end to sinning, so to even consider the possibility of going on sinning is a contradiction in terms. To ponder the thought shows that one does not understand the meaning of his baptism (conversion).

Both in Romans and Colossians Paul emphasizes the "death to sin" aspect of this baptismal theology and the newness of life that is to follow. There is a negative and a positive side to sanctification, the putting off of the old and the putting on of the new.

We need to introduce here a grammatical point that has great theological significance. Paul makes much use of the dialectical relation between the *indicative* and the *imperative*. The distinctive use of these moods has been the subject of much discussion, with several different interpretations emerging.[23] We here suggest what appears to be the best interpretation: The *indicative* speaks of what is the case, whereas the *imperative* is a call to make actual in life that already-accomplished reality. In this case, the apostle speaks of the accomplished fact of baptism, in which symbolically the believer is identified with Christ in His death. The imperative calls the believer to live out, bring to reality, actualize this in his experience. "You are" dead with Christ; now become what you are. As Frank Carver interprets this, "A faith-identification with Christ in His death and resurrection in the fullest sense is one Biblical way of defining the crisis of entire sanctification."[24]

Note the repeated use of the indicative in our passage: **Since you died with Christ** (2:20). **Since, then, you have been raised with Christ** (3:1). **For you died** (v. 3). **You have put off** (v. 9, NKJV), and you **have put on** (v. 10). [Note both positive and negative aspects here.]

On the basis of these already-accomplished facts symbolized by baptism, Paul appeals to the Colossians to both "put off" what is contrary to Christ and to "put on" what is reflective of the image of God as exemplified in Christ. In summary, this is a Christological interpretation of sanctification.

Sermon Suggestions

Topic: **A Strategy for Spiritual Victory**

Text: Col. 2:20—3:17

Introduction: The first question that must be settled before anyone gets serious about Christian growth is conversion, regeneration, the new birth. Our text assumes that this has been accomplished in the words **Since you died with Christ.** On the basis of that decisive event, the question **why, as though you still belonged to it** [the world], **do you submit to its rules ... ?** probes the depths of that conversion. If one has made a complete break with sin through death to sin by being "buried" with Christ in baptism (see Rom. 6:1-4), then one will not **submit to its rules.** As oil and water will not mix, neither will sin and Christ. It is an either/or decision.

Paul's logic follows from the principle that the things of the world **are all destined to perish.** It is only logical that if they perish, those who rely on them will perish too. As William Hendriksen says, "Heaven-born individuals cannot gain satisfaction from earth-born remedies."[25]

A. The Basis of Spiritual Victory (3:1-4)

Since, then hints at a new order, a new life, a new hope. And this is primarily what Paul is describing in the phrase **you have been raised with Christ** (v. 1). The perfect solution for a problem—in this instance, the sinful nature—is Christ and His resurrection power.

The question is ever present when one who has drunk the living water returns to the stagnant waters of sin: "Why?" Hendriksen phrases this query, "Why should they resort to broken cisterns when the Fountain is at hand?"[26] The answer is too often the failure to go on to the new life that Paul enjoins. When one comes out of the gutter of sin and gets a glimpse of something better and higher, he must pursue it with tenacity and determination lest the lowlands of sin become more appealing and he yield to the temptation to return. He must **set [his] heart on things above.** When this is done, life is changed, desires rearranged, and priorities reestablished.

The basis of this new order of existence is that one has **died, and [his] life is now hidden with Christ** (v. 3). Death puts an end to everything that is past, and life is resurrected to new desires, new ways, a new will.

B. A Good Defense (3:5-9)

Any winning team needs a good defense. A good defense is doing whatever is necessary to keep the enemy from penetrating. This is accomplished by putting **to death ... whatever belongs to your earthly nature** (v. 5) in a decisive and final act. This **death** implies that the potential sins listed (v. 5) are no longer alive as options for the will and the heart.

But Paul's advice invokes continued action on our part. We are to rid ourselves of all the marks of the old life (v. 8). Let the Holy Spirit dig out as by the roots the sinful nature, that its weeds and disease no longer contaminate the spirit. It is easy to see that one cannot indulge in such, **since you have taken off your old self** (v. 9).

C. A Good Offense (3:10-17)

Paul's formula for victory is **Put on the new self.** The **new self** aspires to a different order (Christ's order), and the practices of sin are inappropriate, are out of place, do not fit. Holiness is a new order, and sin has no place in this new realm of existence. **Being renewed in knowledge** has reference to the mind/heart being expanded by, inspired by, equipped with, and strengthened from the relationship with Christ, resulting from having **died with Christ** (2:20) and having been **raised with Christ** (3:1). The holy life is, basically, one of relationship, with obedience its key.

In v. 14, Paul says the same thing in the words **put on love.** But love must have shoe leather and an armor. Paul gave this in v. 12. One cannot represent the holy life better than through these expressions. Where love is given priority in the decisions and expressions of life, these actions result.

Another sermon suggestion comes from J. O. McClurkan, who provides the following outline for this section of scripture:
A. There is a *sinful* self to be *crucified* with Christ.
B. There is a *true* self to be *realized* in Christ.
C. There is a *human* self to be *disciplined* by Christ.[27]

Another possibility is to simply take the title:

The New Life in Christ

Introduction: Just as the resurrection of Jesus inaugurated a new order of being in His life as well as the world, so when the believer identifies with Christ in His death and resurrection, he too enters a new realm of existence marked by at least three dimensions according to our text.

A. A New Set of Presuppositions

In 2:3 Paul lays down the principle by which all philosophical presuppositions are to be judged: In Christ "are hidden all the treasures of wisdom and knowledge." On this basis he rejects the implications of the Colossian heresy that do not recognize the Christological basis of the created order (cf. 1:16).

The presuppositions contrary to Christ are referred to in 2:20 (and in 2:8; also Gal. 4:3, 9) as "the basic principles of this world." These assumptions regarding the evil nature of the world led to a faulty asceticism. It enjoined a self-denial that failed to acknowledge the supremacy of Christ and attributed spiritual value to the avoidance of certain items of meat and drink. Its ascetic mottoes are recited by Paul to reject their validity: "Do not handle! Do not taste! Do not touch!" These are principles to which the one who has "died with Christ" is not to be subject.

This aspect of the new life in Christ throws considerable light on the nature of holy living. It is not legalistic and does not entail forms of self-denial on the assumption that any aspect of the created world is essentially evil. Such abstinence *appears* to be spiritual but in fact has little spiritual value (2:23).

The truth of Paul's words in 2:23 are graphically illustrated by the experience of Jerome, the Hermit. "Lying at night on the bare ground, drinking only water and eating only uncooked food, his shriveled skin turning as black as an Ethiopian's, with scorpions and wild beasts for his companions, keeping his body awake by banging his bones against the ground, he lived a life of perpetual austerity." But "pale with fasting, he was assailed with desire for the beautiful dancing girls who came creeping into his imagination, and it puzzled him that they came when his limbs were cold."[28]

B. A New Set of Values

This is the converse of the previous point and must be seen in contrast to worldly presuppositions. The imperative based on having been **raised with Christ** is **set your hearts on things above, where Christ is seated at the right hand of God** (3:1). This is often misinterpreted to be a call to heavenly-mindedness. Such an attitude is not necessarily bad so long as one does not become so heavenly-minded as to be of no earthly use. Actually, it is more an appeal to avoid being so earthly minded as to be of no heavenly use!

Specifically, it enjoins the baptized believer to derive his values from the heavenly realm, or in more concrete terms, from Christ.

The implication of this appeal is that the Christian determines his ethics by a criterion of goodness and not by rules depicting right and wrong. This is the approach Paul always employs in his ethical material. It is reflected in his prayer for the Philippian church (1:10) that they **may be able to discern what is best** and his instruction to them in 4:8 to meditate on the highest values.

What he is saying is consistent with Jesus' own enacted sermon recorded in John 13. The contrast between the value of servanthood shown by Jesus' washing the disciples' feet and their value system that He had earlier characterized as "of this world" (Matt. 20:25-28) is startling and truly illuminates holiness values.

Ordering one's life around a Christ-informed value system eliminates certain behaviors and results in others. The apostle turns to this truth next as a logical consequence of this one.

C. A New Life-style

Two characteristics of this new life-style are important to mention here. The first is embodied in the phrase **Being renewed in knowledge in the image of its Creator** (3:10). This call captures the central NT description of God's intended work of sanctification in human life, to restore humankind to its lost destiny that is modeled by the person of Jesus Christ, who is the perfect image of God in human form.

The second aspect is found in the phrase **Let the peace of Christ rule in your hearts** (3:15). This is one of the most beautiful metaphors in Scripture for maintaining and living out the new life in Christ. The word **rule,** as noted, can be appropriately rendered "keep on acting as umpire" (Williams; cf. Amp.). Better manuscripts support the rendering **peace of Christ** rather than "peace of God" (KJV). The words of Thomas Cook capture the beauty of this figure of speech:

> This arbiter is not peace *with* [Christ], but the peace *of* [Christ], the fathomless ocean of Christ's peace, which He has left as a legacy to His people. "My peace I give unto you." It is that deep repose of spirit which we receive when we enthrone the God of Peace as the Lord of our hearts and lives. When this peace becomes the paramount consideration, everything that disturbs that profound rest of the soul will be instinctively avoided, and every act that would weave the thinnest veil between us and the face of our adorable Saviour, we shall instantly shrink from. A man who is exploring an old well lowers a candle before him, knowing that where that can live, he can live. If the light goes out, he knows that it is not safe to go farther. The peace of [Christ] is the Christian's test-flame. Anything that in the slightest degree disturbs it should instantly be discarded, otherwise the storm has begun which will wreck the fair beauty and happiness of the soul.[29]

Sermon on the Text

Can Life Be Better?

Text: Col. 2:20—3:17

Introduction: Probably the deepest question in the human spirit is "Can life be better than it is?" A phrase to a once-popular song rings with sadness: "Is this all there is?" Sin is good at raising questions but poor at providing answers. But our text provides a positive answer to the question.

A. Death with Christ (2:20—3:1)

1. It is a *decision.* The very language of Paul's Epistle suggests the decisive character of this identification with Christ in His death.

Mother Teresa has this insightful comment: "Often, under the pretext of humility, of trust, of abandonment, we can forget to use the strength of our will. Everything depends on these words 'I will' or 'I will not.' And into the expression 'I will' I must put all my energy."[30]

2. It is a *direction.* **Since you died with Christ to the basic principles of this world . . . set your hearts on things above** (2:20; 3:1). These are decisive acts Paul promotes for the proper development of the decision symbolized by uniting with Christ in baptism.

3. It is a *discipline.* All the imperatives in this passage imply discipline. Harry Emerson Fosdick observed one time that "no steam or gas ever drives anything until it is confined. No Niagara is ever turned into light and power until it is funnelled. No life ever grows great until it is focused, dedicated, and disciplined."

Discipline is closely related to the word "disciple," which means to "bring life along after" or to "pattern after." One cannot bring life along after the ways of Christ without discipline.

B. Life with Christ (3:1-11)

1. There is a *source* for our "new life." **You have been raised with Christ** (v. 1). **Your life is now hidden with Christ in God** (v. 3). Death to that which hinders opens one to the life that helps! The source for this new life is the Resurrection! Christ is an ever-present source and support for the person trying to find a better way. By these inner resources one can move from the "devil made me do it" philosophy to the "Lord helps me do it" possibility.

2. There is a *setting* of the heart and mind (3:1-2). One cannot hope for a better life with continual glances at the old life. There must be a setting of the heart and mind, the emotions and the will, on better things if he is to move toward them.

Someone asked a famous painter when he thought a painting was finished. He answered, "When anything more you do to it will spoil it." A good way to determine if the heart and mind is set on Christ and higher things is to see how much of lower things are still in view, spoiling the walk with Christ.

C. Victory Through Christ (3:12-17)

Death to sin brings death to defeat, failure, and despair. Life in Christ brings victory, growth, and hope. That is what the gospel is all about.

1. There is a *strategy*. **Put to death, therefore, whatever belongs to your earthly nature** (3:5). If there is not a death to the past and to sin, there will never be a victory. The better life comes through a slaying, a removal, of the old. The old life must be "treated as dead" or as having no more influence or pull on us.

There is an Indian word, *Bhakti,* that suggests the death that is required to follow Christ. It means "self committed to another—an utter self-abandonment, until the Other becomes the life of our life, the very center of our being."[31]

2. There is *guidance* through Christ (3:15-16). **Let the peace of Christ rule in your hearts** (v. 15). Let Christ, who wills for us the best, the highest, be the influence, the Judge, the Initiator, the Authority. And when the highest rules and reigns, then peace is the by-product of such an order. From such a peace comes a strength that equips life for both the calm and the critical times.

Let the word of Christ dwell in you richly (v. 16). Dwell, so as to become the Head Resident. As such, He commands and instructs. And what He commands is always right for life, and what He instructs is always "wisdom" of the highest order, enriching life, lifting it to higher levels.

3. There is *strength* through Christ. A lawn food was advertised with the promise that it would help grass to grow thicker and healthier. The ad read, "The shoots grow down before they grow up, and what they find to root in will determine how they grow up." When one puts his spiritual roots into Christ and into the Word of Christ, then the foundations of strength and growth are established. Life will be rich, better in all its expressions, actions, and attitudes.

Endnotes

1. "The Epistle to the Colossians" (Exegesis), in *The Interpreter's Bible* (Nashville: Abingdon Press, 1955), 11:206.

2. *Commentary on the Holy Bible,* 1-vol. ed., abr. Ralph Earle (Kansas City: Beacon Hill Press of Kansas City, 1967), 1050.

3. "Colossians," in *Beacon Bible Commentary* (BBC) (Kansas City: Beacon Hill Press of Kansas City, 1965), 9:407.

4. Quoted in John A. Knight, "Colossians," in *Beacon Bible Expositions* (BBE) (Kansas City: Beacon Hill Press of Kansas City, 1985), 9:213.

5. *The Letters to the Philippians, Colossians, and Thessalonians,* rev. ed., in *The Daily Study Bible Series* (Philadelphia: Westminster Press, 1975), 144.

6. *Explanatory Notes upon the New Testament* (Kansas City: Beacon Hill Press of Kansas City, 1981).

7. Knight, BBE 9:218.

8. Ibid.

9. *Notes.*

10. *Colossians,* 148.

11. Knight, BBE 9:222.

12. A. T. Robertson, *Word Pictures in the New Testament* (Nashville: Broadman Press, 1931), 4:501.

13. Nielson, BBC 9:412.

14. See n. 1 above.

15. J. Kenneth Grider, "The Meaning of Old Man," *Nazarene Preacher,* February 1972, 46.

16. Knight, BBE 9:223.

17. *Notes.*

18. G. Preston MacLeod, "Colossians" (Exposition), *The Interpreter's Bible* (Nashville: Abingdon Press, 1955), 213.

19. Barclay, *Colossians,* 159.

20. Wesley, *Notes.*

21. Robertson, *Word Pictures* 4:505.

22. Wesley, *Notes.*

23. Cf. Richard E. Howard, *Newness of Life* (Kansas City: Beacon Hill Press of Kansas City, 1975); "Some Modern Interpretations of the Pauline Indicative and Imperative," *Wesleyan Theological Journal* 11 (Spring 1976): 38-48; Rob L. Staples, "Sanctification and Selfhood: A Phenomenological Analysis of the Wesleyan Message," ibid. 7 (Spring 1972): 6-8; Gunther Bornkamm, "Baptism and New Life in Paul," in *Early Christian Experience* (New York: Harper and Row, Publishers, 1969). See also comments by Frank Carver, "Biblical Foundations for the 'Secondness' of Entire Sanctification," *Wesleyan Theological Journal* 22, no. 2 (Fall 1987): 12-13.

24. "Biblical Foundations for the 'Secondness' of Entire Sanctification," 13.

25. William Hendriksen, *Philippians, Colossians, and Philemon,* in *New Testament Commentary* (Grand Rapids: Baker Book House, 1962), 139.

26. Ibid.

27. Quoted in Knight, BBE 9:216.

28. Taken from Robert Payne, *The Fathers of the Western Church* (New York: Viking Press, 1951), 99-100.

29. Thomas Cook, *New Testament Holiness* (London: Epworth Press, 1950), 149.

30. Mother Teresa, *The Love of Christ* (New York: Harper and Row, 1982), 20.

31. E. Stanley Jones, *The Christ of the Indian Road* (Nashville: Abingdon Press, 1925), 207.

— 2 —

HOLINESS
AS PERFECTION

_____

STEPHEN GREEN

An Old Testament Call to Perfection

I am the Almighty God; walk before me, and be thou perfect (Gen. 17:1, KJV).

"Nobody's perfect!" So goes the philosophy of today's culture. And it seems that many people are going out of their way to prove their imperfection. Claims to perfection in this ethos seem as out of place as a horse and buggy on an interstate highway during the afternoon rush hour. But this only highlights the dramatic contrast between the ideals of biblical faith and the prevailing cultural mood. God's call is always to the loftiest ideal, and that truth comes vividly to expression in this passage, which is a command to perfection. Out of this divine directive to Abraham, we may learn some important truths about the holiness God requires of His servants.

The great danger of choosing a single verse like Gen. 17:1, however, is the danger of lifting it out of its context with the resultant error of reading one's own concepts into the text. This is especially true when a word like **perfect** is present. We must avoid this pitfall if we are to respect the integrity of Scripture and allow its meaning to arise out of the intention of the writer. This means paying close attention to the historical context and larger unit of scripture of which it is a part.

The Larger Context of the Abraham Story

The Abraham story begins in Gen. 12:1 with the call of Abram. This call was accompanied by a series of promises that included a divine commitment to bless Abram with a son and a multitude of descendants, and through him (and them) bless the whole earth. It is important to note at this point that there is no indication of any ethical qualifications that made Abraham worthy to receive such promises. And even more remarkable is the fact that no demand is laid upon him to follow a specified way of life. There are no stipulations to be fulfilled as part of the covenant agreement except faith in the promises. Abram had no requirements made on him until chap. 17.

The high moment of the Abraham story is found in chap. 22, which portrays a miracle of faith. Up to this point, the story has shown Abraham chasing after, and finally receiving, the promise of a son. Although believing God for the promise was not without some doubt and impatience, Abraham's faith was finally rewarded. But what God had given He now asks to be surrendered. Abraham is told to sacrifice his son Isaac. The power of this part of the Abraham story is seen in the complete trust and obedience of the patriarch. Having received the promised gift, Abraham is now willing to give it up. How was such a dramatic faith possible? Something must have taken place between chaps. 12 and 22 to prepare Abraham for this action of complete sacrifice. What was it? Chapter 17 provides us with a possible answer to that question.

This chapter is comprised of an introductory phrase, mentioning the age of the patriarch, and a series of speeches from God to Abraham. The only time Abraham speaks is in vv. 17 and 18. In his response one can see the struggle of the patriarch to believe the promise of God. The chapter concludes with a narrative section, vv. 22-27, showing the obedient execution of the instructions given by God. A closer look at the details of this chapter is needed.

In vv. 3-8 the promises to Abraham are explained in detail. These promises are understood in the context of a covenant. "Covenant" is a term that describes a relationship between two parties that binds them together in a relation of intimacy.

The record of the establishment of this relation is found in Genesis 15. The meaning of the strange ritual that marked the covenantal bond has a thrilling significance: God pledges His word to Abraham by the symbolic act of "passing between" the halves of the sacrifice, thus saying that if He does not keep His word, may His lot be that of the sacrificial victim. God was actually pledging His own extinction if He is not true to His word. What greater evidence could Abraham have of the faithfulness of God?

The covenant with Abraham anticipates the later covenant between Israel and the Lord. Thus the covenant can be described as "the primary metaphor for understanding Israel's life with God. It is the covenant that offers to Israel the gift of hope, the reality of identity, the possibility of belonging, the certitude of vocation."[1]

The promise is also understood, in vv. 7 and 8, as eternal. The covenant is made not only with Abraham but also with all of his descendants. It is a reference to its timeless validity. The importance of this everlasting covenant can be seen in the similar expression of the Davidic covenant. God's everlasting promise to Abraham was reinforced in His promise to David. Both of these promises have been the greatest source of strength for Israel in her history. An example of this can be seen in the dark days of exile, when the Davidic dynasty was no more, and Israel had lost its land and identity. The people of faith were able to hope as they reminded themselves that God had once covenanted himself forever to Israel. Israel had a future because God would bring them to it, even if by means and in ways that they could not then perceive.

However, we must avoid the conclusion that this makes the covenant unconditional, so that it will be consummated regardless of human response. The promises to Abraham were renewed to Isaac and Jacob and all their successors, and *each of them had to enter into the faith relation* to actualize the covenant provisions for themselves. The eternality of the covenant is from God's side.

The covenant promise is also life changing. Abram was no longer able to understand himself or his wife as before. God's covenant promise brought with it a change of identity that is expressed in the change of name from Abram to Abraham (v. 5) and Sarai to Sarah (vv. 15-16). The popular etymology of his name change is given in the text: "the father of a multitude of nations" (vv. 4, 5, ASV, NASB, RSV, KJV margin). This name change points back to Abram's call in 12:1-3. Abraham being the father of nations and kings is connected with the hope of a universal extension of God's salvation beyond the limits of Israel.

In vv. 9-14 the sign of keeping the covenant is given. Abraham and his descendants will bear the mark of the covenant on their flesh. Circumcision, so important to Jews and sometimes controversial in their history, makes Abraham and his descendants partners in the obligations of the covenant. There are no Jewish practices that are more significant than the sign of circumcision. Though this does not make a child born into a Jewish home automatically a covenant partner, it is a symbol of his special relationship to the God of Abraham, Isaac, and Jacob. Neglecting to circumcise a child was more than merely neglecting a rite, it was a rejection of God's sign. This act was subject to divine punishment as can be seen in v. 14. In Deut. 10:16 it is interpreted as being symbolic of an inward work of grace (see John Wesley's sermon on "The Circumcision of the Heart").

In vv. 17-21 Abraham is responsive to God's promise of a son through his barren wife, Sarah. His first response is curious; he prostrated himself and laughed. This seems to point to a mixture of submission and doubt. Abraham is a man who wants to believe, yet the situation tempts him to rebel against belief. This causes Abraham to offer to God the opportunity of transferring the impossible promise just made to the possible heir who is already in hand. God does bless Ishmael but insists that His promise would be carried through the barren one, Sarah. Isaac would be the heir of the everlasting covenant. God's power has always been **made perfect in weakness** (2 Cor. 12:9). God chooses the impossible situations, so often, to fulfill His promises. In submissive doubt, Abraham continues to be the "father of faith."

Exegetical Notes

The name El Shaddai is of great importance to the patriarchal story. It is God's revelation of himself to Abraham that would continue to remind the patriarchs of the promise (Gen. 17:1; 28:3; 35:11; 43:14; 48:3; 49:25; Exod. 6:3). Many scholars feel that the name originally meant "god of the mountains." The many uses of this name in the Book of Job points to its emphasis upon the power and majesty of God. This is probably why the Septuagint (Greek version of the OT) translated it *pantokratōr,* meaning "Almighty." Therefore, El Shaddai calls all covenant people to two basic responses. The first response is that of submission. This is the all-powerful One who is revealing himself to Abram. The second response is that of hope. The all-powerful One is the One who promises.

The actual address of El Shaddai to Abram contains two commands. The first of these imperatives is "walk in my presence." The command "to walk" is a hithpa'el verb in the Hebrew. This verb form is reflexive, which means that it has reference to oneself. For the Hebrew, "to walk" means to live life out. Life is a walking about. Therefore, God is commanding Abram to live his life in the awareness that it is in the continual presence of El Shaddai.

The second imperative is "be perfect." *Tamîm* is the Hebrew word that has been translated **perfect**. The Septuagint has translated this word with *amemptos*. This is the reason that so many versions have translated this passage "be blameless." There is a difference between the Hebrew word and its Greek translation. The major difference is that "blameless" expresses a subjective judgment, while "perfect, complete, whole, having integrity" reflect a condition. Abraham is called to a condition of *tamîm,* while he lives his life in the awareness of the continual presence of God. Von Rad, in his masterful commentary, points out that *tamîm* is referring to a relational perfection of Abraham toward God. This command would not necessarily mean moral perfection as one living without mistakes, but "it signifies complete, unqualified surrender." The same word is used in Gen. 20:5 (translated as "clear conscience") to refer to relations among men with the sense of "without ulterior motives, unreserved."[2]

In v. 1 God revealed himself as the Almighty One and called Abram to live *tamîm* before Him. Now in v. 2 God reveals His side of the covenant agreement. The word normally used for the establishing of a covenant *(karath)* is replaced by *natan,* "to give." Even though the covenant people are called to maintain their side of the covenant agreement, it is the grace of God that "gives" and guarantees the covenant. The Almighty One makes His original promise new. He binds himself to fulfill what He has promised He would do. In a unique way, God and Abraham will belong to each other as never before (v. 8).

Theology of the Passage

Consideration of the place of Gen. 17:1 in the Abraham story yields several significant theological insights concerning God's call to holiness (perfection).

First, the "Perfect Life" is lived out in the context of the covenant relation. It is not the basis of establishing a relation to God but a way of responding to God's gracious activity that comes to us without respect of our worthiness. The covenant is a covenant of grace. As with Abraham God does not scrutinize our moral worth but freely offers himself to us if we will only respond in faith. If this truth is not preserved—and it is clearly implied by the structure of the story—we fall quickly into works righteousness and lose the gospel.

Second, the "Perfect Life" is lived out in the light of the revelation of a God of power (El Shaddai) whose call to holiness is a "covered promise" that He provides the resources to make it possible. God does not enjoin human effort dependent on our own capacities alone. That would be mockery. He offers not only the gift of His presence but the gift of His power.

What does it mean for God to reveal himself as El Shaddai? In the patriarchal tradition it meant that the promise was secure. This security of the promise can be seen in the continual repeating of the name throughout this tradition (Gen. 17:1; 28:3; 35:11; 43:14; 48:3; 49:25; Exod. 6:3). But why did this name give that type of security? It was because through it the patriarchs understood that God was sovereign over all things. His sovereignty is seen not only in His control over the promise but also in His claim and control over the people of promise. Abram could never understand himself the same. He was forever marked and named by the Almighty One.

Third, the "Perfect Life" is the valid and expected response to the faithfulness of God. The fact that God's promises are unequivocal, eternal, and dependable does not relieve those to whom the promises are given of the responsibility to keep the covenant conditions to which God calls them. To fail here is "antinomian." Walking with God involves more than passive reliance upon the promises. It includes a life-style of faithfulness. The covenant is one of mutual responsibility.

Dietrich Bonhoeffer describes this truth in the opening chapters of *The Cost of Discipleship* as "costly grace." He says:

> Cheap grace means the justification of sin without the justification of the sinner . . . the preaching of forgiveness without requiring repentance . . . grace without discipleship, grace without the cross, grace without Jesus Christ. Costly grace is the treasure hidden in the field; for the sake of it a man will gladly go

and sell all that he has. . . . Costly grace is the gospel which must be sought again and again, the gift which must be asked for, the door at which a man must knock. Such grace is costly because it calls us to follow, and it is grace because it calls us to follow Jesus Christ. It is costly because it costs a man his life.[3]

Gen. 17:1 is a call to "costly grace." In this verse God calls Abraham to a walk of perfection.

Fourth, the "Perfect Life" is characterized by "surrender," "openness," "wholeness." All this is implied by the meaning of the Hebrew word *tamîm*. If one is to insist that "perfect" means without flaw or even moral perfection, then our culture is right, "nobody's perfect." But, by the grace of God, it is possible to live a life marked by the above-mentioned qualities, all of which produce a perfect relation with God.

Although Abraham struggled at the point of fully trusting the promises of God, the story of his willingness to sacrifice Isaac reveals that he had at this point come to the place of total surrender to the will of God. Such submission can only be the expression of absolute trust in the Sovereign Lord who asks for such radical surrender. In NT terms, it is Jesus who is the "perfecter of our faith" (Heb. 12:2), whose design is thereby to bring us to this level of intimacy with our God. One who has been given this "stage of grace" can truly be called "the friend of God."

To be aware of living before the Almighty One is to be called to a life of complete surrender *(tamîm)*. This life of perfection does not mean that there would be no struggle for Abraham, as can be seen as his story continues, but it does mean that he would live in faith-keeping obedience. The greatest challenge that life brought to Abraham was recorded in Genesis 22. In this chapter, God called Abraham to sacrifice his son, Isaac, back to Him. It is interesting to notice the complete surrender and security of Abraham in that chapter. Why? Because it was El Shaddai who called him. The Almighty One who controlled his life also controlled the promise. To understand God as El Shaddai is to respond to His guidance in both submission and security.

Preaching Ideas on the Text

How does one go about preaching this passage? It may be developed using an obvious outline. Some examples of this sermonic style follow:

A. A sermon on the whole Abraham story may go as follows:
  1. The Call (chap. 12)
  2. The Challenge (chap. 22)
  3. The Commitment (17:1)
  4. The Change (chap. 17)
B. A sermon on chap. 17 could be developed as follows:
  1. Costly Grace (vv. 1-2)
  2. Costly Change (vv. 3-16)
  3. Challenge to Grace (vv. 17-21)
  4. Certainty of Covenant (vv. 22-27)
C. A sermon on 17:1-2 may be:
  1. The Revealed God (El Shaddai)
  2. The Realized Self (submission)
  3. The Remembered Promise (security)

Personal Style: When I prepared to preach from this passage, my first move was to establish the problem of the text: unrealized promise. This was done first by finding points of correlation between the Abraham story and the lives of contemporary men and women. After the problem had been established, then I attempted to diagnose why this takes place. This move of diagnosis may or may not be helpful, but it sets up the problem. It is then time to present the good news, God's revelation of himself as El Shaddai. To accomplish this move in the sermon, I went back once again to the Abraham story. Finally, the result of the encounter needs to be expressed in the sermon. The only possible response that any of us can make is that of submission. God then provides the security. Naturally you will want to make this type of sermon your own. My approach is embodied in the sermon below.

Sermon on the Text
Gen. 17:1

One of the greatest challenges to our faith is the unrealized promises of God. These promises can take many forms of expression, but in the final analysis they are only variations on the promise of God to Abram: "By you all the families of the earth shall bless themselves" (Gen. 12:3, RSV). We look into our world and see the dark clouds of curse building up, and wonder, will the promises of God's blessing ever be fulfilled? The curse of sin is felt in all of our lives as we watch our nation, our church, our homes, and even our personal lives stumble and fall short of the blessing of God. Will the promised blessing ever find fulfillment in our own lives?

This is the same question that the patriarch Abram asked. From the time that God called Abram, to His self-revelation as "God Almighty," it had been 24 years. During these years, Abram had alternately believed and doubted, left all security and yet deceptively clung to his life, and finally took the fulfillment of the promise into his own hands (with the result being Ishmael). It was into this situation of unfulfilled hope that God appeared to Abram as El Shaddai, God Almighty!

Now, it is important for us to see what happens to this faithless yet believing one after his encounter with El Shaddai. "The Lord visited Sarah as he had said, and the Lord did to Sarah as he had promised. And Sarah conceived, and bore Abraham a son in his old age at the time of which God had spoken to him. Abraham called the name of his son who was born to him, whom Sarah bore him, Isaac" (Gen. 21:1-3, RSV). The promise was fulfilled! But this was not all that happened. God now asked the doubting believer who had left all and yet deceptively clung to his life to offer up Isaac, the fulfilled promise, to Him as a sacrifice. The most amazing thing about the Abraham story is that he did just that, apparently without wavering in his faith. How could a man who had experienced such a mixture of unbelief and belief stand so strong in his unconditional trust of God? The answer lies in chap. 17.

In chap. 17 we find God revealing himself, for the first time, as El Shaddai, God Almighty. There are many things we could say about this self-revelation of God, but two are of most importance. When God reveals himself as the Almighty One, it brings a security to the promise. In all of the patriarchal tradition the use of the name, El Shaddai, pointed to the security of the promise. The other occurrences of this name can be found in Gen. 28:3; 35:11; 43:14; 48:3; 49:25; and Exod. 6:3. Why was the promise secure? Because it was the Sovereign One who had promised. His sovereignty is seen in His control and claim over all things. So we can stand firm in the assurance that what God calls us to, He will provide for. It reminds me of the confession of the Early Church captured in a contemporary chorus: "He is Lord, He is Lord! / He has risen from the dead, and He is Lord! / Every knee shall bow, every tongue confess / That Jesus Christ is Lord!" The promise is sure because El Shaddai has made it!

Not only is this sovereignty of God experienced as security, but also His sovereignty over all things in my world calls for submission. When God reveals himself as El Shaddai, His sovereignty has a claim over our lives. We can no longer walk as we have in the past, for we are forever changed.

Abram was called to a change that could be heard and seen, for he was called to a new identity (name) and to a sign that showed that this new identity belonged to God (circumcision). But these two outward expressions of submission are but reflections of an inner submission to which the father of faith was called. God said, **Walk before me, and be . . . perfect.** Let us look at the inner qualities that result from responding to the sovereignty of God.

When we are encountered by the Sovereign One, we are called to **walk before** Him. What does that mean? The Hebrew form of this command is reflexive in meaning. Abram is called to be continually conscious and aware that he is walking, living his life out, before El Shaddai. The Sovereign One is not far-off but always with us. We must learn, as Abram, to practice the presence of God. Listen to the prayer of Brother Lawrence, a 17th-century saint: "O my God, since Thou art with me, and I must now, in obedience to Thy commands, apply my mind to these outward things, I beseech Thee to grant me the grace to continue in Thy presence; and to this end do Thou prosper me with Thy assistance, receive all my works, and possess all my affections." To walk before God Almighty is to practice His presence in all the activities of life.

When we are encountered by El Shaddai, we are called not only to practice His presence but also to be perfect. All kinds of images come to our mind when we hear the word "perfect," but what is it to which God is calling Abram? Many times we look at our own lives and see so many failures that we reinterpret this word to mean **blameless** (NASB, NIV, NKJV, RSV). This is exactly what many have done with this word down through the ages, but the call to Abram is not to reflect a subjective judgment of blamelessness. The Hebrew word that is translated **be perfect** is *tamîm*. This word is concerned, not about a feeling, but about a condition. Through the call of Abram, we are also called to *tamîm*. But what does this imply in the lives of people?

Too many people interpret this condition to mean living life without any mistakes. To convince themselves that they are without any moral flaws, they create a system of law. If they keep the law properly, they can call themselves "perfect." This is not what the command to Abram means. As Von Rad says, to be perfect "signifies complete, unqualified surrender." This is exactly what the call of Jesus means when He says, "If any man will come after me, let him deny himself, and take up his cross daily, and follow me" (Luke 9:23, KJV). This complete, unqualified surrender is also what Paul confesses in Gal. 2:20: "I have been crucified with Christ; it is no longer I who live, but Christ who lives in me; and the life I now live in the flesh I live by faith in the Son of God, who loved me and gave himself for me" (RSV).

In this passage, we are not called to a feeling that we are blameless before God, nor are we called to a wooden form of legal perfectionism. We are called to the dynamic of living life honestly and with a complete, unqualified surrender before God. This kind of perfection allows for growth, change, and even confession. This kind of perfection also brings unique change to our very identity. We are no longer Abram, but Abraham. The promise of "blessing" can be fulfilled in and through our lives!

Endnotes

1. Walter Brueggemann, *Genesis.* In *Interpretation: The Bible Commentary for Teaching and Preaching* (Atlanta: John Knox Press, 1982), 154.

2. Gerhard von Rad, *Genesis: A Commentary* (Philadelphia: Westminster Press, 1972), 198-99.

3. Dietrich Bonhoeffer, *The Cost of Discipleship* (New York: Macmillan Publishing Co., 1949), 46-47.

FLOYD PERKINS

Perfection—the Christian's Challenge

We have much to say about this, but it is hard to explain because you are slow to learn. In fact, though by this time you ought to be teachers, you need someone to teach you the elementary truths of God's word all over again. You need milk, not solid food! Anyone who lives on milk, being still an infant, is not acquainted with the teaching about righteousness. But solid food is for the mature, who by constant use have trained themselves to distinguish good from evil. Therefore let us leave the elementary teachings about Christ and go on to maturity [perfection, KJV], not laying again the foundation of repentance from acts that lead to death, and of faith in God, instruction about baptisms, the laying on of hands, the resurrection of the dead, and eternal judgment. And God permitting, we will do so (Heb. 5:11—6:3).

Perfection appears to be every person's goal. Athletes endeavor to break previous records; baseball pitchers endeavor to have more strikeouts each season than the last and more than any previous pitcher in baseball's history; football coaches set their goals toward better performance, and when their players fail to win, they may lose their job. Greater achievement and more perfect performance is not only a goal but also the demand of modern man.

In the Christian way this is not a new idea. Long ago the writer to the Hebrews penned the words "Therefore leaving the principles of the doctrine of Christ, let us go on unto perfection" (6:1, KJV). Although in modern life it is very natural to look toward and expect greater achievement in athletics, more perfect performance in automobiles and electronic devices, and more productive schedules in the work force, it is not uncommon for some to question the validity of such a pursuit in the Christian walk.

Exegetical Section

The Epistle (or sermon) opens with the declaration, "In these last days [God] has spoken to us by his Son" (1:2). In the light of this superior revelation the writer addresses several admonitions, warnings, and appeals to his readers to pursue the provisions made available to them by the new revelation. In 2:1 he urges, "We must pay more careful attention, therefore, to what we have heard." In 3:1 he continues with the exhortation, "Therefore, holy brothers, who share in the heavenly calling, fix your thoughts on Jesus." And he proceeds with a warning that the promise of Christian "rest" through the Son may be forfeited (4:1, 10) through "unbelief" (v. 11, KJV) and by willfully negative responses to the voice of the Spirit. In 5:12-14 he laments that they have not matured in the Christian faith but have remained babies not capable of solid food but still needing milk. This sets the stage for the appeal of the text: **Let us . . . go on to maturity** (6:1).

"Going on" is the great admonition of the sermon. This is the antidote to going back. The overarching theme in the light of which the reader is called to "go on" is the new covenant in Jesus Christ. It is a superior covenant with better provisions than the old. Hence the reader is called to go on to actualize in his experience these better provisions.

The critical issue in the text is the meaning of the key term *teleiotēta*. The KJV renders it "perfection," but most modern versions render it "maturity" (NASB, NIV, RSV).

Certainly the Greek term may be legitimately translated either way; but if it is rendered as "perfection," we must be sure we derive the meaning of the idea of perfection from the writer's intention and not from modern usages that may, in fact, be antithetical or completely different from the biblical use. Only after we have done this can we legitimately move to the use of the term in systematic theology.

Two major considerations must be explored. First is the immediate context, and the other is the way the author uses it in other contexts throughout the homily.

When the exhortation is read in the light of the immediate context, it is clear that the idea of maturity dominates. The concepts of "infant" and, by implication, "adult" can convey no other connotation. But "maturity" in the theological setting of Hebrews may convey a different connotation than either physical or psychological maturity. As H. Orton Wiley says, "Christian perfection therefore means the attainment of the goal of adulthood as it is recognized in the present gospel dispensation. In a spiritual sense this does not so much involve the element of time as the entering into the fullness of the new covenant provided through the blood of Jesus and administered by the baptism with the Holy Spirit. . . . it is accomplished, not by growth alone, but by a divine pronouncement."[1]

Daniel Steele concurs in this evaluation. He says, "It [perfection] is here represented not as something realized by the lapse of time, or by unconscious growth, and, least of all, attainable only at death." He also argued that the Greek preposition translated "unto" embraces both motion to a place and rest in it, and thus cannot mean an aim at an unattainable ideal.[2]

John Wesley, who placed much greater emphasis on progressive sanctification than many of his successors, commonly identified "adulthood" with entire sanctification and specifically saw stages of spiritual development in the three classifications used by John in 1 John 2:12-14: children, young men, and fathers. These are the several stages of the Christian life. "Little children" are Paul's "babes in Christ" (1 Cor. 3:1); "young men" represent a more advanced stage; while "fathers" are the entirely sanctified, corresponding to Paul's *teleioi,* "perfect" or "adult Christians" (1 Cor. 13:11; 14:20).[3]

Adam Clarke apparently assumes the same idea in his comment on the text: "Let us never rest till we are adult Christians—till we are saved from all sin, and are filled with the Spirit and power of Christ."[4]

The term "perfection" (and cognates) is one of the major categories of Hebrews' theology.[5] It is referred to Jesus who is made perfect through suffering and obedience (2:10; 5:8-9; 7:28); neither the law nor Tabernacle ritual could make anything or anyone perfect (7:19; 9:9; 10:1); Christ serves in a "perfect" tabernacle (9:11) and offers a sacrifice (of himself) that is effective in perfecting those who are "being sanctified" (10:14, NKJV; cf. 12:23).

When these references are read in context and then brought together in a composite, as we have done here, the meaning the author gives to "perfection" becomes quite clear, and it is also seen as a corollary to his view of sanctification.[6]

1. Perfection is a functional category. Jesus' perfecting is directly related to the carrying out of the mission for which, as the Son, God sent Him into the world. This mission called for perfect obedience to the Father's will and could only be consummated by His suffering on the Cross.

By analogy, the perfecting (or perfection) of believers involves their actualization of the purpose for which God called them into His kingdom. It does not denote any "finished" or finalized condition signifying absence of flaws but something far more dynamic and realistic. Do we have any clues as to what this entails? No doubt the other uses of the term by the writer address this question.

2. Perfection is not possible under the old covenant but is now made available in the new covenant effected by the work of Christ. From the contents of the passages using the term "perfection," we easily learn that the difference between the covenants is that the old made explicit provision for ceremonial or ritual sanctification, but the new explicitly provides for a *real* sanctification. It is true that the Scripture provides no philosophical explanation of what a real change means, but it is effected by the blood of Christ.[7] A few clues as to the nature of this change may be gleaned by a careful study of the benefits of the new covenant scattered throughout the book.

The implication of this analysis is that "sanctification" or "perfection" in the theology of Hebrews must be viewed holistically. Any aspect of the work of the Spirit (our writer would say "the blood of Christ," since he is appropriating the ceremonial rituals of purification from the OT, in which cleansing is effected by the sprinkling of blood, but arguing that the blood of Christ is infinitely more effective) within the person falls under the rubric of sanctification so defined and would include what systematic theology calls initial sanctification, entire sanctification, progressive sanctification, and even final sanctification or eschatological perfection.

All this fits into the theological structure that informs the entire NT, the tension between the already and the not yet. In this case we are doubtless looking at a perfection of attainment in the context of a perfection of expectation identical to that expressed by

Paul in Phil. 3:12-16. (See exegesis of this passage in this volume.)

Several considerations, however, follow from the immediate context. First, the recipients of this homily are already believers, though immature or imperfect ones. The logical implication would be that the writer is calling them to a further provision of the new covenant in Christ, not "initial sanctification." In modern theological language this could include "entire sanctification," even if it cannot be decisively or exclusively identified as such.

Second, although this maturity or perfection to which they are challenged may be eschatological, the writer indicates in this passage both the possibility and reality of a present actualization of the benefits of the "age to come" (see 6:5). While this consideration does not exclude the idea of an eschatological fulfillment, its point is not to restrict it exclusively to that. In a word, there is implied in the homily a recognition of the possibility of a present perfection.

Third, the perfection in view is related to **teaching** (5:13). Some have concluded from this that the "perfection" is one of Christian doctrine. But more appropriate is the conclusion of Peterson that "fundamental to the problem of the readers is an inadequate grasp of the person and work of Christ." Thus the call to maturity is correlative to the knowledge of the teaching that "the person and work of Christ provides the readers with the certainty that he is ever able to apply to them the benefits of his salvific work and thus bring them to their heavenly destination."[8] In this sense its meaning is similar to that in 2 Pet. 3:18.

One dimension of this passage relating to translation has major theological implications. "Let us go on unto perfection" may be translated "Let us be borne on to perfection." Additionally, v. 3 can be rendered, "and this we will do *with God's help*" (italics added, so TCNT).[9] This highlights the truth that "perfection" or "maturity" is not the result of merely human effort but the consequence of a cooperation between God and man. Theologically this is termed *synergism*, a uniquely Wesleyan-Arminian understanding. This is clearly illustrated by the perfecting of Jesus, the great High Priest. Involved in His perfecting is both suffering and obedience (5:5-10).

Theological Interpretations of Perfection

John Wesley develops a full-length homily based on Heb. 6:1, although it is more a theological treatise than the result of exegeting the text. One clearly cannot draw his observations from the text but from a wide-ranging appeal to theology and experience as well as inferences from Scripture.

He titles his sermon "On Perfection."[10] At the close of his introductory statement he explains, "In order to make this very important scripture as easy to be understood as possible, I shall endeavour,

    I. To show what perfection is;

    II. To answer some objections to it; and,

    III. To expostulate a little with the opposers of it."

Under his first division he declares: (1) "I do not conceive the perfection here spoken of, to be the perfection of angels." (2) "Neither can any man, while he is in a corruptible body, attain to Adamic perfection." (3) "The highest perfection which man can attain, while the soul dwells in the body, does not exclude ignorance, and error, and a thousand other infirmities." In a further passage he explains that an entirely sanctified person may make wrong judgments, may speak wrong words, may commit wrong actions, and in some cases have wrong affections. Because of these infirmities, "every man living needs the blood of atonement, or he could not stand before God." When he comes to his second division, he answers objections raised against his case for Christian perfection with such affirmations as: (1) It is the "general and unlimited promise which runs through the whole gospel dispensation." (2) It is "the command of God, given by St. Peter" (1 Pet. 1:15). (3) It is "the prayer of St. Paul for the Thessalonians" (1 Thess. 5:23). His last division is largely polemical. There he answers direct questions that had been raised in opposition to the doctrine of Christian perfection. Typical of his answers, given in interrogative form, would be, "Why should any man of reason and religion be either afraid of, or averse to, salvation from all sin?"

In his treatment of the subject of Christian perfection in theological context, W. B. Pope follows Wesley rather closely. Note the following condensed outline from his *Compendium of Christian Theology:*

    I. That perfection is the goal of a possible estate is undeniable.

    II. This perfection is evangelical or in other words of pure grace.

III. Christian perfection is relative and probationary.[11]

It is a tribute to Wesley that, in defining both what the blessing of Christian perfection does accomplish in the human heart, and what it cannot accomplish, his ideas may be traced through all the holiness literature of the present day. H. Orton Wiley follows Wesley precisely, concept by concept, when he deals with "misconceptions of Christian perfection,"[12] as does Donald Metz, with some additions, in his book *Studies in Biblical Holiness.*[13]

Sermon Suggestions

Topic: **Spiritual Adulthood**

A. The Tragedy of Immaturity (5:11-14)
B. The Teaching That Leads to Maturity (5:13)
C. The Touchstone of Maturity (the adulthood of Christ)
D. The Tide That Carries Us Toward the Goal (6:1—"Let us be borne on" [lit.] as by a stream)

Topic: **Perfection for Modern Folks**

Text: Heb. 5:11—6:3

It becomes quite obvious from even a casual reading of the Epistle to the Hebrews that the author is speaking to Christians. His words and phrases indicate that there is a level of experience beyond where they are at this stage of their development. The language used here is not the same as emerged in later historical and cultural expressions, but it does address a human need that is the same in all historical and cultural periods, the need to go on to further spiritual progress.

The idea of Christian perfection has been implicit in the writings and teachings of the church from the first, and the call has always been to pursue it with diligence. We suggest three reasons why this is the case, all indicated in our text.

A. Christian Perfection Produces Performance Beyond the Mediocre

Two evidences of mediocrity among those to whom these words are addressed are noted. They were mediocre Christians because they needed to be taught when they should have been teaching others. The author had introduced the High Priesthood of Jesus after the order of Melchizedek and then drew back from developing its implications because his hearers were **slow to learn** (5:11). The Greek word used here is an ethical term for a sluggish intellect, suggesting that the readers were apathetic toward the things of God. As a result they had made no progress in the Christian faith, in fact were on the verge of reverting to a loss of faith. Mediocrity is first of all a manifestation of spiritual laziness. The lack of diligence in developing one's understanding of the implications of the faith results in a dullness that is deadening and unexciting. As E. F. Scott said, "Religion is something different from mere strenuous thinking on the great religious questions, yet it still remains true that faith and knowledge are inseparable, and that both grow stronger as they react on one another. More often than we know, the failure of a religion as a moral power is due to no other cause than intellectual sloth."[14]

They were also mediocre Christians in that they were immature in their faith. This is seen in the diet that they required. Milk is fine for babies but should early give way to solid food if the person is to develop. They were still preoccupied with the foundational truths of religion and had not gone on to build the superstructure of the Christian life on this foundation.

Just as the gardener will never harvest a crop if he repeatedly digs up his seeds to see if they are going to sprout, so the believer will never progress in the faith until he "drives down a stake," accepts the forgiveness of God as a finality, and moves on to higher levels of grace.

B. Christian Perfection Moves the Christian Beyond the Elementary Level of Christian Understanding

The relation between "knowledge" and "growth" is a fundamental premise of the NT (see 2 Pet. 3:18). It is unfortunate that so much teaching and preaching in the Christian church does not move believers beyond the elementary teachings about initial experiences of grace. These truths are indispensable and must be presented for the potential and new converts, but the person who has been in the way for years and still has not been drawn into a study of the profound vistas of grace available in Jesus Christ is suffering from spiritual retardation.

This does not make Christianity a religion of the intellect; it is the recognition that the only basis for genuine growth is an awareness of the goal of adulthood that is found in the person of Christ. This is clearly the "solid food" that our writer wishes his readers to be able to receive.

C. Christian Perfection Leads One into a More Mature Understanding of God's Grace

The writer emphatically states that we go on "with God's help" (6:3, TCNT). This statement should forever cancel out any idea that the perfection of which the author is speaking may be achieved by human effort. It cannot be attained without our participation, but neither is it attained exclusively by human effort. This may appear to be somewhat insignificant and maybe even contradictory, but, in fact, it is of great theological importance, and it is *not* contradictory. It is at this point that the human and the divine intersect in Christian experience. Every work of grace in the human heart is accomplished through the Holy Spirit, but the choice that it should be done is made by man himself. Anytime one meets with the working of God's Spirit in human experience, we will find, at that point, the intersecting of God's indescribable grace and man's responsible choice.

It was Luther who so eloquently preached, with reference to man's salvation, that it is by "grace alone that we are saved and that not by works" (see Eph. 2:8-9). His declaration, with biblical affirmation, was intended to counteract the strong emphasis on "works salvation" that had developed within the Roman Catholic church. As is often the case when correctives are necessary, it was somewhat of an overemphasis. Two centuries later Wesley discovered that a further emphasis was needed to make Christian experience complete. Just as "salvation by faith alone" was not a new doctrine, but a new emphasis on an old one, so Wesley's teaching concerning Christian perfection or entire sanctification was not a new doctrinal belief but was a new emphasis upon one that had been known and believed by devout Christians since the time of Christ. In the same way that the traditional church fought Martin Luther, so the established church of the 18th century opposed John Wesley. Generally, a new departure in religious teaching evokes suspicion and opposition.

Conclusion: If you have been analyzing your own life, and as you have considered your performance as a Christian, you find that you function below par as a professing Christian, leave the mediocre, leave the rudimentary, and press on to perfection.

Endnotes

1. *Epistle to the Hebrews*, ed. Morris A. Weigelt (Kansas City: Beacon Hill Press of Kansas City, 1984), 183.
2. Daniel Steele, *Half-Hours with St. Paul* (Rochester, Pa.: H. E. Schmul, n.d.), 113.
3. *The Works of John Wesley*, 3rd ed. (Kansas City: Beacon Hill Press of Kansas City, 1978), 6:6, 16-17, 419, 488-89.
4. Adam Clarke, *Commentary on the Holy Bible*, 1-vol. ed., abr. Ralph Earle (Kansas City: Beacon Hill Press of Kansas City, 1967), 1259.
5. Otto Michel said: "Understanding Christian perfection is important, indeed central, for an interpretation of the Epistle to the Hebrews." Quoted in David Peterson, *Hebrews and Perfection* (Cambridge: University Press, 1982), 1.
6. W. T. Purkiser says, "One of the chief contributions . . . found in Hebrews is the linking of perfection and sanctification." He cites Oscar Cullmann as arguing that "the author makes the two virtually synonymous." *Exploring Christian Holiness*, vol. 1, *The Biblical Foundations* (Kansas City: Beacon Hill Press of Kansas City, 1983), 196-97.
7. See H. Ray Dunning, *Grace, Faith, and Holiness: A Wesleyan Systematic Theology* (Kansas City: Beacon Hill Press of Kansas City, 1988), for a full discussion of a philosophical model that provides for the possibility of explaining the meaning of "real change."
8. Peterson, *Hebrews and Perfection*, 186.
9. W. T. Purkiser, "Hebrews," in *Beacon Bible Expositions* (Kansas City: Beacon Hill Press of Kansas City, 1974), 11:52-53.
10. *Works* 6:411-24.
11. William Burt Pope, *Compendium of Christian Theology* (New York: Hunt and Eaton, 1880), 3:56-99.
12. H. Orton Wiley and Paul T. Culbertson, *Introduction to Christian Theology* (Kansas City: Beacon Hill Press, 1946), 325-26.
13. Donald M. Metz, *Studies in Biblical Holiness* (Kansas City: Beacon Hill Press of Kansas City, 1971).
14. Quoted in Thomas Hewitt, *The Epistle to the Hebrews*, in *Tyndale New Testament Commentaries* (Grand Rapids: Wm. B. Eerdmans Publishing Co., 1973), 103.

OSCAR REED

Perfection—a Present Obtainment and an Alluring Goal

But whatever was to my profit I now consider loss for the sake of Christ. What is more, I consider everything a loss compared to the surpassing greatness of knowing Christ Jesus my Lord, for whose sake I have lost all things. I consider them rubbish, that I may gain Christ and be found in him, not having a righteousness of my own that comes from the law, but that which is through faith in Christ—the righteousness that comes from God and is by faith. I want to know Christ and the power of his resurrection and the fellowship of sharing in his sufferings, becoming like him in his death, and so, somehow, to attain to the resurrection from the dead.

Not that I have already obtained all this, or have already been made perfect, but I press on to take hold of that for which Christ Jesus took hold of me. Brothers, I do not consider myself yet to have taken hold of it. But one thing I do: Forgetting what is behind and straining toward what is ahead, I press on toward the goal to win the prize for which God has called me heavenward in Christ Jesus. All of us who are mature should take such a view of things. And if on some point you think differently, that too God will make clear to you. Only let us live up to what we have already attained (Phil. 3:7-16).

Many of John Wesley's successors are not a little peeved at him because he left no definite testimony to his own experience of entire sanctification. He felt the Scripture supported the possibility, he vigorously defended the truth against its detractors, he exhorted others to pursue it, and he carefully examined those who claimed it to determine the validity of their profession; but he said nothing about his own status on this point. In fact, Wesley cautioned his followers to be reticent about testifying to such a high state of grace and instructed them to speak of it only to those in sympathy. Why? At least one reason was that professing "freedom from sin" makes one vulnerable to criticism and attacks by cynics, putting one under a microscope with potentially unhealthy consequences. Wesley's later followers were far less cautious and enjoined public and oft-repeated testimony.

Paul, in our passage from Philippians, demonstrated much the same reticence as Wesley. In fact, it is the nearest statement in his extant writings to a straightforward claim to entire sanctification, and this occurs in a somewhat backhanded way and that using a plural pronoun, not a singular one. Furthermore, his testimony sits solidly in the context of a disclaimer, creating a certain ambiguity. But this ambiguity always attaches to redeemed humanity short of the resurrection. Hence we may say, based on this passage, that holiness is both a present obtainment and an alluring goal.

Exegetical Section

Phil. 3:7-16 is a theological argument written in autobiographical form. Its purpose is to warn the Philippian church against those who would undercut the truth of justification by faith. The "dogs" (3:2) are the Judaizing teachers who argue that one must become a Jew first (by circumcision) before he can be a Christian. This is relying on "the flesh" (v. 3) both literally and figuratively. Paul appeals to his own lack of confidence in the flesh, or any earthly achievement, as a basis of acceptance with God in order to nail down the point. He has many credits to his earthly account, but on the ledger of heaven they add up to zero. Consequently he counts them as **loss for the sake of Christ** (v. 7).

At the heart of Paul's argument is the term *righteousness.* He is contrasting the "righteousness which is in [of] the law" (vv. 6, 9, KJV) sought by the Judaizers with the "righteousness which is of God by faith" (v. 9, KJV). This is not a contrast between two standards of ethical righteousness. He nowhere hints that Christians have moral principles unknown to the Jews. The real issue hangs on the fact that there are two kinds of righteousness: ethical righteousness, which comes from keeping the law; and relational righteousness, which arises out of a faith relation to God. These need to be clearly distinguished to avoid confusing justification and sanctification.

Much confusion exists in theological discussions as well as in popular preaching as a consequence of failing to recognize the Bible's distinction between ethical and relational righteousness. From our Greek and Roman cultural heritage we assume that a "righteous" person is one who conforms to some legal or moral standard. When this criteria is applied, no one can be perfectly righteous. But biblical theology knows a righteousness that is accounted to one simply by *being in right relation* with God. Such a person is accounted righteous when he is in a loyal, trustful relationship, that is, when he meets the one condition of the divine-human relation on man's part: *faith.* This is why Gen. 15:6 can speak of Abraham's faith being the basis of God's accounting him as righteous. When appropriated by NT theology, it is a "free gift that God grants to faithful persons through Jesus Christ."[1]

It is crucial to recognize that vv. 12-15 do not refer to relational righteousness. This would subvert the gospel and picture Paul putting forth a supreme effort to earn acceptance by God. It refers here to ethical righteousness, a conformity to a norm that he has not yet reached but toward which he is striving with might and main.

The **prize** (v. 14) is not a reward of eternal salvation but the Christlike character that God desires His people to reflect and to which end He predestines them. It is that **for which God has called me heavenward in Christ Jesus** (v. 14). [See exegesis on Rom. 8:28-29 in this volume, chapter titled "Holiness—God's Predestined Purpose for His People."]

In summary, after establishing the basis of our acceptance with God (justification), Paul then proceeds to speak about the living out of that acceptance (sanctification). As everywhere, Paul does not think of sanctification as a prerequisite for salvation but as the response or outflow of a right relation to God through Christ. He assumes that God has a purpose in mind for His redeemed people that goes beyond mere acceptance. It is "that for which Christ Jesus has also laid hold of me" (v. 12, NKJV). Within the context of this divine purpose there is a tension, and it is here that we discover the holiness emphasis of this passage. Within the sanctified life there is a distinction between a "character perfection" (see vv. 12, 14) and a "realized perfection" (see v. 15).

The same root word *(telos)* is used in reference to both realities. From it the adjective *(teleios)* and verb *(teleioō)* are derived. They can be legitimately translated as either **perfect** or **mature,** and many modern versions choose to render v. 15 as "mature" in order to distinguish the uses of the two terms (NIV, NKJV, TCNT, TLB, Weymouth). Others use synonyms for maturity, for example, "full grown" *(Emphasized NT);* "ripe in understanding" (Conybeare); "spiritually adult" (Phillips). Such terminology is acceptable to Wesleyan theology, since full sanctification is often described in such ways (see John Wesley's oft-used reference to 1 John 2:12-14, where "fathers" are identified with the entirely sanctified). But it is a maturity that is achieved by both *crisis* and *process* as demonstrated by experience.

P. T. Forsyth's statement is illuminating:

> Faith is the condition of spiritual maturity in the sense of adultness, of entering on the real heritage of the soul. It is the soul coming to itself, coming of age, feeling its feet, entering on its native powers. Faith is perfection in this sense. It is not ceasing to grow, but *entering on the normal region of growth.* [2]

If maturity is by faith, it is clearly not exclusively a matter of growth.

Note John A. Knight's excellent contrast between the two uses of these words:

> *Telos,* from which the adjective "perfect" *(teleios)* comes, literally means "end." To the Greek mind it suggested, on the one hand, that which is last, final, or complete; and on the other, that which is accomplishing its purpose or function, mature or full-grown. Both senses are seen in various forms of the word throughout the New Testament. Thus it is used in the sense of "fulfilled" (Luke 22:37; John 19:28), "perfect" or "perfected" (Luke 13:32; John 17:23; II Cor. 12:9; Phil. 3:12; Heb. 2:10; 5:9; 7:19; 9:9; 10:1, 14; 11:40; 12:23; Jas. 2:22; I John 2:5; 4:12, 17-18), "finish" and "finished" (John 5:36; Acts 20:24), and "consecrated" (Heb. 7:28). The adjective *teleios* occurs nineteen times in the New Testament, all of which are translated "perfect" in the Authorized Version, except in I Cor. 14:20, where it

is rendered "men," in contrast to "children," and in Heb. 5:14, "of full-age," in contradistinction to a "babe."

Unless Paul was manifestly contradicting himself—an accusation which even from a literary standpoint would be grossly unfair—it must be asserted that the perfection which he disclaims in 12 (verb *teleioo*) is different from that which he now claims in 15, "Let us therefore, as many as be perfect" (adjective *teleios*). The difference in meaning corresponds to the above different uses by the Greeks.[3]

I want to know Christ (v. 10). This phrase and those that follow in vv. 10-11 may be interpreted as the distinctive Pauline way of speaking of the way of entering into the sanctified life. It is summarized in the concept of identification: with His resurrection, His sufferings, His death, culminating in participating in the final resurrection.

The power of his resurrection (v. 10). It is through the power of the Resurrection that we can become "like him in his death" (v. 10, RSV). That is, knowing Christ comes from an inner transformation in which the believer is dead to the old life and alive to the new (cf. 2 Cor. 5:14-17).

Ralph P. Martin relates the phrase **becoming like him in his death** (v. 10) to Rom. 8:29 and Phil. 3:21 and says:

It involves the teaching and experience of Romans 6, where the death and resurrection of Christ are representative acts in which His people share. His death for sin, and unto sin, carries the implication that in Him we likewise die to the dominion of the old nature and rise to newness of life. When He died at Calvary our death was involved; but its outworking requires the exhortation of Romans 6:11, which is another way of saying, "Be conformed to His death." Death, however, is the gateway to life. Paul dies to himself that he may live to God (Gal. 2:20). Self, represented by his past life as a Pharisee (see verses 4-6), is dethroned—yea, crucified (Gal. 5:24; 6:14), that Christ might be enthroned as supreme Lord.[4]

All of us who are mature [perfect] **should take such a view of things** (v. 15). The KJV renders this mind-set as "thus minded." By this phrase Paul makes an illuminating characterization of the **mature** or "perfect." *The distinguishing mark of those who have obtained perfection is the pursuit of the perfection they have not attained.* This would imply that vv. 12-16 are a description of the sanctified life.

The apostle's language suggests that there were some in the

church at Philippi who were "otherwise minded" (v. 15, KJV). They were apparently claiming to be perfect in the final sense in the here and now. It could possibly be a similar attitude to that found at Corinth where some "professed a spiritual attainment superior to that of the rest of their fellow believers whom they may have despised, in much the same way as the later Gnostics looked down upon those who could never attain the rank of the *teleioi*."[5]

Not that I have . . . already been made perfect (v. 12). What is the nature of the "perfection" not yet attained? Some interpreters think that it is resurrection perfection, while others identify it with the goal of Christlikeness. It is true that the completion or finalization of the process will occur at the final resurrection, but it seems odd to speak of this divine action as a goal to be striven for. "Character perfection" fits the context more logically and is certainly a theme to which Paul gives repeated expression (Phil. 2:5; 2 Cor. 3:18).

Paul Rees's words concur with our interpretation: "I suggest that the 'goal' is *Christlikeness.* I use the term as representing the full-blown flower of all our possibilities in resembling the flawless spirit and life of our Master. This, and nothing less, is the predestined end of our redemption: to be 'conformed to the image of his Son'" (Rom. 8:29, KJV).[6]

Forgetting what is behind and straining toward what is ahead (v. 13). It is possible that this simple phrase connotes more than a willful lapse of memory concerning past successes or failures. It may, in fact, be another way of speaking about putting off the "old self" and putting on the "new self" (Col. 3:9-10). The marks of the old self are inferred in Phil. 3:4-11 and may be summarized as dependence upon the flesh. This self-centeredness must be put behind one—forgotten—and a new center adopted through the enablement of God's grace. This is precisely what Paul says about himself in 2 Cor. 5:16 concerning his perception of Christ. He now sees Him from a completely different point of view. Here, he may be suggesting that he is seeing *himself* from a radically altered point of view.

Theological Exegesis

The implications of these passages provide us with some clear guidance as to the nature of entire sanctification:

First, it is not sinless perfection. Stephen Paine observes, "I do not recall hearing any intelligent Christian testifying to 'sinless perfection.' "[7] And, we might add, no one would, since such a claim could only arise out of a very superficial view of sin or an almost complete absence of self-knowledge. John Wesley's words clearly reject such an interpretation of this view of "perfection": "I believe there is no such perfection in this life as excludes those involuntary transgressions which I apprehend to be naturally consequent on the ignorance and mistakes inseparable from mortality. Therefore *sinless perfection* is a phrase I never use, lest I should seem to contradict myself."[8]

Second, it is singleness of mind or purity of intention. "This one thing I do" (v. 13, KJV) marks the truly "perfect man." When judged by legal righteousness, all persons fall short; but it is a divine possibility to have an intentionality that is pure, that is, unmixed. Even when behavior falls far short of the ideal, if one's *intention* is to do the right thing, he is "perfect" in this sense. Even if attitudes surface that are sub-Christian, and they are contrary to holy intentions, the implication is that they are *willed* to be absent.

Thomas Aquinas, medieval scholar, theologian, and philosopher, identified the possible ways in which perfection may be interpreted. Seen in certain ways, he agreed in the impossibility of its being a present reality. However, when it is interpreted as involving "a total exclusion of everything 'contrary to the motive or movement of love for God,' [it] is possible in this life." Such a perfection may be present in two ways: "[1] in the exclusion from the will of anything 'contradictory to love, that is, mortal sin' and [2] in the will's rejection of anything that prevents the disposition of the soul toward God from being total."[9]

Third, it is evidenced by intense spiritual appetite. The self-satisfaction that marks some who testify to the "second blessing" is incongruous with this understanding of sanctification. Mildred Bangs Wynkoop closes *A Theology of Love* with words that capture the mood of this truth:

> *I have a controversy with Christ.* He will not let me rest. In His presence I cannot relax and rest on my "faith" in Him in a lazy way which dulls moral sensitivity. He will not let me settle for less than my best—not yesterday's best, but *today's* best. When I have done a job, He confronts me with a bigger task— one always too big for me. When I am selfish, He rebukes me

until it smarts. When I am insensitive, He has a way of prodding my conscience into activity. When I cry and pray for a little heaven in which to go to heaven in, He shows me the hell in which other people live. It isn't time for heaven, yet.

Purity is not an end in itself. Purity permits the personality to live in full expression of love to God and man. It is the power of a single-hearted devotion and must be kept intact by a daily fellowship with God.[10]

Fourth, holiness is based upon the foundation of God's free and full forgiveness. It is a response to the gift of God's grace, which offers acceptance without regard for inherent or acquired worthiness.

Preaching Ideas

Paul Rees suggests an exciting outline in his book on Philippians, titled *The Adequate Man.* In his typical style, he has three points in which he says that this text includes: (1) a disclaimer that rules perfection out; (2) a declaration that brings perfection in; and (3) a directive that lights perfection up. This lucidly opens up the three major holiness dimensions of the passage and would allow one to draw heavily upon the exegesis.

Rees develops an additional sermon on this text, using Paul's description of the "thus minded" person, a set of characteristics that we saw in the exegesis would mark the entirely sanctified person. Thus we could speak of this as marks of the sanctified. Here is the two-point outline:

A. This "mind" is one of *perceptive forgetfulness.*
B. A perceptively forgetful mind must be also a *passionately forward* mind.

The following comprehensive outline could become one sermon or two, depending on the preacher:

A. Point (or Sermon) One: *The Foundation of Christian Holiness*
   1. The gift of righteousness, which is by faith in Christ (9*b*)
   2. A knowledge of Christ by the power of His resurrection (10*ab*)
   3. A willingness to share in Christ's sufferings (10*c*)
   4. A commitment to become like Christ in His death (10*d*)
   5. A hope looking forward to the resurrection from the dead (11)

B. Point (or Sermon) Two: *The Realization of Christian Holiness*
1. The setting aside of the past (13*b*)
2. The **straining toward . . . the prize** of the high calling of God in Christ Jesus (13*c*-14)
3. The disposition that makes "setting aside" and **straining** possible (15)

A Sermon on the Text

The Secret of Radiance

Scripture: Phil. 3:7-16
Text: Phil. 3:13-16

Radiance may or may not be an authentic evidence of God's grace, but I have observed that it is usually present in the one who has made a genuine contact with God. The secret is found in our text, which speaks to us of God's great grace, His marvelous hope, and His urgent instructions.

A. *The Marvel of God's Great Grace* (vv. 7-11)

Paul discovered that his pedigree was not enough to earn God's favor. In the light of eternity the privileges of birth and achievement counted for nothing. Consequently, he was willing to lose all things and count them as "refuse" (RSV) in order to gain Christ. "The surpassing worth of knowing Christ Jesus my Lord" (RSV) stands at the center of a marvelous acknowledgment of God's grace.

How easy it is to consider our achievements, our good deeds, or our rank as giving us inherent value in God's sight. It is humbling to have to confess our spiritual bankruptcy, but the free gift of salvation—"knowing Christ"—is certainly worth it.

The marvel of God's grace in v. 9 is His gift of righteousness that depends on faith, with the result that we "may know him, and the power of his resurrection" (KJV) as referred to in v. 10. At least it means that the same power that broke forth on that first Easter morning is the power that is ours when we identify with Christ.

There is one more dimension to that marvelous gift of God's grace in righteousness—that is, to become "conformable" (KJV) or like Him in His death. This intimate relationship can only be explained as death to the former life. Those who die and rise with Christ must exhibit this truth by a separation from their old life and a steady walk in the power of Christ's resurrected life.

B. *God's Grace Results in a Marvelous Hope* (vv. 12-14)

Paul's life now moves in a new direction, but he is not claiming that his conversion has brought him to the final goal. "Not that I have already obtained this or am already perfect," so he presses and strains to make the goal his own, "because Christ Jesus has made me his own" (v. 12, RSV). He would not fall in among the perfectionists in Philippi who claimed the consummation of all spiritual blessings, and neither should we.

With Paul we have a continuing responsibility to constantly pursue the purposes that Christ has chosen for us, and the prize of "the high calling of God in Christ Jesus" (v. 14, KJV) is always a beckoning finger until we are called to be with Him.

Paul, then, has made up his mind on the ground of the gift of God's righteousness and the promise of a final hope to set aside everything in order to run the race and press toward the final goal with the prize that follows. The single-mindedness of v. 13 is correlative to "forgetting what is behind." Nothing is comparable to the goal ahead.

C. *Urgent Instructions* (vv. 15-16)

It is within the context of Paul's commitment that urgent instructions are now given to those who are "perfect" or "mature" to think in harmony with what has gone before. In v. 12 Paul spoke of a perfection toward which he was striving. Now, in v. 15, he speaks of a "realized perfection" that is equivalent to singleness of mind—a purity of intention that pervades all of the heart, mind, soul, and strength of those who follow Christ.

Of perfection, Paul Rees, a prince of preachers, says:

> If there is a whole battery of perfectionisms that we dare not be drawn into because of our loyalty to the Scriptures, let's be sure we do not miss the one unassailable perfectionism that grace provides and the Scriptures declare. Not *absolute* perfection: that were fantastic. Not *legal* perfection: that were to return to the law and to retreat from grace. Not *service* perfection: that were to overlook obvious awkwardness and clumsiness. Not *behavioral perfection:* that were to fly in the face of a hundred flaws in our manners. Not *sinless* perfection: that were to imply a status identical with our "unfallen" Lord.
>
> What then? Let's call it *affectional* and *dispositional* perfection. It is God's own gift to totally committed children of His, who, renouncing self-pleasing and men-pleasing, are imbued with a passionate eagerness to please Him in all things.[11]

E. Stanley Jones, the great missionary to India, speaks to the same point:

> The man who cannot say, "This one thing I do," has to say, "These many things I dabble in." For his soul forces are not fused into one—he is a dabbler instead of a doer. The Holy Spirit cleanses from conflict as well as from contamination. The scattered rays of the sun, not concentrated, set nothing afire; but when they are brought through a burning glass and concentrated at one point, they set that point ablaze.[12]

The urgent instructions of Paul also imply a promise (v. 15). Those who think differently about the "becoming" character of the holy life will be enlightened. God will lead them and us to the truth if our minds are open to the truth of His guidance. How can one stand against such openness? The Lord gives us instructions, and if we do not understand, He is willing to wait until our minds are clear to His revelation. The child of God cannot ask for more!

Many have discovered the *secret of radiance* by entering the fellowship of the perfect in heart through God's sanctifying grace. Have you made that discovery? You can, by the marvel of God's grace, with a singleness of mind that will see in the Christian pilgrimage a journey toward the golden city of our Heavenly Father.

Endnotes

1. Bernhard Anderson, *Out of the Depths* (Philadelphia: Westminster Press, 1983), 100-101; see also George Eldon Ladd, *A Theology of the New Testament* (Grand Rapids: Wm. B. Eerdmans Publishing Co., 1974), 439-40.

2. Paul S. Rees, *The Adequate Man* (Westwood, N.J.: Fleming H. Revell Co., 1959), 83.

3. John A. Knight, "Philippians," in *Beacon Bible Commentary,* 10 vols. (Kansas City: Beacon Hill Press, 1965), 9:339-40.

4. *The Epistle of Paul to the Philippians,* in *Tyndale Commentary* (Grand Rapids: Wm. B. Eerdmans Publishing Co., 1959), 149-50.

5. Ibid., 155.

6. *Adequate Man,* 85.

7. *Toward the Mark* (Westwood, N.J.: Fleming H. Revell Co., 1953), 137.

8. *Plain Account of Christian Perfection* (Kansas City: Beacon Hill Press of Kansas City, 1966), 54.

9. Paul M. Bassett and William M. Greathouse, *Exploring Christian Holiness,* vol. 2, *The Historical Development* (Kansas City: Beacon Hill Press of Kansas City, 1985), 137-38.

10. Mildred Bangs Wynkoop, *A Theology of Love: The Dynamic of Wesleyanism* (Kansas City: Beacon Hill Press of Kansas City, 1972), 361-62.

11. Paul Stromberg Rees, *Prayer and Life's Highest* (Grand Rapids: Wm. B. Eerdmans Publishing Co., 1956), 61.

12. E. Stanley Jones, *Mastery* (New York: Abingdon Press, 1955), 232.

—3—

PRAYERS
FOR HOLINESS

———————

RICHARD S. TAYLOR

An Anguished Prayer for Radical Cleansing

Behold, I was shapen in iniquity; and in sin did my mother conceive me. Behold, thou desirest truth in the inward parts: and in the hidden part thou shalt make me to know wisdom. Purge me with hyssop, and I shall be clean: wash me, and I shall be whiter than snow. Make me to hear joy and gladness; that the bones which thou hast broken may rejoice. Hide thy face from my sins, and blot out all mine iniquities. Create in me a clean heart, O God; and renew a right spirit within me. Cast me not away from thy presence; and take not thy holy spirit from me. Restore unto me the joy of thy salvation; and uphold me with thy free spirit (Ps. 51:5-12, KJV).

All persons who have sinned are guilty before God. But not everyone recognizes this, and of those who do, only a relatively few experience remorse. Every criminal incarcerated in penal institutions is sorry that he has been caught. There are many who deny their guilt, but they are still suffering the consequences of their crimes. Everyone who has a criminal record desires that his record be expunged so that it will not stand as a negative influence in his life, a barrier to success. But few want their crimes expunged from the record book of heaven, and especially its source cleansed from their inner being.

One notable exception to this widespread response to sin was the great Hebrew king, David. When exposed, he did not deny his guilt but reacted by seeking the only effective remedy for wrongdoing and wrongbeing—the forgiveness and cleansing that comes only from God. His prayer of repentance is found in Psalm 51.

This is one of seven penitential psalms, and according to Kyle

M. Yates, Jr., "the most profound."[1] It is the agonized cry of a "broken and contrite heart" (v. 17).

Historical Background

An in-depth study of this very moving psalm requires a careful review of the events in David's life that prompted it (cf. 1 Samuel 11—12).[2] Some might explain what happened as a "midlife crisis." At least there seemed to be an out-of-character lassitude in his leadership. Instead of being in the field with his army, he took it easy at home, where he was swept off his feet by the sudden thrust of a powerful temptation. The result was adultery with Bathsheba and, to cover the consequences, his panicky maneuvers against Bathsheba's husband, Uriah. So in quick succession David found himself guilty of adultery, trickery, deception, and murder.

In view of David's usual sensitivity of conscience it would seem impossible for him to commit these crimes without some feelings of shock, surprise, and shame. But he successfully repressed his anxiety. Doubtless he rationalized that getting rid of Uriah was an unfortunate necessity that Uriah's stubbornness brought on himself; and who could say that he would not have been killed in the war in any case? And anyway, wasn't David king? Couldn't he deploy his soldiers as he saw fit?

When a person starts down this slippery slope, there are no limits to the rationalizations he can employ in blinding himself to reality. It could have been as much as a year that David went on in moral stupor, deceiving himself that all was well, perhaps outwardly as pious as ever. But some time after the child was born, David had a visitor, Nathan the prophet. David was jolted back to his senses, and suddenly he plunged into an agony of remorse. When the dam of self-deception broke, pent-up shame and guilt swept over him.

Exegetical Section

The selection of eight verses out of this psalm (5-12) enables us to focus on the text most germane to holiness preaching. But before any attempt is made to analyze these verses, attention should be given to the previous four, at least (all KJV). Here is David's confession of his sinning. He begins with a plea for mercy: "Have mercy upon me, O God, according to thy lovingkindness." When repentance is hollow, there is always an attempt to plead extenuating circumstances and thus minimize one's guilt. Even Adam said, "The woman whom thou gavest to be with me" (Gen. 3:12, KJV). "Yes, I know I did it, and I shouldn't have, but . . ." David is not hedging in this way. He is not pleading for "understanding." He knows he deserves nothing, so he can only cast himself on the mercy of God. This approach speaks well for the outcome.

"Blot out my transgressions. Wash me throughly from mine iniquity, and cleanse me from my sin." David knows his sins cannot be undone; and he has already been told that the consequences will follow him forever. But he yearns for the record of them to be so expunged that they will no longer stand between him and his God. The washing for which he prays is the Hebrew word meaning, not gentle sponging, but to beat the dirt out with sticks. Don't be easy on me, he is saying, but by whatever means it takes, get the filth out.

"For I acknowledge my transgressions: and my sin is ever before me." "Now that I have stopped hiding and lying and running, I can't get my sin out of my mind. I am haunted by it day and night. Whichever way I turn, there it is, accusing me and tormenting me. I am filled with horror at what I have done." Surface repentance is the result of not feeling deeply about the heinousness of one's sin. David's repentance, by contrast, was profound and heartrending because he experienced his sin to the core of his being.

"Against thee, thee only, have I sinned, and done this evil in thy sight." A possible approach to this is to see that David perceives the profound truth that at the bottom line he is primarily accountable to God, the One whose law he has broken, and whose name he has disgraced. For it is the fact of God that makes wrongdoing sin. If there were no God, no divine power to whom we are accountable, no divine law to which we are obligated, the concept of sin would never arise. There would be no way for a religious vocabulary that included the word *sin* to develop.[3] Man would be related solely to his fellows, and all conduct would have to be interpreted in sociological or legal terms. In the deepest sense, therefore, sin, *as sin,* is only against God. David's acknowledgment that he has sinned against God prompts him to agree with God's judgment: "Yes, thou art just in thy charge, justified in thy sentence" (Moffatt). But having acknowledged God's primacy, we can then see that His relation to man shapes and determines the moral nature of man's relation to his fellows; so that in a secondary sense we can speak of David sinning against Bathsheba, Uriah, Joab, the child, indeed the whole nation.

We now come to David's deeper perception of himself and his sin, as we move into the text proper (5-12). **Behold, I was shapen in iniquity; and in sin did my mother conceive me.** The NIV says: "Surely I was sinful at birth, sinful from the time my mother conceived me." So his collapse cannot be traced to a "midlife crisis" after all. There was a deeper, underlying problem that was natal. He came into the world with a powerful weighting toward sin. It was written profoundly in his very nature—not the nature God had created but the nature Adam transmitted. Another way to explain this is to say that he was born into a race that was alienated from God, and was therefore a participant in the depravity that such alienation breeds.

One can imagine how David came to this awareness. As he struggled with the enormity of what he had done, he must have asked himself a thousand times, "Why did I do it? Why was I so defenseless? Why was I so willing?" There was only one answer. Back of his deliberate sinning was a proneness to sin so deep and subtle that yielding was far easier than resisting. This nature he had doubtless not fully seen before.

The surest evidence of repentance in David is this acknowledgment of his basic crookedness, for the carnal ego struggles to save itself at all costs. Some degree of self-esteem must be preserved, some sense of goodness must be held fast. It is relatively easy to admit specific sins, as long as we can protect ourselves from the implication that we are an evil person. We want to persuade ourselves—and we want others to believe—that this deed is totally "out of character"; it does not reveal the true person, who is really quite decent. So we separate what we have done from what we are, that we might in some way at least salvage our good name from the wreckage. But David's depth is disclosed by his abhorrence of himself, his freedom from any disposition to excuse or spare himself, and his willingness to see that he was thoroughly corrupt.

This verse cannot properly be construed to imply some illegitimacy in David's conception. It is equally unacceptable to read into this an implication of sinfulness in the procreative process, though Augustine came close to it.[4]

Adam Clarke comments: "Notwithstanding all that *Grotius* and others have said to the contrary, I believe David to speak here of what is commonly called *original sin;* the propensity to evil which every man brings into the world with him, and which is the fruitful source whence all transgression proceeds."[5] This does not mean that the body is sinful per se, but that this inherited corruption of nature affects the total person. Paul's prayer for the entire sanctification of spirit, soul, and body (1 Thess. 5:23) would imply that in some sense the body as well as spirit and soul needs sanctifying.

Having finally confessed not only what he did but what he was, David realizes that the cure requires a deeper remedy than forgiveness. Something must be done about the substratum of sinfulness in his makeup. He perceives with fresh clarity what God really wants: **Behold, thou desirest truth in the inward parts: and in the hidden part thou shalt make me to know wisdom.** David discovered himself to be false at the very core of his being. Yet this is where God wants total integrity—in the hidden motives, the real intentions, not only the conscious choices but the dispositional leanings. When truth is their very nature, the bedrock of their character, then men and women will be true to God, to others, and to themselves, no matter what the enticements, inducements, or pressures. It is this inner truthfulness, which is the true wisdom, for which David prays.

Following as it does upon the confession of vv. 5-6, David's prayer for purging **with hyssop** and for a kind of washing (same as v. 2) that will make him **whiter than snow** is doubtless with his deeper need in mind. The hyssop, a very common plant suitable for dipping and sprinkling, was used most significantly in the ceremonial cleansing of a healed leper. But as Clarke points out, the "ceremony was not performed till the plague of the leprosy had *been healed* in the leper; . . . the ceremony was for the purpose of *declaring* to the people that the man was healed, that he might be restored to his place in society."[6] The hyssop is the symbol of the *healing* for which David is praying.

And the washing desired is the kind that beats out hidden dirt, making him **whiter than snow.** To appear white to others is not what he is after. He desires nothing less than cleansing from the impurities that the natural eye cannot detect.

The prayer for **joy and gladness** follows the prayer for purging. David knows that the emotional side of religion must grow out of the moral and spiritual (cf. Rom. 14:17). Furthermore, the joy and gladness so much craved is not for its own sake; it is not a spiritual "high." Rather it is the joy and gladness of restored fellowship with the God he has loved and worshiped and served since boyhood. That sweet communion that he had so greatly prized, and which had ignited his soul in the making of music and in the pouring out of his psalms, had been lost. The result was a suffering that could only be likened to the ache of broken bones. When smitten by divine condemnation, we feel crushed beneath a heavy weight. We feel torn apart. We yearn for our bones to rejoice once more. This is a graphic metaphor, but how can the line be drawn between reality and metaphor? The impact of sin on the body may be literal as well as metaphorical.

In vv. 9-12 we have an encapsulated summary of the petitions of vv. 1-8. They are arranged in an ascending scale, so significantly that the major text could be confined to these verses. First is the *prayer for forgiveness:* **Hide thy face from my sins, and blot out all mine iniquities.** Second is the *prayer for holiness:* **Create in me a clean heart, O God; and renew a right spirit within me.** Third is a *plea for the recovery of the Divine Presence in his heart and life:* **Cast me not away from thy presence; and take not thy holy spirit from me.**[7] Fourth is the *petition for a restored assurance:* **Restore unto me the joy of thy salvation.** Fifth is the *prayer for preservation:* **uphold me *with thy* free spirit.**

However, the words **with thy** are italicized because they are not in the original. The clause should read, "Uphold me with a free spirit." In v. 10*b* he craves a "constant, steady, determined spirit." Here he desires *"a noble spirit, a free, generous, princely* spirit; cheerfully giving up itself to thee; no longer *bound* and *degraded* by the sinfulness of sin."[8] Thus does the vision of an abject but repentant David embrace with holy boldness the whole range of possibilities in grace. By faith he dares to grasp a walk with God deeper and more surefooted than ever—not as a benefit of his backsliding, but out of God's sheer mercy. David is not asking for crumbs but for a full larder.

Holiness is especially pinpointed in the prayer for a clean heart and a right spirit. This requires careful handling. Matthew Henry calls this a prayer "for sanctifying grace." "This," he continues, "every true penitent is as earnest for, as for pardon and peace." Instead of praying for the preservation of his reputation, as Saul prayed, David's consuming concern was "to get his corrupt nature changed."[9]

In praying for a **clean heart,** David is seeking the answer to the natal problem that he has just been confessing. While it is true that *tahor,* "pure, clean," is often used for ceremonial cleanness and the cleanness of forgiveness, it also denotes freedom from filth (Lev. 10:14 et al.), and the cleanness of a healed leper (Lev. 13:17; 2 Kings 5:14). David thought of himself as a moral leper who needed to be healed.

The word for **create** is *bara,* a radical word used for bringing into being something previously nonexistent. David begs for more than patchwork or repair; he wants a pure inner nature—something he has never had before. Nor is this regeneration—making spiritually alive. It is entire sanctification—making every whit holy. "David's prayer," say Conder and Clarkson, "goes to the central depth, the innermost need of our nature."[10]

The two sides of the verse, **a clean heart** and **a right spirit,** may be called parallel in Hebrew poetry structure, but this does not mean that **heart** and **spirit** in this case are exactly synonymous. A right spirit—a devout, obedient, believing attitude—he has had before; therefore the prayer is for its renewal. Sin always affects the spirit, causing it to become depressed, morose, dull, indifferent, self-centered, sometimes caustic and bitter. David desires that his former constancy toward God shall be his again (cf. 2 Tim. 1:7).

When David turns from his own spirit and its renewal to pray that God's **holy spirit** would not be taken from him, he uses **spirit** in a different sense. He now thinks not of a quality but of a presence. While he may not have visualized this **spirit** as the Third Person of the Trinity, he perceived God as the Spirit who is holy, who demands holiness, and whose upholding presence is the sole hope of holiness. He does understand it as "the Spirit who makes holy."[11] "This presence, the very presence of God himself making himself real to my soul, the presence which I have dishonored and almost forfeited, is my only hope. May it [we would say "He" in NT light] continue to convict, enlighten, and enable."

As has many a backslider, during his spiritual stupor David

presumed God's favorable presence; but it was an idle presumption, and his religious exercises—probably as frequent as ever, maybe more so—were but empty forms.

Can This Be Preached?

Here is a yearning, faithful, sensitive pastor, searching his soul for ways to transmit to his people something of the poignancy and passion of this psalm. How can it be done?

Fortunately, neither the pastor nor the people need to commit David's sins in order to identify with his confession and prayer. Any sin separates from God and brings exquisite suffering to the awakened soul. Such pain has been, or will be, the experience of most hearers. Some of them may right now be in David's shoes—maybe even guilty of the same sins. Others may be equally devastated over sin in other forms, perhaps lying, dishonesty in business, emotional infidelity, covetousness and greed, robbing God of His due, neglect of prayer and Bible, twisted priorities, bad attitudes—any one of which will as surely damn the soul as murder and adultery. The pastor therefore can be assured that the Holy Spirit will apply this psalm to his hearers' condition.

Then others in the congregation may still be the complacent cover-up artist that David was before Nathan came. The pastor senses their perilous state and prays to preach a Nathan-like sermon, which the Spirit can use to explode in their soul like a bomb, shattering their alibis and hiding places.

The pastor needs to pray over this passage until he feels profoundly its passion and is enabled by the Spirit to transmit something of its urgency and authenticity, as well as explain verbally the profoundly basic doctrinal ideas that are here.

What is the fundamental stance of this psalm? It is the stance and predicament, not of a worldling who has never known God, but of a backslider whose reputation is impeccable, whose walk up to this time has been above reproach, and whose devotion to God has been such that God called him "a man after mine own heart" (Acts 13:22, KJV). This means that the message is to Christians, not outsiders.

It is the example of a truly devout believer who is deceived by his own carnal heart. It is this that makes the passage a holiness text par excellence. It is a study in double-mindedness. It is the story of a man whose awakened spirit is mature enough and sensitized enough to perceive the state of his very being as being corrupt, equally as well as he perceives the wrongness of his actions and their guiltiness. He grasps the truth of a double need and dares to pray for a double cure.

If we turn the coin over, we can see hope written large on the other side. In a way this is one of the most encouraging and comforting passages in the Bible. This is true because whenever an awakening has occurred, there are with it feelings of despair, shame, and hopelessness. But this psalm, which on one side is a pouring forth of a broken heart, is on the other side a most eloquent articulation of possibilities. It is an inspired scripture, and every such prayer is a covered promise (Wesley). The entire Bible, focusing on Christ on the middle cross, assures those who pray as David that what they humbly pray for is exactly what a merciful God, through Christ, is pleased to provide. David is asking for a lot, but in the matchless divine economy it is not too much. Therefore we can preach the privileges of (1) a pure heart, (2) a right spirit, (3) the indwelling Spirit, (4) the daily upholding, (5) the restored joy and fellowship, and (6) the revitalized ministry in the congregation, with joyous affirmation.

Several sermonic suggestions may be made:

Topic: **Inner Healing**
A. The Nature of True Repentance
    1. Confessing with sorrow and honesty what we have *done*
    2. Confessing with shame and honesty what we *are*
B. The Extent of Available Healing
    1. Total forgiveness (v. 9)
    2. Total sanctification (v. 10)
    3. Total recovery of God's presence and power (v. 11)
    4. Total recovery of the joy of salvation (v. 12)

Conclusion: "A broken and a contrite heart" God will "not despise" (v. 17, KJV).

Topic: **Inward Truth**

Text: **Behold, thou desirest truth in the inward parts: and in the hidden part thou shalt make me to know wisdom** (v. 6, KJV).

The inward parts are "the innermost being" (NASB)—the real person, which only God sees.

A. Truth in the inward parts can be defined by the word *integrity.*
1. Integrity is moral principle that cannot be bought.
2. It is unity between the inward and the outward—what we seem to be and what we really are. (It is more than "truthfulness" about our untruthfulness!)
B. The reason God desires truth in the inward parts is twofold:
1. It is the only possible ground of fellowship between us and God. It is impossible for an acceptable relationship to be sustained except on the basis of complete honesty (Rev. 21:7-8).
2. Only as God sees truth in our inward parts can He use us (cf. vv. 13-15).
C. God has made provision for us to be made true in the inward parts.
1. This is that holiness of heart and character that is the supreme objective of all God's redemptive ministrations.
2. But we must see the implications. God's total redemptive plan in Christ presupposes that in our natural selves we are not truthful in the inward parts. David's discovery (Jer. 17:9). As soon as Adam and Eve sinned, they became untruthful; that is, they manifested a disposition to blame others and excuse themselves.
3. The first step in experiencing truth in the inward parts is the discovery and acknowledgment of our falseness.
4. The second step is to pray David's prayer (v. 10), and believe that God the Holy Spirit, for Christ's sake, will do for us and in us what all our striving cannot accomplish in a thousand years—*make our inner nature true.*

Topic: **The Highest Boon of Divine Grace**

Text: **Create in me a clean heart, O God** (v. 10, KJV).

The possession of a clean heart is the highest blessing known to man. For in this he is most recovered from his lost estate, he is most Christlike, he is most truly himself, and only with a clean heart is he fit for fellowship with God either on earth or in heaven. Furthermore, only in the possession of a clean heart can all the other blessings of redemption be sustained. Growth in grace, a happy spirit, daily victory over sin, a meaningful prayer life, and effectiveness in service—all these blessings will be blocked by an unclean heart.

A. Notice the sense of need that prompts this prayer: David's discovery of a profound uncleanness.

1. *The uncleanness that David saw consisted of a deep affinity for evil.* His heart was a lodestone to sin. His sinning had been too easy. He was too vulnerable.

2. *As much as he loved God, he loved himself more—in the pinch.* This self-love became the spring of disloyalty to God.

B. In praying for a clean heart, exactly what does David have in mind? What kind of a heart is a "clean" heart?

1. *He is obviously praying for more than forgiveness.* See context. Expiation or forgiveness is the first step.

2. *He desires a heart free from filthiness.* When sin is seen in its true nature, it appears as dirty and filthy.

3. *David desires a rectified moral nature:* a nature free from secret falseness; a nature with a spontaneous affinity for right instead of wrong; a nature no longer divided or double-minded. David desires that the "grain" of his nature shall mesh with the "grain" of God's nature.

C. How can a clean heart be "created"?

1. *Only by God.* The Hebrew word *bara,* used here, is never linked with any agent other than God. Obviously a clean heart is beyond our own power.

2. *But not without our cooperation.* As in David's case we must see our need and confess our need and pray for a miracle of grace in our very nature. On the level of moral purity the "perfecting" of holiness requires a thorough self-purging (2 Cor. 7:1). God's "creative" action includes the grace that we utilize in doing our part, but it is also a direct action of the Spirit on our inner selves—beyond anything we can do. This is sheer miracle, the nature of which we can neither fathom nor duplicate. It is nothing less than the undoing, at the heart level, of the perversion caused by the sin of Adam.

D. Is David's prayer answerable?

This question is the real bottom line issue. Is David simply being rhetorical and idealistic? Is he praying for that which in this life is impossible?

1. *This is an inspired prayer, which implies divine possibilities.* Every petition is pregnant with promise.

2. *The entire NT supports David's faith.* The power of God to

create a clean heart is affirmed or implied in (1) the declared purpose of the Atonement (John 17:17-19; Eph. 5:25-26; Titus 2:11-14); (2) the core effect of Pentecost (Acts 15:8-9); the direct ministry of the Holy Spirit (2 Thess. 2:13; 1 Pet. 1:2); the promise of entire sanctification (1 Thess. 5:23-24); the special genius of new covenant privileges (Rom. 8:1-4; Eph. 1:4; Heb. 10:16; cf. Jer. 31:31-34; Ezek. 36:25-27).

3. Yes, David's prayer is answerable, for us as well as for him. But it is conditionally answerable. We must follow David in his honest confession and his earnest petition, and be persuaded that as we confess, commit, and believe, God the Holy Spirit will perform the miracle in our hearts. Then *stand back and let Him do it!*

Endnotes

1. Kyle M. Yates, "Psalms," in *The Wycliffe Bible Commentary,* ed. Charles F. Pfeiffer and Everett F. Harrison (Chicago: Moody Press, 1962), 54. Other penitential psalms are 6; 32; 38; 102; 130; and 143.

2. In defense of the title (ascribing the psalm to David on the occasion of his sin against Bathsheba and Uriah) see Adam Clarke, *Commentary on the Holy Scripture,* vol. 2 (New York: Abingdon Press, n.d.). Also Franz Delitzsch, *Commentary on the Old Testament,* trans. James Martin (reprint, Grand Rapids: Wm. B. Eerdmans Publishing Co., 1984).

3. One definition of *sin* in the Merriam-Webster *Third New International Dictionary* is: "a transgression of religious law: an offense against God."

4. Paul M. Bassett and William M. Greathouse, *Exploring Christian Holiness,* vol. 2, *The Historical Development* (Kansas City: Beacon Hill Press of Kansas City, 1985), 97.

5. Clarke, *Commentary.*

6. Ibid.

7. This is one of the three references to the Holy Spirit in the OT, the other two being Isa. 63:10, 11; though there are numerous references to "my spirit" and "the spirit of the Lord."

8. Clarke, *Commentary.*

9. *Matthew Henry's Commentary on the Whole Bible* (reprint, Wilmington, Del.: Sovereign Grace Publishers, 1972).

10. E. R. Conder and W. Clarkson, "Psalms" (Homiletics), in *The Pulpit Commentary,* ed. H. D. M. Spence and Joseph S. Exell (reprint, Grand Rapids: Wm. B. Eerdmans Publishing Co., 1950), 8:398.

11. David Hill, *Greek Words and Hebrew Meanings* (Cambridge: Cambridge University Press, 1967), 211.

BRUCE PETERSEN

Paul's Prayer for the Philippian Church

And this is my prayer: that your love may abound more and more in knowledge and depth of insight, so that you may be able to discern what is best and may be pure and blameless until the day of Christ, filled with the fruit of righteousness that comes through Jesus Christ—to the glory and praise of God (Phil. 1:9-11).

Where is a Christian to find a pattern for living the Spirit-filled life in contemporary society? Many options are offered today. Some would try to emulate those persons showcased by television's "Lifestyles of the Rich and Famous." From this viewpoint, Christianity is nothing more than showy materialism. Some media evangelists preach a gospel of "Jesus wants you to be rich." Whatever your heart desires, all you need to do is "name it and claim it." Little mention is ever made of spiritual surrender and sacrifice.

Others find Spirit-filled living to mean a certain legalistic style of dress or activity. Often it is nothing more than wearing clothes and hairstyles that are 20 years out of date. Legalism is just another form of trying to fit a mold that will impress people.

Emotionalism is another proposed answer to a sanctified lifestyle. How high you jump is more important than how straight you walk. Ethical values are secondary to experience and feelings.

While many in the current religious scene preach these values of exterior Christianity, Paul prays that the Philippian Christians would have quite a different life-style based on a true change of heart. The Spirit-filled life begins with a specific encounter with the Holy Spirit. But what then? This passage gets very specific with the way we live in the Spirit day by day. It gets right down to the basic motivations of the heart, and the concepts Paul gives work just as well for contemporary man today.

Exegetical Section

Paul's prayer includes four petitions: (1) **that your love may abound more and more in knowledge and depth of insight.** (2) **That you may be able to discern what is best.** (3) That you **may be pure and blameless until the day of Christ.** (4) That you may be **filled with the fruit of righteousness that comes through Jesus Christ.** These four petitions encompass the very essence of Christian holiness and, as Stephen W. Paine said, is "a prayer so radical in its grasp and far reaching in its extent that a whole Christian life may be lived in its scope."[1] We will examine each petition for its significance in the life of holiness.

Petition One

This is a concern that Paul reiterates verbatim in his prayer for the Thessalonian church (1 Thess. 3:12). Since love is such a multifaceted reality, we must ask what kind of love is in view. It is the Greek word *agapē*, which, according to the NT, is the highest form of love. Its source is God himself. This love is connected with the will far more than the emotions and thus can be commanded (Matt. 22:37). It is a self-giving love that does not demand anything in return. Since it originates in God, it is God's kind of love and elicits the same kind of love in response. Thus it can appropriately be called divine love.

Abound *(perisseuē)* is in the present tense, indicating a continuous process. The word means to overflow like floodwaters, superabundant, without measure. Paul desires love to rise to its most expansive expression. The nature of this love suggests that as it grows, it is supplanting self-love. This is the point of John Wesley's answer to the question, "When does inward sanctification begin?" He said, "In the moment a man is justified. . . . From that time a believer gradually dies to sin, and grows in grace."[2]

This love is to abound in **knowledge** *(epignōsei)* and **depth of insight** *(aisthēsei)*. The knowledge of which he speaks refers, not to intellectual development, but to a grasp of spiritual truth on a practical level. It is a knowledge of the heart and not the head. Such knowledge comes directly from the Holy Spirit. The word translated **depth of insight** is used only here in the NT. It means the ability to apply knowledge to the everyday situations of life. This provides love with discrimination so that it is not unregulated, just as knowledge gives love direction.

Petition Two

That you may . . . discern. The Greeks used *dokimazein* (discern) to refer to the testing of metal or of coins and, as a result, to "approve" (KJV). **Discern** is not just the ability to distinguish right from wrong, but to choose the best from the good, or the things that matter over the things that don't. Moffatt translates the phrase, "enabling you to have a sense of what is vital."

The apostle's concern is that the Philippians develop a taste for the higher values. He enjoins the same thing more explicitly in 4:8—"Finally, brothers, whatever is true, whatever is noble, whatever is right, whatever is pure, whatever is lovely, whatever is admirable—if anything is excellent or praiseworthy—think about such things." The words of Susanna Wesley put this ethical principle of the holy life in classic form: "Whatever weakens your reason, impairs the tenderness of your conscience, obscures your sense of God, or takes off the relish of spiritual things, whatever increases the authority of your body over mind, that thing for you is sin."[3]

Petition Three

That you may . . . be pure. *Eilikrineis* is translated "sincere" by the KJV. There are two possible derivations of the word. One means to judge by holding something in the light of the sun, thus "suntested." It probably comes from the art of pottery making. A vase or urn was held up to the sun, and the light shining through would reveal if it had been patched. From this practice comes the Latin term from which *sincere* is derived, meaning "without wax." It implies a transparency of character and motive.

In Wesley's *Plain Account,* the question is asked, "Does then Christian perfection imply any more than sincerity?" He answered: "Not if you mean by that word, love filling the heart, expelling pride, anger, desire, self-will; rejoicing evermore, praying without ceasing, and in everything giving thanks."[4] He goes on to suggest that few use the term in that sense, but he seems to think that that *is* the biblical significance of it. It would be safe to say that sincerity in human relations is an essential aspect of the sanctified life.

Another possible meaning is "to whirl around as a sieve." In this metaphor, every impurity is removed by extraction. The resultant purity pertains to the inner life, to a pure heart.

Blameless *(aproskopoi)* means to be whole or complete in one's life around others. It can refer either to walking without stumbling (taking "offence," KJV) or causing someone else to stumble (giving "offence"). The latter seems more feasible as a corollary to "sincerity" or "purity," referring to holiness in human relations.

Against the impurity of our world, the Wesleyan understanding of purity stands in stark contrast. If purity is not possible in this present world, Paul would not be praying for the Philippians' hearts to be pure. "Purity" is a work of God's grace. It should be noted that purity refers to man in relation to God, whereas blamelessness deals with our relation to our fellowman. Purity is related to our motives, while being blameless refers to our performance.

The question might be raised whether it is possible to be totally blameless before others, since it is possible to be misunderstood. Obviously, we cannot be responsible for the responses of others to us. We do have a measure of accountability to others to make sure we do not stumble before them or cause them to stumble. People will always see our actions from a different perspective and thus may misjudge our motive.

Petition Four

[That ye may be] **filled with the fruit of righteousness.** This phrase can mean we are filled with the righteousness of Christ, which leaves no room for unrighteousness. But the more likely meaning refers to the fruit of the Spirit elaborated in Gal. 5:22-23. This clearly defines Paul's understanding of holiness as *ethical in nature.* The phrase **that comes through Jesus Christ** identifies the paradigm for the fruit, thus reinforcing the idea of holiness as *ethical* rather than *emotional* or *ceremonial.* The contrast between ethical and ceremonial holiness is dominant in the prophetic denunciation of cultic activity unaccompanied by moral behavior (cf. Amos 5:24). Holiness is more than a ceremonial trip to a mourners' bench; it is a representation of the fruit of the Spirit according to the character of Christ.

This phrase is also, for Paul, a synonym for being *filled with the Spirit.* His teaching is the climax of a long development of understanding about the Spirit-filled life.[5] Thus the normative NT under-standing of the Spirit-filled life is embodied in the phrase **filled with the fruit of righteousness.** It is neither an "emotional fullness" nor a "charismatic fullness" but an "ethical fullness" (Daniel Steele).

The culminating statement of the prayer affirms that the holy life—defined by these four petitions—is **to the glory and praise of God.** Thus, holiness does not self-consciously direct attention to itself but seeks to magnify the Lord, and certainly the life described here would cause all but the most caustic skeptic to give God the glory.

Theology of the Passage

Samuel Chadwick once said that "Paul's prayers are the best expositions of his theology."[6] In them we may see many of his basic concepts of the Christian life. It is certainly true of his prayer for the church at Philippi.

As in so many Pauline passages, we recognize the apostle's concern for the ongoing dimension of the holy life. He is never content with the status quo either in his own life or that of his converts. Christian living should be an exciting, romantic pilgrimage. Believers should always consider themselves as "becomers."

The essence of this dynamic pilgrimage is love. Love is not a quantity that one receives in a moment as a complete reality; it is a relation that may be pure (unmixed, in Wesley's terms) in an instant but that continues to develop throughout all of life.

Love is one of Paul's favorite subjects. He is not implying that the church of Philippi lacked love. Rather, he desires that the quality of their love will expand beyond measure. Karl Barth states, "Love will have to be taken here as a concentrated expression for the highest, ultimate human potentiality which Paul sees realized in the Philippians as members of the body of Christ: they love."[7] But love cannot be construed to mean loving those we like when we feel like it. Paul removes the frothy emotion by stating that love should increase in **knowledge and depth of insight.** Knowledge without love may result in egoism (1 Cor. 8:1), while love without knowledge is sentimentality. Love without the practical application through **depth of insight** can have a worthy motive but do great harm to the recipient. Love implies doing, but it must be doing what is right and worthy of effort.

The life of love cannot be scientifically demonstrated; it can only be validated through practical living. Paul prays that the church will develop the ability to **discern what is best** in life. The idea is to test something with the purpose of approving or rejecting it. The best things are certified or given a stamp of approval. The best may not always be what is for our comfort; but if it contributes to the achieving of God's purpose for us, it is truly the best.

Love, as both Paul and Jesus interpreted it, has a dual dimension. It is directed toward both God and neighbor. The qualities referred to in v. 10 are somewhat ambiguous, but there is at least the possibility that both these dimensions are included: "pure," referring to the vertical; and "blameless," to the horizontal.

The NIV translation of **pure** over "sincere" (KJV) may be preferable in this age, when many think it doesn't matter what you believe as long as you are sincere in your belief. But the original meaning of sincere carries a somewhat different connotation. Purity focuses on our relation with God. Its territory is the inner life that no one else can see. Craftsmen would hold pottery or cloth to the sun for inspection to look for imperfections. If it passed the test, it was pure. It can also refer to the process of removing impurities so that metal is unmixed or without alloy. Such a process involved rocking the material around in a sieve. The implication is plain. Further purification of some areas of our lives, even after we are sanctified, can only take place through suffering and conflict. To be pure means a transparency of heart before the Holy Spirit. Only He can cleanse the life of impurities so that we can pass the test of exposure to the Son.

Inwardly pure hearts manifest outwardly blameless lives. Since the world cannot see inside, their only evidence of Christ's presence is the way we live. Paul is not advocating some lofty, idealized lifestyle that is impossible to attain. Rather, Christians are normalized to live as God planned from the beginning. There is no need to stumble (Jude 24) or to cause others to stumble. This does not imply we will not make errors in judgment or be misunderstood. However, God knows the motive of our hearts.

The total thrust of the passage is a call to bring one's life more and more into conformity to the full measure of holiness embodied in the person of Christ. In Him we see love perfected, absolute transparency, complete dedication to the "best" as perceived by the Father and the full expression of the fruit of the Spirit. As Friedrich Schleiermacher so beautifully put it, "the fruits of the Spirit are therefore nothing but the virtues of Christ."[8] Once again, the Pauline theology declares that holiness is Christlikeness.

Preaching Ideas on the Text

One possibility could be titled "Let Love Abound." A. Abounding Love's Expression. True *agapē* love is more than a feeling, it is action expressed through (1) Loving God, (2) Loving the brothers, and (3) Loving the world. B. Abounding Love's Understanding. More than a feeling, love involves the intellect. (1) Through **knowledge** we relate to God more intimately. (2) Through **depth of insight** we relate to men more effectively. C. Abounding Love's Transformation. More than mere feeling, God's love has the power to change us. Purity creates a transparent character.

Another could be titled "Holiness Is Fruitfulness." A. The Seed (v. 9, **love may abound**). (1) The *agapē* seed cannot be counterfeited by man or Satan. (2) Planting such seed anticipates an increase— **abound more and more.** B. The Sower (v. 11, Jesus Christ). (1) The Sower sows *agapē* seeds that come from His very nature. (2) The Sower sows seeds that will last (v. 10, **until the day of Christ**). C. The Harvest (v. 11, **the fruit of righteousness**). (1) A top-quality harvest—**pure and blameless** (v. 10). (2) A great quantity of harvest— **filled** (v. 11).

A sermon could simply be titled "A Prayer for God's Church." Paul prays that the Philippian church and, by implication, our church will be: A. A Loving Church (v. 9). (1) A love that is ever reaching out—**abound.** (2) A love based on the Bible—**knowledge.** (3) A love that is lived out practically—**depth of insight.** B. A Discerning Church (v. 10*a*). (1) Developing the best in ministry. (2) Developing the best in people. C. A Holy Church (v. 10*b*). (1) Honoring a godly life-style. D. A Helpful Church (v. 10*b*). (1) Setting a proper example. (2) Eliminating any hindrances. E. A Growing Church (v. 11). (1) Growing inwardly—**filled.** (2) Growing outwardly—fruitful.

Sermon on the Text

The Marks of a Spirit-filled Life

Introduction: My wife and I recently began shopping for a new clothes washer. After listening to several salesmen, I had become very confused about washers. I was interested in knowing what made one washer better than another. In our search for the truth we turned to a nationally known buyers' guide. This source listed the marks of a good, quality clothes washer. Using these criteria, we were able to buy the kind of washer we really wanted and needed.

What are the marks of a Spirit-filled Christian? Perhaps Paul himself had been asked that question. We see his real concern for the Philippian church in the context of our scripture. It is with love and affection that he prays for this church that he helped found. His concern is not for buildings or programs. He prays not that they will increase their staff, their finances, or their attendance. Paul was concerned that they know and exhibit the basic qualities of Spirit-filled living. As Spirit-filled people, we need to possess the true marks of a sanctified life as Paul sets forth in our text.

A. *Abounding Love* (v. 9)

1. A definition of love is certainly in order. Paul uses the word *agapē* to distinguish this love from other loves. *Agapē* love is more than just a feeling inside. Rather, it is an act of the will. It means loving someone who perhaps does not deserve our love but needs our love anyway. We know about *agapē* love most clearly as we look at the way God has loved the world. When we are filled with the Spirit, the indication of that fullness is God's *agapē* love, which permeates every area of our being. This should never be confused with some type of flabby emotionalism. We love, not because we feel like it, but because God has loved us.

2. Note the development of love—**abound**[ing]. The Greek word for abound means to overflow, as a river cascades over its banks in flood season. Paul is praying that a raging flood of love will wash over the church with such power and might that it will never be the same. It wasn't that these Philippians had demonstrated no love before. Paul wanted their love and ours to increase by a multiplied measure. Floods of water are normally destructive, but a flood of love can be very constructive to life.

3. The direction of love is through **knowledge.** The word Paul

uses for knowledge does not mean what we might commonly understand to be intellectual or educational development. This knowledge is a practical understanding of spiritual truths. It is very possible for someone to have a Ph.D. from a world-renowned university and still be lacking in this kind of knowledge. On the other hand, there are those who have never had the opportunity to have much formal education but who have great understanding of spiritual truths because of their study of the Bible. Isn't it interesting how God gives direction to this abounding love. Love is given direction and force as we apply spiritual principles.

4. There is also the discrimination of love, indicated in Paul's words **depth of insight.** This conveys the further understanding of knowledge as it applies to everyday practice. It is possible to express love indiscriminately and really do more harm for the Kingdom. A young man recently came to my door, collecting funds to help the youth of the city. It would have seemed that the loving thing to do would be to reach down and give generously. However, I began to inquire about the organization he represented. After much hesitation he told me he was part of a well-known aggressive cult. My giving generously out of a heart of love could have brought harm to the kingdom of God if I had not exercised **depth of insight.**

5. Love needs to flood our lives, but it needs to be a controlled flood. The best way to make a raging flood useful is to anticipate the need by building a dam on the river. Such a dam can control the waters from a damaging flood and also harness the energy for positive good. This is the nature of Paul's prayer for our lives. We need the mark of abounding love.

B. *Adjusting Priorities* (v. 10a)

1. The word that is translated **discern what is best** had a very interesting meaning in Paul's day. It referred to the testing of metal or coins to see if they were really genuine, and, if they were, to give a stamp of approval. In the Old West during the gold rush days the miners would have to take the raw ore they had collected into town to have it tested to determine the amount and quality of the gold. Paul is praying that we will test our activities and priorities so that we can really determine what is the best for us. A spiritual Christian needs to develop a test to prioritize life.

a. What is proper? This is a test to determine what is right from what is wrong. One of the basic premises for a Spirit-filled

Christian is that he will avoid wrong or sin completely. Part of determining what is best is rejecting what is worse for our lives.

b. What is prudent? This is not a question of determining right from wrong but determining the best from the good. It is a truly wise man who finally recognizes the fact that there are more good things to do in life than there is time to do them. There are many legitimate and desirable things that can rob us of the time to do the most important things. A new convert told me that before he became a Christian, he played softball three or four nights every week. After coming to Christ, he realized that although softball was good fun, it was taking some of the time he needed to spend with his family. Now he is perfectly content to play one night a week on the church softball team and invest the rest of his time in other productive endeavors for the Lord.

c. What is providential? This question deals with what God is guiding us to do. The divine priority is clearly stated in Matt. 6:33: "But seek first his kingdom and his righteousness, and all these things will be given to you as well." God does not allow for bargaining or substitutions for His will. Our prayer needs to be: "God's will—nothing more, nothing less, nothing else."

2. Adjusting priorities calls for real discipline in our own private lives. The use of time, resources, and abilities should be of primary concern to the Christian. There are things grabbing and pulling from every angle to gain a part of our time and energy. A motto on the desk of a well-known leader in world missions perhaps gives us the best warning: "Beware of the barrenness of a busy life."

C. *Appealing Character* (v. 10*b*)

The most attractive person ever to live on this earth was Jesus himself. Even as a young lad of 12 Jesus was developing into an attractive individual, improving intellectually and physically. Jesus strengthened His relationships horizontally and vertically. Just as Jesus grew in favor with God and man, we need to follow His example.

1. We are to be **pure** before God. The word **pure** has two definitions. The first refers to the extraction of the impure from the pure by swirling in a sieve until only the pure remains. Obviously, we can be pure before God only if everything that is impure is taken away. We cannot do this, but God can through the cleansing power

of His Holy Spirit. The second definition refers to the examination of an object under the light of the sun to inspect for flaws. Craftsmen would hold new cloth or finely shaped pottery in direct sunlight. If no flaws appeared, it would be declared pure by the worker. It is important for us to notice that God is the One who does the inspecting and not man. God is able to look at the heart, while man can observe only what is on the outside. It is possible for us to be pure in heart before God through the complete work of Christ on the Cross.

2. We are also to be **blameless** before men. This means simply that we are to live without stumbling. While this may appear to be difficult from a human perspective, we do find some encouraging words in the Bible about victory. Jude 24 states, "To him who is able to keep you from falling and to present you before his glorious presence without fault and with great joy." God calls us to a life of rejecting sin, but He empowers us so that such a life is possible. We must also be careful that we do not cause others to stumble. A blameless life is one that provides an example to follow, not a detriment to the kingdom of God. In D. Paul Thomas' portrayal of the life of P. F. Bresee he has a scene where this great Christian leader is discussing the union of several branches to form one denomination. One of the issues separating the groups was the wearing of wedding bands. Thomas has Dr. Bresee dropping his own wedding band into a cup and then commenting on how many wonderful leaders were gained as a result of such a compromise. Bresee was one of those men who exhibited the twin qualities of purity before God and blamelessness before men.

D. *Abundant Fruit Bearing* (v. 11)

1. The origin of this righteousness that Paul prays for is very clear. He states that it **comes through Jesus Christ.** There is no room in the sanctified life for any kind of inflated self-righteousness. We need to recognize the fact that without Christ we have no righteousness at all. Without Jesus we are nothing.

2. The obligation of this righteousness is not specifically stated in this text but is implied in its imagery. If we are going to bear fruit, we must remain in the vine (John 15:4-5). Any branch that is separated from the vine will begin to shrivel up because the life-giving fluids flow from the vine to the branches. It is impossible for a separated branch to ever bear such fruit.

3. The outgrowth of righteousness is the natural development

of fruit bearing. The normal reason for having a fruit tree is to bear fruit. A person usually plants a large apple orchard, not to see the apple blossoms in the spring, but to see the apples red and ripe in the fall. In Matthew 21 Jesus passed a fig tree that had only leaves. Jesus placed a curse on this tree, and when the disciples returned, it was shriveled up. Jesus was trying to illustrate to them the point that a profession without accompanying fruit is unacceptable to God. The life of the Spirit-filled Christian ought to be constantly bearing fruit. What an exciting thing to be literally filled with fruit. While visiting a farm, I was taken by a very small peach tree along the lane. It was not tall. In fact, the size of the tree itself made it very unimpressive. The thing that startled me was the amount of fruit on that small tree. Each branch was literally weighted to the point of touching the ground. Luscious ripe peaches were hanging everywhere from the branches. I thought as I left, That peach tree is literally filled to overflowing with fruit. Our lives are to be bearing that fullness of fruit that makes us worthwhile in the kingdom of God.

How do you recognize a person who has been filled with the Spirit? The identifiable qualities are detailed in our text as Paul prays that these marks will be evident in the life of every believer. Yet we don't achieve these qualities by human effort alone. They come about as a result of our asking the Holy Spirit to fill us and seeing the results of His fullness in our lives. The raw material is brought in by the Holy Spirit. How we develop those marks is partially our responsibility. I join Paul in prayer that as people observe your life and mine, they will recognize the marks of true Spirit-filled living.

Endnotes

1. Stephen W. Paine, *Toward the Mark* (Westwood, N.J.: Fleming H. Revell Co., 1953), 35.

2. *Plain Account of Christian Perfection* (Kansas City: Beacon Hill Press of Kansas City, 1968), 42.

3. *Manual of the Church of the Nazarene*, 1985 ed., par. 904.7.

4. *Plain Account*, 84.

5. See H. Ray Dunning, *Grace, Faith, and Holiness: A Wesleyan Systematic Theology* (Kansas City: Beacon Hill Press of Kansas City, 1988), chap. 13.

6. Quoted in W. E. McCumber, *Holiness in the Prayers of St. Paul* (Kansas City: Beacon Hill Press, 1955), 11.

7. Karl Barth, *The Epistle to the Philippians* (Richmond, Va.: John Knox Press, 1962), 21.

8. *The Christian Faith* (Edinburgh: T. and T. Clark, 1960), 576.

MELVIN McCULLOUGH

Holiness as Inner Resource

For this reason, I bow my knees before the Father, from whom every family in heaven and on earth derives its name, that He would grant you, according to the riches of His glory, to be strengthened with power through His Spirit in the inner man; so that Christ may dwell in your hearts through faith; and that you, being rooted and grounded in love, may be able to comprehend with all the saints what is the breadth and length and height and depth, and to know the love of Christ which surpasses knowledge, that you may be filled up to all the fulness of God (Eph. 3:14-19, NASB).

It has been my discovery in numerous conversations with my church family, in interacting and counseling with fellow pilgrims, and in my pulpit ministry, that the issue of strength and integrity in the interior of a person is one of the most urgent needs many Christians feel today. Producing books and seminars to help people organize and succeed in their careers and personal lives is a high-growth industry in the Western world. But more significant for followers of Jesus Christ is the crucial need for power and order in the inner life. The public life can seemingly be well put together, but it is hollow and soft if the private part of one's life is disorganized and weak.

It was the **inner man** (v. 16) that concerned Paul when he wrote a letter to young Christians at Ephesus. He knew that deep in our private lives our self-esteem is shaped; our basic motives, values, and commitments are made; and our deep devotion and communion with the Lord is maintained. For Paul this was a strategic battle zone because over against the Lordship of Christ in the inner

161

life is what the Bible calls sin—that which resists Christ's control and authority. The sinful nature creates inner conflict and disorder, where wrong motives and values can be tucked away and brought to the surface in unguarded moments. And here is the crucial relevance of what the Spirit wants to say through Paul: The only adequate solution to this inner disarray is the inward work of the indwelling Christ, who mysteriously but definitely assumes sovereign authority over our inner lives upon our personal yielding, our invitation, and our continuing availability. And when the strength and might of the risen Lord flows through the inner life, we discover the joy and the fulfillment that caused the apostle, in spite of the unpleasant Roman prison conditions, to break forth into praise: "Now to Him who is able to do exceeding abundantly beyond all that we ask or think, according to *the power that works within us*" (v. 20, NASB, italics added).

Exegesis

Background. In two places in the Ephesian letter the writer identifies himself as Paul (Eph. 1:1 and 3:1), and the church fathers and Christian leaders of the second century substantiated this as authentic. The title "To the Ephesians" was attached to the Epistle from the earliest manuscripts. The lack of personal greetings and intimate details as might be expected from one who lived and served for three years in Ephesus (Acts 19—20) would support the idea that this letter was written to be circulated among the other Christian congregations in western Asia.[1]

Three clear statements indicate that Paul was a prisoner when he wrote the letter (Eph. 3:1; 4:1; and 6:20). Of the three imprisonments of Paul in Acts, it seems most reasonable that Ephesians (as well as Philippians, Colossians, and Philemon) was written when he was a prisoner in Rome. There is a similarity in language and subject matter among these letters, and the references to the "praetorian guard" (Phil. 1:13, NASB) and to the saints "that are of Caesar's household" (4:22, KJV) would support the idea of a Roman setting.[2]

Knowing the context in which Paul lived and wrote enables me as a preacher to make it clear that this is not abstract theory. Here's a servant of God with a pastor's heart. Paul knew these Christians in

Asia because he had lived among them, shepherded them, loved them, and faced their problems with them. Also, this was not a letter coming from some detached ivory tower. Some people are confident they could be more holy and more spiritually dynamic if their circumstances were different. Paul is saying, "I know you have hassles and pressures and disappointments and broken relationships." He's aware of what it feels like to hurt because he is in prison, and there were no organizations working for the improvement of penal conditions in the Roman world. But in spite of the outward circumstances, he had found ultimate meaning in his life, and he could write about a real world and say that it is possible to be resourced through the Holy Spirit in the inner person (Eph. 3:16) and deeply rooted in the love of Christ (v. 17) in a way that enables you to deal with the problems of a harried and stress-filled world.

Textual Notes. The specific content of Eph. 3:14-19 is a prayer that the readers will experience a "personal strengthening which issues in higher knowledge and completer work."[3]

For this reason (v. 14) is Paul's way of telling us that he's been on a detour that started with v. 2. He repeats this connecting phrase from v. 1. Thus the antecedent is 2:1-22. The **reason** is the free offer of mercy and grace to the Gentiles. All in the human family are invited to be reconciled to God by the Cross so that they may enter into a covenant relationship with God and be incorporated into His household. Paul prays that these new Christians may come to experience the new life in Christ in its abundant fullness.

Since nearly all NT references to prayer suggest that standing was the usual attitude (see Mark 11:25), Paul's mention of his prayer posture (**I bow my knees**—3:14) suggests his earnestness in praying for these new Christians. There is urgency here. And there is deep intimacy because Paul directs his petition to the God who is **Father.** To pray to the Father is to know that you have a God who is personable and approachable and sensitive to the deepest needs of your life.

To be strengthened with power (v. 16) is not a result of a changed attitude resulting from human effort, but is a divinely given experience. It is granted by God **according to the riches of His glory.** As H. C. G. Moule states, God is able to do this because He is "Lord of the resources of an eternal nature and heavenly Kingdom."[4] (The phrase **to be strengthened** is an aorist infinitive suggesting a completed act or a reality seen in its wholeness. It is a reality that may be experienced in a moment but is a whole life provision.) And the strengthening is no mere external propping up. It occurs **in the inner man.** As Richard Taylor writes, "The Spirit is his Resource on which he is absolutely dependent. This is the Spirit who strengthens inwardly as a divine dynamo."[5]

So that Christ may dwell in your hearts through faith (v. 17) is another aorist infinitive that describes the same spiritual blessing as in v. 16. Not only does **dwell** describe critical action, but also the word carries the idea of Christ making His home in our hearts as an ongoing relation. **"In your hearts** means at the center of the whole personality."[6] Christ taking control of the inner life is a work of grace, a gift received **through faith.**

It is the inward strengthening by the Holy Spirit and the inward mastery of the Lordship of Christ that enables the disciple of Jesus Christ to be **rooted and grounded in love** (v. 17). These biological and architectural metaphors (**rooted** and **grounded)** describe the established and growing relationship that we know once there is the solid and deep attachment to God by the divine work of grace.

Another exciting evidence of the work of the strengthening Spirit and the indwelling Christ is the supernatural ability to **comprehend with all the saints** (v. 18) and **know the love of Christ which surpasses knowledge** (v. 19). There are divine realities and spiritual principles and a perceptiveness that are not known by intellectual pursuit alone. The opening up of the deep things of God comes through the Word and by the ministry of the Holy Spirit. **Know** here is an existential word signifying more than intellectual comprehension. It is a personal relation that includes self-knowledge and the transformation of the knower.

In the climax of his prayer, Paul earnestly prays that these new followers of Christ **may be filled up to all the fulness of God** (3:19). Again the tense of the verb **filled** is aorist and suggests that this is a definite experience not gradually acquired but available now to the believer, but nonetheless one that is a whole life possibility.

To a culture where there is an obsession to fulfill the self, Paul offers an unusual solution. Here is a paragraph (3:14-19) containing an earnest prayer for the inward strengthening of the readers by the Holy Spirit, the presence of the indwelling Christ, their enlargement in their comprehension and knowledge of the love of Christ, and the realization in them of the divine fullness (perfections).[7]

Theological Exegesis

The structure of Eph. 3:16-19 makes it difficult to be dogmatic in determining the central focus of the prayer. Willard Taylor, in his Christological Epistles course at Nazarene Theological Seminary and in later writings, viewed Paul's prayer as a petition for spiritual fulfillment in the life of the believer. He concluded that the primary focus was on the last clause, **that you may be filled up to all the fulness of God** (3:19). He writes, "To be strengthened by the Spirit, to have Christ dwelling permanently within, and to be filled with all the fullness of God are one and the same experience."[8]

Within the holiness movement Wesleyans have experienced and proclaimed that by faith in Christ the believer may enter into a richer relationship with God. Each phase of the prayer of Paul is recorded in the original Greek with words that suggest that this experience can become a reality at a definite point in time.[9] This deep, inward encounter with the Lord brings the believer into a more victorious, fulfilling Christian life.

The NT generally and Paul more specifically speak of the inner and outer person. "Therefore we do not lose heart, but though our outer man is decaying, yet our inner man is being renewed day by day" (2 Cor. 4:16, NASB). These two dimensions of human beings are vitally related. The inner expresses itself in the outer, and the activity of the outer is an index to the inner person. **The inner man** (Eph. 3:16) is known only to God and the individual person, while the outer person is seen and known to all.

The NT (and Paul) use **heart** to refer to the total inner person in contrast to the outward and visible. In this passage, however, it is used as "the seat of religious experience."[10] The heart determines what a person is and the motivation for what he does—his character and his conduct. It is clear that the experience of the heart is strategic if the divine life is going to flow and shine through our humanity.

It is the deep, invigorating work of the Spirit at the heart level that makes disciples identifiable in the crowd. The Holy Spirit, the indwelling Christ, and the God who fills make it possible for the gospel to be incarnate in relationships and in the structures of society. God in His perfect plan of redemption goes to the heart of the matter and addresses humankind in the inner person (Eph. 3:16) so that the people of God may have the inner resources for behaving and living as a holy people (1:4).

Preaching Ideas

Eph. 3:14-19 is filled with preaching possibilities. An alert preacher can get an amazing amount of illustrative material from the whole field of energy and what it takes to keep an industrialized society going.

Two major points emerge from the text; one might be to use the subject: "God's Energy Plan." While the cost and conservation of energy have dominated the media in recent times, it took the Soviet author Alexander Solzhenitsyn, speaking to Harvard graduates, to get the attention of Western society about the spiritual energy shortages that threaten our survival. While Solzhenitsyn did not flesh out in any detail an answer for the spiritual energy shortages, a spiritual energy specialist known as Paul urges young Christians to be filled with the Holy Spirit (Eph. 5:18) and **to be strengthened with power through His Spirit in the inner man** (3:16).

A. God's energy plan shapes us at the core of our moral being. Building specifically on 3:16, the preacher can talk about the Holy Spirit giving power where it counts the most—within. Another key idea is to address the fact that in our culture we are often "other-directed" rather than "inner-directed." A third subpoint might be that the Holy Spirit provides inner resources to cope with the external pressures of life. Here the second work of grace becomes extremely practical. Power at the core of our being speaks to a felt need.

B. God's energy plan is designed to shine through and light up the surface of our lives. Here the preacher will talk about the relational implications of the inward strengthening of the Spirit and the overflowing fullness of God. Perhaps the Spirit-energized life gets its best handles as we are a loving people (3:16-17). Further, the Spirit-energized believer probably shines through most effectively by becoming more Christlike. The Spirit testifies of Jesus, who dwells in our hearts through faith (v. 17). The meaning of the original language is to the effect that Christ may make His home in our hearts. But He can't be at home without making His presence known in our life-style and relationships.

Topic: **In Search of Excellence**

Another possibility for preaching from this great passage is to capitalize on the passion for excellence in some quarters. *In Search of Excellence* is more than the title of a book. The Word of God calls us to a life of spiritual excellence. One might focus on Paul's petition for divine fullness. The commentators understand the fullness of God to include all the gifts and graces that God has promised to bestow on the human family in order to effect His full salvation.

A. In a society that is generally concerned only with the cosmetics of life, the Word calls us to the excellence of inner beauty. Here the subpoints might focus on the excellence of character shaped by the inward work of the Holy Spirit (3:16) and the excellence of love at the motivational level of life (**rooted and grounded in love,** v. 17).

B. The divine excellence of spiritual discernment. One subpoint might deal with the truth that one may **comprehend** or "grasp" (v. 18) by the inward ministry of the Holy Spirit. Are we growing? Why are we not growing? The Holy Spirit is Teacher, and there are divine truths that can only be known by the teaching of the Spirit through the Word. Another subpoint might be the importance of laying before the church ("all the saints") what the Spirit is teaching. It is not to be a mere subjective matter but is to be tested within the context of the church.

Sermon

The Search for Fulfillment

Scripture: Eph. 3:14-19 (NASB)

Introduction

1. For a generation our society has been obsessed with the search for the fulfillment of self, and the theme song has been "I've Gotta Be Me!" And this preoccupation to "find ourselves" has caused the culture to worship fame, success, materialism, and celebrities. And the result is we have a world full of spiritually empty, self-absorbed, and hollow people.

2. And in the midst of our kind of world we have the Church, those who are followers of Jesus Christ. It could be our finest hour in history. People all around are searching for fulfillment, and the Church alone can provide a spiritual vision for searching people.

But the Church sometimes has been contaminated by the culture and has endeavored to market the Good News in such a way as to satisfy the people who want the "what's-in-it-for-me gospel." Almost unaware we can sing the theme song "I've Gotta Be Me!" In asserting ourselves as the culture is encouraging us to do, we are faced with the tremendous responsibility of deciding who we are; and not being sure, we get our cues for what we should be from the wrong sources, and we fail to make the commitments along the way that will enable us to be the unique, fulfilled persons God has destined us to be.

What kind of self are we projecting on the video screen of our imagination? Does that picture represent the fully developed self the Lord intends us to be? Many of us are standing at the crossroads in our spiritual journey, looking at two destinations. We might call one of these roads self-assertion. We might label the other self-surrender. The destination of self-assertion is achievement of our purposes, professional goals, and the structuring of our own personality according to the way we see that it should be structured or according to the models we have decided we want to emulate. The other road is the way of self-surrender to the Lord's plans for us, and its destination is the transformation of our personality into His image.

3. At the gateway of spiritual fulfillment is the willingness to be obedient in letting God transform our lives from the inside out. We have read from a letter that the apostle Paul wrote to the Christians in and around the city of Ephesus. In Acts 19 there is the record of Paul's evangelistic mission to Ephesus where he found 12 disciples. It was about the most unfulfilled church family that you can imagine. They weren't making a perceptible impact on the more than 200,000 who lived in their metropolitan area. After Paul had opportunity to get acquainted, he scanned their faces and talked with them about God's great redemptive plan to bring every believer to this highest level of fulfillment and effectiveness; then he wrapped it up with one final question that they would never forget: "Have ye received the Holy Ghost since ye believed?" (Acts 19:2, KJV). And typical of young believers, these new Christians responded, "We have not so much as heard whether there be any Holy Ghost."

Paul baptized these believers in the name of the Lord Jesus, and he laid hands on them; then the Holy Spirit filled their lives, and incredible things started to happen. They spoke with a new boldness. There were extraordinary miracles in their midst. The name of Jesus was magnified. There was a new spiritual discernment. A new energy of love overflowed. There was a dynamic power that flowed through their spiritual veins.

4. Not only did Paul visit the Christians and pray that they might be filled with the Holy Spirit, but also he wrote a personal letter reminding them that they might experience and live spiritually fulfilling lives.

And in the midst of the letter we have this prayer in our Scripture lesson. Paul never rises to a higher level than in his prayers. When he wrote this, he was not at the local Hyatt Regency. He was in prison; but as he thought about these young Christians whom he had shepherded, his love brought him to his knees. It was customary for the Jews to stand for prayer with arms outstretched toward heaven. But in this case Paul writes, **I bow my knees** (Eph. 3:14).

5. Paul is praying with deep emotion for these "saints who are at Ephesus" (Eph. 1:1, NASB). He is praying for those who had been dead in their trespasses and sins but have been made alive by the grace of the Lord Jesus (2:1, 5). And he is praying that they might move to a higher and more fulfilling level of spiritual development. The verb tenses of these petitions suggest that he was praying for a crisis commitment in their lives, a specific spiritual experience that would put these young believers in touch with the true source of spiritual fulfillment.

A. The Source of Spiritual Fulfillment: An Inward, Transforming Attachment to the Lord

1. Inward Spiritual Strengthening by the Holy Spirit

Paul is clear that there can be no spiritual fulfillment unless things are made right at the core of our moral being. By his use of the three Persons of the Godhead, Paul is saying that this abundant life comes from an inward relationship and yielding, so that our lives are resourced from the inside out. And the inward attachment to the Lord presupposes a detachment from the superficialities of life. An authentic attachment to the Lord will transform all other attachments. It will save us from superficial relationships that strip us of time, energy, and spiritual power.

In what things or relationships are we finding our identity, our security, and our fulfillment? God's Spirit is speaking through the Word to remind us that there is nothing that is more important to us than our inward connection to the Lord. There's the true source of spiritual fulfillment.

Once there is openness and yielding to God's purpose, we are prepared for the inward strengthening that will bring lasting fulfillment. Paul describes this inward attachment as a power that invades the private life of the individual through the work of the Holy Spirit. He writes, **That He would grant you, according to the riches of His glory, to be strengthened with power through His Spirit in the inner man** (Eph. 3:16). There's no ultimate spiritual fulfillment until the inner reservoir of life is plugged into the might and energy of God through the work of the Holy Spirit. Over against self-sufficiency that creates stress and strain and inadequacy, Paul is setting forth Spirit-sufficiency.

There is a preoccupation today with burnout, tension, and stress. And there are important and helpful techniques for coping with stress in much of the literature that is making its way to our library shelves. But the Scripture gives us the most significant dimension if we're going to deal with the external pressures of our lives. Essential for dealing with the stress that pulls at all of us is the lifting grace of the Holy Spirit within.

Dr. Hans Selye, who has been probably the best authority on what stress does to the human mind and body, says the greatest need in the Western world is for inner reserves. In an uncertain economy, with the fear of nuclear holocaust, and with the stress on the contemporary family, we need inner resources to be able to live peaceful and effective and fulfilled lives in spite of all of the external pressures that push in upon us.

It's the inner person that makes the outer person. If your interior life is weak, it cannot help but surface. The call by the apostle is a call to an inward attachment and reliance on the Lord that is made possible by the strengthening with power by the Holy Spirit in the inner person.

2. Inner Mastery by the Indwelling Christ

Further, the indwelling of Christ brings an inner mastery at the center of your personality that is an essential element of spiritual fulfillment. It is a gift given by faith when we turn over the absolute control of our inner lives to the sovereignty of Jesus Christ. Paul prays, **That Christ may dwell in your hearts through faith** (Eph. 3:17). By the use of the word **dwell**, Paul conveys the idea of Christ making His permanent home at the center of our lives.

The *New York Times* asked the founder of McDonald's what he believed in. He replied, "God, my family, and McDonald's hamburgers." And then he added, "And when I get to the office, I reverse the order." He may have been trying to be amusing in the interview. But that's a tragic truth in the lives of too many professed believers. Many who have followed Jesus Christ have been tempted to put Christ as the first priority of their lives on Sunday mornings but maintain these private areas for themselves. Are there rooms in our spiritual lives that we have not permitted Jesus Christ to fully occupy? There can be no authentic spiritual fulfillment until we let Christ take every nook and corner of our individual lives. A. W. Tozer, in his book *The Pursuit of God,* has a powerful prayer that addresses the issue of the Lordship of Christ:

> Father, I want to know Thee, but my coward heart fears to give up its toys. I cannot part with them without inward bleeding, and I do not try to hide from Thee the terror of the parting. I come trembling, but I do come. Please root from my heart all those things which I have cherished so long and which have become a very part of my living self, so that Thou mayest enter and dwell there without a rival. Then shalt Thou make the place of Thy feet glorious. Then shall my heart have no need of the sun to shine in it, for Thyself wilt be the light of it, and there shall be no night there. In Jesus' Name, Amen.[11]

Spiritual fulfillment is on the way when we determine in a moment of time, as the aorist tense suggests, that there will be no rival to Christ in our lives. And this is to happen, as the phrase **in your hearts** suggests, at the center of our whole personality.

3. Overflowing Fullness from the Presence of God

The climax of Paul's prayer is in the last part of Eph. 3:19: **That you may be filled up to all the fulness of God.** These new Christians at Ephesus are not in their humanity to be deified, but they are to be filled with the fullness of God until the very presence of God is to overflow their lives. Spiritual fulfillment comes from time to time as we are conscious of the spilling over of the presence of God in our spiritual journey. There is so much being said and written these days about skills and marketing and management techniques, but the foundation for fulfillment in work in the Kingdom is a relationship between the disciple and his God.

What a difference it makes in worship when the presence of God is so real to the worshipers that it overflows to touch the whole church family. What a difference it makes in an individual's Christian walk when he is stirred at the deepest level by a sense of deep encounter with God who fills our lives with His presence from the inside out.

The word here, as in all three of these crucial petitions, is an aorist verb, which means it is a positive experience available now to the believer. You can be filled. You don't have to wait until you die to experience this spiritual fulfillment. You don't have to wait until you grow another year or two. The invitation is to detach yourself right now from the things that are superficial and attach yourself to the strengthening Spirit, the indwelling Christ, and the God who fills to overflowing.

B. The Manifestation of Spiritual Fulfillment: The Resources That Flow Through Transformed People

1. The Fulfillment of Spiritual Perceptiveness

Once we have learned to be our authentic selves by losing ourselves in the Lord, then the transformation will shine through in our living, our attitudes, and our relationships. Our security is not in our adequacy but in His unlimited power surging through us, changing our personalities, guiding us, and expressing His wisdom and His love.

This fulfilled living is characterized by a divine perceptiveness, which is the Lord's gift. This profound experience of the Spirit-filled and Christ-indwelt life enables us **to comprehend with all the saints** [Christians] **what is the breadth and length and height and depth** (Eph. 3:18).

There are divine realities that are not known by intellectual pursuit alone. It would be easier to buy a book and find an easy formula or quick fix or three easy steps. But the inward attachment, the dynamic relationship with the living God cultivates a spiritual sensitivity to the spiritual principles that the Lord wants to demonstrate as He shapes our character and life-style.

There is a spiritual wisdom that brings fulfillment. There is a divine perceptiveness that is manifested in our ethical decisions and in the way we treat people with justice. This is the mark of people who are marching to a different drummer.

2. Fulfilled Living Manifested by Love as a Constant Principle of Life

Paul prays in Eph. 3:16 that his audience might be strengthened within so that they might be **rooted and grounded in love** (v. 17) and so that they might **know the love of Christ which surpasses knowledge** (v. 19). The love that is cultivated in our attachment to the Lord enables us to express love in the most practical ways in our lives.

Some of us get the feeling we could be more loving and more fulfilled if we didn't have so many problems to try to cope with, or if we had a different automobile, or if the circumstances of life were different. But remember, Paul is writing in prison, and he's saying that we can be a loving people even when we walk the path of suffering or lose our job or end up in jail. Later Paul writes about loving relationships in marriages, in families, on the job, in the church, when we get angry, when we need to forgive, when kids need to be disciplined, when tough love needs to be demonstrated. Spiritual fulfillment comes when great doctrines and great scriptural themes are lived out in the most practical ways. G. K. Chesterton admonished, "Let your faith be less a theory and more a love affair!"

Conclusion

1. Spiritual fulfillment is inward attachment to the Lord and the fulfillment of letting His life flow through ours, blessing us now and preparing us for tomorrow.

That is illustrated vividly in the life of Eric Liddell in *Chariots of Fire*. At the Paris Olympics in 1924, the Christian athlete denied himself the right to participate in running on Sunday. He held firm beliefs about observing the Lord's day. It was a visible evidence for him of his inward attachment and his detachment from the superficialities. He would not contradict his convictions and refused to run the race for which he had spent years of arduous preparation.

Later that week, because of the generosity of a friend and the intervention of the Lord, Liddell was given the opportunity to enter another race. In that event he won the gold medal by placing first in the event. He denied himself, and the Lord took care of the tomorrows. Liddell gave the Lord all the glory for the victory of the gold medal. The denial of self enabled him to discover a wonderful level of fulfillment. And it was that resource that enabled him later as a missionary to give a stirring witness for Christ in a Japanese concentration camp during World War II. And when I look at the life of Eric Liddell, I say, "There is one who found real fulfillment."

2. Wherever human beings become available to the Lord, there follows a transformed and fulfilled life. Give Him the gift of your life, and He will transform you and enable you to be the unique, fulfilled person that He has destined you to be in all your future days.

Endnotes

1. Willard H. Taylor, "The Epistle to the Ephesians," in *Beacon Bible Commentary* (Kansas City: Beacon Hill Press, 1965), 9:129-33.

2. Ibid., 133-34.

3. B. F. Westcott, *St. Paul's Epistle to the Ephesians* (Grand Rapids: Wm. B. Eerdmans Publishing Co., 1950), 51.

4. H. C. G. Moule, *Studies in Ephesians* (Grand Rapids: Kregel Publications, 1977), 96.

5. Richard S. Taylor, *Exploring Christian Holiness,* vol. 3, *The Theological Formulation* (Kansas City: Beacon Hill Press of Kansas City, 1985), 188.

6. Willard H. Taylor, "Ephesians," 195.

7. S. D. F. Salmond, "Ephesians," in *Expositor's Greek Testament,* ed. W. Robertson Nicoll (London: Hodder and Stoughton, n.d.), 3:311.

8. Willard H. Taylor, "Galatians—Ephesians," in *Beacon Bible Expositions,* ed. William M. Greathouse and Willard H. Taylor (Kansas City: Beacon Hill Press of Kansas City, 1981), 8:164.

9. D. Martyn Lloyd-Jones, *The Unsearchable Riches of Christ* (Grand Rapids: Baker Book House, 1979), 117-18.

10. G. E. Ladd, *A Theology of the New Testament* (Grand Rapids: Wm. B. Eerdmans Publishing Co., 1975), 475-76.

11. A. W. Tozer, *The Pursuit of God* (Harrisburg, Pa.: Christian Publications, 1948), 31.

—4—
HOLINESS
AS LOVE

———————

PAUL BASSETT

Holiness as Love in Relation to Others

*O*we *no one anything, except to love one another* (Rom. 13:8, RSV).

I went to a reception the other day. Ostensibly I went to honor someone for something. Really I went because the culture in which I live says that it was my duty to go. I owed the honoree respect, I was told, even though I knew him well enough to think him a bit of a twit. And now, as he said to me that afternoon, he "owes" me "one."

That's life, isn't it? One social or legal obligation after another.

In such straits, what are we to make of the apostle Paul's word on it?

Exegesis

Paul's potent phrase fell on ears fine-tuned to social and legal niceties. Every normal inhabitant of the empire knew and accepted the duties of keeping to one's own place and of treating others as befit theirs. So, Paul's advice that none should overrate himself (Rom. 12:3) came across as good sense. And so did his words about using one's gifts for the good of the whole (vv. 4-8), and his words about living in harmony and guarding against conceit (v. 16). Even the counsel that one "overcome evil with good" would have pleased thoughtful Roman pagans (v. 21).

And, while Paul and the pagan Roman would mean something different by the word "god," that Roman would agree that all should subject themselves to the governing authorities, since "God" had instituted them. Roman society deeply revered law and order, believing it to be both the cause and an effect of their having aligned themselves with the very purposes of the gods or of the universe itself.

But in putting the matter of how the Roman Christians should treat one another in terms of love, Paul inverts the usual cultural understanding. The usual inhabitant of the empire simply did not think about social obligation—about serving and being served—as an expression of faith in God or of the love of God or neighbor. Social position, they thought, comes from God or the gods, and the gods do not need to explain their distribution. Social obligation was to be in line with social position. It had to meet one criterion: the maintenance of the harmony of Rome and therefore of the universe. It might express love, or it might not. That made little difference.

Paul does not destroy the notion of social obligation. He tells Christians quite plainly that they should recognize social position and meet legal obligation even in a sinful society. But, for him, these things are not means by which one presses toward higher goals, they are not instruments for maintaining the stability of society or the harmony of the universe. In fact, he stands such a perspective on its head.

The Christian actively recognizes social position and meets legal obligations, even in a sinful society, because he has been "transformed by the renewal of . . . mind" (Rom. 12:2, NBV, RSV). So this recognition of social position and this meeting of obligations must not be signs of conformity to this world. Instead, they are proofs of "the will of God, what is good and acceptable and perfect" (v. 2, RSV) by God's standard. They are instruments for expressing transformation. They convey the rejection of conformity to the world's way of looking at life. No longer rungs on the ladder to social and legal stability and harmony, no longer symbols of commitment to the values of this world, active recognition of social position and social and legal obligation become channels conveying gratitude and utter allegiance ("spiritual worship," v. 1, RSV, Paul calls it) to the one everlasting society and kingdom.

That's why Paul can go on at length about social and legal obligation and then say, **Owe no one anything.** He is not about to destroy them. He insists that they are, for the Christian, utterly transformed—**except to love one another.**

Paul underlines his point by turning from social position and social and legal obligation in Roman society to what he recognizes as sacred law, the Ten Commandments. "Keep the commandments," he says, "but remember that their true fulfillment lies in loving the neighbor, not simply in keeping the law" (cf. 13:8-10).

Then, as if to put an extra line under the point, Paul reminds the Roman Christians that the "Great Day," the "Day of the Lord," is at hand. So, it's time to "cast off the works of darkness and put on the armor of light . . . Put on the Lord Jesus Christ, and make no provision for the flesh, to gratify its desires" (13:11-14, RSV). It's time to meet social and legal obligation, not in an expression of conformity to worldly values, but as an expression of our present transformation and of our future hope. It's time to meet them as exercises of love, for the full manifestation of the kingdom of love is near at hand.

So Paul puts the matter on a very different basis from that developed by the world. And it's not just a matter of a call to higher ideals. It's a matter of living in a different world while also living in this one.

Theological Exegesis

We need to take a look at the spiritual-theological "backstage" to all of this before we venture on to current application.

Our first observation "backstage" is this: We will misinterpret the Christian ethic if we see it only as some sort of refinement of a non-Christian ethic.

When described solely in terms of how one behaves, and often even when described in terms of attitudes and motives, as best these may be determined, Christians will not differ appreciably from non-Christians. In fact, in some situations Mafiosi may act with more decorum, more honorable motives, or healthier attitudes (at least as we mortals can judge such things) than Christian saints.

To put our backstage observation positively, we turn first to Paul, then elsewhere.

Paul's theme in Romans is God's power to save and how that salvation is to find expression in our lives (1:16-17). Paul is not reporting on how to be saved; he is exhorting the saved on how to live.

So, putting negative and positive together, **Owe no one anything, except to love one another** becomes a revolutionary instruction to people already transformed, to people whose way of looking at things has been completely renovated. Changed behavior does not and cannot create a changed life, but a changed life creates the possibility of and the necessity for changed behavior. And even where the change is not obvious, even where the behavior still isn't all that different from the behavior of one whose life is unchanged, it would be the height of folly to overlook the difference in perspective, the difference in *why* life is lived as it is.

Our Lord spoke clearly of these things in the conversation with Nicodemus (John 3:1-21). Nicodemus saw what Jesus did and drew the conclusion that Jesus was "a teacher come from God." On the surface of things, at the level of words and perhaps even at the level of intention, Nicodemus had things right. But Jesus thoroughly confused him by telling him that he really had no idea of the "kingdom of God," that he knew nothing of the real content of what it means to be sent from God, to do signs, to teach true righteousness. Authentic knowledge and inauthentic may sound quite similar, but authentic knowledge comes only as one is born again, born of the Spirit of God.

To be born again, one must not simply believe Jesus but believe *in* Jesus. And that means that however "together" one may believe oneself to be, or believe others to be, however "with it" or "aware," that confidence must submit to the confession that apart from what God in love has done through Jesus, the Son, all are lost, eternally lost. Whatever our kind call light and wisdom, truth and goodness, the true Light and Wisdom, Verity and Goodness have come into the world as a divine gift named Jesus. And to see that, we must be reborn. And to be reborn, we must see that and appropriate it. We must believe in Him, absolutely, utterly, with a love that issues from a pure heart, good conscience, and unfeigned faith (see 1 Tim. 1:5, KJV).

Believing in Jesus means believing in God's love, believing in it absolutely; believing in it as one reborn in order so to love. And this is true transformation, for if there is one thing in which we do not believe, on our own, it is the saving power of love, not even in the saving power of divine love. On our own, we would trust almost anything but love to save us—money, a quick wit, "street smarts," power, position, national identity, religious identity, ideological correctness, and so on.

Having come to trust divine love to save us, and divine love alone, as it is in Jesus Christ, we find all of our interpersonal relationships set on a very different foundation. **Owe no one anything, except to love one another,** then, means so to trust God and so to trust what God has done for us in Christ—all of it as an expression of divine love—that we refuse to look upon any aspect of any of our relationships with others in terms of earthly obligation. The only obligation in our vast network of relationships will be the obligation to love. And that obligation arises from the fact that we are ourselves divinely loved.

Our refusal to let "obligation" fuel our relationships with others expresses our protest of the way in which the whole world now operates, socially and legally. And it expresses our life commitment to that world into which we have been born anew, which will one day come in fullness.

So let's come to cases with all of this.

Application

Sometimes we see it and sometimes we don't—the absolutely radical character of the life to which God in Christ calls us. And sometimes we see it and sometimes we don't—that all earthly social and legal systems anchor themselves in self-interest. From the best of them to the worst, they express the fundamental characteristic of fallen human nature, absolute self-centeredness. And over against them stands the call of our Lord, and the provision of His grace, to and for life that is His in loving service to others.

Of course, certain aspects of some earthly social and legal systems encourage and even produce high ideals and environments of mercy, justice, and freedom. God, in mercy, oversees and directs the establishment of systems even in this fallen world to keep us from doing each other in and to provide some opportunity for speaking to us of our sinfulness and of the possibilities of salvation from it, a salvation that should, in turn, contribute to the reconstitution of earth and its societies to faithful reflections of what God intended in the first place.

But God also sent Christ, who came and died and rose again, and promised to come again to establish His kingdom in glorious fullness. And this tells us that something was and is radically afoul in every system all of the time.

We must keep this fact at the very forefront of our way of looking at life. No matter how good an earthly social or legal system may appear to be—and some may be quite good over long periods of time—our commitment to Jesus Christ should testify that it is tainted with sin. Perhaps the given system is not caught up in "reveling and drunkenness, . . . debauchery and licentiousness, . . . quarreling and jealousy" (Rom. 13:13, RSV). In fact, it may do a fair job of curtailing these and other less immediately destructive attitudes and practices such as petty falsehoods and self-protective deceits and mean and small reasons for rewarding and punishing. But the Christian will remember that Christ died for all of it because it came under the power of the evil one.

To allow such systems to dictate obligations to us is to set at naught the person and work of Christ, to nullify the grace of God. And that is every bit as serious as it sounds. It is never authentic love that makes such worlds go round. It's reciprocation. It's knowing one's place and demanding what is due it. It's knowing who is what and carefully giving each his due, unless one can get by for less, or unless for selfish reasons one wishes to give more in order to get more.

Paul's exhortation to **owe no one anything, except to love one another** simply cannot be fully heeded by developing programs of self-discipline or self-improvement. To respond to this exhortation, one must be reborn and empowered by the Holy Spirit. Putting it in Paul's language in Rom. 12:1-2, one must present oneself a living sacrifice, one being transformed by the renewing of the mind.

Only as one constantly and entirely protests worldly systems of obligation and only as one constantly and entirely, unreservedly, opens oneself to transformation, sacrificing that which has provided personal identity from a worldly point of view, can one really be truly debt-free, except for the obligation to love.

God's radical act in becoming human in Christ Jesus enables us—indeed, calls us—to that which is equally radical. As God made it His obligation, His only obligation as well; and as it took the radical act of incarnation for God to fulfill that obligation, so it takes the radical act of rebirth, of transformation, for us to respond as Paul, under divine inspiration, has directed.

Saying No to Kant

Let me tell you a bit about someone very influential in our lives though few would even recognize his name. He was Immanuel Kant, and he lived 200 hundred years ago. He was from German-speaking East Prussia, which is now part of the Soviet Union. And he taught at the University of Königsberg (now Kaliningrad), where he became the most famous university professor of his time. He was so predictable that it was said that folks set their watches by him.

Kant influenced all of us by insisting that doing one's duty for duty's sake is an essential ingredient of morality. He used this as an argument against those on the one hand who said that we are morally obligated to do only that which is rational and against those on the other hand who said that we are morally obligated to do only that which will have results that our senses can declare good. We have a conscience, he said, and it doesn't always function according to reason or experience. The fact that it doesn't and yet continues to press us must be taken very seriously, said Kant. Conscience is working at moral levels far deeper than the mind or the senses, and it must be heeded. Walt Disney put Kant's point in popular terms that have stuck with us: "Always let your conscience be your guide."

This sounds like good advice. But is it Christian to do one's duty for duty's sake and always to let one's conscience be one's guide? Let's examine the matter by way of the apostle Paul's letter to the Romans, 13:8-10. Apparently some persons in the Christian church in Rome raised the question whether Christianity, with its demand that God alone be worshiped, released them from their social and legal obligations to the Roman state and to Roman customs and manners.

Paul must have surprised them a bit by saying that God had instituted the government and its attendant social system, and that for that reason they were to be careful to give everyone his due—taxes, honor, courtesy, whatever.

But Paul went on to say something equally as surprising. The Christians in Rome are to give everyone his due, but not as if it were his due. The Christians are to conform to the laws and customs, but not for the same reasons that the ordinary pagan conforms to them.

The ordinary non-Christian Roman conformed to Roman laws and customs because he believed that those things had developed as expressions of the very will of the gods or, some would say, of nature. Of course, they believed that they had a right and a responsibility to improve upon those matters, to bring them even closer to the will of the gods or of nature, or to correct them if there had been slippage; but they believed that basically they were fixed in nature itself and must not be contradicted. So, one had the responsibility to discover one's place in the social system and to play by the rules of that place. They had a deep sense of social obligation—of what they owed to others and of what others owed to them. Failure to meet such obligations threatened the whole system. It brought disharmony to the very universe itself and threatened the very well-being of both the individual and of the society.

Paul's response to the question of the church at Rome concerning the Christian's response to social and political obligation is rooted in his understanding of the person and work of Jesus Christ. And it has broad implications concerning the Christian's relationships to others in any situation.

Some of the Pharisees and other religious authorities tried hard to trap Jesus into pitting allegiance to God against allegiance to the state and to do it in such a way as to bring Him to the notice of the civil government as a troublemaker. So it was that they raised the vexing question of taxes.

To pay taxes was to support idolaters and even their idolatry, for certain civic functions were accompanied by sacrifices to the pagan gods. And, while it had begun just before Jesus' day and was not yet universal, the empire knew the practice of sacrificing to the genius of the emperor himself. These sacrifices were often paid for out of the public purse. So, those who asked Jesus about the legitimacy of paying taxes to Caesar asked a valid question. But they asked it on the basis of illegitimate presuppositions and with illegitimate motives.

First of all, their basic question was obviously not about whether or not they should submit to the government or support it. They supported it quite willingly when it served their purposes— such as at the time of the Crucifixion. But more to the point here, they assumed that the kingdom of heaven really must be kept distant from the systems of earth. At least they believed this abstractly. They could not see that the heavenly kingdom yearns to penetrate and to convert earthly systems. They assumed that if Jesus really were Messiah, He could have no positive relationship whatsoever with worldly systems. They could more easily see the heavenly kingdom being soiled by the earthly than the earthly being converted by the heavenly. And that attitude indicates a profound lack of faith and a misunderstanding of their own history. It says either of two things: that God cannot finally overcome evil, or that whatever victory there is over evil must take place in some place other than our real world, which God himself created.

Enter now the fact of the incarnation and the resurrection of our Lord. It all took place in our real world, and the One who was incarnated was incarnated in flesh as human as the humanest human you and I know. The One who was raised from a death as dead as the deadest we know was "this same Jesus" (Acts 1:11). And by His death He conquered sin and death—not in some never-never land of imagination or ideals, but right there just beyond the wall of old Jerusalem. We can go to the spot today. And what's more, what was done at that spot is applicable to anyone, anywhere, at any time on the whole globe.

When Jesus rose, He did not even visit Pilate, let alone utter some malediction on governments that crucify good people for reasons of political expediency. He did not march to the next meeting of the Sanhedrin and declare them legally powerless. The government stayed in place, the religious system stayed in place, customs and taxes and honors remained as they were. Rather, He instructed His people to go into all the world and preach and teach the Good News, and to make disciples. And He sent them that other Person of the Trinity, the Holy Spirit, to empower them to penetrate and convert the very systems that had done Him in.

Jesus owed no one any of this. He did what He did strictly out of love. And it's precisely because of His fidelity to love—in fact, He is love itself—even to the point of utter humiliation, that the heavenly kingdom can penetrate and convert the earthly. In fact, so thorough are that penetration and conversion that we are saved not merely in our sin or in spite of our sin but, praise God, from our sin. And we are made the very children of God.

But we are all of this in this present world, not to the point of full glorification but to the point of full sanctification. We are in the world, but we are not of the world. And our being in the world is not some sort of Divine Plan B any more than the Incarnation and

186 / Biblical Resources for Holiness Preaching

Resurrection here were some sort of divine contingency plan. That divine purpose for our being here is as positive as was the divine purpose for our Lord. In fact, it is the same purpose: the redemption of the world itself.

This means that we, owing God everything, owe the world nothing. Nothing at all. But as our purpose is that of our Lord, we offer in debtless abandon His love, His redeeming love. In this sense, and in this alone, are we debtors: to give everyone the Good News. The Good News that they too, as we and as their Lord, can be in the world but not of the world, reconciling that world to God.

So, good-bye to notions of duty for duty's sake. We will do all for the sake of Christ and to the glory of God. And we will do it in this present world, where some require taxes, and some require honor, and some require custom. We will fulfill their requirements, not because we, children of the Heavenly King, owe those things to them, but because we would speak to them even through their own systems of the absolute love and grace of our Lord.

This requires of us that we abandon completely any worldly way of looking at our relationships to others. For that, grace alone suffices, and that grace is promised to us: "You shall be my witnesses" (Acts 1:8, RSV).

We will do our duty, but not as duty. We will see our duty as an opportunity to penetrate the world with the good news of Christ. We will do it freely, joyfully, lovingly; for after all, it is the love of Him who owed no one anything but loved the whole world that we witness to.

Sermon Ideas

Topic: **Authentic Possibility Thinking**

Introduction: Robert Schuller's notion that we replace negative thoughts with positive, replace emphasis upon limitations with emphasis upon possibility, has captured many. And, carefully put, it lies at the very foundation of Christian living. But it must be carefully put, or it becomes an instrument of pagan, secular self-centeredness. Let's examine it in the light of Christian truth and act accordingly.

A. *Exegesis*

    1. Our text may be understood only in the context of Rom.

12:1—13:14. Paul is talking about life as a living sacrifice and about life lived out of a transformed mind. That is the quality of the authentically Christian life. Further, such a life is lived under the inspiration of the coming day of the Lord.

2. In the light of these things, Paul states a principle, both negatively and positively. Negatively: One should not think of oneself more highly than one ought (12:3). Positively: One should owe nothing to anyone but to love (13:8).

3. This, in a context in which squaring one's social and political accounts was considered a religious duty. The Romans had a keen sense of social structure and believed that in spite of its flaws, their system basically expressed the will of the gods or of nature. The system was dependent upon everyone's recognizing his place and its social and political obligations—those paid by it, those owed to it.

4. Paul sets about to answer the expected and pressing question: How is the Christian, citizen of a kingdom very different from the Roman system, to respond to the social and political demands of this world? His response is: The Christian conforms outwardly to most worldly expectations, but not because the Christian feels some sense of social or political obligation or is caught up in some sensitivity to place. Rather, the Christian makes of such worldly demands opportunities to express the love of Christ in the light of having been completely transformed in mind and in the light of the coming day of the Lord.

B. *Exposition*

1. Here is a radical life-style that will not always appear to be so radical on the surface. Of course, from time to time, the radical nature of this life-style will express itself precisely and clearly in behavior. But fundamentally, it is a radical change in perspective, and that change governs all behavior. Here we ponder the incarnation of Christ. Phil. 2:5-11 helps very much. So do such passages as Isa. 53:1-3. Jesus' contemporaries were not sure what kind of person He was, but all believed Him to be a man and not a celestial being. In large part, this was because of His willing obedience to the usual social and political systems. They took His obedience as compliance, as full conformity, or at least as willing compro-

mise with their systems. They took His occasional contradictions of their systems as rebellion only. They could not see that He worked from a different groundwork. He did not come either to destroy the world or to approve it, but to convert it, to transform it, to prepare it for the coming day of the Lord.

2. The divinely chosen mode for expressing this mission is that of servanthood. The mode is one of giving, not one of gaining. That is to say, rather than asking the question of who owes what to whom, Christ "took upon himself the form of a servant and became obedient even to the point of death—and death upon a cross at that" (Phil. 2:7-8, author's paraphrase). He owed no one anything. In fact, all owe Him everything, even life itself (cf. John 1:3).

3. Having submitted as He did, "God therefore highly exalted him" (Phil. 2:9). Paul refers here to the resurrection and ascension of Christ and of His current place "at the right hand of the Father" (author's paraphrases). But even yet, while the systems of this earth will pass away, they are not currently destroyed. And in the meantime, we are exhorted to exhibit the mind—the outlook—of Christ, submitting to societal demands, but out of a spirit of loving service, not out of a sense of obligation.

C. *Application*

1. The Christian is quite correct to avoid the very appearance of evil. So, from the very outset, we understand that Paul is not advising us to do absolutely everything that society demands of us. Or, to put it another way, we are to conform to society's demands only insofar as responding may be an expression of divine love—forgiving, redeeming love. And that is precisely the point: While we must from time to time resist honoring society's demands, we resist on the ground of love and love alone, just as we conform on the grounds of love and love alone. We owe no one anything—but to love.

2. This means that we reject absolutely any worldly notions of obligation. We do not do what we do out of a sense of duty, nor do we demand of others that they owe us anything. This is what it means to be a living sacrifice, to be transformed in mind, to have the mind of Christ. It is a life of radical servanthood in a world that takes lordship to be the ideal.

3. This is the life-style through which God proposes to overcome evil, to gain ultimate victory, to redeem the lost, to
make Christ Lord indeed. God is not concerned to destroy
the world, at least not yet. God is "not willing that any should
perish, but that all should come to repentance" (2 Pet. 3:9,
KJV). God yearns to convert, and to do it through our debtless way of living, a way of living that points to the Redeemer
and is possible only through Him.

Conclusion

Here, then, is authentically Christian possibility thinking. Will
we open ourselves to it? (Read, with appropriate editorial adjust-
ments, Eph. 3:16-21.)

Topic: **We Christians and the World's Customs**

Introduction: We Christians want to avoid worldliness, for Christ's
sake. But how then do we avoid boorishness and self-righteousness
as well?

A. Paul writes here specifically to the Christians in Rome. He and
they know well the importance of the question of civil and social
obligation in the world's capital.
Paul states his basic rule in such matters:
1. The Christian cannot be indifferent to the political-social
structure. God instituted it (Rom. 13:1).
2. But the Christian must not confuse civic or social righteousness with Christian righteousness, which is by faith (cf. Rom.
13:5).
3. The Christian must not use spiritual superiority as an excuse
for ducking any justified human demand (cf. Rom. 13:2).

B. Paul goes beyond the basic rule, however, to give us a positive
principle: Christians do nothing out of obligation. They do all
things out of love (Rom. 13:8-10).
1. The Christian submits to the civil and social structure as a
means of practicing love and nothing but love. (Remember,
Paul is writing here with his eye on society as it is redeemable.
He's not laying down a law of absolute submission in all
things whatsoever. Some aspects of society are totally contradictory to the practice of love and cannot bear its expression
at all.)
2. The Christian does not keep civil and social obligation in

order to love any more than the Christian keeps the Ten Commandments in order to love. Exercising the love of God is the Christian's way of keeping obligations.

3. The Christian opens himself, then, to the faithful fulfillment of all civic and social obligations as means of expressing the love of God in Christ given to him.

C. Paul has given us in this text a specific application of Jesus' prayer for us: that we be in the world but not of it. Christians have usually emphasized the importance of the "not of it" and have nearly forgotten that our Lord did pray that we might be "in the world." We are not taken out of it when we become His own (cf. John 17:15-16).

1. Here is a specific example of being a living sacrifice. That is to say, even in the keeping of civic and social obligations, one shows "what is that good, and acceptable, and perfect, will of God" precisely by turning what society sees as obligation into a quite willing expression of God's love, even for sinners. Sacrifice may come at the point of the world's miscalculation of our reasons for doing what we do (cf. Rom. 12:1-2, KJV).

2. Here we must consider Christ and what He has done for us. See Phil. 2:5-11, noting that it's not a matter of our producing in ourselves a mind like Christ's but a matter of having Christ's mind, which is possible only as Christ grants it to us. Truly, He owed no one anything; truly, He loved, even to the point of absolute servanthood and submission to the socio-political system.

3. Such openness, such love, are gifts of grace, and they replace all else that is there in our relationships, our characters. He "emptied himself of all but love" (Charles Wesley). We cannot empty ourselves, and if we could, the remainder would not be love. But by the grace of God, we can present our bodies a living sacrifice; we can be transformed by the renewing of our minds.

D. The Christian's day-to-day activities often appear to differ little from those of the worldling. But there is a profound difference. The worldling responds to earth's call and political systems in terms of obligation. The worldling constantly thinks in terms of who owes what to whom. And there are debts of honor, debts of taxes, debts of custom. The Christian is not to live that way. The

Christian takes love as his only obligation, so the giving of honor, the paying of taxes, the submission to custom, are done not to pay off social or political obligations, nor are they done to accrue IOUs for ourselves. Rather, we give honor, pay taxes, and follow custom, seeking to make such activities vehicles of divine love.

1. We Christians are to be radical people. But our radicalness is not always expressed in contradiction of the ways of the world. Our radicalness lies in our perspective, which may or may not call for such contradiction in behavior. We do not see the world and its ways from a point of view that contradicts that of the worldling, however. In the place of self-interest constraining us, the love of Christ constrains us. We seek not so much to contradict the world as to convert it. But to do this, we must ourselves be radically transformed.

2. The definition of *radical* is not ours to make. We take Christ as our definition. But even this process is not one over which we have control. We open ourselves to letting Christ define himself in our lives. Christ gives himself, His radical self, to us, and that changes everything about us, especially the way in which we relate to the world. Owing Him all, we can owe the world nothing. Loving Him, we love the world as He loves the world.

3. Nothing less than total commitment, total surrender underlies such a radical life and perspective. To **owe no one anything, except to love one another** is to abandon completely the way in which the worldling looks at life. It is truly to accept the gift of "the mind of Christ" (1 Cor. 2:16).

Conclusion

To be truly Christian is to be truly nothing but Christian. It is to have the mind of Christ. He owed no one anything but loved unreservedly. We are called to this same sort of life and promised grace to live it. Why do you do what you do? Why do you respond to the demands of earthly systems as you do? Are you thinking in terms of paying off debts, or of creating debts that others must pay off? Or have you renounced such selfishness, for Christ's sake, in order that His love might be set loose in a sinful world?

DON W. DUNNINGTON

Holiness as
Love of God

Hear, O Israel: The Lord our God, the Lord is one. Love the Lord your God with all your heart and with all your soul and with all your strength (Deut. 6:4-5).

In a world like ours, what does it mean to love God with all of your heart? In a world filled with hate and hunger, money and meaninglessness, slums and Star Wars, poverty and pain, affluence and evil—in a world like this, what does it mean to love God? In a world so divided and among people so internally fragmented, can we talk meaningfully of loving God with all of our heart, soul, mind, and strength? (See Mark 12:30; Luke 10:27.) If the answer is yes, then the next question is, how?

Persons like Mother Teresa of India point us toward the answer to both questions. Her life and ministry among the poor and outcasts of Calcutta demonstrate her belief in the possibility and desirability of loving God. Writing on this great text—"Thou shalt love the Lord thy God with thy whole heart, with thy whole soul and with thy whole mind"—she declares, "This is the commandment of the great God, and he cannot command the impossible. Love is a fruit in season at all times, and within reach of every hand. Anyone may gather it and no limit is set."[1]

The work of Mother Teresa and others like her shows us how to love God wholeheartedly and challenges us to follow this way of servanthood to others. In *Something Beautiful for God* Malcolm Muggeridge tells of his experiences with Mother Teresa and shares his impressions of her lifework. In one interview she shares her feelings regarding the relationship between her work and her love for God: "The work is the only expression of the love we have for God. We have to pour love on someone . . . the people are the means of expressing our love for God."[2] In another place she declares that "in heaven we will see how much we owe to the poor for helping us to love God better because of them. . . . Our hearts need to be full of love for him and since we have to express that love in action, naturally the poorest of the poor are the means of expressing our love for God."[3]

Muggeridge sums up her outlook on life like this:

> For Mother Teresa the two commandments—to love God and to love our neighbor—are jointly fulfilled, indeed, inseparable. In her life and work she exemplifies the relation between the two; how if we do not love God we cannot love our neighbor, and if we do not love our neighbor we cannot love God.[4]

It is possible, even in a world like ours, to talk meaningfully about a wholehearted love for God. Indeed, we must speak of such love. People are hungry to find something that will bring meaning and purpose to their existence. This ancient text is God's gracious call for people the world over to orient their lives around Him and to find meaning in the fulfillment of His will.

Exegetical Section

According to some scholars, there is no book of more importance to the OT than the Book of Deuteronomy. And there is "no Old Testament book more basic for understanding the New Testament than Deuteronomy."[5] It is one of the OT books most frequently quoted in the NT—83 times altogether. Elizabeth Achtemeier goes so far as to suggest that Deuteronomy's message is "an Old Testament foreshadowing of the New Testament gospel and it is no accident that its words are often heard from the lips of our Lord."[6]

While it is difficult for us to know the exact historical setting, Deuteronomy comes to us in the form of three addresses of Moses to the children of Israel. The essence of the book is preaching about the law of God. It is for a people who need to be reminded of God's covenant relationship with them (4:31; 7:9; 26:16-19; 29:1-9). He has acted redemptively on their behalf (4:38; 6:20-25; 7:8) and calls for their obedience (13:3-4). The people must avoid anything that compromises loyalty to God. Deuteronomy also reminds the people that God is fighting for them (3:22; 20:1ff.; 31:6-8) and that He is vitally concerned with the cause of the poor and underprivileged (10:17-22; 15:4, 7).

Peter Craigie points out that Deuteronomy is "a book about a community being prepared for a new life. . . . There is a call for a new commitment to God and a fresh understanding of the nature of the community of God's people."[7]

At the heart of Deuteronomy there is a call for Israel to respond in love to God's gracious, redemptive activity on their behalf. The term that is used for love is "suggestive of the intense, interior, personal love of one family member for another."[8] At least 12 times in the book Israel is called to manifest this heartfelt love for God (5:10; 6:5; 7:9; 10:12; 11:1, 13, 22; 13:3; 19:9; 30:6, 16, 20).

The primary text presenting this call for love is 6:4-5. It has been regarded for 2,000 years as one of the most important Hebrew texts. Known as the "Shema" (from the first word of v. 5 in Hebrew), this passage is recited twice daily by devout Jews. It is also known as the "Great Commandment" because of the central place given to it by Jesus in His teaching (Matt. 22:37; Mark 12:28-34; Luke 10:27). **Hear, O Israel** . . . appears to be a set formula in Deuteronomy (4:1; 5:1; 6:3, 4; 9:1; 20:3) and functions as a call to obedience. **Israel** includes "the forefathers, the present Israel and even those who were yet to be (5:3); i.e. God's word through Moses had permanent significance for Israel."[9]

"The Lord our God is one Lord" (RSV). The margin of the RSV text shows how the four words (Yahweh, our God, one) in this ancient confession of faith may be translated: "The Lord our God, the Lord is one"; or "the Lord is our God, the Lord is one"; or "the Lord is our God, the Lord alone." This verse became the basic formula of absolute monotheism, the distinct Hebrew belief in one and only one God. In the midst of polytheistic cultures, it was essential for Israel to have a clear understanding of the nature of Yahweh. God was not just one among many gods, He was the only God. This verse stresses both the unity and the uniqueness of God and thus "puts positively what the first commandment of the Decalogue states negatively."[10]

Having called for the attention of the people and declared who God is in v. 4, the passage moves on to define what man's attitude toward Him should be. "It is not to consist in a fearful and servile recognition of his sovereignty, and therefore a dutiful obedience to his will, but in a glad and wholehearted response to him—a response of the total self, which only the word love can express."[11]

"You shall love the Lord your God . . ." (RSV). In Deuteronomy we find the earliest references in the Bible of the use of **love** to describe the proper attitude of men to God. Over and over again the writer affirms that what God most wants is the wholehearted devotion of His people, as noted in earlier references. The love called for here is sought in response to God's covenant love already demonstrated repeatedly to the people (cf. 7:9). Deuteronomy reflects the idea expressed much later by the NT writer: "We love, because he first loved us" (1 John 4:19, RSV). The primary duty of the Israelite was not to serve different gods indiscriminately, "but to devote himself, with undivided allegiance, and with the pure and intense affection denoted by the term 'love,' to the service of the one Jehovah."[12]

S. R. Driver summarizes the basic understanding of the term **love** as it is used in Deuteronomy. It is

1. a duty which follows naturally as the grateful response to Jehovah for the many undeserved mercies received at his hands (6:12; 10:12f).
2. It involves the fear and service of God (6:13; 10:12; 11:13).
3. It impels those who are filled with it to the conscientious observance of all God's commands (11:1, 22; 19:9; 30:16).
4. It appears as the most inward and the most comprehensive of all religious duties, and as the chief commandment of all (Mk. 12:29f).[13]

"Heart . . . soul . . . might" (RSV). "Heart in Hebrew psychology is primarily the seat of the mind and will, together with a whole range of psychical emotions. Soul . . . is primarily the source of vitality which dies when the body does. . . . the two words mean that one is to love God with his whole being. This is reinforced by the third phrase . . . with all your force or strength."[14]

Verses 6-9 show the great importance of the two verses we are studying. "These words" were to be held in highest importance in the lives of the people. They were to be memorized, taught to the young children, talked about all the time in every place, and always held before their eyes. These verses (4-9) along with Deut. 11:13-21 and Num. 15:37-41 came to comprise Israel's basic affirmation of faith.

Theological Exegesis

In order to fully understand this text, we must remember that the command to love is given in the context of God's gracious activity to His children. The function of this passage is to remind Israel of God's love and faithfulness to them throughout their history and to call them to a renewed commitment of their lives to His purposes. The response God desires from His people is love.

In the beginning man was created to live in a harmonious relationship with the Creator. This relationship was disrupted by sin in the Garden of Eden. The law was given to provide guidance to a redeemed people so that they might live out God's will for their lives. It addresses the relationships that were disrupted by the Fall and thus depicts man's created destiny.

Deut. 6:4-5 reminds the people of Israel that love for God is the very essence of that law. At the very heart of those relationships that constitute man's destiny is this matter of love. God enables His people to respond to His grace by loving Him with all of their being. It is this love toward God that is the greatest fulfillment of the law.

It is, of course, impossible for men to love God with all of their heart in their own strength. The power and influence of sin is too great. The only way that we can possibly respond to the command of the text is through the grace, strength, and freedom that God himself gives to those who turn to Him. As persons hear the call of God to respond in love, they are also enabled by the power of God's Spirit to obey. As noted earlier, this response does not consist of a fearful and servile recognition of God's sovereignty and therefore a dutiful response to His will, "but in a glad and wholehearted response to him—a response of the total self, which only the word love can express."[15]

All of the great writers and teachers in the holiness tradition have understood that love is the great fulfillment of the law and that love is the very essence of the holiness message. When John Wesley was asked in 1744, "What is implied in being a perfect Christian?" he replied: "The loving God with all our heart, and mind, and soul (Deut. vi. 5)."[16] Later he added that "this implies, that no wrong temper, none contrary to love, remains in the soul; and that all the thoughts, words and actions, are governed by pure love."[17] In another place when Wesley explains what is "implied in the being altogether a Christian," he says:

First. The love of God. For thus saith his word, "Thou shalt love the Lord thy God with all thy heart, and with all thy soul, and with all thy mind, and with all thy strength." Such a love is this as engrosses the whole heart, as takes up all the affections, as fills the entire capacity of the soul, and employs the utmost of all its faculties.[18]

Adam Clarke also sees love toward God as the essence of holiness:

Love to God and man can never be dispensed with. It is essential to social and religious life; without it no communion can be kept up with God; nor can any man have a preparation for eternal glory whose heart and soul are not deeply imbued with it. Without it there never was true religion, nor ever can be.[19]

There is perhaps no better theological commentary on Deut. 6:4-5 than the explanation Clarke gives regarding the meaning of the words heart, soul, strength, and mind. His comments merit inclusion here:

1. *He loves God with all his heart who loves nothing in comparison to Him,* and nothing but in reference to Him; who is ready to give up, do, or suffer, anything, in order to please and glorify Him; who has in his heart neither love [n]or hatred, hope nor fear, inclination nor aversion, desire nor delight, but as they relate to God, and are regulated by Him. Such a love is merited by that Being who is infinitely perfect, good, wise, powerful, beneficent, and merciful. He merits and requires it from His intelligent creatures; and in fulfilling this duty the soul finds its perfection and felicity; for it rests in the Source of goodness and is penetrated with incessant influences from Him who is the essence and centre of all that is amiable; for his is the God of all grace.

2. *He loves God with all his soul,* with all his life, who is ready to endure all sorts of torments, and to be deprived of all kinds of comforts, rather than dishonour God; he who employs life, with all its comforts and conveniences, to glorify Him in, by, and through all; to whom life and death are nothing, but as they come from, and lead to God; who labours to promote the cause of God and truth in the world, denying himself, taking up his cross daily; neither eating, drinking, sleeping, resting, labouring, toiling, but in reference to the glory of God, his own salvation, and that of a lost world.

3. *He loves God with all his mind,* with all his intellect, or understanding, who applies himself only to know God and His holy will; who receives with submission, gratitude, and pleasure,

the sacred truths which He has revealed to mankind; who studies neither art nor science, but as far as it is necessary for the service of God, and uses it at all times to promote His glory; who forms no projects nor designs but in reference to God, and to the interests of mankind; who banishes, as much as possible, from his understanding and memory, every idea which has any tendency to defile his soul, or turn it for a moment from the centre of eternal repose.

4. *He uses all his abilities, both natural and acquired, to grow in the grace of God,* and to perform His will in the most acceptable manner: in a word, he who sees God in all things, thinks of Him at all times, having his mind continually fixed upon God; acknowledges Him in all his ways; who begins, continues, and ends all his thoughts, words, and works to the glory of His name; continually planning, scheming, and devising how he may serve God and his generation more effectually; his head, his intellect, going before; his heart, his affections, and desires, coming after.

5. *He loves God with all his strength* who exerts all the powers and faculties of his body and soul in the service of God; who, for the glory of his Maker, spares neither labour nor cost; who sacrifices his body, his health, his time, his ease, for the honour of his divine Master; who employs in his service all his goods, his talents, his power, his credit, authority, and influence; doing what he does with a single eye, a loving heart, and with all his might; in whose conduct is ever seen the work of faith, patience of hope, and labour of love.

O glorious state of him who has given God his whole heart, and in which God ever lives and rules! Glorious state of blessedness upon earth, triumph of the grace of God over sin and Satan! State of holiness and happiness far beyond this description, which comprises an ineffable union and communion between the ever blessed Trinity and the soul of man! O God! let Thy work appear unto Thy servants, and the work of our hands establish upon us! The work of our hands establish Thou it! Amen. Amen.[20]

Application

It is not enough for us to merely seek to understand the significance of this text for ancient Israel. Just as it called them to a central allegiance to Jehovah, it calls us to the same total life response to God. We must ask ourselves how such a call applies to our contemporary situation. While we will not all be in the same situation as Mother Teresa, we are all called to live out in everyday ways a full obedience to the call of love. How does this central holiness text apply to some of the basic concerns in our lives?

Home and Family. One of the greatest causes of dissension and strife in homes and families is the spirit of self-centeredness. As individuals within a family assert their own way, it often creates conflict with others who want things to go their way. Tension, stress, and anger result unless there is some willingness to defer one's own interests out of concern for the other person. It is at this point that a full devotion to God expresses itself in love for neighbor—the neighbors who live closest to us, our families. In Philippians we are instructed to be possessed by the "mind" of Christ, which will enable each of us to "look not only to his own interests, but also to the interests of others" (2:5, 4, RSV). As husbands and wives and brothers and sisters truly love God with heart, soul, and might, the result will be greater harmony in the home.

Personal Values. It is impossible to love God with all of your heart and at the same time be devoted to other gods. This text, along with others like it in Deuteronomy, reminded the people of God that, despite the claims of their pagan neighbors, there were no other gods; **The Lord our God, the Lord is one.** In a positive way it reminds us that our value choices must be made in harmony with the values and priorities of the God whom we love and serve. We cannot profess to love God with all our hearts and then devote our lives and resources to those things contrary to His will and purpose. "'The expulsive power of a new affection' claims our attention as the chief dynamic of the sanctification of the soul. Love for God subordinates and reorders all lesser loves."[21]

Furthermore, to teach our children "these words" (6:6, RSV) is primarily to model their meaning by the way we live in our relationships with other people and in the way we use the things God allows us to have. Those who know us best will know whether our profession of love for God is the true basis of our life or just the mouthing of empty religious phrases.

Career and Vocation. This great OT text cuts across all the boundaries we use to divide and compartmentalize our busy lives. It calls for a complete devotion to God in every dimension in life, including our career or vocation. All of life is regarded as sacred and set apart for God. This means that we will seek to express love for God in our careers or vocations. Such a commitment will call for us to examine the purpose of our work, the effect or impact of our work on society, and the nature and quality of our relationship with fellow workers (both those who are in positions over us and those for whom we are responsible). We will ask questions like, can I glorify God in this job? Is this vocation in harmony with causes that benefit others?

Living life with a deep love for God will mean that our goals for employment are not primarily status, personal gain, or worldly success, but service to others. Such a claim sounds radical in our society, but loving God in the way described in Deut. 6:4-5 is a radical way to love, and it has serious *implications for almost every area of our lives.* Although it may begin this way, loving God is certainly not just a private, personal experience to be enjoyed by the believer. It is an experience with God that impacts one's private and public life. It directs the way I live at home and in the public arena. It influences my opinions and choices in the realm of business, education, and politics as I love others and seek their best welfare because of my love and devotion to God. "And this commandment we have from him, that he who loves God should love his brother also" (1 John 4:21, RSV).

Preaching Ideas

There are several ways to approach this text in preaching. One helpful sermon suggestion comes from Frank Carver. Under the title or theme of "A Life Set Free" he develops three points: (1) A life set free to acknowledge God properly (v. 4) in *(a)* a life response and *(b)* a personal confession; (2) A life set free to love God adequately (v. 5) *(a)* as the only appropriate response (v. 5a) and *(b)* with the total being (v. 5b); and (3) A life set free to serve God effectively (vv. 6-9) *(a)* out of an inner dynamic (v. 6), *(b)* in the home (v. 7a), and *(c)* in every sphere of life (v. 7b).[22]

James Wolfendale also offers a very usable outline for preaching on this text. After reminding us that these verses assert that "Jehovah is one, indivisible and supreme God, and worthy of love supreme and undivided," he observes that: (1) God is worthy of our love and service because *(a)* He alone is God and therefore deserves our homage, and *(b)* He is a Living Being, on whom we can think and with whom we can converse. (2) God requires us to love and serve Him with entire self-surrender. This means we serve Him *(a)* Affectionately, "with all thine heart"; *(b)* Intelligently, with all thy mind"; *(c)* Energetically, "with all thy might"; and *(d)* Entirely, "with all thy soul." God must be loved above all creatures and things and with our total personality. (3) God's relationship to us is a motive to prompt this required service: *(a)* Jehovah was Israel's God and had shown himself such; *(b)* His presence had been seen and His goodness displayed in wonderful ways.[23]

A very simple and direct way of dealing with Deut. 6:4-5 is to address it with the familiar journalistic questions: (1) Who is speaking? God is giving His word through His servant Moses. We hear God's word through the Bible, the Record of His dealings with men. (2) To whom is He speaking? In the context of the passage He is speaking to the people of Israel who are confronted with the idolatry and pagan notions of the people around them. The word of God here also speaks to people of God in all ages who are tempted to put their trust in man-made gods. (3) What is the message? Love God. Worship Him alone. (4) How? With all of your life. (5) Why? Because He alone is God and because He first loved us (1 John 4:19). (6) When? Now and always. (7) Where? Everywhere—you should always be reminded of these words and seek to perpetuate them forever (vv. 6-9).

Why Love God?

Some of the great texts in the Bible are deceptively simple. Clearly articulating great doctrinal truths, they beckon the preacher in their direction. Upon arriving at the text and spending time with it, the preacher suddenly realizes that the truth is so important and so clear that little can be done other than to repeat it over and over again. All attempts to break it up into neat divisions appear superfluous. How do you preach from such passages?

Deut. 6:4-5 strikes me as such a text. What do we find to say beyond merely repeating the words of the scripture: **Love the Lord your God with all your heart . . . ?** What more can the preacher say?

This is not the first time these words have beckoned me and then resisted, as artificial and superficial, my attempts at a homiletical treatment. Several years ago I turned to the words of the Shema in search of a sermon. Because I believed the passage to be so central to the holiness message, I wanted to preach from it. The text put me off. I saved my study notes; a sermon never materialized.

I feel a little bit the same way this time. I have studied the passage thoroughly. I have read what many others have written about it. I sense the text probing me, challenging me, and continually opening me up to a fuller, more thoroughgoing response to God. In my meditation and reflection on these words I keep coming back to this central affirmation: *It is absolutely important and essential for us to love God.* My thoughts about this affirmation come together best around two questions: (1) Why is it essential and important for us to love God? and (2) What does it really mean to love God?

The writer of Deuteronomy suggests three good reasons why it is essential and important for us to love God. *We love God,* first of all, *because of who he is.* "The Lord is our God, the Lord is one" (v. 4, RSV margin). Yahweh had revealed himself to the people of Israel. He had chosen them to be the people through whom He demonstrated His love for the world. God had let them know that He was not just their God as one god among many but God alone over all creation. The Lord, speaking to the people of Israel through Isaiah, makes this point clear: "You are my witnesses . . . and my servant whom I have chosen, that you may know and believe me and understand that I am He. Before me no god was formed, nor shall there be any after me. I, I am the Lord, and besides me there is no savior" (43:10-11, RSV).

We also love God because of what He has done for us. This admonition to love God comes to the people in the context of a book designed to remind Israel of her covenant with the God who delivered her from the bondage of Egypt. He made himself known to her in the very act of redeeming her. By grace she was brought into a very special relationship with God.

In Jesus Christ God made himself known to the whole world as a saving, redeeming God who desires to bring men and women into a relationship with himself. "In this the love of God was made manifest among us, that God sent his only Son into the world, so that we might live through him" (1 John 4:9, RSV).

A third reason why we love God is that *this is the way He wants us to respond to His love.* Over and over again in Deuteronomy the people are instructed by the Lord to respond to His gracious activity by loving Him (5:10; 7:9; 10:12; 11:1, 13, 22). The motivating force behind the love we are to have for God is His prior love for us. We do not love Him in order to win His favor. He has already shown us His gracious, steadfast love and now instructs us in how to respond. "We love him, because he first loved us" (1 John 4:19, KJV).

If we fail to understand this point, we can become trapped in a legalistic concept of holiness, striving in our own strength to be what God wants us to be without recognizing that in Jesus Christ God has already done all that is necessary for us to be holy. We do not earn holiness; God works it within us as He enables us to respond to His grace in love.

We have good reasons for loving God. *But what does it really mean to love Him?* Many Christians familiar with the Great Commandment have been concerned with this question. Chuck Colson's concern led him to ask a number of believers how they loved God with all their heart. The responses were typical. One answered in the words of the Scripture: "Well, by loving Him with all my heart, soul, and mind." Another said, "By maintaining a worshipful heart, offering myself as an acceptable sacrifice." Colson pushed for specifics, and the person began talking about his devotional reading and prayer life. Others cited faithful church attendance and tithing as ways they loved God. A few spoke of sins they used to commit but had now forsaken. Many tried to say that loving God was a feeling they have in their hearts. Colson concluded that "most of us, as professing Christians, do not really know how to love God. Not only have we not given thought to what the greatest commandment means in our day-to-day existence, we have not obeyed it."[24]

The writer of Deuteronomy felt the command to be so important that he said you should love God "with all your heart, and with all your soul, and with all your might" (RSV). Furthermore, in the verses that follow (6-9), precise instructions are given regarding how succeeding generations are to be taught this essential word. We are to love God with our total being and to teach others to love Him in the same way. The question, however, is still there. How do I love God in this way?

When we study Deuteronomy and other parts of the Bible, we are not left without an answer. John's answer is clear: "For this is the love of God, that we keep his commandments" (1 John 5:3, RSV). A review of the Deuteronomy passages calling for the people to love God will show that love to be expressed in obedience to the commandments. The beginning of loving God, says Colson, is a "passionate desire to obey and please God—a willingly entered-into discipline." We must know His commands. We must know and obey the Scriptures, "the key to loving God and the starting point for life's most exciting journey."[25]

It is far easier to speak of love for God in terms of some sort of emotional response to Him. But the love God desires is love expressed in wholehearted, down-to-earth, day-by-day obedience to His will. Love as obedience requires the commitment of the heart, soul, mind, and strength. It is not based in passing feelings or fleeting interests but upon deep conviction about who God is, what He has done for us, and what He expects from us in response.

To love God with this single-minded, obedient allegiance is the heart of the holiness message. John Wesley advised, "Let your soul be filled with so entire a love to Him, that you may love nothing but for His sake."[26] He went on to pray:

> O grant that nothing in my soul
> May dwell, but Thy pure love alone!
> O may Thy love possess me whole,
> My joy, my treasure, and my crown.
> Strange fires far from my heart remove—
> My every act, word, thought, be love![27]

When God answers this prayer in our lives, by shedding His love abroad in our hearts (Rom. 5:5), we are enabled to respond to the Great Commandment. We are enabled by grace to live obedient lives in response to His great love for us. Loving God in this way impacts every area of life—our values, our priorities, our stewardship, our relationships, and our vocations. Our love is expressed by obedience to His Lordship over every dimension of our existence. Love for Him controls, motivates, and dominates our lives. This commandment—the one Jesus called the greatest—is based on costly grace and calls for radical discipleship.

Endnotes

1. Malcolm Muggeridge, *Something Beautiful for God* (New York: Ballantine Books, 1971), 47.

2. Ibid., 78.

3. Ibid., 55, 93.

4. Ibid., 108.

5. Elizabeth Achtemeier, *Deuteronomy/Jeremiah,* in *Proclamation Commentaries* (Philadelphia: Fortress Press, 1978), 9.

6. Ibid.

7. Peter Craigie, *The Book of Deuteronomy* (Grand Rapids: Wm. B. Eerdmans Publishing Co., 1976), 7.

8. Achtemeier, *Deuteronomy/Jeremiah,* 635.

9. J. A. Thompson, *Deuteronomy,* in *The Tyndale Old Testament Commentaries* (Downers Grove, Ill.: InterVarsity Press, 1975), 81.

10. Edward Blair, *Deuteronomy,* in *The Laymen's Bible Commentary* (Richmond, Va.: John Knox Press, 1964), 37.

11. Ibid.

12. S. R. Driver, *Deuteronomy,* in *The International Critical Commentary* (Edinburgh: T. and T. Clark, 1895), 91.

13. Ibid.

14. G. Ernest Wright, *Deuteronomy,* in *The Interpreter's Bible* (Nashville: Abingdon, 1953), 374.

15. Blair, *Deuteronomy,* 37.

16. John Wesley, *A Plain Account of Christian Perfection* (Kansas City: Beacon Hill Press of Kansas City, 1966), 41.

17. Ibid., 51.

18. W. Stanley Johnson, "Christian Perfection as Love for God," *Wesleyan Theological Journal* 18, no. 1 (Spring 1983): 53.

19. Adam Clarke, in *Great Holiness Classics,* vol. 2, *The Wesley Century,* ed. T. Crichton Mitchell (Kansas City: Beacon Hill Press of Kansas City, 1984), 340.

20. Ibid., 338-39.

21. Johnson, "Christian Perfection," 56.

22. Frank Carver, "The Interpretation of Deuteronomy 6:4-9," *Preacher's Magazine* 54, no. 2 (Dec.-Jan.-Feb. 1978-79): 58-61.

23. James Wolfendale, *Deuteronomy,* in *The Preacher's Complete Homiletic Commentary* (Grand Rapids: Baker Book House, 1974), 132-33.

24. Charles Colson, *Loving God* (Grand Rapids: Zondervan Publishing House, 1983), 15-16.

25. Ibid., 40.

26. Wesley, *Plain Account,* 13.

27. Ibid., 14.

W. T. PURKISER

Holiness as Perfect Love

And so we know and rely on the love God has for us. God is love. Whoever lives in love lives in God, and God in him. In this way, love is made complete among us so that we will have confidence on the day of judgment, because in this world we are like him. There is no fear in love. But perfect love drives out fear, because fear has to do with punishment. The one who fears is not made perfect in love (1 John 4:16-18).

Contemporary Focus of Text

No topic is more widely discussed today than love—in newspapers and magazines, on television and radio, in serious studies and frivolous comment, by both secular and religious people. But because love is so often parodied and misrepresented by the sources, it is important to hear what God's Word has to say about it. At this point, the writings of John in the NT speak most clearly.

Modern man is also tormented with uncertainty. Against this background, John speaks with assurance: **We know and rely on the love God has for us** (v. 16). Those filled with anxiety and fear—of the future, of failure, of loneliness, of poverty, of judgment—are pointed to the love that offers an antidote for fear (v. 18).

John's portrayal of NT love undercuts the moralism and legalism that are the bane of so much modern Christianity. God's love is not to be earned; it is the free gift of grace—in Paul's words, "not by works, so that no one can boast" (Eph. 2:9).

Today's Christians need the motivational power of God's kind of love—what Thomas Chalmers called "the expulsive power of a new affection." It is "Love divine, all loves excelling," as Charles Wesley phrased it, and it conquers and controls all the lesser loves of life.

And God's love is "tough love," taking away the fear of judgment, but not setting aside the legitimate demands of justice. In the face of all sentimental expressions of love, John insists that "this is love for God: to obey his commands. And his commands are not burdensome" (1 John 5:3).

Exegetical Section

The context of 1 John 4 is particularly important. John wrote his first letter against the background of a heretical movement generally known as Gnosticism. The Gnostics held many variant views, chief of which was that matter is totally evil and that salvation is gained through a higher form of knowledge to which they alone were privy. Because they thought the body is evil, the Gnostics denied the incarnation of Christ and in practice taught that sin is unavoidable in this life.[1]

John wrote the Gospel in order that "by believing you may have life in his name" (John 20:31); he wrote the first letter "to you who believe in the name of the Son of God so that you may *know* that you have eternal life" (1 John 5:13, italics added). Knowledge of eternal life does not come through Gnostic speculation but by faith evidenced by love.

The letter is admittedly difficult to outline. One helpful division employs John's three statements about God, and our human response:

1. God is Light, chap. 1. Our response is to walk in the light (1:7).

2. God is Life, chaps. 2—3. Our response is to be born of God (3:8-10).

3. God is Love, chaps. 4—5. Our response is to live in love (4:16).

John is rightly known as "the apostle of love." We need to understand the meaning of love as John uses the term. The NT uses two Greek words for love: *philia* and its verb form (25 times)—the love that is aroused by the excellence, beauty, or worth of its object;

and *agapē* and its verb form (225 times)—for love that results from the disposition or nature of the one who loves. In 1 John, the writer uses *agapē* and its verb form 46 times, 27 times in chap. 4 alone.

Agapē has often been called "God's kind of love," for it is used most consistently of God's love and its reflection in our lives. It is not primarily emotional (liking) but volitional (caring). In NT terms, one can love those he does not particularly like.

That master of NT word studies, William Barclay, says that *agapē* "is the attitude which, no matter what the other person is like, and no matter how we may feel emotionally towards him, will seek the other person's good, and which will never hate. The opposite of this Christian *agapē* is not hate; the opposite is indifference. This Christian love is undefeatable caring."[2]

Verse 16, **we know** (KJV, "have known") is the translation of a Greek verb from which *Gnostic* is derived. It is in the perfect tense and describes a condition already accomplished whose effects remain.

Rely on is the rendering of the most common Greek verb for "believe." It means both to accept as true and to put confidence or trust in. Saving faith is more than mental acceptance of truth about the Savior; it is trust in and reliance on Him to do what He has promised. In its full NT meaning, it always implies obedience.

Lives in (KJV, "dwelleth in") is the English equivalent of a Greek verb that literally means to remain or abide in. It carries the thought of continuance, endurance, a settled dwelling place.

Lives in God, and God in him (v. 15) relates to Jesus and is the equivalent of Paul's "living in the Spirit" (Gal. 5:16, 25, KJV; Col. 1:8).

Verse 17, **made complete** ("perfect" in v. 18) is from the Greek *teleios,* "having reached its end, finished, complete, perfect."[3] Perfection is a difficult idea for us to come to terms with, since today it implies absolute flawlessness, and to relate it to anything human seems presumptuous in the extreme. William Barclay notes that "*teleios,* at least in the New Testament, if we may put it so, does not imply philosophical or metaphysical perfection; it implies functional perfection. It describes that which achieves its end and purpose."[4]

Confidence is literally boldness. The Greek term originally meant boldness in speech, but the term was extended to include courage or daring in any area.

World is from *kosmos*—here, not the world in opposition to the will of God, but the world of human society.

Verse 18, **fear** is *phobos,* from which we get our term *phobia.* It is not our instinctive reaction to the threat of danger, but dread compounded by guilt. Here, it is fear of God's judgment, the fear of an unsanctified heart in the presence of divine holiness.

Theological Exegesis

First John 4:16-18 emphasizes Christian assurance in the face of the multitude of questions that confront the believer. We are taught to rely on the love that manifested itself on the Cross and continuously in our lives as grace sufficient for all our needs.

It is important to note that John is not concerned here with the question of the *ordo salutis,* the order of salvation. He is portraying, rather, the wholeness or completeness of God's redemptive work. Divine love is born within us when we are born of the Spirit in Christian conversion (Rom. 8:9). It is made full or complete when the sanctifying Spirit fills the heart of the consecrated, believing Christian.

This second epoch of entire sanctification, heart purity, or perfect love, is noted most clearly in 1 Thessalonians (cf. 1:2-10; 2:13; etc., with 3:10-13; 4:3-8; 5:23-24) and elsewhere throughout the Epistles where those who are already believers are instructed to go on to "completion" (e.g., Rom. 6:11-14; 12:1-2; 1 Cor. 3:1-3; 2 Cor. 7:1; Gal. 5:16-25; Eph. 3:14-19; 4:22-25; Col. 3:1-10; Titus 2:11-14; Heb. 6:1-3; 12:14-17; 13:12-13; James 4:8; etc.).

In these verses in 1 John, the writer turns to the positive principle in holiness that underlies the call to cleansing in 1:7 and 3:1-3 and the holy living enjoined in 3:4-10. It is the perfection of God's love by the indwelling fullness of His sanctifying Spirit.

An exposition of these verses should include reference to John Wesley's use of them in defining Christian perfection. He wrote, "Both my brother and I maintained . . . That Christian perfection is that love of God and our neighbour, which implies deliverance from all sin. . . . It is nothing higher and nothing lower than this,—the pure love of God and man . . . It is love governing the heart and life, running through all our tempers, words, and actions."[5]

In one of his letters, Wesley wrote, "I want you to be all love. This is the perfection I believe and teach. And this perfection is consistent with a thousand nervous disorders."[6]

Such perfection is possible only in union with Christ. In another letter, Wesley wrote, "Our perfection is not like that of a tree, which flourishes by the sap derived from its own root; but like that of a branch, which, united to the vine, bears fruit, but severed from it is dried up and withered."[7]

Paul S. Rees reminds us that "perfect love does not insure perfect practice. It would be a mistake to imply that it does. What *may* be insured is a perfect purpose; and in the perfecting of that holy purpose, constantly renewed by the Holy Spirit, the practice will be constantly corrected upward."[8]

The result of perfect love is a more Christlike conduct: **In this world we are like him** (v. 17). John consistently emphasizes the fact that the only genuine evidence of true love is obedience. This aspect of Christ's teaching is recorded in the Gospel (14:15, 21, 23; 15:10) and in 1 John 5:3. It underlies John's insistence on a holy life (2:4-6, 15-17; 3:18; 4:19-21; 5:18).

John also teaches that the proof of the love of God in us is our love for those around us. This is the acid test (3:10-11, 14; 4:7-8, 11, 20-21).

It is important to note that God's love is "tough love." It does not do away with accountability for sin. God's holy wrath against evil is the other side of His infinite love for the sinner. To love God is to hate all that threatens those God loves.

Vignettes on Love

First Corinthians 13 is a worthy parallel to John's teaching about love. Years ago, Henry Drummond described the nine ingredients in what he called "The Spectrum of Love" in 1 Cor. 13:4-6:

Patience—Love "suffereth long"
Kindness—"and is kind"
Generosity—Love "envieth not"
Humility—Love "vaunteth not itself, is not puffed up"
Courtesy—"Doth not behave itself unseemly"
Unselfishness—"Seeketh not her own"
Good temper—"Is not easily provoked"
Guilelessness—"Thinketh no evil"
Sincerity—"Rejoiceth not in iniquity, but rejoiceth in the truth" (KJV).[9]

It has often been pointed out that the fruit of the Spirit in Gal. 5:22-23 may be considered varied expressions of love. "The fruit of the Spirit is love" (v. 22). Joy is love singing, peace is love resting, patience is love enduring, kindness is love sharing, goodness is love's character, faithfulness is love's habit, gentleness is love's touch, and self-control is love in charge.

Augustine said that in order to know whether a person is a *good* person, "one does not ask what he believes or what he hopes, but what he loves."[10]

Love must grow or it will die. Edwin C. Lewis notes, "At a given time, the perfection of holy love may obtain in Christian experience. The acme is reached. But time moves on, bringing new possibilities, new demands, new experiences. If the acme still remains where it was, it is the acme no longer. It can be kept only as it is exceeded. This is the logic of love. Perfect love is therefore perfect love only as it is a continual *going on unto* perfect love."[11]

E. Stanley Jones tells of meeting a devoted and beloved bishop whose life had been spent in Africa. After his first year in Africa as a missionary, the mission council voted to send him home as one unable to get along with his fellow missionaries. Then they decided to give him another chance if he would promise to read the 13th chapter of 1 Corinthians, Paul's great "Hymn to Love," every day. He did. He was transformed, and the very people who were going to send him home elected him their bishop.[12]

John Greenleaf Whittier, the Quaker poet, wrote the much-loved lines:

> *I know not where His islands lift*
> *Their fronded palms in air.*
> *I only know I cannot drift*
> *Beyond His love and care.*

Love must at times be tough to be true. Discipline is an evidence of love as much as the expression of approval. The mother who cuddles her child in love expresses the same love when she slaps the little hand that reaches out to touch a red-hot stove.

Love is really the only enduring motivation for Christian service. A tourist who saw the difficult circumstances under which a missionary was working said to him, "I wouldn't do that for a million dollars!"

The missionary quietly replied, "Neither would I. But for the love of Christ, that's different."

Samuel Taylor Coleridge wrote:

> *He prayeth best, who loveth best*
> *All things both great and small;*
> *For the dear God who loveth us,*
> *He made and loveth all.*

Psychiatrists generally agree that mental health depends on one's capacity to love. Dr. Rollo May writes, "To be capable of giving and receiving mature love is as sound a criterion as we have for the fulfilled personality."[13]

When Tigranes, king of Armenia, was taken captive by the Roman legions under Pompey, he was led before the monarch to receive the sentence of death together with his family. Tigranes pleaded that he alone be sacrificed—that his dear ones might go free. The self-sacrificing love of the captive so moved Pompey that he ordered the release of the whole family. On their way home, Tigranes said to his wife, "What did you think of the emperor?"

"Indeed," she said, "I never saw him."

"You never saw Pompey?" her husband exclaimed. "Where were your eyes?"

She replied, "They were fixed on the one who offered to die for me!"

A British minister tells of a Yorkshireman whose son had caused much trouble. He was telling a friend that the lad had gone off again.

"If he were mine," his friend said, "I would send him abroad and cut him off without a shilling."

"So should I," answered the father, "if he were yours!"

Love, to be effective, must be expressed in concrete terms. The cynic remarks,

> *To love mankind, to me's no chore;*
> *My problem is the man next door!*

Or again,

> *To walk in love with saints above,*
> *That will be wondrous glory;*
> *To live below with those we know—*
> *Well, that's another story!*

The expression of love in action brings results. The late publisher Bennett Cerf told of a woman who went to her family counselor and said, "I hate my husband! I not only want to divorce him, I want to make things as tough for him as I can."

The counselor said, "I know just what you should do. Start showering him with compliments and indulging his every whim. Then, just when he knows how much he needs you, start divorce proceedings. You'll really fracture him!"

The woman decided to take the advice. Six months later, the counselor met her at a dinner. He asked, "Are you still following my suggestion?"

"I am," she said.

"Then how about filing your divorce papers?"

"Are you out of your head?" countered the wife. "We're divinely happy! I love him with all my heart!"

The quality of love in a congregation is directly related to its growth, according to a study conducted by Dr. Win Arn of the Institute for American Church Growth. The study surveyed more than 8,600 persons from 39 different Protestant denominations to measure their "love-care quotient." The results showed that churches with lower quotients declined, while those with higher ratings grew. The study concluded that "growing churches are more loving—to each other and to visitors—than declining churches." Arn concluded that "a church that loves people is a church that grows. Learning to love, or to love again, is the most important first step for a church that wants to grow."[14]

Preaching Ideas on the Text

God Is Love—1 John 4:16-18

Introduction: Glasgow's William Barclay declares this to be "probably the greatest single statement about God in the whole Bible."[15]
A. We Can Count on God's Love
    1. He proved it by the sacrifice of His Son, v. 9
    2. He certifies it by the gift of His Spirit, v. 13
    3. We can trust and rely on His love, v. 16
B. God's Love Is Transforming Love
    1. **In this world we are** [made] **like him,** v. 17; cf. 3:2-3
    2. Perfect love drives out fear of judgment, v. 18

Conclusion: "We love because he first loved us," v. 19. We find heart purity and power for holy living by responding to God's loving call.

God's Cure for Man's Phobias—1 John 4:16-18

Introduction: Ours is a fearful, frightened age—the "Age of Anxiety"
A. Fears That Trouble the Heart
    1. Fear of the future, of poverty, of illness
    2. Fear of death and the judgment, v. 18
B. Faith Points the Way, v. 16. There is a certainty we can believe and rely on.
3. God's Perfect Love Drives Out Fear, v. 18, by forgiving the past and purifying our hearts.

Conclusion: In His sanctifying Spirit and perfected love we may face eternity without fear.

Sermon on the Text

Living in the Love of God

Text: **God is love. Whoever lives in love lives in God, and God in him** (1 John 4:16).

Introduction

One of the miracles of Scripture is the way great truths are put in few words. One has only to think of some of the three- and four-word texts in the Bible: "God is able" (2 Cor. 9:8); "Jesus is Lord" (Rom. 10:9); "All have sinned" (Rom. 3:23); "My grace is sufficient" (2 Cor. 12:9).

But the greatest of them all are John's words, **God is love.** They are twice repeated in this chapter: in v. 8 in connection with knowing God, and in the text in connection with the very nature of God—what God is.

"Love," of course, is a word of many meanings—all the way from Hollywood to heaven. Spelled "luv," it can stand for a small pickup truck or disposable diapers. It can be changeable and fickle. The young man proposing to his girlfriend said, "I'm not wealthy, and I don't have a sharp convertible and a luxury yacht like Jerome Green, but I do love you!"

To which the girl replied after a moment's thought, "I love you, too. But tell me a little more about Jerome!"

When John speaks of the love of God, he uses a distinctive NT word, *agapē.* This is the kind of love that expresses the nature of the one who loves rather than the inherent worth of the one loved.

It was a wise young woman who said, "There are three kinds of love: *if* love, *because* love, and *anyhow* love." Human love tends to be "if" or "because" love: "*If* you are worthy or *because* you are good, I love you." God's kind of love is *anyhow* love—quite beyond the measure of man's mind.

> *Could we with ink the ocean fill,*
> *And were the skies of parchment made;*
> *Were every stalk on earth a quill,*
> *And every man a scribe by trade;*
> *To write the love of God above*
> *Would drain the ocean dry;*
> *Nor could the scroll contain the whole,*
> *Though stretched from sky to sky.**
>
> —F. H. LEHMAN

*From "The Love of God." Copyright 1917. Renewed 1945 by Nazarene Publishing House.

John gives us here two great truths about the love of God.

First, he talks about the assurance of God's love. That God is love is not something we wish for or speculate about. Because "the Father has sent his Son to be the Savior of the world" (v. 14), **we know and rely on the love God has for us** (v. 16).

The proof of God's love for us is the gift of His only begotten Son. Back in v. 9 we read, "This is how God showed his love among us: He sent his one and only Son into the world that we might live through him."

The "Golden Text" of the NT is also from John's pen: "For God so loved the world that he gave his one and only Son, that whoever believes in him shall not perish but have eternal life" (John 3:16). Here is *"God,"* the greatest Lover; *"so loved,"* the greatest degree; *"the world,"* the greatest number; *"that he gave,"* the greatest act; *"his one and only Son,"* the greatest Gift; *"that whoever,"* the greatest invitation; *"believes,"* the greatest simplicity; *"in him,"* the greatest Person; *"shall not perish,"* the greatest deliverance; *"but have,"* the greatest certainty; *"eternal life,"* the greatest possession.

> *I sometimes think about the Cross,*
> *And shut my eyes, and try to see*
> *The cruel nails, the crown of thorns,*
> *And Jesus, crucified for me.*
>
> *But even could I see Him die,*
> *I could but see a little part*
> *Of that great love which, like a fire,*
> *Is always burning in His heart.*[16]

It is this love that gives us our highest value. The story is told of a strange advertisement in the personal column of a city newspaper: "Reward: $200 for return of rag doll lost Tuesday near 4th and I streets." Just think—$200 for a handful of rags scarcely worth two cents! Its value was measured by the brokenhearted love of a little girl.

God's love is personal love. We must not let John 3:16 dissolve into vague generalities. God so loved *me* that He gave His one and only Son, that *I,* believing in Him, should not perish but have eternal life!

Second, John moves on to talk about the perfection of God's love. What the KJV translated as "Herein is our love made perfect," the NIV renders, **Love is made complete among us so that we will have confidence on the day of judgment** (v. 17). Both "perfect" and

complete are valid translations of the NT Greek term *teleioō*. It is defined as "to bring to an end by completing or perfecting,"[17] in which "to bring to an end" means "to fulfill the purpose of."

Perfect and *perfection* are words likely to be misunderstood in our day. What in Bible times meant to be "whole, entire, complete, fulfilling its purpose" now suggests what is utterly flawless—such that any change would mar it.

John's point is that when we fully come to live in love and love lives in us, the Spirit of God makes His indwelling presence real within us (v. 13). We experience the love of God to the degree that we allow His Spirit to fill our hearts—as Paul says in Rom. 5:5, "God has poured out his love into our hearts by the Holy Spirit, whom he has given us." This is the same term, "to pour out," that Peter uses in Acts 2:17, 18, and 33 to describe the infilling of the Holy Spirit at Pentecost.

This is not to deny that the Holy Spirit is given to every Christian. Jesus tells His disciples before Pentecost that they knew the Spirit and had Him with them. But, He said, "He . . . will be in you" (John 14:15-17). Our regenerating Life is to become our sanctifying Lord—and when He does, we live in love, God lives in us, and His love is made complete in and among us, **so that we will have confidence on the day of judgment** (1 John 4:17).

John Wesley described holiness of heart as "Christian perfection." Even in his day the use of "perfection" was misunderstood, and Wesley explained that the perfection of which he spoke was simply that commanded by the Savior in the Gospels, "Love the Lord your God with all your heart and with all your soul and with all your mind and with all your strength. . . . Love your neighbor as yourself." Then Jesus added, "There is no commandment greater than these" (Mark 12:30-31).

Love is perfect in the NT sense when it is the expression of a heart cleansed by the baptism with the Holy Spirit (Acts 15:8-9). It is perfect when it excludes all rivals. The perfection is not of us, it is of God and His indwelling Spirit. Christian perfection is not to be a perfect person or even a perfect Christian, but a Christian completely yielded to the sanctifying will of the Father.

Because God loves us and we love Him, we are able to love our brothers and sisters. Indeed, John is adamant that this is the practical test of our devotion. One has only to run through chaps. 3 and

4 of this priceless Epistle to grasp this truth: "Anyone who does not do what is right is not a child of God; nor is anyone who does not love his brother" (3:10; cf. 3:11, 14-15; 4:7-8, 11-12, 20-21; 5:1-2).

Conclusion

God loves us enough to accept us just as we are; He loves us *too much* to leave us as we are. His love is liberating and transforming. Even **in this world we are like him** (v. 17).

This is our challenge in a love-starved world: to experience the love of God ourselves, and to reflect that love in our relationships with those around us. May God help us to open our hearts to His forgiving and cleansing love!

Endnotes

1. Cf. Wayne E. Caldwell, "Gnosticism," in *Beacon Dictionary of Theology* (BDT), ed. Richard S. Taylor (Kansas City: Beacon Hill Press of Kansas City, 1983), 235-36.

2. *The New Testament: A New Translation* (London: Collins, 1969), 2:314; cf. also William M. Greathouse, "Agapē," BDT, 31-32.

3. W. E. Vine, *Expository Dictionary of New Testament Words* (London: Oliphants, 1958), 3:173-74.

4. *New Testament* 2:319.

5. *The Works of John Wesley,* 14 vols. (Kansas City: Beacon Hill Press of Kansas City, 1978 [reprint of 1872 edition]), 11:393, 397.

6. *Letters of the Reverend John Wesley,* ed. John Telford (London: Epworth Press, 1931), 4:188.

7. Ibid., 5:204.

8. *Prayer and Life's Highest* (Grand Rapids: Wm. B. Eerdmans Publishing Co., 1956), 46.

9. From Henry Drummond, *The Greatest Thing in the World, and Other Addresses* (London: Collins Cleartype Press, n.d.).

10. "Enchiridion," chap. 117, in *Works of Augustine,* ed. M. Dods (Edinburgh: T. and T. Clark, 1873), 9:256.

11. "The Ministry of the Holy Spirit," *Revival Pulpit* (August—September 1944), 158.

12. *Mastery: The Art of Mastering Life* (New York: Abingdon Press, 1955), 188.

13. *Man's Search for Himself* (Bergenfield, N.J.: Signet, 1953), 238.

14. Reported by the Nazarene News Service, 1986.

15. *The Letters of John and Jude,* rev. ed., *Daily Study Bible Series* (Philadelphia: Westminster Press, 1976), 98.

16. Quoted by Ian Macpherson, *The Art of Illustrating Sermons* (New York: Abingdon Press, 1964), 46-47.

17. Cf. Vine, *Expository Dictionary* 3:174.

—5—

HOLINESS AS
RESPONSE TO
THE GOSPEL

ROGER L. HAHN

Law and the Spirit

There is therefore now no condemnation for those who are in Christ Jesus. For the law of the Spirit of life in Christ Jesus has set me free from the law of sin and death. For God has done what the law, weakened by the flesh, could not do: sending his own Son in the likeness of sinful flesh and for sin, he condemned sin in the flesh, in order that the just requirement of the law might be fulfilled in us, who walk not according to the flesh but according to the Spirit (Rom. 8:1-4, RSV).

Contemporary Western man responds to law in a way diametrically opposed to the response of the Bible. The Bible views law positively, as Psalms 1, 19, and 119 amply demonstrate. Our instinctive reaction to law is negative, though we may affirm its value and importance. Rarely does a North American driver not involuntarily ease up on the accelerator when seeing a highway patrol car, regardless of how slowly he may be traveling.

This negative reaction to law is also a part of our Protestant heritage. Law has been set in opposition to gospel. "You are not under law, but under grace" (Rom. 6:14) has been used to justify a wide range of negative attitudes toward the OT. Though such a view of the OT is common, it does not reflect the apostle Paul's understanding.

A correct understanding of Paul's view of the OT law may never make us feel comfortable in the courtroom or around a highway patrolman, but a right view of the biblical law is vitally important for our spiritual well-being. Legalism and antinomianism both reflect wrong thinking about the role of law for the Christian, and

223

both lead to wrong living by the Christian. Paul's delightful resolution of the problem of law is the Holy Spirit!

Paul taught that the Spirit could take possession of the law and internalize it ("write it in the heart" is the biblical phrase, e.g., Jer. 31:33) so that the believer would be empowered to fulfill God's original purpose for the law. Very little contemporary teaching on the Holy Spirit has dealt with this significant role of the Spirit. Our text is the key passage in which Paul deals with the law and the Spirit.

Exegesis

Rom. 8:1-4 is a transitional section in Paul's letter to the Romans bringing to a climax Paul's treatment of the law. Law will hardly be mentioned again in the letter, though it had been at the center of attention in the first seven chapters.

The reading of the oldest and best manuscripts for v. 1 is "Now there is therefore no condemnation for those who are in Christ Jesus" (author's trans.).[1] Verse 1 is best understood as picking up the thought of 7:6. Chapter 7, vv. 7-25 had developed Paul's understanding of sin and the law. Sin had taken advantage of the law and had caused deception, death, and condemnation. However, having clarified sin's misuse and abuse of the law, Paul returns in chap. 8 to the role of the Spirit, which he had mentioned in 7:6.

Condemnation does not merely refer to the juridical sentence, which would mean the opposite of justification. Rather, Paul's thought here is of the actual punishment brought about by the sentence. The point is that those who are in Christ Jesus have no need to continue suffering the consequences of sin controlling the law.[2] There should be freedom from the anguish described in 7:7-25, and v. 2 precisely makes that point.

Such freedom is available **now . . . for those who are in Christ Jesus,** a phrase alluding back to 6:2-14 and 7:4. It is those who have been baptized into union with Christ who may enjoy such freedom.

Every phrase of v. 2 is exegetically important. The opening **for** indicates that it is the Spirit who gives the freedom from the condemnation described in v. 1. The subject is **the law of the Spirit of life in Christ Jesus. The law of the Spirit** has been understood as the authority of the Spirit,[3] the order or principle of the Spirit,[4] the

"Spirit himself in his ruling function,"[5] the religion or way of life of the Spirit,[6] and the principle or system of the Spirit.[7] However, such interpretations reflect modern presuppositions and force Paul into using the word "law" with very different meanings within the same context. It is better here, as always in Paul, to understand law as the Torah or law of the OT. The phrase **of the Spirit** is the common genitive of possession, and the apostle is speaking of the Spirit taking possession of the law as opposed to sin and death possessing the law as was the case in 7:7-25.

Paul further describes the Spirit as the **Spirit of life.** He often associates the Spirit with life in his letters, though this is the first such direct association in Romans. The close relationship of the Spirit and life can be seen in the fact that the apostle spoke of "newness of life" in 6:4 and of "newness of the Spirit" in 7:6. As 2 Cor. 3:6 makes clear, it is the Spirit who makes alive. Thus, several have translated Paul's phrase **the Spirit of life** as "the life-giving Spirit."[8]

The phrase **in Christ Jesus** may modify either **life** or **set . . . free.** The Greek text is more naturally understood if **in Christ Jesus** describes the sphere or basis of the freedom available to believers. In the light of v. 3 it is best to understand that this freedom has been accomplished by means of the work of Christ.

The freedom is **from the law of sin and of death.** The genitives **of sin and of death** should be understood as possessive genitives. Sin's law or sin's possession of the law is what created the bondage described in Rom. 7:7-25. "The law is holy and the commandment is holy, just, and good" (7:12), but "Sin, taking advantage through the commandment, deceived me and killed me through it" (7:11). But when the Spirit takes possession of the law, the believer is set free from the bondage that arises from sin's possession and manipulation of the law. Since Paul had noted in 5:12 that death's tyranny functioned by means of sin, it is natural for him to link sin and death here in v. 2.

Though the Greek text of v. 3 is abrupt, the meaning is quite clear.[9] "God condemned sin—that which was impossible for the law because it was weak through the flesh." This rearrangement shows how the opening clause should be related to the main sentence. God did what the law could not do: He condemned sin. "Condemned" means more than simply pronouncing the sentence of condemnation. The law could pronounce the sentence, but it could not carry out the sentence. As in the case of **condemnation** in v. 1, the reference here is to the carrying out of the sentence. Paul's point is that God broke sin's power, which is exactly what the law could not do.[10] The means by which God accomplished this victory over sin was the Cross.

Paul describes Christ as being **in the likeness of sinful flesh.** This appears to be a carefully nuanced description. To have simply described Christ as "in the likeness of flesh" would have implied the Docetic error of denying the full humanity of Jesus. However, he appears to have wanted to emphasize that Jesus' "fleshness" was the very human flesh in which "sin [had] gained a foothold and dominated the situation until the grace of God drew near."[11] But to say that Christ came "in sinful flesh" would have contradicted the sinlessness of Christ that Paul affirmed in 2 Cor. 5:21. So, it is **in the likeness of sinful flesh** that describes the genuine incarnation of the Christ who knew no sin. Though other interpretations have been proposed,[12] this traditional understanding remains the best explanation of Paul's phrase.

Paul specifically refers to the Cross by use of the ambiguous phrase "and concerning sin." The Greek expression, *peri hamartias,* can be translated as "concerning sin." However, it was also the regular phrase used in the Greek OT for a sin offering. Though the general meaning, "concerning sin," is not out of place here, the structure of Paul's thought from Rom. 3:25 on suggests the sacrificial metaphor.[13]

God condemned sin in the flesh by sending His Son—"in order that the righteous requirement of the law might be fulfilled in those of us who walk not according to the flesh, but according to the Spirit." The purpose construction (in order that) that begins in v. 4 makes the fulfillment of the law the purpose of God's condemnation of sin. As Cranfield notes, purpose clauses expressing God's purposes are also result clauses.[14] God has successfully condemned sin in the flesh by means of the work of Christ, and as a result we who walk by the Spirit fulfill the righteous requirement of the law.

"The righteous requirement," or **the just requirement**, best translates the Greek word *dikaiōma,* which is the subject of **might be fulfilled.** "Righteousness" (KJV) lacks the idea of requirement, while the NASB translation of "requirement" does not show the relation to the concept of righteousness inherent in the Greek root. The translation in the plural, "righteous requirements" (NIV), misses the significance of Paul's use of the singular. The singular "brings out the fact that the law's requirements are essentially a unity, the plurality of commandments being not a confused and confusing conglomeration but a recognizable and intelligible whole, the fatherly will of God for His children."[15]

That "the righteous requirement of the law might be fulfilled" immediately brings Jer. 31:33-34 and Ezek. 36:26-27 to mind. The way in which the Spirit would cause Israel to walk in the Lord's statutes in Ezek. 36:27 and the lack of the necessity of teaching because the law had been internalized in Jeremiah both find their true fulfillment here in Rom. 8:4. However, the passive construction of the verb must be recognized.[16] Paul does not say, "In order that we might fulfill the righteous requirement of the law," but "In order that the righteous requirement of the law *might be fulfilled* in us." It is no human effort or achievement that fulfills the demand of the law. It is the grace of God that accomplished what was impossible for the law because it was weak through the flesh: victory over sin.

The fulfilling of the law's righteous requirement is accomplished "in those of us who walk not according to the flesh, but according to the Spirit." To "walk according to the flesh" is to live with human resources and strength as one's only frame of reference. To "walk according to the Spirit" is to live with the Holy Spirit as Guide and Resource for life.[17] The grace of God working in us to fulfill the righteous requirement of the law is activated by the Spirit's control over the believer's life.

Theological Exegesis

Several significant theological themes converge in Rom. 8:1-4. The role of the law in the Christian life, the reality and extent of Christian freedom, and the relationship of Christology and pneumatology in Paul's thought all intersect in this passage.

In Paul's thought generally, and in Romans specifically, the Holy Spirit internalizes or makes subjective the objective work of Christ. The Spirit takes the work of Christ and imprints it upon the believers' hearts. This is clearly portrayed in Romans 5. Chapter 5, v. 8 declares, "God demonstrates His love toward us because while we were still sinners, Christ died for our sake." Chapter 5, v. 5 had noted, "The love of God has been poured out into our hearts through the Holy Spirit who has been given to us." The objective fact of Christ's atoning death on the Cross is moved from fact to our hearts by the Holy Spirit. The reality of Christ *for me* is accomplished by the work of the Spirit.

In similar fashion the Spirit actualizes the work of Christ in Rom. 8:1-4. By sending His Son, God pronounced an effective condemnation of sin in the flesh. However, the actual defeat of sin in the flesh is accomplished in the lives of believers by the Spirit's liberating possession of the law. It is only those who walk according to the Spirit—that is, out of the resources and direction of the Spirit—who experience in their own lives freedom from the law of sin and of death. Paul will note in 8:16 that it is the Spirit who bears witness with our spirit that we are the children of God.

The failure to maintain the close relationship of the Spirit to Christ is disastrous for the Christian life. When the work of Christ becomes the only focus and the Spirit's applying that work to the heart of the believer is de-emphasized, scholasticism and pharisaism are almost inevitable. Apart from the Spirit, theories of the Atonement become more important than the experiencing of reconciliation with God, theology is divorced from life, thought from action, and there is a form of godliness but no power. When the Spirit takes center stage and Christ is relegated to the wings, subjectivism and emotionalism become almost inevitable. Apart from the content of the life, death, and resurrection of Christ, religious feelings become more important than integrity of faith and life. Experience is divorced from theology, emotion from its basis, and there is much sound and fury but no glory. The Spirit must make alive and internal the work of Christ in our lives, and Christ must give definition to the role of the Spirit.

Paul also deals with the reality and extent of Christian freedom in this passage. Sin does enslave. Christ does set free from the bondage of sin. That is the dramatic announcement of Rom. 8:2-3. Sin by its possession and use of the law ensnares people. Whether by rebelling against the demands of law or by substituting requirements of law for relationship with God, everyone finds himself caught in the law's agenda. But the good news of the gospel is that what was impossible for us to do in our human ability, God has done by the death of Christ. Sin's stranglehold over us has been broken; God has pronounced and is carrying out a sentence against sin; and God has given the Holy Spirit possession of the law so that we might walk in newness of the Spirit's life.

Christian freedom is not license to do whatever we please. Rather it is the freedom to fulfill God's original intention for the law. It is the freedom that comes from the Spirit writing the law on our hearts and internalizing it in the very fabric of our thinking and being. Christian freedom is the freedom given to the Holy Spirit to empower and direct us in the fulfilling of God's purpose in our lives. Far from being lawless, Christian freedom is freedom to love in a law-fulfilling way (Rom. 13:10). As 8:4 makes clear, that freedom is experienced in the daily life of believers who conduct their lives according to the Spirit.

The Spirit's possession of the law helps us understand the role of law in the life of the Christian. The history of the church has revealed a sad tendency toward one of two extremes. There has always been a segment of the church that overemphasized the concept of law. Law became an end in itself. Obeying all the requirements of the law has been seen as the essence of the Christian faith. This extreme emphasis on legalism has been a constant source of paralysis and dryness in the life of the church. When the law is overemphasized, the Spirit has no freedom to create and sustain life.

On the other hand, there have always been those in the church who rejected law completely. They have often, mistakenly, claimed Paul as their authority. Law is placed in opposition to the gospel. Good works, discipline, and order are rejected as legalistic. The law's instrumental value is rejected in an extreme reaction to the legalism of others. The moral failures of antinomians are legion.

For Paul the law is neither bad nor good in itself. Law has a place in God's total provision for the human race. It does provide order and structure for life; it is pedagogically necessary before discernment can develop; and it can provide the frustration that may lead us to Christ. In fact, in general terms it describes the will of God for us in a number of typical life situations. What Paul saw, as had Jeremiah and Ezekiel before him, was that the Spirit could take possession of the law and enable the believer to discern the will and purpose of God that lay (and lies) behind the individual statutes and commandments. The Spirit could then enable the believer to apply that will of God stated in a particular command in an entirely new situation for which no statutes or commands had been given.

In this fashion, a Spirit-directed Christian will be able to meet any new circumstance in any place in life and to discern the will of God in that circumstance. Judaism, via the oral tradition, continued to create new laws to interpret the written law for each new generation and new situation. Eventually the process became so complex and massive that it collapsed under its own weight. How much simpler was the Christian way! The Spirit would write the law on the believer's heart and enable that believer to discern God's will in each new situation. That the kind of life lived by such a Spirit-directed Christian is Christlike should come as no surprise. The whole point of Jesus' great antitheses in Matt. 5:21-48 is the fulfillment of God's original purposes in various segments of the law.

Application

Rom. 8:1-4 is stated in general terms. No particular application of it is given in Romans, although it is likely that the Roman readers saw immediately some very direct applications to their own situation. Because of its general expression it is widely and easily applicable. It is especially useful and important in the discussion of the role of law and of Christian freedom.

The balanced view of law given in this passage is extremely important for a church and people seeking the middle road between legalism and antinomianism. Large segments of the holiness movement have rejected legalism in the final third of the 20th century, and rightly so. However, a significant number of people are being taught to think in an antilegalistic mode, but with no positive content to replace the legalism of the past. Many, especially young people, are practical antinomians and have no sense of discipline, structure, or direction for the Christian life. They are completely vulnerable to materialism and sensationalism. In a self-centered, pleasure-seeking society they are tossed about by every faddish wind. Their witness to the world is a nonwitness.

Rom. 8:1-4 reminds us that life in the Spirit is not life in the winds of fashion and fads. The Spirit operates from an objective baseline: the law. The Spirit has no interest in creating legalists. Neither is life in the Spirit the creating of rules to govern behavior in every circumstance. Nevertheless, the Spirit is not free form. There is always a discernible shape to the life formed by the Spirit, and it is always the form of Christlikeness. Christlikeness happens to always be in the form of the will and purpose of God revealed in the law written on the heart.

In days in which much of Christianity is contentless, and many holiness people are adrift between legalism and antinomianism, Rom. 8:1-4 is immensely important. Choices in sexual morality, choices in financial philosophy, responses to sin in multiplex forms, and ministry to people trapped by personal and systemic evil must arise from the law written on the heart. If it is not the Spirit who possesses the law who guides us, it will be an evil wind that blows in our midst.

Preaching Ideas

There are a variety of ways in which this passage can be preached. One could easily present this text as a map showing major points in one's journey in the Spirit. Verse 1 describes "The End of Condemnation." This means the end of the kind of confusion described in Rom. 7:14-25. It comes to an end when one enters the sphere of **in Christ Jesus** (8:1). Verses 2 and 3 describe "The Beginning of Freedom." Freedom from bondage to sin is described in both vv. 2 and 3, and v. 2 describes the freedom from death that is given by the **Spirit of life.** Verse 4 points to the actual road, "The Way of the Spirit." This is a path characterized by walking according to the Spirit and not according to the flesh. It is also characterized by having the law written on our hearts as the echo of Jeremiah 31 and Ezekiel 36 suggests.

The text may also be approached from the perspective of freedom. Verse 2 suggests "Freedom from Sin," which consists of "Freedom from Condemnation" (v. 1) and "Freedom from Death" (v. 2). Verses 2 and 3 suggest "Freedom from the Law." This denotes "Freedom from Legalism's Bondage" (as implied by v. 2) and "Freedom from the Law's Weakness" described in v. 3. Finally, v. 4 suggests "Freedom from the Flesh," which is accomplished by walking according to the Spirit (v. 4*b*) and leads to the fulfilling of the law's righteous requirement (v. 4*a*).

The response of the Trinity to sin is also seen here (one could speak of a triple whammy on sin). Verse 3 speaks of "God's Condemnation of Sin." This is done in sin's special arena, the flesh (v. 3), and it accomplishes God's original purpose for the law (v. 3*a*). Verse 3 also describes "Jesus' Sacrifice for Sin." This is done significantly as a sinless Son (v. 3*c*) and as a Sin Offering (v. 3*d*). "The Spirit's Victory over Sin" is outlined in vv. 2 and 4. Verse 2 describes the believer as set free from the law of sin and death, while v. 4 points to the fulfillment of the law by those who walk according to the Spirit.

Sermon

The Spirit and the Law

Introduction

The gospel proclaims the good news that we can be saved by faith in the grace of God shown to us in Christ. Our salvation does not depend on the fulfillment of the law nor on works of law, but only on the grace of God available to us by faith in Christ. What relief this Good News brings to us who have become exhausted from trying to be good enough to satisfy God. Most of us have never succeeded in fully satisfying our parents or our spouse, and so the task of satisfying God seems to lie far beyond hope of accomplishment for us. Yet that sense that we ought to be doing just a little bit more gnaws at us. Others among us have rebelled against gnawing guilt, and we now seethe with anger at the whole concept of obligation and rules. Almost all of us live with a sense of resentment against and fear of the law. Is there anyone among us who does not involuntarily ease off the accelerator and check our speedometer when we see a patrol car? Though in theory we may affirm the value of law and order, in reality the law makes us nervous. We really do not understand the Psalmist's line, "Oh, how I love Your law! It is my meditation all the day" (Ps. 119:97, NKJV). In fact, our feeling about law is quite contrary to the way Scripture understood law, particularly God's law. Our text is one of Paul's significant statements about the role of the law as he makes the transition from the failure of legalism to life in the Spirit. Three things are crucial for understanding this passage. We must come to grips with the purpose of the law, the powerlessness of the law, and the possessor of the law. First,

I. The Purpose of the Law

A. The first basic purpose of the law is to order our lives in such a way as to free us from the evil consequences of sin. The apostle states in Rom. 7:10 that the commandment or the law was for the purpose of life. In Gal. 3:19 he specifically declares that the law was added because of transgressions. If there was no sin in the world, there would be no need of the law. If we, and everyone else, just naturally did what is good and beneficial, there would be no need for the law. But we don't, and neither does anyone else. The law has been given to us to restrain us from a series of choices that would be devastating to our lives.

B. A second purpose of the law is to show the sinfulness of sin. In Rom. 7:12-13 Paul states that the law, which was designed to bring life, had brought death in order that sin might be shown to be sin. Sin, you see, is quite good at making out as if it really was good. The agony of a devastated spouse and emotionally sliced-up children never enters the mind of two people tempted toward an illicit relationship. Only the sense of fulfillment and excitement and drama ever enters their consciousness. Sin never shows its own ugly sinfulness. But the law does. It forever holds up a mirror reflecting the blackness and ugliness of sin. That is part of its purpose.

C. A final purpose of the law is to bring us to Christ. Paul understood that the ultimate purpose of the law was to lead us to Christ. Conscientious attempts to obey the law in human strength bring failure and frustration. Rejection of the law leads deeper in the ugliness and consequences of sin. Ultimately there is no place to turn, no answer, except Christ. That is the story of Rom. 7:14-25. When finally the sinner cries, "Oh, wretched man that I am! Who will deliver me from the body of this death?" then God through Jesus Christ is able to transform a life.

The threefold purpose of the law is to order our lives, to ever remind us of the ugly sinfulness of sin, and to bring us to Christ. But the purpose of the law is really in the background of Paul's thought in our text. He is more specifically concerned with

II. The Powerlessness of the Law

In Rom. 8:3 Paul states that the purpose of the law was, in fact, impossible for the law to accomplish because of its weakness through the flesh. The law was powerless to set free from sin; it did not provide an adequate sacrifice for sin; and it was powerless to motivate a virtuous life.

A. The law was powerless to set free from sin. Verse 2 speaks of freedom from the law of sin, but v. 3 tells us that the law was not able to accomplish that freedom. The law that had as its purpose to protect us from the consequences of sin, in fact, actually led us deeper into sin. Paul indicates that sin took possession of the law. The law became the slave of sin. As a slave of sin the law certainly couldn't provide us with freedom from sin. As the ancient proverb instructs, "Physician, heal yourself" (Luke 4:23). The law is powerless to provide freedom from sin. In part that is because

B. The law did not provide an adequate sacrifice for sin. Verse 3 goes on to say that God did what the law could not do by sending His own Son in the likeness of sinful flesh and for sin. That last phrase, **for sin,** or "concerning sin," should be translated as "as a sin offering." God sent His Son as a sin offering. The writer to the Hebrews makes it quite clear that the sin offerings prescribed by the law were inadequate. Jesus is the better, the adequate, the once and for all Sin Offering. The law is powerless to deal with the issue of sin. Perhaps even more telling to us is that

C. The law is powerless to motivate toward right living. In human experience the law frequently motivates evil. How many of us, when we are told not to do something, are not immediately possessed with the desire to do the forbidden thing? Especially when we are children, the prohibition of the law immediately motivates a disobedient testing of the law. In contrast to that, God sent His own Son in the likeness of sinful flesh. The strongest motivation is based on personal relationship. The law is powerless to motivate us; but the love of God demonstrated by His sending His Son to the Cross—that love of God constrains us, it compels us to do far more than the law ever imagined.

Paul makes the powerlessness of the law quite clear, but even that is not his main point. He would never have emphasized the powerlessness of the law unless he had had something positive to offer in its place. The apostle's real concern in our text is

III. The Possessor of the Law

A. As far as Paul is concerned, the problem is not the law. After all, he states in Rom. 7:12 that the law is holy, just, and good. The problem is in the possessor of the law. Paul understands that the law never comes to us in a neutral way; it never comes on its own two feet. The law is always under the control of or possession of something else. Either sin possesses and controls the law, or the Holy Spirit possesses and controls the law. That is the point of Paul's somewhat strange-sounding phrases in v. 2: the law of the Spirit and the law of sin. The grammatical construction is a simple possessive: the Spirit's law and sin's law. There are not two different laws, but two very different agents controlling and using the law. The powerlessness of the law is a result of sin possessing the law and perverting it from God's purpose. But when the Spirit takes possession of the law, God's will can be accomplished in our lives, and that is the joyful climax of Paul's argument in our text.

B. The Spirit-possessed law sets us free. The good news of v. 2 is that when the Holy Spirit takes control of the law and begins to work in our lives, there is freedom from sin's control and use of the law. The powerlessness of the law is overcome by the power of the Spirit, and the purpose of the law is fulfilled in our lives. A very practical result is victory over sin. The power of sin in our lives lies in its control of the law and the way the law is manipulated to bring us into bondage. The Spirit sets us free from that bondage and, as v. 1 declares, there is no more condemnation for those of us who are in Christ Jesus. Sin and its condemnation is not the will of God for a Christian, but the power of sin exercised in its control of the law must be broken by the Spirit. The freedom that results, however, is not freedom from the law.

C. The Spirit-possessed law sets us free to fulfill the law's righteous requirements. This is the message of v. 4. W. M. Greathouse tells a story of a lady who was married to a very harsh, demanding husband. He had a list of rules specifying all the duties that she was to obey every day. Every evening he held inspection and gave a report on all her failures. Naturally, her love for him grew cold and died. She was a slave, not a wife, and she lived each day in the bitter fulfillment of duties. Perhaps providentially her husband died. After some years she remarried, but her new husband was just the opposite of the first one. He was kind and tender. His primary interest in their relationship was bringing joy and fulfillment to her. Quickly she responded in similar fashion. One day while cleaning out some old files, she ran upon the list of rules her first husband had written up. To her amazement she discovered that she was fulfilling every single rule and even more for her new husband![18]

The problem was not the duties or rules. The problem was in the owner and enforcer of the rules. Under new ownership the rules had become written on her heart. In fact she was free from the rules. Her freedom did not mean that she quit taking care of the house; it meant that the bondage was gone, and the rules were simply part of a whole life expressing love to her new husband. The Spirit-possessed law does not set us free from God's will. Rather, as we walk according to the Spirit, the righteous requirements of the law are simply small parts of a whole life of love dedicated to the Lord we love.

Conclusion

We live in a time in which there is growing resistance to the law. In our church we have come through a time of rejecting legalism, and rightly so. There is no room in biblical Christianity for legalism. But too many of us and too many of our children have rejected legalism and have thrown the baby of the law out with the bathwater of legalism. And now we have no understanding of a right way in which the law operates and continues to be significant for us. Legalism is one way in which sin can control and possess the law. But the answer is not no law, but the Spirit-possessed law. Only then can the purpose of God for the law be accomplished. Only then is there freedom from sin. Only then can the goal of law, which is Christ being formed in us, be reached. My prayer for you is that you will allow the Spirit to take control of the law and set you free.

Endnotes

1. Translations are by the author.
2. F. F. Bruce, *The Epistle of Paul to the Romans: An Introduction and Commentary,* in *Tyndale New Testament Commentaries* (Grand Rapids: Wm. B. Eerdmans Publishing Co., 1962), 159.
3. William Sanday and Arthur Headlam, *A Critical and Exegetical Commentary on the Epistle to the Romans,* in *The International Critical Commentary,* 5th ed. (Edinburgh: T. and T. Clark, 1902), 190.
4. Matthew Black, *Romans,* in *New Century Bible* (London: Marshall, Morgan, and Scott, 1973), 114.

5. Ernst Kasemann, *Commentary on Romans,* trans. Geoffrey W. Bromiley (Grand Rapids: Wm. B. Eerdmans Publishing Co., 1980), 215.

6. C. K. Barrett, *A Commentary on the Epistle to the Romans* (New York: Harper and Row, Publishers, 1957), 155.

7. C. H. Dodd, *The Epistle of Paul to the Romans,* in *The Moffatt New Testament Commentary* (New York: Harper and Brothers, Publishers, 1932), 119.

8. Barrett, *Romans,* 155; and C. E. B. Cranfield, *A Critical and Exegetical Commentary on the Epistle to the Romans,* ed. John A. Emerton, vol. 1 of 2 vols., *The International Critical Commentary* (Edinburgh: T. and T. Clark, 1975), 376.

9. Sanday and Headlam, *Romans,* 191-92; Cranfield, *Romans,* 378.

10. Cranfield, *Romans,* 382-83.

11. Bruce, *Romans,* 161.

12. See Cranfield, *Romans,* 379-81.

13. H. C. G. Moule, *Studies in Romans,* in *Kregel Popular Commentary Series* (1892; reprint, Grand Rapids: Kregel Publications, 1977), 139.

14. Cranfield, *Romans,* 383.

15. Ibid., 384.

16. Kasemann, *Romans,* 218.

17. Moule, *Romans,* 140.

18. William M. Greathouse, *Romans,* vol. 6 of *Beacon Bible Expositions* (Kansas City: Beacon Hill Press of Kansas City, 1975), 119-20.

HAL A. CAUTHRON

Holiness—a Matter of Dying

I have been crucified with Christ; it is no longer I who live, but Christ who lives in me; and the life I now live in the flesh I live by faith in the Son of God, who loved me and gave himself for me (Galatians 2:20, RSV).

Evangelicalism has become a popular and accepted cultural phenomenon in recent years. That popularity has included the wide and regular use of many typical evangelical terms or expressions, such as "born again." This language-borrowing by the wider culture is a result of the increased visibility of evangelical conversion, including professions of faith by contemporary celebrities. Such professions of faith have often been made in response to an evangelical entreaty to "receive Christ." But too often that invitation has been given or heard from within a decidedly unevangelical mind-set. It has been interpreted by either the speaker or listener as an invitation to get something for nothing. Popular understanding of evangelical conversion has too frequently exhibited a "What's in it for me?" attitude. And many evangelical preachers have been willing to let that attitude go unchallenged. The result is that far too many who call themselves "born again" Christians understand little or nothing about the discipleship, the ethical response, which is at the heart of the gospel's offer of grace. Conversion has come to be only an experience.

Such a situation cries out for a forthright declaration of the gospel's call to a holy life. Christ's grace is offered freely to us, just as we are. But that grace will not leave us simply as we are. It will change us. It will call from us and produce in us a different sort of life than that which we have been living before conversion.

239

This is the truth to which the apostle Paul testifies in Gal. 2:20. He writes about the radical change effected by the power of the gospel. He can capture its radical nature by speaking in terms of the contrasts of death and new life. Here is a text worthy to be heard in the contemporary setting.

Exegesis

I have been crucified with Christ. What prompts Paul to make this rather startling claim? The answer to that question can be found by placing his statement within its context. Paul's affirmations in Gal. 2:20 come within a paragraph (vv. 14-21) where he writes about the truth of justification by faith. This is his first discussion of this central gospel truth in the Epistle. He has stated that truth in both positive and negative terms in 2:16: "A man is not justified by works of the law but through faith in Jesus Christ . . . because by works of the law shall no one be justified" (RSV). Paul writes in these terms in order to counteract criticisms of his gospel message that have arisen among the Galatian churches.

These criticisms have been leveled by some who have been "troubling" (1:7, NBV) the Galatian believers by insisting that these Gentile converts must submit to the rite of circumcision in order to be fully Christian (1:7-10; 5:2-12). Paul's opponents have criticized him for preaching a gospel that abandons the careful Jewish observance of the law. In their opinion, to preach justification by faith and not by works of the law is to make Christians become no better than "Gentile sinners" (2:15, RSV). This is so, they must have argued, because such a gospel message prompts people to ignore the ethical demands of the law, and thus they are "found to be sinners"; but this then makes of Christ "an agent of sin" (2:17, RSV). To Paul's critics this conclusion would have been a decisive argument against the gospel of justification by faith apart from works of law.

However, it is this concluding assertion that Paul forcefully denies: "Certainly not!" (2:17, RSV). It could be said that those who seek to be justified before God by faith are "found to be sinners" in at least two senses. First, they come to recognize and accept the fact that they have no standing before God on their own merit, but only on the basis of God's grace. They acknowledge that they receive God's word of forgiveness as a gift. They have surrendered any claim to special treatment by God and have in that sense admitted that they are sinners in need of mercy. Second, when such persons live out the implications of their gracious acceptance before God, they do not revert to a life based upon "works of the law" (v. 16, RSV). They continue to live as those who are constantly accepted before God on the basis of His grace. And their nonlegalistic living may bring them to ignore certain of the specific provisions of the law. This was exactly the course of action followed by Peter early in the episode at Antioch, recounted by Paul in the previous paragraph (see 2:11-14).

But Paul's response to both these ways of understanding "sinners" is to deny that either of them makes Christ "an agent of sin" (2:17, RSV). He in fact turns his opponents' argument back upon them. The very thing that they are urging upon the Galatians, a turning to works of the law once one has been justified by faith, that is, submitting to circumcision, will in fact constitute one a transgressor. "But if I build up again those things which I tore down, then I prove myself a transgressor" (2:18, RSV). This assertion highlights the radical nature of the gospel that Paul is defending. Turning back to the works of the law as the basis of one's standing before God would in fact place one outside of God's revealed will and intent. That is the meaning of "transgressor" in this verse: one who breaks, opposes, or otherwise goes against what God has shown to be His intention and purpose for humankind. Paul is convinced that God has revealed in Jesus Christ that the law was never intended to be the way in which human persons found acceptance with God. The attempt to be accepted by God on the basis of works of the law puts one in direct opposition to what God has revealed in Christ, namely, justification by faith. And such an attempt in fact makes one a "transgressor." Paul effectively stands his opponents' argument on its head.

It is clear that Paul's reference to "those things which I tore down" (2:18, RSV) does mean his abandonment of works of law as the means of justification. He makes this meaning unmistakable by his very next statement: "For I through the law died to the law, that I might live to God" (2:19, RSV). The radical nature of Paul's gospel comes into focus again here. He asserts that he has ceased to live under the power and dominion of the law. He has been released from its domination and has entered upon a new life "to God." This understanding of his relationship to the law is the reason Paul argues so forcefully against reverting to works of the law as the means of justification. It is important to note that Paul can speak of believers as having died to sin (Rom. 6:2) in the same way as he speaks of their having died to the law (cf. Rom. 7:4-6). Here is a fundamental element in Paul's understanding of the law. He can define one and the same experience as death to sin and death to law. In his view, to be under the law is to be vulnerable to the power of sin, for as he says in another place, "The power of sin is the law" (1 Cor. 15:56, RSV). It is the law that provides sin a beachhead in its invasion of human life and experience (see Rom. 7:7-11).

But one is prompted to ask just how Paul could have died to the law "through the law." An answer to that question must take into account Paul's former life as a Pharisee. He was utterly dedicated to the observance of the law, even to the meticulous carrying out of the oral interpretations of the law characteristic of the sect of the Pharisees. He has given his own testimony earlier in Galatians: "I advanced in Judaism beyond many of my own age among my people, so extremely zealous was I for the traditions of my fathers" (1:14, RSV). He testifies in a similar manner in Philippians: "As to righteousness under the law blameless" (3:6, RSV).

Paul's zeal for the law led him to violent persecution of the Church in the attempt to destroy it (see Gal. 1:13; Phil. 3:6). After his conversion he came to view that activity as utterly sinful (see 1 Cor. 15:9). And he understood that the law had been incapable of demonstrating the sinfulness of that course or of preventing his pursuit of it. After his encounter with the resurrected Christ on the Damascus road he saw that the law had in fact led him into sin. He writes elsewhere, "The very commandment which promised life proved to be death to me. For sin, finding opportunity in the commandment, deceived me and by it killed me" (Rom. 7:10-11, RSV). Paul had been deluded by sin into thinking that meticulous observance of the law would lead him to "life." But as he came to see, through an encounter with the resurrected Jesus, life did not lie in that direction, only death. His experience, as he now reflects upon it from a believer's perspective, was that even a perfect observance of the law did not provide him right standing before God. And he now sees that it was sin's own deceitfulness that had led him to expect such in the first place.

But Paul's death to the law resulted from more than his own individual experience. It is inseparably connected to the person and destiny of the crucified Jesus. Thus we come to the declaration of our text, **I have been crucified with Christ** (Gal. 2:20, RSV). The end of Paul's attempt to gain a right standing before God through works of law results from his identification with the crucifixion of Jesus. Paul's death to the law is seen by him as a full participation in the death of Christ. This idea is clearly conveyed by the word that he chooses to use. That word literally says, "I have been crucified together with Christ."

The basis for this claim can be seen when we note another context in which Paul uses this same verb. In Rom. 6:6 Paul writes, "We know that our old self was crucified with him so that the sinful body might be destroyed, and we might no longer be enslaved to sin" (RSV). This affirmation follows immediately Paul's earlier statements in the same context: "Do you not know that all of us who have been baptized into Christ Jesus were baptized into his death? We were buried therefore with him by baptism into death" (Rom. 6:3-4, RSV). Identification with and personal appropriation of the death of Christ comes at baptism or conversion. When one ceases to trust one's own efforts at keeping the law and begins instead to trust in God's grace as the basis of a right standing with God, at that point one also identifies with the crucifixion of Christ. Through faith Christ's death becomes one's own death. And that death is beautifully symbolized by the outward rite of baptism.

Paul makes this connection between Christ's death, the believer's death with Christ, and the believer's death to the law on the basis of two important presuppositions. The first is his own understanding of Christ's relation to the law. That relationship is briefly described a few verses later in Galatians: "Christ redeemed us from the curse of the law, having become a curse for us—for it is written, 'Cursed be every one who hangs on a tree'" (3:13, RSV). In His death Christ exhausts all that the law can require of Him, dying as one who has transgressed the law. The law can make no more demands upon Him once He has died. Its authority claims are at an end when a person is dead. Paul applies this very principle to believers elsewhere (see Rom. 7:6). By suffering crucifixion, Jesus incurred the condemnation of the law, but in dying He also satisfied the law's last demand. And in Paul's view what happened to Jesus

was not just for himself. It was for "us." Here is the second important presupposition mentioned above. We may in faith make the
death of Christ our own death because it was indeed His death on
our behalf. The last portion of Gal. 2:20 makes this clear: . . . **the
Son of God, who loved me and gave himself for me** (RSV; cf. 3:13
above).

It is no longer I who live, but Christ who lives in me. Paul's
affirmation in this portion of Gal. 2:20 takes on special significance
when one realizes the peculiar grammatical construction that he
uses in the original Greek. He emphasizes the **I** subject of the verb
live by repeating the pronoun, separate from the verb form, which
also expresses the pronoun subject. His words might be translated
more literally, "I live no longer I." The RSV rendering would effectively carry the emphasis that this wording conveys if the **I** were
underlined and if it were given emphatic voice inflection when read
aloud, thus: "It is no longer *I* who live." Paul also writes in a way
that contrasts this first phrase with the phrase that follows. The
latter might be literally translated, "but lives in me Christ." The
ordering of the words in the original language calls attention to the
contrast between **I** and **Christ.** Each of these is the last word in its
respective phrase. Paul uses this grammatical parallelism to highlight the contrast of these two ways of living.

Paul's declaration implies that his former way of life, before he
came to identify with the crucifixion of Christ, was a way of life that
focused upon the "I." Herein lay what he now sees as the futility of
the attempt to be justified before God by works of the law. That
attempt was misdirected because it grew out of a fundamentally
sinful existence, an existence that was at its center self-referring
rather than God-referring. Human sinfulness means primarily the
usurping of God's rightful place by humankind. The attempt to be
right before God on the basis of human achievement (works of law)
is the most subtle form of human sinfulness. It involves trying to be
one's own savior, that is, to be sovereign over one's ultimate destiny.
Paul's recognition of these realities is demonstrated by another reference: "So then, I of myself serve the law of God with my mind,
but with my flesh I serve the law of sin" (Rom. 7:25, RSV). The
expression "I of myself" is the key here. It is grammatically similar
to the "I live no longer I" of Gal. 2:20. Thus we may conclude that
the condition described here is the same self-referring kind of situ-

ation that Paul implies in Galatians. One in this state may be able to recognize the validity of God's righteous requirement and thus "serve the law of God with my mind." Nonetheless one is still bound in this condition so that "with my flesh I serve the law of sin." The attempt to be justified before God by works of the law is ultimately futile because it is based upon a sinful misappropriation of the law.

Paul now sees that he was in this predicament all during his preconversion experience. But now he can declare, "I live no longer I, but lives in me Christ!" Such a declaration is possible on account of the resurrection of Christ himself. Paul has died with Christ, and he has begun already to live with Christ, or rather, the resurrected Christ has begun to live in him. Here we read Paul's own testimony regarding the experience he describes in his letter to the church at Rome: "We were buried therefore with him by baptism into death, so that as Christ was raised from the dead by the glory of the Father, we too might walk in newness of life" (6:4, RSV). This means in an ultimate sense that believers will come to share fully in the resurrection life of Christ, as Paul says in the very next verse: "For if we have been united with him in a death like his, we shall certainly be united with him in a resurrection like his" (RSV). But the reality toward which that Christian hope looks is not only a future reality. It is a present experience for believers. "So you also must consider yourselves dead to sin and alive to God in Christ Jesus" (v. 11, RSV). The operative power of the old order was sin, which reigned through the law. The operative power of the new order of things is the resurrection life of Christ. That new life is communicated and maintained by the Spirit, whom the resurrected Christ bestows (see Gal. 3:26-29; 4:6; 5:16-25).

And the life I now live in the flesh. This reference to **flesh** does not carry the negative ethical connotations that it will have later in Galatians (3:3; 4:23, 29; 5:13, 16-17, 19, 24; 6:8) and that is also present in Romans 8. Here it signifies merely life in the "mortal body" (Rom. 6:12; 8:11; cf. 2 Cor. 10:3). When Paul uses **flesh** with the distinctive ethical meaning that he gives it, living life **in the flesh** means living an unregenerate life. "Those who are in the flesh cannot please God. But you are not in the flesh, you are in the Spirit, if in fact the Spirit of God dwells in you" (Rom. 8:8-9, RSV). Although Paul speaks in Gal. 2:20 of living **in the flesh** in the neutral sense, nonetheless, there remains a tension between life in the mortal body and life in Christ. The life of the new age to come, "in Christ," has already begun; but mortal life, **in the flesh,** has not yet come to its end. That is why Paul goes on to make the additional declaration in the remaining portion of this phrase.

I live by faith in the Son of God. Faith is the bond of union with the resurrected Christ. Through faith Paul has identified with the crucifixion of Christ as his own crucifixion. And through faith he continually identifies with the resurrection of Jesus as the ground of the new life he already lives, although he continues living in the mortality of the flesh. This is another way of describing life in the Spirit (see Rom. 8:9-11). One entrusts oneself to the present living reality of the resurrected Christ. One is led by the Spirit in terms of this trust (see Gal. 5:25).

Who loved me and gave himself for me. Paul can speak of divine love for humankind with either God or Christ as the subject of that love (cf. 1 Thess. 1:4 and 2 Thess. 2:13). And when Paul describes the death of Christ as a being "given up" (cf. ASV), either God can be the subject, or Christ can be the subject of the reflexive action, as in the present statement (cf. Gal. 1:4—"who gave himself for our sins," RSV). It is divine love that is exhibited in the cross of Christ. And the whole of Christian experience is response to that love so unmistakably demonstrated.

Theological Exegesis

There are a number of truths or principles that our text highlights or at least leads us to acknowledge. First, Gal. 2:20 taken with its context emphasizes the connection between justification and sanctification. We must keep in mind that, theologically, justification refers to a relative change, or a change in relationship or standing before God. Human persons are declared by God to be in right relation or standing before Him, on the basis of God's grace. God makes this declaratory judgment in spite of human sinfulness. The gospel of Jesus Christ calls us to accept or believe as fact that we are acquitted of our guilty past. Our exegesis above has shown that Paul's chief concern in Gal. 2:15-21 is with this reality, justification by grace through faith.

We also need to remember that, in its fullest sense, sanctification refers to a real change of human character and moral quality in respect to sin. It means God's work of grace whereby human persons are transformed ultimately into the image and likeness of Christ. This work begins in the new birth, or regeneration, when we receive the new life of Christ. It reaches a decisive stage of perfection in love in the experience and life of Christian perfection. It will ultimately come to its goal when we share fully in the resurrection life of Christ in heaven. Paul's words in Gal. 2:19-20 not only emphasize the relative change of justification, as defined above, but also speak of the real change of sanctification. His use of the figures of death and life underscores the reality of his transformation from a former way of life to a new way of life. Such a transformation must be thought of as God's sanctifying grace, in the broadest sense of that term. And the principle that we should affirm out of this is the truth that justification leads to sanctification. The doctrine of justification affirms that God's love accepts human sinners as we are. The doctrine of sanctification insists that God's love will not leave us simply as we are. Rather, God's love will eventuate in our ethical transformation into the image of Christ and our being fitted for the presence of a holy God.

A second truth that we ought to infer from our text is that the new life about which Paul writes includes or involves a change of lordship or sovereignty. Paul testifies that the law's rule over his life has come to an end. He has died to the law so that he may live to God. His former way of life was one dominated by the necessity of obeying the law. It was in truth a way of life dominated by his own sinful, self-centered attempt to gain a right standing with God on the basis of works of law. He was attempting to be his own savior, to assure or insure his ultimate destiny by his own efforts. But he is now released from the law's domination, which was in fact the domination of sin. He has come under the dominion and sovereignty of the resurrected Christ to such an extent that Christ now lives life through Paul.

The sovereignty or lordship issue is central to the truth of the gospel. When we are justified, Jesus Christ becomes sovereign over our guilty past. We cease our efforts to atone for our wrongdoing. We submit to His rule of grace and accept just as we are His offer of forgiveness. But when we are thus free from our guilty past, when we have received new life from God, we must then face the sovereignty issue in terms of sanctification. The issue becomes: How are we going to live the new life that God has given us—in continued sinful self-centeredness, or in radical God- and other-centeredness?

A third truth that we learn from consideration of our text is that both the cross *and* the resurrection of Christ are central to the doctrines of justification *and* sanctification. Identifying with the *crucifixion* of Christ by faith means an end to the attempt to be right with God through works of law, that is, justification. But such a faith commitment also means a change of lordship, or indeed a change of the central motivation of one's religious life, from self-centered to God-centered, that is, initial sanctification, the new birth, or regeneration. Conversely, one is brought to faith in God's justifying grace because God *resurrected* Jesus. We know that we are not presuming upon God when we trust in His grace for justification because God has already vindicated Jesus by raising Him up. The resurrection was Jesus' own "justification" before God. It showed that the law's verdict upon Jesus—"accursed"—was not God's verdict. Furthermore, actively living out the new life begun at conversion means experiencing the power of the resurrection life of Christ in an ongoing way. That dynamic life means being enabled to say yes to the Lordship of Christ in a more profound or ultimate way in terms of our future, that is, progressive and entire sanctification.

The context of Gal. 2:20 makes clear the truth that justification is received or appropriated by faith, that is, by trusting God's revelation of His grace in the cross and the resurrection of Jesus. Paul's words in the verse itself make the further claim that God's sanctifying grace is also received by faith. The new life that Paul claims to be living, or rather to have living in him, is possible through **faith in the Son of God.**

Our text also affirms the truth that this new life that a believer comes to know is a lived-out response to the love of God in Christ. This is the dynamic of the resurrection life of Christ at work in the believer. The law had its constraints, but the love of Christ has even stronger constraints. The motivating principle of Christian living is no longer the self-centered attempt to be worthy of God's favor. It is rather the selfless giving of gratitude and profound appreciation for all that God has done for us and in us by His grace.

Application

Our text expresses truth that is quite relevant to the issues raised in the opening section above about minimal concern for the ethical dimensions of the Christian life that is frequent in popular evangelicalism. Our study of Gal. 2:20 has disclosed the importance of ethical considerations insofar as Paul's understanding of the gospel is concerned. We have heard him testify that the reality of justification by grace through faith included, in his own life, the reality of a dynamic change that could be described with such radical images as death and life.

Paul's testimony illustrates the gospel's call to a holy life. Such a life can be characterized as a self-abandoning surrender of one's former way of life. That former way of life could be that of a religious legalist, such as Paul's was before his conversion. Or it could be the life of a profligate, self-indulgent sophisticate in our day and age. In either case, the truth of justification by grace through faith includes the realization that one stands before God as a sinner, and that there is only one hope for a remedy to that situation. That hope is God's own offer of His forgiving grace through the cross of Christ. But such a self-surrender involves a change of lordship. It means that one need no longer be the unwitting or unwilling slave of sin. One can discover true freedom, the kind of freedom that Paul is careful to describe later in Galatians. It is the freedom that comes from serving a new sovereign, the Lord Jesus Christ.

Paul's testimony in Gal. 2:20 also illustrates that the gospel's call to a holy life holds out the prospect of God's own enablement for that life. The dynamic of holy living is not one's own ingenuity, cleverness, or moral fortitude. One does not receive justification by faith and then sanctification by works. One is sanctified by grace just as surely as one is justified by grace. The grace of sanctification is the grace of the resurrection life of Christ, effective in the life of the believers. That grace is the source of the hope that we too can be transformed into the image of Christ himself. The power of the resurrection life of Christ is the power of self-emptying, self-giving love. By God's grace the love of Christ is formed in our lives as we experience the resurrected Christ living through us. This prospect is sufficient reason to be optimistic rather than pessimistic about the possibilities of grace wrapped up in the gospel's call to a holy life.

Preaching Ideas

The following skeletal outlines depend for content on the careful appropriation of the exegesis. They can be either three sermons (in series) or made into one sermon by changing the topics into three main points.

Topic: **Holiness—a Matter of Dying**
A. Christ's Crucifixion: Holiness Provided
  1. Experiencing the Law's Condemnation
  2. Experiencing Sin's Power
  3. Experiencing These for Us
B. Our Cocrucifixion: Holiness Appropriated
  1. Experiencing an End to Our Current Way of Life
  2. Experiencing a Change of Lordship in Our Lives
  3. Experiencing These by Faith in Christ's Cross

Topic: **Holiness—a Matter of Living**
A. Christ's Resurrection: Holiness Vindicated
  1. God's Seal of Approval on Jesus
  2. God's "Renewing/Recreating" of Jesus
  3. God's Response to Jesus' Trusting Commitment
B. Our Coresurrection: Holiness Imparted
  1. We Live Under a New Lordship
  2. We Live in Christlike Love
  3. We Live Through Trust in Christ's Resurrection

Topic: **Holiness—a Matter of Trusting**
A. Trust in the Cross of Christ
  1. It Becomes Our Death to Sin
  2. It Becomes Our Death to Self
  3. It Becomes Christ's Work for Us
B. Trust in the Resurrection of Christ
  1. He Becomes Our New Lord
  2. His Life Becomes Our Life
  3. His Love Becomes Our Aim
C. Trust in the Midst of Life's Realities
  1. With Our Continued Limitations and Weaknesses
  2. With Our Failures and Mistakes
  3. With Our Confidence in God's Dynamic Grace

Sermon

Holiness—a Matter of Dying

The biblical call to a holy life makes clear the means by which we may expect to experience the holiness of God. The words of Paul in Gal. 2:20 highlight an important dimension of those means. The possibility of ethical transformation into the likeness of Christ comes to focus in the cross of Christ. The reality of holiness, created in human heart and personality, necessitates the reality of dying. Holiness is *provided* by God through the death of Christ. Holiness is *appropriated* by us through our faith identification with Christ's death.

God's provision for holiness is accomplished in the life and experience of Jesus. Paul makes it plain a few verses later in Galatians that Christ's death on the Cross involved His experiencing the condemnation of the law. In Gal. 3:13 Paul quotes from Deut. 21:23 the verdict of the law upon Jesus: "Cursed be every one who hangs on a tree" (RSV). Jesus dies a sinner, at least as far as Paul's earlier Pharisaic understanding of the law was concerned.

But for Jesus to have died in this way means that in His dying, He experienced the power of sin. Death is, as Paul makes clear in other contexts (Rom. 5:12; 1 Cor. 15:56), the outcome or consequence of sin. That Jesus died at all suggests that He was under the power of sin.

This experience of Jesus is not simply His own personal destiny, in Paul's way of thinking. It is rather His experiencing of the law's condemnation and of sin's power on our behalf. Paul's words in the latter portion of our text make that truth abundantly clear: **the Son of God, who loved me and gave himself for me.** This same idea had been presented earlier in Gal. 1:4 and will be emphasized again in 3:13. In the latter passage, Paul insists that Jesus, by accepting upon himself the condemnation, the "curse" of the law, in fact redeemed us from the law's curse. It was indeed "for us" that Jesus experienced the law and sin's power.

But the key to understanding the importance of these experiences of Jesus lies in our being able to recognize that once Jesus had experienced death, there was nothing more that the law could exact from Him, or that sin could do to Him. His dying was, in a very real sense, a dying to law and to sin. He was freed from any further obligation to or demand from the law. It is here that the work of Jesus begins to have redemptive significance. He has experienced *all* that any human being can be made to endure in terms of the law's condemnation or sin's unrelenting and autocratic dominion. Death is the end of both of these when anyone dies.

It is because Jesus has shared the common experience of sinful humanity that we can *appropriate* God's provision for holiness. The dying that we must experience in order to know God's provision of holiness is a dying to our former way of life. It is a dying such as Paul described when he spoke of dying "to the law" (Gal. 2:19). Paul experienced an utter severing of his former relationship to the law when he came to know the grace of God in Christ. We must die in the same way to our sin-dominated way of life if we are to experience the holiness that God has graciously provided.

Paul's death to the law took on a particular quality that must characterize our death to our current way of life. Paul the Pharisee was seeking to be right before God on the basis of his own good works, by "works of the law" (RSV). But that attempt was in its very nature sinful, for it was the attempt to be his own savior, to insure his eternal destiny himself. So Paul's death to the law was really a death to a way of life in which he had been his own sovereign or lord. It meant a dying to the self-centered, self-referring way of being religious that was the focus of his Pharisaism. And the death that we must die in order to experience the holiness that God has provided is a death like that. We have to experience a change in lordship or sovereignty in our lives. As Paul put it in our text, **It is no longer *I* who live, but *Christ* who lives in me** (italics added).

But the death we are called to die is not solely our own experience. It is a sharing in the crucifixion death of Christ through faith, until Christ's death *for* us becomes *our* death along with Him. We must come to place our total confidence, our complete trust, in the cross of Christ. We must come to rely only upon God's offer of His grace as the source and means toward the holiness to which we are called. We are in no way made holy by our own efforts. We are made over into the image of Christ by God's grace alone. Our appropriation of holiness, our dying, must bring us to the end of ourselves so that we may begin to truly and genuinely trust in God's provision in Christ.

DAN BOONE

Follow-through

Therefore, I urge you, brothers, in view of God's mercy, to offer your bodies as living sacrifices, holy and pleasing to God—this is your spiritual act of worship. Do not conform any longer to the pattern of this world, but be transformed by the renewing of your mind. Then you will be able to test and approve what God's will is—his good, pleasing and perfect will (Rom. 12:1-2).

Indecisive, fluctuating, vacillating, unpredictable, hot and cold, undisciplined, directionless, tossed by every wave, blown by every wind—do you know people like this? Our churches house many. I imagine you know them:
—people who can't quite make up their mind
—people who scale the heights at each revival and sink to the depths when the refrigerator breaks
—people who glowingly speak of the power of the Word and gorge themselves on TV
—people who are against homosexuality, abortion, and pornography, but have never sharpened their thinking to effectively punch it in the nose
—people who are placid and innocuous as Christ's servants in the world.
Paul calls for decisive action. **Offer your bodies as living sacrifices . . . to God.** Make a firm decision, the kind of decision that is reflected by a steady aim and direction. Contemporary man needs to hear the call of Paul: Make a moral decision. See it through. Stick with it. Don't waver. Don't conform. Be transformed. Live it out. Quality decisions followed by consistent implementation bring a

simple saneness to lives that vacillate and fluctuate. Our text is a call that will liberate us from directionless living.

Exegetical Section

Paul wanted the Roman believers to know that his itinerary included a trip to Spain that would allow him to make a long-desired stopover in Rome. He had no hand in planting the church there, but his interest is evident. To us, his full exposition of the Christian gospel makes the news of his upcoming trip pale by comparison. But to the Romans, seeing and hearing Paul was an exciting prospect. Romans may well be viewed as Paul's portfolio, containing a reasoned presentation of the gospel that he hoped they would support by furthering his mission to Spain.

Chapters 1—11 progress logically, moving from greeting in 1:1-7, to glory in 11:33-36. The major themes are man's exceeding sinfulness, God's righteous judgment, the function of the law, justification by faith, death to sin and life in Christ, life according to the flesh versus life according to the Spirit, future glory, and God's sovereign workings in the history of the Jews for the sake of the Gentiles. The theological section ends with a fitting doxology in which Paul marvels at the sovereign wisdom of God.

"Oh, the depth of the riches of the wisdom and knowledge of God! How unsearchable his judgments, and his paths beyond tracing out! 'Who has known the mind of the Lord? Or who has been his counselor? Who has ever given to God, that God should repay him?' For from him and through him and to him are all things. To him be the glory forever! Amen" (11:33-36).

The next four chapters deal with the practical application of truth to the redeemed life. This section opens with the appeal that is our text. Life in the church, state, and society are full of issues that serve as the platform for Christian responsibility.

The book closes with Paul's itinerary (15:23-33) and personal greetings (16:1-27).

Therefore . . . in view of God's mercy. The great doxology of 11:33-36 would be a fitting conclusion, but where we would put a period, Paul pens a **therefore** and makes a transition from proclamation to exhortation. With one phrase he connects his theological treatise with his impassioned plea: **in view of God's mercy.** The basis of his exhortation (**offer your bodies ... to God**) is the merciful activity of a God who has revealed His righteousness in Christ, enabling sinful man to experience justification, sanctification, and glorification.

Offer your bodies as living sacrifices. The language and feel of 12:1 is sacrificial. Envision the OT worshiper bringing an unblemished, choice lamb to the Temple as a sacrifice to God. The sacrifice had one of two functions. It could be offered as atonement for sin in quest of reconciliation, or as a celebration of reconciliation found. Paul has already shown in his letter that God has provided the final sacrifice for atonement of sin. "God presented him [Christ] as a sacrifice of atonement, through faith in his blood" (3:25). "You see, at just the right time, when we were still powerless, Christ died for the ungodly. ... God demonstrates his own love for us in this: While we were still sinners, Christ died for us. ... We also rejoice in God through our Lord Jesus Christ, through whom we have now received reconciliation" (5:6, 8, 11). We cannot offer this sacrifice. God has offered it for us. In view of His merciful provision, we can respond with an appropriate sacrifice that celebrates our commitment. God's act enables our act.

Offer or "present" *(parastēsai)* is an aorist infinitive, calling for a decisive action. It denotes activity that commences a way of life. It is an operative word in sacrificial terminology. To "offer" an animal in sacrifice is a concise action that bears ongoing results. As the OT believer decisively presented an animal for sacrifice, Paul calls the Roman Christians to place themselves before God in an act of dedication by presenting their bodies as living sacrifices. The argument of Romans 6 gives even more weight to Paul's call for decisive action:

> Do not offer the parts of your body to sin, as instruments of wickedness, but rather offer yourselves to God, as those who have been brought from death to life; and offer the parts of your body to him as instruments of righteousness.
>
> Don't you know that when you offer yourselves to someone to obey him as slaves, you are slaves to the one whom you obey—whether you are slaves to sin, which leads to death, or to obedience, which leads to righteousness?
>
> I put this in human terms because you are weak in your natural selves. Just as you used to offer the parts of your body in slavery to impurity and to ever-increasing wickedness, so now

offer them in slavery to righteousness leading to holiness *(vv. 13, 16, 19).*

As realistically as we once placed ourselves on sin's altar to do its deeds, we now offer ourselves upon the altar of God to serve Him.

The **body** is offered. A correct understanding of this indicates that Paul is setting forth man in his entirety. The body is the instrument by which all human service is rendered to God. It is the organ in which we experience our responsibility before God.

Holy and pleasing to God. These two concepts, descriptive of the living sacrifice, are also reminiscent of the OT sacrificial imagery. All that was set apart from common, profane use, and thereby dedicated to God, became holy. Holy in Romans 12 also carries the thought of being set apart for service to God, placed totally at His disposal. As the animal was burned, the aroma was well-pleasing to God. He accepted the sacrifice. When we offer ourselves totally to God with determination to serve Him, He accepts us. He is well-pleased with us. These two descriptives also feed into the motives of the believer who is decisively offering himself. God does not accept just any sacrifice. Malachi chided the priests:

"A son honors his father, and a servant his master. If I am a father, where is the honor due me? If I am a master, where is the respect due me?" says the Lord Almighty. "It is you, O priests, who show contempt for my name. But you ask, 'How have we shown contempt for your name?' . . . When you bring blind animals for sacrifice, is that not wrong? When you sacrifice crippled or diseased animals, is that not wrong? Try offering them to your governor! Would he be pleased with you? Would he accept you?" says the Lord Almighty.

"Now implore God to be gracious to us. With such offerings from your hands, will he accept you?"—says the Lord Almighty.

"Oh, that one of you would shut the temple doors, so that you would not light useless fires on my altar! I am not pleased with you," says the Lord Almighty, "and I will accept no offering from your hands. My name will be great among the nations, from the rising to the setting of the sun. In every place incense and pure offerings will be brought to my name, because my name will be great among the nations," says the Lord Almighty.

"When you bring injured, crippled or diseased animals and offer them as sacrifices, should I accept them from your hands?" says the Lord. "Cursed is the cheat who has an acceptable male in his flock and vows to give it, but then sacrifices a blemished animal to the Lord. For I am a great king," says the Lord Almighty, "and my name is to be feared among the nations" *(Mal. 1:6, 8-11, 13-14).*

It is not a matter of "any old goat will do." God desires sacrifices that are calculated to please Him. He despises empty commitments, watery promises, heartless gestures flung to Him in thoughtless emotion. David knew this when he wrote, "You do not delight in sacrifice, or I would bring it; you do not take pleasure in burnt offerings. The sacrifices of God are a broken spirit; a broken and contrite heart, O God, you will not despise" (Ps. 51:16-17). His offering to God was one that David knew would be pleasing. Paul calls on the Roman believers (and us) to offer a God-pleasing sacrifice, their (our) total being for His service.

This is your spiritual act of worship. I must admit, I prefer the translation "reasonable service" or "reasonable act of worship" (author). **Spiritual act of worship** *(logikēn latreian)* has given commentators much to write about. The first word means logical, reasonable, or fitting. The second word is used exclusively in the NT to speak of the service man renders to God. **Worship** in its larger context encompasses all service to God. Paul is telling them that to offer themselves to God is exactly what one who has received His mercy should want to do. Mr. Spock would say, "It's the logical thing to do." It is our fitting response. It is an act in character for those calculating how they might please God. As the knee reacts to the doctor's tap with a reflex instrument, so should the heart of redeemed man logically offer the service of himself to God.

Do not conform any longer to the pattern of this world (Rom. 12:2). Two kingdoms coexist in the world. The kingdom of God has invaded the kingdom of darkness, and "our struggle is not against flesh and blood, but against the rulers, against the authorities, against the powers of this dark world and against the spiritual forces of evil in the heavenly realms" (Eph. 6:12). The forces of evil have saturated this dark world with their values, idols, attitudes, and mind-set. Rom. 1:18-32 is a glimpse of the pattern of this world. The schema of the kingdom of darkness stands against the mind-set of Christ. But God has invaded the darkness in the person of Jesus Christ. The new age has broken through into the present age. The result is that we may "declare the praises of him who called [us] out of darkness into his wonderful light" (1 Pet. 2:9). We are no longer living with darkened understanding and hardened hearts. Therefore, Paul says, **Do not conform** *[syschēmatizesthe]* **any longer to the pattern of this world.** Living sacrifices refuse to be shaped by a dying age and a dark kingdom. They fit a new schema: the kingdom of God.

But be transformed by the renewing of your mind. Transformed *(metamorphoō)* is used four times in the NT and is rendered "changed," "transfigured," and **transformed**. It carries the idea of changing from one form to another. Jesus was "changed" before their very eyes on the Mount of Transfiguration (Mark 9:2, NBV, Williams). The biological concept of metamorphosis enables us to grasp the idea in the development of the butterfly. It is interesting that Paul changes words in v. 2. How easily he could have written, "Do not be conformed to the pattern of the world, but be conformed to Christ." Rather, he selects a more dynamic word that denotes an ongoing process whereby one becomes less and less what he once was, and more and more what he is called to be. The caterpillar becomes a beautiful butterfly. Children of darkness become children of light. Foreigners and aliens become members of God's household. "Old man" becomes "new man." Death becomes life. A metamorphosis occurs within and among those who implement the decision to offer themselves totally to God.

One of the best descriptions of this change is a "renewed mind." The perspective changes. How we view ethics, morality, relationships, values—it all takes on a new perspective. We develop a renewed mind-set, a way of thinking. Believers have the mind of Christ and view things according to the Spirit. "Those who live in accordance with the Spirit have their minds set on what the Spirit desires" (Rom. 8:5).

Then you will be able to test and approve what God's will is—his good, pleasing and perfect will. Paul closes his exhortation with a picture of the result. If one decisively acts in offering himself to God, and implements that decision by a refusal to conform to the world's pattern, and by a renewing of the mind, *then* he will be a living demonstration of what God desires for man and from man. He will be living proof of God's **good, pleasing and perfect will.**

Theology of the Text

Grace is seen as the prior and ongoing activity of God that

enables man to make an offering of himself. Trace the roots of all holiness in man, and those roots will lead to the grace of God and His merciful activity toward man. Holiness preaching that begins with man's dutiful working, rather than God's gracious act in Christ, will very rapidly call for more than can be humanly delivered.

However, this passage does support our Wesleyan understanding of synergism. There is a cooperation between God and man. Our salvation is a relationship, initiated by God, entered into by man, and sustained by a faithful God and an obedient, responsive man. Holiness theology must hold these two realities in tension. Remove the tension, and either God is a demanding, legalistic judge watching us struggle our way to holiness, or man is a passive zombie waiting for the mystical blessing. Synergism is seen in the active/passive blending of verbs and commands: **offer your bodies, do not conform, be transformed, you will be able.**

The sacrificial theme also makes this a great holiness text. That which is sacrificed to God is set apart, holy. This shade of meaning adds to the biblical understanding of what it means to be holy. A holiness preacher can easily connect the dots between the OT understanding of separation to God and a current-day understanding of what it means to be devoted to and for the use of God. This bridge of understanding, however, will be cold and mechanical unless we see that what we offer to God is not things done or even chunks of our lives, but ourselves in these bodies in total. The sacrifice is man in all his relationships and connections. This is the devotion that pleases God and reflects His holiness.

Finally, this passage is in the mainstream of the great movement of Scripture. God is at work restoring man to His likeness and image. This restoration has many components, one being man's crucial decision to respond to grace offered by a total devotion of himself to God. Apart from this responsible decision, the renewal of man in God's image is arrested, thwarted, and brought into danger. Rom. 12:1-2 helps us explain the importance of a moment's decision that is in keeping with newfound grace, and also enables an ongoing restoration. On the basis of a continuing justification, man is able to respond in full cooperation toward his sanctification. This will lead in ever-increasing measures toward man's full glorification or final renewal in the image of God.

Preaching Themes

1. God's provision, man's response

Paul assumes that the Roman believers can offer themselves totally to God, stop conforming to the world's pattern, and have renewed minds that model the perfect will of God. Quite an assumption about fickle humans! To leap from the depravity of Rom. 1:18-32 to the heights of 12:1-2 is some feat. But let's not miss "the enabling phrase": **in view of God's mercy.** Man's ability to offer himself is an impossibility, apart from God's merciful activity in Jesus Christ. His quickening work enables a new obedience within man. This new obedience responds as faith that works by love to follow the Lord Jesus. Man at his highest level of moral response is a testimony to God's enabling mercy. Man at his lowest level of moral response is a testimony to what God will not do: work out our salvation in us. Man without God cannot achieve holiness. God without man will not force the issue. God has acted mercifully; man must respond in obedient faith.

2. Gateway to a life-style

God's quickening work results in the new birth, new life, and a new road. As believers journey this road, decisions are demanded. Paul calls for decisiveness in a crucial act—offer yourselves to God. It is a gateway that one comes to on the road of moral responsibility, a gateway that one goes through to continue his journey begun in justification. It is a crisis decision that meshes with a life of obedience, opening the gate to an ongoing process that continues throughout the journey. Mildred Bangs Wynkoop writes:

> This commitment is *reasonable.* And *reasonable* meant to Paul, not simply an acceptable idea, but the conclusion to which all right thinking drives one. ... Paul's exhortation in Rom. 12:1-2 ... is not then an added "upper story" to justification, nor a Christian alternative to higher or lower levels of grace, nor a luxury enjoyed by the excessively devoted and almost fanatical fringe enthusiast. It is, rather, the theological point of his whole argument. *The whole-body presentation is not the maximum Christian attainment but the minimal Christian commitment.* As the Roman letter proceeds, it is seen that all of Christian living, with all its problems and vicissitudes, lies beyond this particular point.[1]

Not all the Roman believers had obeyed in offering themselves.

Deep spiritual antagonisms remained in their hearts. Christians do not always do the logical thing. Paul knew it. And he knew that such antagonism was not in character with the work God had begun in them. Thus the **Therefore, I urge you, brothers!**

The gateway of crisis decision enables us to continue the journey we've begun. The gate is not our destination. We are destined to be conformed to His glory. The gateway must not be glamorized to the degree that the road beyond it is dull, placid, and uninviting by comparison. The road beyond the gate contains the issues in which the decision made at the gateway is affirmed and put into practice. Romans 12—15 describes the road and its many issues: spiritual services through use of gifts (12:3-8), love that evidences itself in a variety of ways (12:9-21), submission to governing authorities (13:1-7), being clothed with Jesus rather than darkness (13:8-14), and dealing nonjudgmentally with the weaker brother (14—15). We can write many more chapters of the road beyond the gate. We would, no doubt, add our current issues that test our gateway decision: materialism, business ethics, sexual morality, stance on social issues, and so on. The Christian life does not end at the gate, it travels on down the road, implementing a life-style of obedience that is enabled by the gateway decision.

3. The Christian's yes and no

Believers are called to be in the world but not of the world. A disciple of Jesus is the salt of the *earth* and the light of the *world* (Matt. 5:13-14). When we live out our holiness in the midst of an evil age, we are "on location," exactly where God wants us. The straight and narrow road that we walk is not necessarily different turf from the broad road that leads to destruction. Both roads traverse the same turf. As a matter of fact, the narrow road leading to life is the middle of the road, flanked on both sides by the broad road. The difference is not in the turf but in the direction of the traffic. Those on the narrow road are headed in the opposite direction.

It takes a determined mind-set to travel upstream against the traffic of the world, to be in but not of the world, to be distinctively different. Two words are necessary: yes and no. Paul's exhortation is paraphrased by J. B. Phillips, "Don't let the world around you squeeze you into its own mould." Here is the Christian's no! Conformity to the pattern of the world requires nothing. Be passive, do nothing, coast, and you will be shaped by the world. Walk in the world without a determination to resist conformity, and the pattern of the world will subtly emerge. Lethargic Christians are open game to the shaping influences of Satan through avenues such as TV seepage, pop music seduction, visual stimulation, materialistic security, and humanistic logic. Casual, placid, innocuous Christians will lack the keen edge of thinking that resoundingly shouts, "No!" to these molding pressures.

The life-style of the Christian must involve more than resistance to conformity, or the watching world will see only a negative legalism. The no is accompanied by a yes. **Be transformed by the renewing of your mind. Then you will be able to test and approve what God's will is—his good, pleasing and perfect will.** The growing believer says yes to the continuing, transforming renewal of his mind. Such a renewed mind not only detects the patterns of the world but also discerns the things of God. Paul wrote to the Corinthians:

> We have not received the spirit of the world but the Spirit who is from God, that we may understand what God has freely given us. . . . The man without the Spirit does not accept the things that come from the Spirit of God, for they are foolishness to him, and he cannot understand them, because they are spiritually discerned. . . . But we have the mind of Christ *(1 Cor. 2:12, 14, 16).*

This yes to the renewing of the mind in Christlikeness is the heart of spiritual growth. Godly patterns emerge in daily habits, revealing the sanctification of time, entertainment, relationships, possession, conversation, sexuality, bodily health, priorities, and attitudes. Transformed people, renewed in their mind-set, begin to grow increasingly in likeness to their Lord.

> *From glory to glory He's changing me,*
> *Changing me, changing me;*
> *His likeness and image to perfect in me—*
> *The love of God shown to the world.*
> *For He's changing, changing me*
> *From earthly things into heavenly;*
> *His likeness and image to perfect in me—*
> *The love of God shown to the world.**

*"2 Corinthians 3:18," *Exalt Him: A Hymnal Supplement* (Kansas City: Lillenas Publishing Co., 1984), no. 69.

This changing, renewing process enables one to have a Christ-perspective on societal issues such as materialism, abortion, pornography, euthanasia, the poor, world peace, and hunger. The world will challenge the Christian mind-set, seeking to belittle, shame, or argue the believer into its mold. But the Christ-mind will not yield because it has a transformed perspective that is pleasing to God. He will become the proof and model of thinking that affirms the good, pleasing, and perfect will of God.

Preaching Rom. 12:1-2

A pastor might approach this passage in three connected sermons. The first sermon would highlight the dignity and majesty of the life that God's mercy has made possible. In a second sermon, the call for a reasonable decision to offer oneself to Christ could be sounded. The third sermon would describe the life-style of a living sacrifice who resists conformity to the world's pattern and is being transformed by the renewing of his mind-set. The outline of the three sermons follows.

Sermon 1: **The Sky's the Limit**

Introduction: Establish the thought that in almost every field there is a limit to what can be accomplished. The limit usually lies in (1) the adequacy of resources, or (2) the commitment of a person. As far as our walk with God is concerned, the sky's the limit. He has provided all the resources through His mercy.

A. God's Merciful Provision (12:1)
   Use this beginning of the sermon to give a brief overview of God's work as presented by Paul in Romans 1—11.
B. Man's Marvelous Potential (12:1-2)
   Elevate the estimation of what can happen in human lives. We can be
   1. A living sacrifice (v. 1)
   2. Holy (v. 1)
   3. Pleasing to God (v. 1)
   4. Distinctly different (v. 2)
   5. Christ-minded (v. 2)
   6. Living proof of God's will (v. 2)

Conclusion: Paul assumes the attainment of such potential. What limits you?

Sermon 2: **The Most Reasonable Thing You Could Do**

Introduction: It is reasonable for parents to discipline, students to study, athletes to exercise, pianists to practice, salesmen to sell. They are expected to "act in character," to do the reasonable thing. The Christian life begins with a turning toward God in faith that obeys. Is it not the most reasonable thing to expect that such an attitude continue to characterize the Christian? Paul calls for "your reasonable service" in Rom. 12:1-2, KJV.

A. It is reasonable to respond to God's merciful provision. (12:1)
   Review the thrust of sermon 1.
B. It is reasonable to offer sacrifice to the One who saves you. (12:1)
   1. Build the OT scene of a worshiper presenting sacrifice after being rescued from Egypt.
   2. Explain the call of Paul to present, not dead animals, but living bodies to God.
C. It is reasonable to believe that God accepts our sacrifice. (12:1)
   1. He makes us holy.
   2. He is pleased.

Conclusion: Paul exhorts the Roman believers toward such a decisive commitment because some have acted "unreasonably." Shall we not keep offering to God a faith that obeys and do "the most reasonable thing"?

Sermon 3: **The Vocabulary of the Sanctified**

Introduction: Computer people are hard to talk with. Their vocabulary is complex. Their terms are gibberish to those of us without personal computers. The vocabulary of the sanctified is simple. It contains two words: yes and no.

A. No—to the world's pattern (12:2)
   1. The pressure to conform
   2. The passivity that compromises
   3. The persistence that continues (to say no)
B. Yes—to a transformation (12:2)
   1. A metamorphosis of life
   2. A mentality for learning
      Deal with the expanding mind-set of Christ that affects every area of living.

3. A model of loving.

Define the life that approves God's will and pleases Him.

Conclusion: We know the words. When, where, and why to say them will write the story of our growth in Christlikeness.

Sermon on the Text

Follow-through
Rom. 12:1-2

We see it all the time.

A struggling family sets a budget to get finances under control. Limits are imposed on spending. Credit cards are scissored. A record-keeping system is established. On paper, debt is liquidated. Everyone agrees: This is the answer to our problem. Two months later, family finances are a fiasco. Why? Lack of follow-through.

A sinking company calls in a specialist. Surveys are taken among employees. The organization is examined from top to bottom. The specialist presents the cure: Hire these, fire those, cut this out, put this in. It all makes sense. The specialist goes back to HQ. Nothing changes. The company goes under. Why? Lack of follow-through.

The Sunday School is declining. The chairman calls a meeting. The problems surface. Solutions are reached. Unity, excitement, and vision permeate the meeting. Twenty percent growth is anticipated. Everyone has a role. Midyear checkup reveals continuing decline. Why? Lack of follow-through.

A believer responds to an inner urge to offer himself totally, unreservedly to God. He kneels at an altar of prayer. To the depth of his knowledge, he commits himself to God for service. He testifies to a deep work of God that thoroughly sanctifies him. Three months later, we find him undisciplined in life-style, excusing himself from service to God, eking out a religious routine that is dull at best. Why? Lack of follow-through.

Paul, in Rom. 12:1-2, exhorts the believers in Rome to follow through on their commitment to God. We need the same encouragement today. Most of us want a relationship with God that works like the electric ice-cream freezer: We put in all the right ingredients, plug it in, and come back later to discover something thoroughly divine. We tire quickly of turning the old crank that mixes the ingredients. Let the electric motor do the follow-through. Human nature is essentially lazy when it comes to homemade ice cream and spiritual development. We like to have it, but we'd rather not be responsible for it.

Let's listen to Paul's exhortation and note the three ingredients of good follow-through.

First, good follow-through begins with *a firm decision.* There must be a fixed, concise choice to follow through. Paul's call for a firm decision is obvious: **Offer your bodies as living sacrifices.** There is something final about the whole idea of being a sacrifice, something that doesn't have one eye on the back door. When OT man selected a choice bull to present as a whole burnt offering, he was making a firm decision. The animal was slain, skinned, cut into pieces, and placed on the altar to be consumed by fire. This was total commitment. The animal begins to char and burn. It goes up in smoke as an aroma that pleases the Lord. We never hear of a worshiper crying out as the sacrifice reaches the well-done stage, "Wait! Stop the sacrifice! I want my bull back. I've decided that I cannot afford to make this sacrifice." The thought is ridiculous. The language of sacrifice is a vocabulary of totality, intentionality, and finality. When we think sacrificially, we think of commitment without reservations, loopholes, or escape clauses.

Consistent follow-through must have a fixed point from which to operate, a point that does not fluctuate, a point that stays fixed. Paul appeals to the Roman believers to make a firm decision, to fix a steady point, to present themselves to God. The attempt of a Christian to bring a disciplined direction to a life still revolving around the service of self is futile and doomed to defeat. Competing "lords" want to begin at different points, neither of which is firmly fixed and indisputably uncontested. If we would ever know the steadiness and consistency of Christlike living, we must make that firm decision to offer ourselves unreservedly to God.

> Take my life, and let it be
> Consecrated, Lord, to Thee.
> Take my hands, and let them move
> At the impulse of Thy love.
> Take my will and make it Thine;
> It shall be no longer mine.
> Take my heart; it is Thine own!
> It shall be Thy royal throne.
> —FRANCES R. HAVERGAL

Knowing that we do not drift into such a decisive commitment, Paul summons all urgency in his exhortation: **I urge you, brothers, in view of God's mercy, to offer your bodies as living sacrifices.** Follow-through begins with a firm decision.

The *second* ingredient of good follow-through is *the rejection of competing agendas.* Excursion from the fixed point of a firm decision will eventually lead to oblivion. Every action and choice must carry the intent and purpose of the original decision.

The world in which the Christian operates has set its own agenda. The bottom line of that agenda is simple: Serve yourself. Approach every decision and issue with the question, "What's in it for me?" Follow-through on the world's agenda is as easy as doing what comes naturally, because "Those who live according to the sinful nature have their minds set on what that nature desires" (Rom. 8:5). The world has imbedded its agenda in us. Self-centeredness is deeply rooted. Those who offer themselves as **living sacrifices** die to this agenda and take on a new purpose. Where they once offered themselves to sin as instruments for the implementation of its agenda, they have now offered themselves to God for the accomplishment of His work.

Though there is a firm, fixed decision that rejects the world's agenda, the Christian is not free of its pressure. Satan still operates in this evil age, seeking to mold us according to the spirit of the age. He will use every resource available to him to squeeze us into his mold. Paul's command rings loudly: **Do not conform any longer to the pattern of this world.** Reject its agenda. Throw off its influence. Refuse to be shaped by its perspective. Remember your firm decision. Operate from the fixed point of your commitment to God. Do not yield to the things that squeeze you. Be who you are—a living sacrifice that is holy and pleasing to God.

Good follow-through begins with a firm decision, is maintained by a rejection of competing agendas, and, *third,* is implemented by *a renewed mind.* The Christian is transformed by the renewing of his mind, so that he can prove by his life what God's good, perfect, and pleasing will is.

The old adage tells us that it is a woman's prerogative to change her mind. It is not, however, the prerogative of a **living sacrifice** to casually decide that he wants to reverse his decision. The act of offering ourselves to God looses a transforming power within us that reorients our way of thinking.

Executives are told to "think big," "think growth," "think positive." They know that as a man thinks, so is he. Paul exhorts the Roman believers to "think Christ." If we would follow through on our firm decision, we must be transformed by the renewing of our minds. We will learn to look at life from Christ's perspective, to have His mind-set, to get His viewpoint, to implement His way of looking at things.

This transformed mind-set will gradually come to see the many pockets of life under the Lordship of Jesus Christ, yielded to Him in obedient service. Time is a gift to be invested for Him. Recreation is a pleasure afforded by His love. Our sexuality is a precious gift to be enjoyed as per His instructions. Our bodies are temples that house the living God. Relationships are the test of character. Our attitudes are reflections of what lies in our motives. Priorities are sanctified by Him. The renewed mind seizes every issue and views it from Christ's perspective, with a determination to please and serve the Father in our response. Good follow-through is impossible apart from this transformed mind-set.

The struggling family, the sinking company, the declining Sunday School, the fluctuating Christian—all suffer from a lack of follow-through. The Word of God bears truth that rescues us from such shoddy, directionless living. (1) Make a firm decision to offer yourself to God as a living sacrifice, holy and pleasing to Him. (2) Reject the competing agenda of the world that seeks to squeeze you into its mold. (3) Think with a transformed perspective and deal with every issue from a Christ-mind-set. The first we can do in a moment of deep faith. The second and third evidence, the quality and content of that firm decision, is magnified in daily practice.

On June 16, 1973, Denise and I offered ourselves to one another in a God-witnessed covenant of marriage. We celebrated a firm decision to be faithful to one another for the rest of our lives. Today that decision still lives. It lives every time one of us rejects covenant-destroying options. It lives every time we refuse to behave toward one another according to the pattern of the world. It lives every time we deal with practical issues from the perspective of Christ. It lives every time we act toward one another in a God-pleasing way. We're following through on a firm decision. We like the results.

Offer yourself to God—totally, unreservedly. Then follow

through. Refuse to conform to the world's pattern. Be transformed by the renewing of your mind-set. You'll be a living demonstration of a life that is good, fulfilling, and pleasing to God. It's all in the follow-through.

Endnote

1. Mildred Bangs Wynkoop, *A Theology of Love: The Dynamic of Wesleyanism* (Kansas City: Beacon Hill Press of Kansas City, 1972), 332.

—6—

HOLINESS—
THE DIVINE
STANDARD

What Does God Require?

Who *may ascend the hill of the Lord? Who may stand in his holy place? He who has clean hands and a pure heart, who does not lift up his soul to an idol or swear by what is false* (Ps. 24:3-4).

Contemporary Focus

When Sam and Virginia began attending our church, I was delighted. They were impressive young professionals with two teenage children. After a few services Sam indicated that they had decided to join our friendly church, and I made an appointment to spend an evening with them discussing the covenant of church membership.

It was a pleasant two hours, but soon I learned that I would eventually have to talk to them about the difference between *inclusive* and *exclusive* membership. Conversation showed that they had little knowledge of the new birth and had had no such experience. There were also habits of the flesh and some casual attitudes in matters of morals that gave me concern.

After a while I invited them to accept Christ as a personal Savior, but they were hesitant to do so. I had no option but to explain that in the United States some churches have *inclusive* membership. These churches have concluded that the best way to build the Kingdom is to accept all people into the fellowship of the church, assuming that after they get into the fellowship, they may eventually become Christians. I explained that that was the case with our Sunday School, and that no confession of faith is necessary in order to become a member of the school.

Our church, however, is one of many churches for whom membership is *exclusive.* I explained that while I did not like the sound of the term *exclusive,* I agreed with its meaning. It simply means that one is to be a believing Christian before becoming a member of our church. I expressed my hope that they would continue in the fellowship, would soon come to know Christ as Savior, and that then, as the confessions of the church became their own, they would join the membership of the church.

The passage that is before us has to do with the qualifications for entering into the house of the Lord. But a far more serious issue is at stake than joining a denomination. Here, it is a question of standing with acceptance in the presence of the holy Lord God. Apparently the ancient Hebrews were exclusive also.

Exegetical Section

This psalm consists of three sections with different styles and subject matter, but the three probably arise out of the same cultic situation. The psalm is presumably a part of the liturgy of the autumn festival, at the climax of which the Lord as the King is to appear (vv. 7 ff.). Verses 1-2 speak of God's dominion over the earth; vv. 3-6 are a liturgy like Psalm 15 that is designed to be used at the entry of the Temple and provide a basis for entering into the celebration that is to follow; vv. 7-10 supply the liturgy that is used during the Epiphany of Yahweh in the Temple.

Our text is the first portion of what came to be called the "Entrance Torah." The question (v. 3) was raised by the pilgrims who had come to celebrate the feast and had assembled outside the wall. The answer (vv. 4-5) is given by the priest and, as is true of Psalm 15, focuses on the basic moral requirements of purity of mind and action.

The fact that this well-known ritual is placed in this psalm immediately following the grand statement of the power of creation is very significant. In a number of places the OT argues the power of God as the One who created all living things (1 Sam. 2:8; Ps. 74:16-17; 89:11-12; 95:4-5). It is just this powerful God that the worshiper expects to encounter, and the reaction has two strong expressions: (1) There is joyful confidence, for a God of such power will certainly provide blessings unmeasured (v. 5). (2) But it is also true that great responsibility is laid upon the follower of such a God.

The interface between these two aspects of OT faith embodies the essence of OT piety. Martin Luther reflected the same tension in this kind of piety in his expositions of the Ten Commandments as follows: "We shall fear God, and we shall love Him."

When one considers the cultic rites of purification that were common in that day, one is all the more impressed by the profound insight reflected by the priests' response. There is no call for a trip to a ceremonial fountain. There is no suggestion of a price to be paid for animals that might be sacrificed. The only qualification is the moral purity of the worshipers in both hand and heart. When moral purity is the prerequisite for communion with God, the cult out of which this ritual came has little, if any, control over the details of worship. It makes this text all the more amazing and demonstrates the profound inwardness of the OT covenantal religion.[1]

Theological Themes

The first and most obvious truth of this psalm is the sovereignty of the creator God. The earth and all that is in it is the Lord's. His power founded it when the firmament was chaotic. He provides stability in the midst of the instability of the seas.

The language of vv. 1-3 reflects the appropriation of a motif that is prominent in the Psalms and runs throughout both the OT and NT. The sea (the symbol of chaos) or the sea monster is the standard symbol of evil. God is pictured as overcoming the chaos at the creation (see Gen. 1:1-3) and thus demonstrating His power over it. Thus evil both in the realm of nature and within human nature is subservient to the Creator. As J. H. Eaton puts it: "The Text presupposes that God has gone out to battle against the Chaos forces and by his victory ensured an ordered and meaningful world. What it now depicts is the triumphant return of the Creator-King to his throne."[2]

The second truth is raised in the form of a question. What are the requirements of any who would worship such a God? Were Yahweh a lesser god, the question would not be so burning. But in the light of who He is, who ought His worshipers to be? The answer is given in three requirements: (1) **Clean hands** is a reference to freedom from the guilt of sinful deeds. It stands for what a person does. (2) **Pure heart** indicates that the foundation of one's actions must be clean. External purity is not enough to prepare one to stand in the presence of the One who created and knows the heart. It stands for what a person is. (3) Truthful tongue. **Who does not . . . swear by what is false** or "In order to deceive." The creator God is also the God of truth, and those who would know His presence cannot deal falsely.

While vv. 5-6 are not a part of the text, they are a part of the setting and have insights helpful to the message. It is important to the author not only to list the entrance qualifications for those who would enter the sanctuary but also to comment on the benefits. (1) Such an individual will receive blessings from the all-powerful God who shall now function as his Savior (v. 5). (2) He will also benefit as a part of the people of God. He is a part of the godly party. Others may boast of their affiliations as they wish. But these are those who not only seek the face of God but seek after it much as Jacob did, wrestling with the angel until dawn (v. 6—see interpretation).

Application

There are problems that often arise when a church does not grow. The people may become satisfied with themselves, exclusive and ingrown. Commitment to the mission of the church may be replaced with concern for the preservation of the status quo.

There are also problems that arise when a church grows rapidly or strives to do so. Identities are often lost, expectations are less clear, standards of behavior that have long been revered may be challenged, and familiar methods and patterns are changed. I once heard a general church leader ask at a time of rapid growth, "Are they joining us or are we joining them?" As the church continues to grow, the question will be asked again, no doubt.

A proper question at such a time has to do with the legitimacy of the inclination of organizations, even the church, to become sectarian and then legalistic in its standard of acceptance. Is it right for a local congregation to refuse full participation to some new Christian simply because he does not share some of the views of the denomination's heritage, even though it is a revered heritage? On what basis can we say no to persons who are eager to share not only the fellowship of the congregation but also the membership of the church? Is there any basis on which we may become exclusive? Was I right in treating Sam and Virginia as I did (see opening illustration)? What if they had agreed to pray the sinner's prayer of confession? What if they had promised to quit the sinful habits in question? How much transformation can be expected in a new convert's life? These are pertinent questions for any dynamic and growing congregation.

Were we willing to be satisfied with a simple sectarian and legalistic evaluation, the task is simpler. The letter of the church law and an insistence on the acceptance of our traditional patterns of procedure, behavior, appearance, and vocabulary are simply imposed. In such a case they are clearly "joining us." There would then be no fear that we will change.

But since we too propose to be a part of "the generation of those who seek him" (v. 6), our function as "keepers of the gate" is less arrogant. We understand that we too are to stand before the awesome presence of the Creator of the universe. So, while as leaders of the church we cannot disregard the standard for entry into her sacred fellowship, that standard must and will be established and enforced by God himself, upon others and upon us.

This only compounds the quandary. For while we must not arrogantly impose our own standard upon those who would enter into the holy place, we must announce, and in some sense enforce, God's standard. We cannot maintain the sanctity of the temple and the holiness of His people and also be casual about those who enter there. The currently popular mood that refuses to stand in judgment on any other person ignores the command of God and the role that He imposes on the priestly function. The question of the psalm must still be asked, **Who may stand in his holy place?** It implies that there are some who are not presently prepared to be there. The priest must call back from within the gate and announce the requirements laid down by the all-powerful and holy God.

These truths make this ancient psalm particularly applicable to our time.

Preaching Ideas

Since the question of whether a church should be more inclusive or exclusive is one on which almost everyone has an opinion, I suggest that the sermon might be introduced with an example, either of an extremely high standard or an unbelievably low standard. Maybe both could be illustrated briefly. This would get the hearers to take a position on the issue and immediately involve them in the message. It could then quickly be shown that this issue is not a new one. Men have been asking this question for a long time. Move then to the text, pointing out that the question has no adequate, man-made answer. We must hear God's response.

Most preachers have viewed the text as having three parts with some combination of (1) cleanness of hands, (2) purity of heart, and (3) truth of tongue, although occasionally the emphasis is upon the first two aspects: (1) clean hands, (2) pure heart.

In order to provide a rationale for the demand for purity, brief emphasis might be placed on vv. 1-2 with comments upon the awesome power and holiness of the God of creation. Such an introduction would call for an outline as follows: (1) Pure Conduct; (2) Pure Thoughts; and (3) Pure Speech. Each of these major points calls for several subheadings. E. R. Conder has an interesting development in *The Pulpit Commentary* that points out that the hand in the Scripture is a symbol of: (1) work, (2) earning and paying, (3) mutual faith and honor, (4) power and conduct, and finally, (5) that it must be washed. He then quotes the famous soliloquy of Lady Macbeth: "What! will these hands ne'er be clean? . . . All the perfumes of Arabia will not sweeten this little hand." But he adds, "The blood of Jesus Christ cleanseth from all sin."[3] Point 2, "Pure Thoughts," calls for a discussion of motive and the radical nature of the work of God that changes not only a man's actions but also his intent.

Point 3, "Pure Speech," calls for an emphasis on the importance of the spoken word in the economy of God. A conclusion would emphasize the cleansing references in the NT that make it clear that the Holy Spirit is the sanctifying and purifying Agent who prepares God's people to stand in His presence.

Sermon on the Text
What Does God Require?

Introduction

Some churches require a congregational vote before anyone

can be received into the fellowship of the local church. We have never practiced that here in a congregation where I serve. Were we to do so, how would you vote on the three following cases? *Case one* is a recent convert. He is filled with joy by his new experience in the Lord. He confides to his pastor that he has lived a homosexual life-style most of his adult life, senses that it is wrong, has left such conduct behind, but acknowledges an occasional temptation to return. *Case two* is a husband and wife team. They recently moved to our city and have a long and consistent background in a fundamental, Bible-believing church. They want to know our stand on evolution, TV, and prayer in the schools, as well as our political preference. *Case three* is a young medical doctor and his wife who recently moved to town. They graduated from one of our colleges but have expressed their view that the church is too strict in its standards. They acknowledge using beverage alcohol socially on occasion.

For which of these would you vote to become members of the local church? All of them? None of them? Which? Do you find it a hard question?

The question of God's requirement for acceptance into His presence has been in the human heart for a long time. All the way back in David's time, as the people approached the place of worship, they considered the holy God of majesty and deliverance who dwelt there and cried out, **Who may ascend the hill of the Lord? Who may stand in his holy place?** You'll find that question raised in Ps. 24:3. As you look at the context, it isn't hard to believe that it is a question posed by God himself. When you glance at the opening verses of this psalm, you see a litany of awesome praise for the great God who created the universe (vv. 1-3).

Man has the ability to raise such questions. God not only raises such questions but answers them as well. His answer to this question of the ages is found in our text (v. 4). *What does God require of one who would stand in His presence?*

A. Clean Hands

The first answer is cleanness of hands. The hands are a symbol of many things in the Scripture. They symbolize work (Pss. 95:5; 111:7; Eccles. 9:10), paying and receiving (Prov. 10:4), faith and honor as in a pledge (Gen. 14:22; Deut. 32:40), and power in prayer

(Isa. 1:15; 1 Tim. 2:8). God seems to be saying that in all these ways one who stands before the Lord must be "clean."

1. But is this not an impossibility? How can any of us qualify if this is the demand? Did the Psalmist fail to understand what he was saying? Isn't he the one that acknowledged, "Surely I was sinful at birth, sinful from the time my mother conceived me" (Ps. 51:5)? Doesn't the Scripture also say, "There is no one righteous, not even one" (Rom. 3:10)? Didn't Paul, with NT insight, finally conclude that "all have sinned, and come short of the glory of God" (v. 23, KJV)? And just to make sure that none boasted in a self-righteous retort, he declared, "You, therefore, have no excuse, you who pass judgment on someone else, for at whatever point you judge the other, you are condemning yourself, because you who pass judgment do the same things" (2:1).

If this is the standard, we are hopeless in our own resources. Shakespeare spoke for all of us when he had Lady Macbeth cry out, "What! will these hands ne'er be clean? . . . All the perfumes of Arabia will not sweeten this little hand." There appears to be no hope for any of us.

2. But if meeting the requirement of clean hands is a human impossibility, then the only answer is a divine provision. The Scripture tells us there is one. David, in his prayer of repentance, cried out in confidence, "Cleanse me with hyssop, and I will be clean; wash me, and I will be whiter than snow" (Ps. 51:7). John, having looked upon the ministering, dying, and resurrected Christ, could say, "If anybody does sin, we have one who speaks to the Father in our defense—Jesus Christ, the Righteous One" (1 John 2:1). And again, "If we confess our sins, he is faithful and just and will forgive us our sins and purify us from all unrighteousness" (1:9).

God requires that we have clean hands if we are to stand in His presence. The one provision for the cleansing of these vile hands is the cleansing blood of Jesus made available by faith in the new birth.

B. Pure Heart

1. Again, it appears that if this is the requirement before one can stand in the presence of God, we have no hope. It is difficult enough to discipline our outward deeds. But it is impossible to discipline the inner thoughts, desires, imaginings. Jeremiah said it

for all mankind, "The heart is deceitful above all things and beyond cure. Who can understand it?" (Jer. 17:9). Our Lord knew the human heart and said, "For out of the heart come evil thoughts, murder, adultery, sexual immorality, theft, false testimony, slander" (Matt. 15:19). Surely God's standard can be met by no mortal whose heart is as Jesus describes it.

2. Is there also a divine provision for this prerequisite? This liturgy is not intended as a requirement placed so high that no one can enter into the holy Presence. The God of *creation* who provokes such awe (vv. 1-2) is also the Source of the clean heart. David says it clearly in his hymn of repentance: *"Create* in me a pure heart, O God" (Ps. 51:10, italics added). A clean heart is the creative work of Almighty God, the ramification of which is amplified beautifully in the NT and often identified with Pentecost. Peter compares the experience of the Gentiles at the house of Cornelius with the experience shared by the disciples on Pentecost when he said, "God, who knows the heart, showed that he accepted them by giving the Holy Spirit to them, just as he did to us. He made no distinction between us and them, for he purified their hearts by faith" (Acts 15:8-9).

According to H. Orton Wiley, there are five divinely appointed means to a pure heart (sanctification): (1) The originating cause is His love (1 John 4:10). (2) The meritorious cause is the blood of His Son (1 John 1:7; Heb. 13:12). (3) The efficient cause is His Holy Spirit (1 Pet. 1:2; 2 Thess. 2:13). (4) The instrumental cause is His truth (John 17:17; 1 John 2:5). (5) The conditional cause is faith (Acts 15:9; 26:18).[4]

The command for a pure heart is not merely an OT misunderstanding. Jesus said, "Blessed are the pure in heart, for they will see God" (Matt. 5:8). Such a command is disheartening save for the provision of the creator God who provided for the heart to be wholly sanctified by His creative power. With this provision it is the hope of glory.

C. Truth of Tongue

Since the cleansing of the hands is readily identified with the conversion experience in which deeds done in the past are forgiven, and since the purifying of the heart is easily identified with the experience of entire sanctification, done as an instantaneous and creative work in the heart of the believer, it would be easy to slide by

282 / Biblical Resources for Holiness Preaching

the third of the three great requirements that God imposes on all who would stand in His presence. We must not do that. There is a life-style that must characterize those who would enter the presence of God, and it is marked by a disciplined integrity.

1. But as it is impossible to have clean hands by our own effort, or a clean heart by our own doing, so is the life-style of disciplined integrity impossible by our own virtue.

2. By this time in the message we are coming to suspect that whatever God has commanded, He has also provided. Jesus promised that when the Holy Spirit came, He would "guide you into all truth" (John 16:13); and Paul could write to the Philippians, "And the peace of God, which transcends all understanding, will guard your hearts and your minds in Christ Jesus" (4:7).

Conclusion

Have you cast your vote yet on which of the candidates should be accepted for church membership? Of course you haven't. You see by now that the real issue is not entrance into the membership of any local congregation. The real issue is preparing to enter into the presence of an eternal God. *What does God require of one who would stand in His presence?* And the question is not one regarding which I am a passive spectator, to cast or not to cast my vote. Rather, I am the one upon whom the requirement is placed. And my eternal destiny hangs on the answer.

The old prophet had asked, "What does the Lord require of you?" and he answered, "To act justly and to love mercy and to walk humbly with your God" (Mic. 6:8). It is not unlike the searching question of David.

The NT more often raises the question, "What does the Lord provide for you?" And the answer is, "Abundant grace!"—grace to forgive the sinful deeds, so that your hands are clean; grace to sanctify the vile heart, so that it is pure; grace to provide strength and guidance for a life-style that is characterized by integrity.

The God of creation calls you into His presence. He lists the prerequisites to enter His presence. He provides grace in full measure so that we may be prepared. Accept His provision today.

Endnotes

1. This analysis draws extensively from Artur Weiser, *The Psalms* (Philadelphia: Westminster Press, 1976).

2. J. H. Eaton, *Psalms* (London: SCM Press, 1967). See also Bernhard Anderson, *Creation and Chaos.*

3. *The Pulpit Commentary,* ed. H. D. M. Spence and Joseph S. Exell (Chicago: Wilcox and Follett, Publishers, n.d.), 17:175.

4. H. Orton Wiley and Paul T. Culbertson, *Introduction to Christian Theology* (Kansas City: Beacon Hill Press, 1946), 316.

H. RAY DUNNING

Holiness as the Prerequisite for the Beatific Vision

Make every effort to live in peace with all men and to be holy; without holiness no one will see the Lord (Heb. 12:14).

Dr. Timothy Smith was speaking in a series of opening convocation chapels at a Nazarene college. His text on Tuesday morning was Heb. 12:14, from which he articulated a sound Wesleyan message on the ongoing life of holiness. The next morning in chapel, as he stood up to speak, a new freshman student in his first week at college spoke up from the front pew and challenged this professor from Johns Hopkins University. "Were you telling us yesterday that you don't have to have the second blessing to get to heaven?" Quietly and unabashedly, Dr. Smith replied politely, "What I was trying to say was that there will be no Christians in hell." This fascinating incident highlights the tension that often exists between a popular reading of this great text and a sound exegetical understanding of it.

Exegetical Section

There are few verses more brilliant in meaning when viewed in the larger context, and at the same time more susceptible to misinterpretation when the context is ignored. It is illuminated from both the passage preceding and the one following, each making its own contribution to exposing the significance of the exhortation. Little

285

is gained in this instance by putting the particular words under a microscope, since the context alone informs their meaning.

It is important to begin with the largest context—the book itself. While disputes among scholars are many, we opt for the view that sees this document as an exhortation to Jewish Christians who are being persecuted for their faith and pressured to return to the old way of the law. The earnestness of the unknown author's appeal betrays the reality of the situation. His apologetic rests on the basic foundation truth that the Mosaic covenant has been superseded by a new and better way. The bulk of this argument revolves around the priestly work of Christ as being better than the old priesthood because it offers a better sacrifice and mediates a better covenant with better provisions that the Mosaic covenant merely foreshadowed.

In a careful study of the priestly service as described in relation to the sacrifices in Leviticus 1—7, it becomes apparent that these services have to do with the purification of the people of God rather than with the justification of the alien sinner, that is, with sanctification. It should be noted that no provision is made for a sacrifice for "willful sin." Those that pertain to any form of transgression specify that they are for "inadvertent sin." Willful or high-handed sin is handled by the offender being expelled from the community unless he repents, and such repentance reduces the willful transgression to an inadvertent one.[1] This explains the otherwise enigmatic statement in Heb. 10:26: "If we deliberately keep on sinning after we have received the knowledge of the truth, no sacrifice for sins is left." Therefore the sacrifices of the cult are designed to maintain the covenant relation by removing the impurities that stand as obstacles to fellowship between the worshiper and a holy God.

Thus the central thrust of our author's claim is that Jesus' sacrifice of himself provides a *real* sanctification in contrast to a ritual sanctification. The cultic offerings did provide for a ritualistic removal of the ceremonial defilement that attached to inadvertent sin, but as the Hebrews author puts it: "For this reason it can never, by the same sacrifices repeated endlessly year after year, make perfect those who draw near to worship. If it could, would they not have stopped being offered? For the worshipers would have been cleansed once for all, and would no longer have felt guilty for their sins" (10:1-2). In a word, he is exalting the greater benefits of the new covenant and exhorting his readers to press on to actualize these benefits in their own lives.

The problem is that they are being hindered in doing so by their circumstances, especially the fainthearted (note 12:12). Hence the author both warns them against going back (or failing to go on) by emphasizing the disastrous consequences of this course of action (or nonaction) and urges them to go forward by holding before their eyes the delights of this new relation to God opened up in the blood of Jesus Christ.

There is great need for encouragement for these people. He seeks to provide this by emphasizing the faithfulness of God to persons in the past. In doing so, he articulates the definition of faith that captured John Wesley's imagination: It is "the substance of things hoped for, the evidence of things not seen" (11:1, KJV). The point of this way of putting it is to emphasize that faith lays hold of the promises of God, and God will make good on His words of promise to those who cling to them. This is made clear by the list in chap. 11. T. W. Willingham once worked through the list of heroes and heroines of faith in this great chapter, demonstrating in a series of sermons that in every case the faith of the person could be traced to a promise that God had previously vouchsafed to them. The emphasis may not be on the greatness of *their* faith so much as upon the dependableness of God's word in faithfully fulfilling His commitments. F. F. Bruce is doubtless correct when he argues that they are "witnesses" in the sense that "by their loyalty and endurance they have borne witness to the possibilities of the life of faith. It is not so much they who look at us as we who look at them—for encouragement."[2]

All this sets the stage for the particular way in which the author in chap. 12 seeks to exhort his readers to pursue the full benefits of the new covenant that include real sanctification and ethical holiness. This exhortation climaxes with 12:14.

In 12:1-13 he suggests two ways in which the goal is to be pursued: (1) by laying aside hindrances, especially "the sin which so easily ensnares" (NKJV) or "which clings so closely" (RSV). This obviously refers to the athletic imagery of foot racing, where every hindrance is eliminated to speed the runner on his way toward the finish line. This divesting includes both legitimate practices and alliances that hamper our Christian race as well as the inward principle of sin that in the NT is understood as self-centeredness, the essence of fleshly (carnal) mindedness.

The "sin that so easily entangles" cannot be understood as a "besetting sin" in the sense of a particular weakness or habit or other type of specific sin. It can only refer to the "principle of sin" that is in need of eradication from the human heart. And incidentally, the metaphors used in this passage—for example, "root of bitterness" in 12:15 (KJV), the term "eradication" used here, or even the term "heart"—should never mislead us, as it has some, into thinking that such "inbred sin" is other than a perverted relation, certainly not some sort of entity of a quasi-material nature.

(2) The second way of pursuing holiness is to "cash in" on the chastening of our Heavenly Father. This refers specifically to the opposition that they are facing and that provides the occasion for their temptation to go back rather than to go on. Such persecution can become either a stumbling block or a stepping-stone. Such ideas may sound strange to some of our traditional notions, but Wesleyan theology has, from Mr. Wesley himself, learned that discipline may become a *means to holiness.* The proper response to the difficulties of life may bring us more and more into conformity to the image of Christ that is the essence of true holiness. Our writer puts it like this: "that we may be partakers of his holiness" (v. 10, ASV).

All these exhortations are reinforced by inviting the readers to gaze upon the example of Jesus. This does not suggest that holiness is simply imitating Christ, but rather the challenge is to pursue with joy, determination, and faithfulness the destiny to which God calls *us* in the same way that our Lord pursued the destiny to which His Father appointed *Him.* Both goals are defined in terms of "perfection," which implies a functional meaning rather than static flawlessness. The "perfection" of the Savior is in His completing His mission. The "perfection" of the believers is in being what God has called them to be.

It is in this sense that Jesus is referred to as the "pioneer . . . of our faith" (12:2, RSV). He has been perfected through suffering, and this is "perfecting in the sense of completing and fulfilling the qualification of the high priest . . . His people follow, enabled to do so because he has both led them and arrived before them."[3]

All this exhortation is given in the context of confidence that the faithfulness of God will fully provide what He has promised. It is on this solid footing that Mr. Wesley based his belief in the possibility of deliverance from all sin in the here and now. God's promises, along with His commands, prayers for perfection, and examples of perfection (the latter three being "covered promises"), assure us that He will make good on His word. Hence faith is the evidence of the yet unseen reality that the reader is exhorted to lay hold of.

In the broader context, we see the people of God as a pilgrim people, or as Ernst Kasemann dubbed them, "the wandering people of God." The Church is compared to the people of Israel in the wilderness period when they were in transition from the slavery of Egypt to the conquest of Canaan. Theirs was to be a temporary camp and not a permanent abiding place, since they had a destiny to which they were called. They could not rest until this destiny had been reached; hence they were a people on the move, going somewhere—to a place of God's appointing.

Likewise, the larger context of NT theology provides us with more light on the text. All experience, in the NT understanding, occurs in a tension between the no longer and the not yet. The "age to come" has broken into history and may by faith be entered into now (see Heb. 6:5), but it is present in only an anticipatory way. Its fullness awaits the consummation when Christ returns in glory to usher in the fullness of the Kingdom.

Much rabbinic theology had put off until the future age of salvation the benefits of righteousness, justification, and sanctification. But the central proclamation of the NT is that those benefits are now available because of the work of Christ overcoming the principalities and powers and potentially releasing man from their control (see Col. 2:15). The same truth is expressed by Hebrews using the liturgical language of the OT cult to refer to the spiritual meaning of what Jesus accomplished by His death on the Cross.[4] It is furthermore illuminating to be aware that the liturgical setting of Hebrews comes to expression in its use of "the blood of Christ" as an efficacious agent in the way that Paul ascribes the effects of "grace" in the Christian life to the work of the Holy Spirit.

When these two great contextual insights are focused on the appeal to pursue peace and holiness in 12:14, it yields the following picture:

The call to holiness is a call to a real possibility and yet one that remains an unfinished reality. Both of these are true at one and the same time. John Wesley has captured this truth in his repeated insistence that "there is no *perfection of degrees,"* that is, "none which does not admit of a continual increase."[5]

Holiness is a completed reality in the work of Christ (10:10), that is, in an objective sense. But if it is a *finished* reality in experience, that is, in a subjective sense, it places a finality to the Christian pilgrimage that stultifies the whole of life. Nothing could be more deadening than to claim a "state of grace" that is the end of all growth. Far better, with the NT and John Wesley, to see the possibilities of grace for this life as freedom from sin and yet a lifelong pursuit of ever more perfect conformity to the image of God that is the essence of true holiness. Here is a delicate truth to preach; like all balanced positions it is easily tipped to one side and readily misunderstood. But the grandeur of the truth makes it worthwhile to take the risk in order to challenge the people of God to "go on to holiness" in the glory of the holiness they have already been given.

In the text, there is an important correlation between the two relationships that stands at the heart of biblical sanctification: to the other person and to God. The believer is exhorted to pursue "peace with all men." Scholars disagree as to the inclusiveness of this appeal. If it is taken in the broadest sense, it then should be recognized as having the same limitation implied by Paul in Rom. 12:18: "If possible, so far as it depends upon you, live peaceably with all" (RSV). But strong scholarly opinion supports a limitation of the reference to all Christians and thus is an appeal for peace within the church. The statement in v. 15 as to the results of the springing up of the "root of bitterness" seems to support this interpretation.

The second appeal is to pursue purity within the church. Almost all commentators agree that this is the more important of the goals, since they insist that it implies that one should not seek peace at any cost, but that holiness should be the prior consideration. However, when we recognize how intimately biblical faith connects the two relations (to God and others) in its understanding of what the Christian life is about, it is difficult to easily separate the two. If, in fact, the corporate dimension is in the author's view (as so often is the case with NT calls to holiness, e.g., 1 Thess. 5:23), and he has in mind peace in the church, the two are inseparable. Jesus would not allow right relation to God without right relation to one's brother (see Matt. 5:23-24; 6:14-15).

Holiness in this text must be informed by the larger context of the Book of Hebrews, as we have been surveying it. The term itself does not carry any static, uniform connotation. Here, it is virtually equivalent to the "perfection" that refers to functioning according to the divine will. See Heb. 6:1 for almost the identical implication of this text. It involves a real change of an ethical nature that can only be effected by the blood of Christ or by the Holy Spirit (see above for theological equivalence of these concepts). It is completely untenable, theologically and exegetically, to translate the word *hagiasmon* as "consecration," as a few versions do (e.g., Amp., Barclay, Moffatt, Williams).

After the statement of the exhortation to pursue **peace with all men** and that "holiness [without which] no one will see the Lord," the author utters three warnings if his appeal is ignored. These are easily distinguished in the KJV since they each begin with the word "lest." They also increase in intensity or seriousness as they build to a powerful climax.

"Lest any man fail of the grace of God" (v. 15). The word rendered "fail" may mean "fall from" or "fall short of" a privilege or a standard or a provision. In the light of the larger context (as above) it seems unequivocal that the latter is the more appropriate rendering. As the RSV puts it, "See to it that no one fail to obtain the grace of God." It assumes that grace offers the present possibility of holiness, and that the problem lies in failing to appropriate these gracious provisions.

"Lest any root of bitterness springing up trouble you, and many thereby be defiled" (v. 15). This danger draws upon a similar metaphor in Deut. 29:18 that refers to "a root bearing poisonous and bitter fruit" (RSV). The word rendered "springing up" carries the idea of "quickly germinating," and the bitterness implies language or spirit or both. It is amazing how the touchiness of self-centeredness can quickly and sometimes violently erupt even in persons who apparently are normally self-controlled.

The result of this outburst is seen to have social implications ("Many thereby be defiled"). Doubtless (as above) it refers to the disturbance that such an uprising of carnal-mindedness may cause within the community of faith. Such behavior can be footnoted in numerous instances, even among so-called holiness people. Nothing upsets the equilibrium of the church or militates against its witness like internal squabbles resulting from the root of bitterness springing up.

The final warning (vv. 16-17) has the most seriousness attached to it, since it implies the possibility of rejection if one does not respond to the words of encouragement to pursue the goal of God's appointing. Its significance depends upon recognizing the distinction between the birthright and the blessing. Esau is not necessarily an immoral person in the ethical sense, but "profane" (KJV) or secular or "worldly-minded" (NEB) in the light of the incidents that inform this reference. The birthright is spiritual in nature including headship of the clan and priesthood of the family. The blessing was a material inheritance including the lion's share of the father's possessions. Esau despised his spiritual inheritance (to be seen as holiness, the birthright of the children of God) and thus lost (by Jacob's deceit, to be sure) the material inheritance that he desired profoundly. But he had sold the greater good and by doing so forfeited the lesser.

As T. C. Edwards points out, the birthright "carried with it the great promise given to Abraham with an oath on Mt. Moriah."[6] Hence we see the unity of the passage once more as focusing on the idea of "promise." God has promised His children a real sanctification that He has provided for them in the sacrifice of His Son, and they are called to pursue with total dedication the actualization of this benefit in their lives. Only in this way will they be enabled to see God both now and hereafter, since only "the pure in heart . . . shall see God" (Matt. 5:8, KJV).

Theological Exegesis

The theology that comes to expression in this text includes the major motifs of the Book of Hebrews, since it is, in fact, a rather summary verse. It highlights:

1. The sanctifying provision of the new covenant. In contrast to the old covenant, the new relation in Jesus Christ makes available a real transformation of human nature. Nowhere does the writer explain how this is possible except to indicate that it is by the effective agency of the "blood of Christ." Whereas the blood of the OT sacrifices sprinkled on the appropriate person or place effected a ceremonial purity, Jesus' blood has real transformational power.

2. The necessity of the pursuit of God's provision. This involves a dynamic understanding that includes not only the pursuit of the "perfection" that is available to believers now under the conditions of existence but also a continued pursuit of the holiness that will never be a full possession until the final consummation. There is no place in the believer's life for a static state of being; it is always to be a "going on" from grace to grace.

3. The importance of interpersonal relations in the holy life. Not only are we a part of a great company of believers of the ages past, but also we live in the midst of contemporary Christians. It is one aspect of the sanctifying work of Christ to create unity among those who are His brothers (and sisters).

4. The great danger of failing to pursue holiness. It is unequivocal that acceptance with God occurs at the moment of justification by faith, but refusal or neglect of the search for the fullness of grace will eventually invalidate that faith. Certainly bad consequences follow from not allowing the Spirit to take and maintain control of our existence both internally and externally.

Sermon Suggestions

Numerous sermon possibilities present themselves, but all must draw upon the context to give content to the text.

If one likes alliteration, he could speak about (1) the Promise of Holiness, (2) the Provision for Holiness, and (3) the Pursuit of Holiness, with the last point emphasizing the outcome being the vision of God.

Using the text (12:14) as the point of reference, one could draw sermonic material from the context leading up to it. Here one could emphasize the necessity for "laying aside" everything that stands in the way of the pursuit of Christlikeness (which is the essence of NT holiness). This builds upon the exhortation in 12:1 and involves a negative emphasis, so it should probably be concluded with a positive affirmation concerning the great benefits of this negative action. Emphasis should also be placed upon the fact that "inbred sin" (the sin that clings closely) is not removed or eliminated solely by human effort but only as we put ourselves in touch with the transforming blood (grace) of Christ.

A similar, but more positive, emphasis could be made by bringing the issue of "chastisement" (12:8, KJV) to bear on the pursuit of holiness. This involves a bit more careful study of 12:2-13 than we have provided in our exegesis here, but the point is that the thrust of this passage is summed up by 12:14. As suggested in the foregoing, this is an idea clearly seen by John Wesley, namely, that there are *means to holiness*. The sum of the point is that circumstances may become the occasion for the development of Christlikeness (holiness) dependent upon the response we make to them. One of Wesley's most illuminating sermons along this line is "On Patience" from James 1:4: "Let patience have its perfect work, that ye may be perfect and entire, wanting nothing" (his version). The possibility of a holiness sermon on this passage is his equation of "perfect patience" with "perfect love of God," which constrains us to love every soul of man, "even as Christ loved us." This is the sum of *entire sanctification.* Keep in mind that "tribulation worketh patience" (Rom. 5:3, KJV), and it is simple to see that the gift of perfect patience (perfect love) is the outcome of an interaction of the grace of Christ and proper response to the untoward irritations of life. Other passages that support the same idea when correctly exegeted are Rom. 8:28-29 and James 1:2-8.

One could also develop a sermon on the dual dimension of sanctification explicit in the text as involving both a horizontal ("peace with all men") and a vertical ("and holiness") aspect. There is no holiness but social holiness, said John Wesley, and here we have it embodied in biblical teaching.

Finally, it is as natural as breathing to identify "God's Reasons for Being Sanctified" or "for Pursuing Holiness" in the three items following the text. Here one should probably preach from the KJV, since its use of "lest" identifies the points so clearly that the simplest reader can follow and even repreach the sermon from his own Bible. The NIV uses "see to it" but mentions it only twice, whereas there are three warnings of the danger of failing to go on to the perfection or holiness that God has provided in the blood of Christ.

Endnotes

1. See Jacob Milgrom, "Sacrifice," in *Interpreter's Dictionary of the Bible,* supp. vol., ed. Keith Crim (Nashville: Abingdon, 1976).

2. F. F. Bruce, "The Book of Hebrews," in *New International Commentary on the New Testament* (Grand Rapids: Wm. B. Eerdmans Publishing Co., 1984).

3. Robert A. Spivey and D. Moody Smith, Jr., *Anatomy of the New Testament* (New York: Macmillan Publishing Co., 1974), 419-20.

4. G. E. Ladd, *A Theology of the New Testament* (Grand Rapids: Wm. B. Eerdmans Publishing Co., 1974), 571-87.

5. Sermon "Christian Perfection," in *The Standard Sermons of John Wesley,* ed. Edward H. Sugden (London: Epworth Press, 1961), 2:156.

6. "Hebrews," in *The Expositor's Bible* (New York: A. C. Armstrong, 1903).

ROBERT W. SMITH

Keeping the Temple Clean

Do not be bound together with unbelievers; for what partnership have righteousness and lawlessness, or what fellowship has light with darkness? Or what harmony has Christ with Belial, or what has a believer in common with an unbeliever? Or what agreement has the temple of God with idols? For we are the temple of the living God; just as God said, "I will dwell in them and walk among them; and I will be their God, and they shall be My people. Therefore come out from their midst and be separate," says the Lord. "And do not touch what is unclean; and I will welcome you. And I will be a Father to you, and you shall be sons and daughters to Me," says the Lord Almighty. Therefore, having these promises, beloved, let us cleanse ourselves from all defilement of flesh and spirit, perfecting holiness in the fear of God (2 Cor. 6:14—7:1, NASB).

Contemporary Focus

Recently a young minister was discussing the condition of his church. He said that many people who had once attended no longer came because "nothing was happening." He was troubled because his attendance was low; I was troubled because I was unable to determine what these people were attempting to find but had failed to find.

Although programs and fellowship are vital to the social needs of all Christians, the gospel of Jesus Christ makes the church unique. The principle that ideas are the foundation of meaningful activity cannot be ignored by people seeking that elusive "something" in a local church. People searching for a church home should

295

seek answers to the following questions: (1) What does this church believe about Jesus Christ? (2) How does this belief make a difference in individual lives, in personal relationships, and in the community? The answer to these questions reveals the relevance of a local church.

In 2 Corinthians Paul is struggling against an idea about the gospel of Jesus Christ he judged to be wrong (cf. 11:1-15). In Paul's absence, preachers came to Corinth proclaiming a "new" gospel that was based on visions, revelations, and miracles. They had convinced many Corinthians that their brand of "power Christianity" was superior to the vulnerable "cross-shaped Christianity" that they had heard from Paul. The battle lines were drawn by an idea about the gospel of Jesus Christ.

If we are to understand the message of 2 Corinthians, we must first understand Paul's gospel. His gospel is centered in the cross of Jesus Christ. Thus, the Christian preacher will affirm Paul's paradoxical statement, "I will rather boast about my weaknesses, that the power of Christ may dwell in me. . . . for when I am weak, then I am strong" (12:9-10, NASB), without excuse or compromise.

Exegetical Section

The church has no greater task than the responsible interpretation and proclamation of the Bible. The preacher cannot proclaim the Word of God if careless exegesis has resulted in a message never intended by the biblical writers. Responsible biblical interpretation acknowledges that each verse has an immediate context —the paragraph in which it is found—and that each paragraph contributes to the intention of the entire book. Thus, for example, the preacher cannot separate 2 Cor. 6:17 from its context and declare that all Christians must isolate themselves from contemporary society because it is evil. This message would not be faithful to the biblical text and would serve to destroy the possibilities for evangelism in our day.

In dealing with any passage of Scripture, the primary exegetical task is to identify its "big idea." Once this is found, the "big idea" is related to the dominant idea of the book as a whole. Based on the literary structure of 2 Cor. 6:14—7:1, I conclude that the "big idea" is embodied in 6:16: **We are the temple of the living God.**

The passage begins and concludes with an apostolic command. The first command is negative, **Do not be bound together with unbelievers** (6:14). The second is positive, **Let us cleanse ourselves from all defilement of flesh and spirit, perfecting holiness in the fear of God** (7:1). The first command warns the Corinthians against making close ties with unbelievers. The second urges them to take positive steps in developing a Christian life-style that is clean and pure. These apostolic commands are directly related to the affirmation in v. 16: **We are the temple of the living God.** This statement refers to that which enables the Christian to maintain his identity in the midst of a secular world, an identity that reflects the holiness of God.

The five rhetorical questions that follow the first command (vv. 14-16) are practical. They clarify the problem exposed by the command. Christians are not to be bound together with unbelievers because there is no partnership between righteousness and lawlessness; no fellowship between light and darkness; no harmony between Christ and Belial; nothing in common between a believer and an unbeliever; no agreement between the temple of God and idols. The last point provides a smooth transition from the command and its clarifications to the major statement of the passage.

The radical nature of the major statement demands support from an authoritative source. Paul offers this support by citing several quotations from the Hebrew Bible. The exegete must be careful to note that the "big idea" of the passage is not explicitly stated in the quotations. Rather they establish the major statement within the broad perspective of God's revelation. This is significant for Paul's theological argument. What was true for the Temple in Jerusalem remains true for the "new" temple. God continues to dwell among His people, and His dwelling place must be undefiled. The quotations support this fact.

A second apostolic command follows in 2 Cor. 7:1. The content of the command is also related to the temple imagery of the major statement. It is grounded in the promises of God that Paul set forth in vv. 16-18. Once again the exegete must interpret the command within the context of Pauline theology, or the point of the passage will be missed. The Christian life is a life of faith. The Christian is justified by faith (Rom. 5:1; Gal. 2:15-21) and is called to walk by faith (2 Cor. 5:7). For Paul, then, faith in Jesus Christ is the essence of Christianity. Therefore, to force the apostolic commands in 2 Cor. 6:14 and 7:1 to the center of the interpretation of this passage is to misunderstand Pauline Christianity. The Christian is exhorted to adopt a life-style characterized by self-cleansing because Paul is convinced that the dwelling place of God has been reestablished within the Christian community.

The following structural outline has been established:

A. First Apostolic Command (6:14*a*)
B. Clarification of First Command (6:14*b*-16*a*)
C. Major Statement (6:16*b*)
D. Support for Major Statement (6:16*c*-18)
E. Second Apostolic Command (7:1)

The exegete is now faced with the most difficult problem presented by this passage. Paul declares that God has chosen a new dwelling place. The location of this divine dwelling place must be identified while remaining faithful to the biblical text. Two options are available. Paul may be saying that God's new dwelling place is the individual Christian (cf. 1 Cor. 6:19-20). If this is his intention, then the significance of human existence is raised to a level seldom defined in the modern church. Or, he may be saying that the church is the new dwelling place of God on earth. If this is so, then the church as the temple of the living God cannot be ignored by modern Christians. The church is no longer an option. It defines the very dwelling place of God in the midst of a godless world.

Frank Carver states that "the NT Church as the temple of God is a familiar figure (I Cor. 3:16-17; Eph. 2:20-22), related to the Church as the body of Christ."[1] Most commentators agree that Paul identifies the church as God's new dwelling place. This interpretation does not deny the importance of God's relationship to individual believers, for the integrity of the church is located in the integrity of individual lives. Therefore, the apostolic commands enable individual Christians to capture a vision of living as the people of God in the present age. It is not enough to know who we are. We must also know how to live in the light of who we are. Paul's commands, then, are grounded in the theological interpretation of God's new dwelling place on earth (the imperative is grounded in the indicative).

Paul says that our self-cleansing takes place as we are **per-**

fecting holiness in the fear of God (2 Cor. 7:1). What does Paul want to emphasize by adding this statement to his command to **cleanse ourselves from all defilement of flesh and spirit?** The Greek word *epiteleō,* which the English term "perfecting" translates, has a narrow range of meaning in the NT. Four interrelated descriptions of *epiteleō* can be determined from its use in the Greek NT: (1) end, bring to an end, finish something; (2) complete, accomplish, perform, bring about something; (3) fulfill, of a saying of Scripture; (4) lay something upon someone, accomplish something in the case of someone.[2] Paul claims that self-cleansing establishes the quality of holiness in the Christian life. The internal work of God becomes visible in the self-discipline of the Christian. In the NT, "holiness is both a gift and a task."[3] Second Cor. 7:1 emphasizes how the Christian is able to maintain this quality of holiness. God, through the activity of the Holy Spirit, sanctifies the believer. The believer, in turn, perfects or brings to completion the purity of holiness in the realm of daily living. Thus, NT holiness is not an illusion. Through Spirit-empowered self-discipline the Christian is able to remain undefiled.

How does this call to self-cleansing and holiness fit into the argument of the letter? The pagan environment of Corinth presented a continual threat to the existence of the small Christian congregation struggling to establish its theological identity and mission. Likewise, the threat posed by the "false apostles" could destroy the infant church (cf. 2 Cor. 11:13). Paul knew that without specific boundaries against these encroaching threats it would be impossible for the Corinthians to develop a church grounded in the gospel of Jesus Christ. In spite of this setting, it is difficult for most commentators to place this passage within the broad structure of 2 Corinthians. Ralph Martin, however, "sees 6:14-7:1 as integral to Paul's closing argument begun in chap. 5 and completed in 7:3 ff. It is not a digression but a logical development."[4] The passage continues Paul's "appeal to his alienated children to believe his Gospel of reconciliation and thereby to break with the unbelieving world with which—however unwittingly—they have identified themselves."[5]

Theology of the Text

As 20th-century Christians we are unable to grasp the revolutionary character of Paul's affirmation, **We are the temple of the living God** (2 Cor. 6:16). Jewish worship excluded the layman from the inner precincts of the Temple *(naos)*. This area was reserved for the ministry of the priests. Here, in the most holy place, the high priest made atonement for the sins of all Israel on the Day of Atonement, Yom Kippur. Paul declares that the church has become the temple of God and that no one is excluded from God's presence.

From Paul's perspective the idea of holiness includes the church. Although Paul states that the individual Christian is accountable before God (Rom. 14:12), he always relates the individual to a group, the church of Jesus Christ. The tension between the individual and the church is found throughout Paul's letters. Paul is certain that the church is more than just another institution within society; it is the temple of the living God (2 Cor. 6:16). No other organization can make this claim. In 1 Corinthians 1—4 Paul asserts that the splintered Corinthian congregation could form a basis of unity in "the message of the cross" (1:18-25). Next, he declares that Jesus Christ is the Foundation of the church, in 3:10-11. Then, in 3:16, he supplies the basic principle that makes the church unique: "Do you not know that you are a temple of God, and that the Spirit of God dwells in you?" (NASB). This principle is reiterated in 2 Cor. 6:16.

The NT church was not a building. It was composed of individuals from various backgrounds who shared a common faith in Jesus Christ as their Lord. First Corinthians 12 tackles the difficult problem created by the tension between the Christian as an individual and the church as a group. Paul's discussion reaches its climax when he states that "you[, as a local church,] are Christ's body, and individually members of it" (1 Cor. 12:27, NASB). Whenever Paul speaks of the church, this idea is the foundation of his teaching.

Since the church is a group of individuals, the purity of the church depends on the purity of each individual. The apostolic commands in 2 Cor. 6:14 and 7:1 reveal Paul's concern to maintain the purity of the church. Paul, however, is absent from the Corinthian congregation and unable to model the purity he expects the church to exercise. Therefore, he writes to them with the authority of "an apostle of Christ Jesus" (2 Cor. 1:1), anticipating that they will obey his words.

The Corinthian situation becomes more complex when we realize that "like Paul and other Christian proclaimers, the opponents of Paul thought of themselves as envoys of Christ, as Christ's personal representatives."[6] How can the challenge presented by this dilemma be resolved? The popular way to overcome the dilemma is by choosing sides according to the personality traits of the preachers. If the Corinthians should use this method, Paul knew that he and his gospel would be rejected. In person he seemed meek and unimpressive (2 Cor. 10:1, 10), and his speech was contemptible and unskilled (10:10; 11:6). Added to this, he did not accept the support of the Corinthians for his ministry (cf. 11:7-9). He accused the Corinthians of only "looking at things as they are outwardly" (10:7, NASB). Thus, the gospel of "power Christianity," which the false apostles proclaimed, appeared more appealing than Paul's "message of the cross."

Therefore, Paul furnished the Corinthians with his own method for solving the dilemma. Simply stated, his idea of the gospel of Jesus Christ is the criterion of judgment for the Corinthian church. Paul could not force them to accept his gospel and apostolic authority. He could only present his idea of the gospel and demonstrate how it related to all the details of his life. The cross symbolized Paul's idea of the gospel. He exposed his weakness to the Corinthians and declared that Christ was at work in him (cf. 2 Cor. 11:23-33; 12:7-10).

Application

Paul issues his apostolic commands in 2 Cor. 6:14 and 7:1 in order to maintain the purity of the Corinthian church. The contemporary holiness preacher should endeavor to proclaim these commands in the same way. They are given to individuals who have been filled with the Spirit. The life of holiness does not originate in a personal response to the apostolic commands. For if the life of holiness finds its source in obedience, then it is the result of our own good works rather than faith. Paul's exhortation to self-cleansing must never be interpreted as self-sanctification. Colin Williams states that "the great strength of Wesley's doctrine is in his awareness that the work of sanctification is a gift, a divine work wrought by God and to be accepted by faith."[7]

The life of holiness, however, does demand rigorous self-discipline. No longer can the believer follow the path of least resistance. For the holy life is lived in a world that has little regard for godliness. If the believer is to live effectively in a non-Christian environment, the boundaries between right and wrong must be clearly established, and principles of godliness must control behavior.

Values shape the life-style of individuals. Therefore, the believer will always be distinguished from the unbeliever by a distinct set of values. According to Paul, Christian values not only are personal but reach out and include the church as well. In fact, Paul exhorts the Corinthians to self-cleansing because the church is identified as the temple of the living God. In that Paul's theological perspective is shaped by the Cross, the success of the church is never evaluated by its physical size or its political influence. The church, as the temple of God, embodies the weakness and vulnerability of its individual members. Nevertheless, as the Temple in Jerusalem was to be undefiled, so is the church of Jesus Christ.

The holiness message does not separate individuals from society or from other religious groups. It creates the possibilities for a new society within society and proclaims a message of full salvation to all humanity. The mission of the Christian church is not to intimidate the world by its power. Its mission is to present the gospel of Jesus Christ to everyone and to show a skeptical world that purity is stronger than power. The church as the temple of God must never accommodate its message to the cultural values of society in its attempt to be relevant. The holiness of God is not to be confined to dusty theological books in a seminary library. Neither is it to be kept within the sacred walls of a building called the church. The holiness of God is to be experienced in the everyday relationships of men and women who have entrusted their lives to Jesus Christ and who know what it means to experience the presence of God in the community of believers. Apart from this sphere, the message of holiness is meaningless!

Preaching Ideas

Three sermon ideas immediately leap from this passage and beg to be preached.

The first sermon focuses on the "big idea" of the entire passage, **we are the temple of the living God** (2 Cor. 6:16). The other parts of the passage serve to illuminate this truth. The sermon could begin with a brief account of God's promise to dwell among His people. This word was first spoken to Moses as the children of Israel camped in the wilderness. The first point would establish the significance of Paul's theological designation of the church as the temple of the living God. The preacher could stress the fact that Christians have unrestricted access to the presence of God in the community of believers. A second point could emphasize the apostolic commands (6:14; 7:1) and exhort believers to accept self-cleansing as a vital part of their relationship to God and to the church. "We Are the Temple of God" would be an appropriate title for the sermon.

A second sermon, "Holiness and Human Responsibility," would use 2 Cor. 7:1 as its text. After explaining that many individuals struggle against irresponsibility, the first point could emphasize the necessity for Christians to perfect the quality of holiness in their lives by a life-style that represents the holiness of God. The preacher could realistically develop a model of life that exemplifies a responsible relationship to God. The second point could emphasize how this responsible life-style is related to the church as the temple of the living God. We take responsibility for our own lives so that we may become responsible to the body of Christ. Do not forget the importance of the Cross in Paul's thought. The unity of the church is found in the cross of Christ.

A third sermon could find its center in the promises of God cited in 2 Cor. 6:16-18. This sermon would be more difficult to prepare, but the impact of its message could provide hope to Christians searching for identity in contemporary society. The first point could place the promises in their historical and theological contexts in the Hebrew Bible. The preacher could emphasize that the roots of our Christian faith grow out of these promises. A second point could point out the four "I will" statements by which God speaks to His people. Then the two statements beginning with "they shall" and "you shall" could stress God's concern to establish family ties with His people. A final point could affirm that those who have faith in Jesus Christ are now the people of God. The "big idea" of the passage could be used to solidify this point.

Sermon

Keeping the Temple Clean

Purpose: To encourage Spirit-filled believers to accept personal responsibility for the continuing purity of their lives.

Introduction

Western culture does not attribute great value to custodial duties. The qualifications for janitorial work seldom include a college education or specialized training. Janitorial service is rarely given adequate monetary reward. We take the janitor for granted. We only respond when the job has not been well done.

Second Cor. 7:1 establishes a job description for Spirit-filled Christians. Our job is to keep our part of the temple of God clean. We cannot ignore the value God gives to this job.

How can we fulfill this vital, God-given job?

A. *We Recognize the Value of the Temple* (2 Cor. 6:16)

1. God's Presence Makes the Temple Significant

Exod. 25:8 records an incredible request. The God of all creation asks Moses to construct a sanctuary as His dwelling place on earth. The remaining chapters of Exodus provide elaborate details for the construction of the Tabernacle and the ministry of the priesthood. Had we seen the Tabernacle in its wilderness setting, we would have been overwhelmed by its splendor. Later, during the reign of Solomon, a permanent dwelling place for the presence of God was built. After the destruction of Solomon's Temple, a second Temple was constructed, and finally a third under the reign of Herod the Great.

Although each Temple was magnificent, it was the presence of God that made the Temple unique among all the buildings of the world. For this reason, the Israelites took great care to protect its purity.

2. God's Temple Is No Longer a Building

Paul proclaimed that the coming of Jesus Christ into the world created a new relationship between God and humanity. He identified the children of Abraham as those who share Abraham's faith in God (Romans 4). He went so far as to relocate the dwelling place of God on earth. Where is God's dwelling place now? It is the church! If we could capture the importance of this fact, it would revolutionize the 20th-century church. The church is more than buildings and budgets, more than programs and policies; it is the dwelling place of God on earth. Its purity must be maintained so that the presence of God may be revealed to the entire world.

B. *We Locate the Source of Contamination* (2 Cor. 6:14)

1. Our Secular Environment

Ancient Corinth was a cosmopolitan city dominated by paganism. How could the Christian church, with no buildings and limited resources, make an impact in a city in which there were magnificent pagan temples and alluring worship rituals? The contemporary church must answer the same question as it is asked in our cultural setting. Our day is filled with marvelous attractions that appear innocent in themselves but that make no claim to honor the God in whom we have entrusted our lives. "In God We Trust" is stamped on our coins but is only frequently confessed as an important principle of life. Undisciplined leisure time has made us all susceptible to the lure of questionable forms of entertainment. Where is the presence of God in such a world as ours? How can we keep the temple of God clean when the filth of our world swirls around us? The apostolic command in 2 Cor. 6:14 demonstrates Paul's concern for this issue.

2. An Unacceptable Gospel

To make matters worse, the Christian church is unable to identify and proclaim a common message of the gospel. Some equate the gospel with success and talk about a "bottom line" as though the gospel of Jesus Christ were a commodity on the New York Stock Exchange. Others isolate themselves from society by a life-style that could compete with the austere monastic orders of the Middle Ages. The church of Jesus Christ must never forget that it can be contaminated by a misconception of the gospel. Paul's admonition against being bound together with unbelievers does not merely apply to our culture; it also involves the doctrines and teaching we confess. This is not a new problem; Paul faced it in Corinth (cf. 2 Cor. 11:4).

Thus, the church can be contaminated from within as well as from without. The gospel must become so clear to us that we can keep the temple of God clean from either form of pollution.

C. *We Carry Out the Challenge of Our Job Description* (2 Cor. 7:1)

Having established the internal and external sources of contamination, what does our job description call us to do?

1. The Janitor and the World

The life of holiness is directly related to the holiness of God. We are concerned about holy living because we serve a holy God who has cleansed our hearts from sin. Therefore, the apostolic command to accept a life-style of cleansing is not a burden. It clarifies our personal activity in everyday Christian living.

As spiritual janitors we must understand that sin separates humanity from God. We must not participate in activities that pollute the temple of God. Although the world has never been a friend of the church, we must keep the values of the church from being swallowed up by the values of our culture. The janitor's "mop and bucket" are, in reality, a discerning mind and the gospel of Jesus Christ by which the values of the world are cleansed from the temple of God.

2. The Janitor and the Church

We are responsible for our own purity before God. After we have adopted Paul's call of self-cleansing as a way of life, we can begin to encourage others to adopt a similar way of life in order that the temple of God may be kept clean. The self-discipline of cleansing refers not only to the avoidance of sin but also to ideas, and specifically to our idea, of the gospel. The cross of Jesus Christ serves as our symbol of a life willing to take the risk to stand against the values of a secular culture. Any other symbol would distort the gospel Paul gave his life to proclaim.

Conclusion

The imagery of this passage is so vivid that it is difficult to miss Paul's point. Am I willing to become a janitor in the temple of God? Am I willing to pick up a mop and bucket and begin to take responsibility for the spiritual cleanliness of my life so that the temple of God may remain undefiled?

God has cleansed our hearts from sin. Now we can do no less than to keep our lives—our part of the temple—clean.

Endnotes

1. Frank G. Carver, "The Second Epistle of Paul to the Corinthians," vol. 8 in *Beacon Bible Commentary,* ed. A. F. Harper et al. (Kansas City: Beacon Hill Press of Kansas City, 1968), 565.

2. Walter Bauer, *A Greek-English Lexicon of the New Testament and Other Early Christian Literature,* trans. W. F. Arndt and F. W. Gingrich, 2d ed.; rev. and aug. F. W. Gingrich and F. W. Danker (Chicago: University of Chicago Press, 1979), 302.

3. Carver, *Beacon Bible Commentary* 8:567.

4. Ralph P. Martin, *2 Corinthians,* in *Word Biblical Commentary,* ed. David A. Hubbard (Waco, Tex.: Word Books, Publishers, 1986), 40:195.

5. Ibid.

6. Dieter Georgi, *The Opponents of Paul in Second Corinthians: A Study of Religious Propaganda in Late Antiquity,* trans. Harold Attridge et al. (Philadelphia: Fortress Press, 1986), 32.

7. Colin Williams, *John Wesley's Theology Today* (London: Epworth Press, 1962), 186.

—7—

HOLINESS
AND
MINISTRY

————

DANIEL SPROSS

Holiness in the Pastoral Epistles

For many, the term *holiness preaching* conjures up a very narrow image. They understand a holiness sermon to be the proclamation of a particular structure of religious experience. This is not difficult to explain, since that view was almost inevitable with a movement that emerged out of the controversies of the post-Civil War holiness revival. However, now that the clouds of doctrinal battle have cleared away, it is more appropriate to recognize the comprehensive nature of holiness preaching.

The way holiness should pervade the whole of the minister's function and inform all his preaching can be seen most clearly in those letters addressed to ministers, the ones we refer to as the Pastoral Epistles: 1 and 2 Timothy and Titus. And yet they have not been widely used as a resource for understanding the holiness message. They have been appealed to as resource for addressing the issue of the inspiration of Scripture, the expectation of church leaders in terms of personal behavior and conduct, or the role of women in the church. Rare indeed is the classical holiness sermon based on and drawn out from the Pastoral Epistles, despite the fact that they are significantly endowed with the terminology of holiness.

How can this be explained? It is quite possible that the concepts of sanctification and holiness occurring in the more frequently used texts found in Romans, 1 and 2 Thessalonians, and 1 and 2 Corinthians may be more explicit, definite, and clear than those to be found in the Pastorals. In the settings of these earlier Pauline letters, the force and thrust of the passages may lend themselves more readily to the preaching task.

Yet if the holiness message is indeed to be found "within the warp and woof of the entire Bible," then part of the concern of the holiness preacher ought to be to find it, examine it, and proclaim it from every sector of the canon. It is even possible that the greater effort required to mine the less overt sections may result in some new and fresh insights that will broaden, deepen, and enrich the total understanding of the holiness message itself. That clearly seems to be the case with the letters looked at in this essay.

Exegetical Considerations

One of the first steps in carrying out the exegetical task is determining the historical setting, which includes identifying the principals involved, both author and recipient(s). In looking at these historical-critical issues in the Pastoral Epistles, the main concern for those who hold to the traditional view of the Pauline authorship is finding a place in our existing knowledge of his ministry where they fit. Simply stated, the issue is whether these Epistles were actually authored by Paul or were written later than Paul's own lifetime, incorporating his thought as well as interpretations of his thought to address issues that emerged in the church after his death. The significant point for exegesis is that the situations addressed in the Pastoral Epistles do indicate a later point in time and a somewhat different setting than previous letters of Paul tend to address or that can be identified in Luke's account of his ministry in Acts. The acceptance of that point makes it possible to move beyond the arguments about authorship and dating that dominate much contemporary discussion and permits interpretation to proceed, informed by the concerns about the actual life setting of the Pastorals. These letters are addressed to younger men charged with the responsibility of setting in order the Christian church in and around Ephesus (Timothy) and Crete (Titus). They are given instruction concerning their own personal work and character as ministers and guidelines for developing a Christian community that truly reflects the gospel of Christ. Our analysis of the Pastorals will take two forms. First, we shall consider the meaning and uses of key terms within the letters. Second, we will examine the concept of "sound doctrine" that plays such a central role in these Epistles in order to better understand the minister's task of "preaching scriptural holiness." Properly understood, "sound doctrine" appears to be inclusive of significant holiness content, particularly in the setting of the situations at Ephesus and Crete.

Holiness Vocabulary

The standard sanctification/holiness vocabulary appearing in the Pastorals includes terms based on the Greek root *hagios,* which means "holy" or "set apart"; terms based on the Greek root *katharos,* which means "pure" or "clean"; and terms based on the Greek root *hosios,* which means "holy" or "devout."

The Pastorals provide an interesting array of such terms. In 1 Timothy the term *hosios* occurs in 2:8; the term *hagiasmos* occurs in 2:15; the term *hagiadzō* occurs in 4:5. The cognates of *katharos* occur in 1:5 and 3:9. In 2 Timothy, *hagios* appears in 1:9, *hagiadzō* appears in 2:21, and *katharos* appears in 1:3 and 2:22. In Titus, there are no cognates of *hagios,* but there is one occurrence of *hosios* in 1:8. There are two cognates of *katharos* in Titus, *katharos* in 1:15 and *katharidzō* in 2:14.

However, the mere presence of holiness terminology does not necessarily indicate a clearly presented foundation for the preaching of biblical holiness. When holiness vocabulary is employed in strings of synonymous terms all pointing to the basic redemption event, for instance, sound exegesis requires that care be exercised in attempting to impose a more narrow understanding upon the passage than the context will admit. We must thus ask the critical question, "How are these terms used?" In 1 Tim. 1:5, the concept of "pure" *(katharas)* is used to describe the "heart" and is parallel to the use of "good" (which modifies "conscience") and "sincere" (which modifies "faith"). [See exegesis of this text in this volume.] In 2:8, "holy" *(hosious)* is used to modify "hands." In 2:15, the hope of salvation for women (or for their children) is dependent upon their continuance in faith, love, and sanctification *(hagiasmō)* with self-restraint. In 3:9, the concept of purity *(kathara)* is used to modify the conscience of the deacons. In 4:4, it is suggested that everything created by God is good, and in 4:5 it is proposed that all things are sanctified *(hagiadzetai)* by the Word of God and prayer. In 2 Tim. 1:3, the concept of pure *(kathara)* is used to describe the conscience (as in 1 Tim. 3:9). In 1:9, holy *(hagia)* is used to describe the nature of the calling with which they had been called. In 2:21 the concepts of cleansing and sanctification are linked together. The man that cleanses himself *(ekkatharē)* will become a vessel for honor sanctified *(hēgiasmenon),* and useful to the master. The latter trio of terms (cleanses, sanctified, and useful) are obviously synonymous in this context. In Titus 1:7-9, a list of six parallel qualifications for the *episcopos* is provided, including holy or devout *(hosion).* In 1:15, there is a significant discussion on the concept of purity *(katharos).* It is stated that to those who are pure *(katharois),* all things are pure *(kathara);* in contrast to this purity are those who are defiled and unbelieving. The contrast here makes it obvious that unbelief and defilement are opposed to being pure. Belief carries an implicit purification within it. In 2:14, it is stated that Christ gave himself for us in order to redeem us from all lawlessness and to purify *(katharisē)* a people unto himself. Purification is inextricably linked to redemption here. [See exegesis on this text in this volume.]

What holiness preaching resources are then available from the above survey? One thing to keep in mind is that there are two major uses of "holiness vocabulary" in the NT. One is ceremonial and the other is ethical. The latter is the normative use and demonstrates that holiness in Christian experience extends to all aspects of the life of the believer in ethical ways. The believer is called to a belonging that involves an ethical transformation of his being. Even when the language is semantically ceremonial (e.g., purity, cleansing, etc.), it is informed by the normative ethical understanding and entails moral renewal. This is to radically disagree with George Eldon Ladd in his otherwise excellent book when he says of such language in the Pastorals, "When applied to Christians, holiness or sanctification is not in the first place an ethical concept although it includes an ethical aspect."[1] This view, like the typical Reformed interpretation, fails to take into account the transformation of the concept of sanctification that actually began with the eighth-century prophets, but it prefers to stay with the idea of imputed rather than real, ethical holiness.

There is one ceremonial use of the language in the Pastorals (1 Tim. 4:5), while the remainder reflect the ethical understanding. This means that all the uses referred to above highlight some aspect of the believer's existence that is to be holy in nature.

We see the importance of holiness in worship (1 Tim. 2:8). In the East it is the custom to raise one's hands when praying. The point here is that the worshiper must be morally and spiritually fit, since hands represent character (see Ps. 24:4 and James 4:8). This truth is reinforced by the next phrase rendered "without anger or disputing." As Donald Guthrie says, "Such attitudes of mind are as alien to the holy place of prayer as sullied hands. Not merely pure actions but pure motives are essential to Christian worship."[2]

In two places, "pure" *(kathara)* is used to modify conscience (1 Tim. 3:9; 2 Tim. 1:3). It is usually translated "clear," but it carries a deeper significance than simply a conscience free from a sense of guilt. Paul fully understood that conscience is not of itself a reliable guide. Therefore it is essential that conscience have an objective criterion of truth or right to give it proper content. Thus we agree with G. E. Ladd when he concludes his analysis of the Pauline view of conscience: "All this suggests that the conscience of the Christian must always be exercised in the light of the divine revelation in Jesus Christ."[3] In this sense, a "clear" or "pure" conscience is one that is informed by the character of Christ.

The reference in 1 Tim. 2:15 is so obscure and difficult that it is best passed by here, but we can note the correlation of holiness and usefulness in 2 Tim. 2:21. It appears that this primarily refers to separating oneself from the false teachers to avoid being contaminated by them, but it could conceivably involve purging oneself from the similar elements in one's own nature.

In Titus 1:15, there is a distinctive characterization of the "pure." At least one implication here is that holiness does not entail a faulty asceticism based on a cultic impurity. Finally there is the point made that those who hold places of leadership in the church must be holy in character and behavior (vv. 7-9).

Holiness as Sound Doctrine

The concept of holiness as sound doctrine lies at the heart of the endeavor to discover holiness preaching resources within the Pastoral Epistles. What is the basis for that interpretative connection? Can it be sustained exegetically, or is it merely that which is hoped for theologically? A careful study of the concept can yield some fruitful results.

The young ministers are encouraged, even commanded, to *teach* sound doctrine. The term **teach** *(didaskō)* suggests the idea of causing someone to accept something. It includes the imparting of information, the passing on of knowledge, or the acquiring of skills.[4] The aim of all teaching is "to communicate knowledge and skill with a view to developing the pupil's abilities, but not to force his will in a particular direction."[5] However, in the Septuagint, it does *not* primarily denote the communication of knowledge and skill, "but means chiefly instruction in how to live, the subject matter being the will of God."[6] The ordinances and judgments of God are to be learned and understood, yet clearly an act of will is required to obey and keep them. "The term *didaskalos* is always marked by the fact that it has a volitional as well as an intellectual reference."[7] These "teachings" may be taught by God himself, by the father of the family, or by the righteous and godly ones who know the will of God.[8] This basic understanding of the meaning of "teaching" or "instructing" carries into the NT.

The teaching of Jesus was considered by early Christianity to bring the hearer into direct confrontation with the will of God. In fact, it seems that the dominical teaching constituted the accepted source of ethical *didachē* by the apostles (see Paul's references in 1 Cor. 7:25 et al. to "word from the Lord," by which he means Jesus). Teaching in the Pastoral Epistles is likewise identified with Jesus' teaching (1 Tim. 6:3). The *didaskalos* (teacher) is "one who indicates the way of God from the Torah."[9] Since the Torah, or law, serves to provide guidance for the people of God in their living out the covenant relationship, and that is defined to be "holy living," we are given further insight into the connection between the function of teaching and sanctification. Furthermore, in the Pastoral Epistles it is assumed that what is taught will be "good" or "sound *[hygiēs]* doctrine" *(didaskalia),* and that doctrine will, in turn, be passed along.[10]

The term "doctrine" *(didaskalia)* "refers to the authoritative tenets accepted by a particular body of believers or adherents," referring in the OT to "Torah, the teaching of Moses as found in the Pentateuch." It is generally taught that in the Pastoral Epistles it likewise "suggests a fairly fixed body of orthodox thought."[11] But the question is, Is this an appropriate understanding in the light of the context, especially in the light of the modification of "doctrine" by "sound" *(hygiainousa)?* When the concept of doctrine is modified by one of the cognates of *hygiēs* ("sound" or "healthy"), significant implications emerge. The Greek term *hygiēs* means "to be healthy," and "healthy is what is balanced according to the order of the whole."[12] It also includes the meaning of "strong," "active," or "judicious."[13] In the Septuagint, health is a part of life that is a divine gift. It is often a translation of the Hebrew *shalom,* which denotes man's well-being.[14] In the Gospels, "health" is a sign that the age of salvation has dawned.[15] In the Pastoral Epistles, sound doctrine is "connected with the summons to a correct and orderly walk."[16] We need to examine the larger context, rather than just the terms, to see what implications may be drawn from the correlation of "sound" with "doctrine."

What becomes readily apparent in 1 and 2 Timothy and Titus is that there is definite opposition to be overcome. Paul's basic theological teaching *(didaskalos)* and preaching *(kērygma)* and even his apostolicity were coming under attack, and those whom Paul had left in charge when he departed were trying to withstand those attacks. Likewise they themselves were coming under increasing opposition from groups that were not remaining faithful to the gospel that Paul had proclaimed. The primary thrust of each of the letters in the Pastorals is encouragement and exhortation: encouragement to those who are striving to remain faithful to the teaching of Paul; exhortation to combat the opposition with sound doctrine *(hygiainousē didaskalia)* in the Pauline tradition. In attempting to determine the significance of the idea, an overview of each letter in terms of a structural analysis will be helpful.

Clearly the Thanksgiving section, so pivotal in several of the previous Pauline Epistles, is of lesser significance in the Pastoral Epistles. This can probably be attributed to the severity and intensity of the attacks on the Pauline teaching and preaching, as is also the case in Galatians. Also worthy of note is the brief use of the standard Body section in each of the Pastoral Epistles. What appears to have happened is that the section consisting of exhortations and admonitions has been significantly expanded to include a great deal of material that would typically have been covered in the Body section as in previous letters. It is possible that this reflects the importance of that kind of material in relation to the situation in these churches after Paul's departure. It appears that matters that concerned the writer must be addressed in the stronger mode of imperatives, rather than the more typical mode of indicatives. The significance of this structural analysis is magnified when an analysis of the content of the letters is made.

In 1 Timothy, the introduction (1:1-2) is followed immediately by instructions to guard against teaching "strange doctrines" (author's trans.) *(heterodidaskalein)* (1:3-4 and 6-7). The "strange doctrines" are contrasted (1:5, 8-11) with the goal of Paul's instructions based upon the law when used lawfully, summarized in 1:10 as "sound doctrine." This is reinforced in 1:12-17 with a Pauline testimonial to the grace and mercy of God experienced in his own life.

A charge to Timothy is found in 1:18-20. Chapter 2 contains a teaching of prayer and godly conduct, while 3:1-7 deals with the conduct that is befitting an "overseer" or "bishop," and 3:8-13 deals with the conduct that is befitting "deacons." The chapter concludes with a general exhortation to the church (3:14-16) regarding proper conduct. Then 4:1-4 deals with serious concerns about false teaching described as "demonic doctrines" (author's trans. if not noted) *(didaskaliais daimoniōn)*, which is followed by a section of instructions for Timothy (4:6-16), including an emphasis (v. 12) upon Timothy being an example for all the congregation. After that, 5:3-16 deals with the problem of the widows and also speaks to the issue of proper conduct for this class of church members. Verses 17-20 are an admonition concerning the "elders," followed by an exhortation to Timothy (5:21-25). In 6:1-2 is contained a word concerning the behavior of slaves, followed by a warning against "false doctrine" in contrast to "sound words" (6:3-10). The battle for the faith is the focus of 6:11-16, followed by instructions for the wealthy in 6:17-19 and the conclusion in 6:20-21.

The central role of behavior is easily recognized here, but its crucial place is further emphasized when it is seen that the key verse of 1 Timothy is 3:15: "[That] you may know how one ought to behave in the household of God, which is the church of the living God" (RSV).

Second Timothy begins with an address, salutation, and thanksgiving (1:1-5). In 1:6-18, there is a recounting of Christian tradition and suffering that includes a reminder of the holy calling with which they have been called (1:9) as well as an exhortation to "hold to the standard of sound words" that have come from Paul. 2:1-13 is an exhortation to be strong despite suffering; 2:14-19 proposes a strategy against heresy by advocating the ability to accurately handle "the word of truth." The remainder, 2:20-26, is an inducement to shun passion and controversy while seeking love and peace, and it includes the reminder that if anyone "cleanses himself," he will be "a vessel for honor, sanctified, useful to the Master, and prepared for every good work." Then 3:1-9 provides an identification of the character of the heretics, while 3:10—4:8 is an exhortation to follow Paul's example in teaching and preaching the Word, with emphasis on teaching (*didaskalia* in 3:10 and 3:16, *didachē* in 4:2), sound teaching *(hygiainousēs didaskalias)* (4:3), and an emphasis on preaching the Word *(kēryxon ton logon)* (4:2). The final instructions to Timothy run from 4:9 to 4:18 and include a warning against those who opposed Paul's teaching (4:15; literally, it says they opposed his "words"). The letter closes with 4:19-22.

Titus begins with a long ascription identifying the sender in 1:1-3 as part of the opening in 1:1-4. The qualifications of elders is the concern of 1:5-9, with an interesting compounding of related concepts in 1:9 that includes holding fast "the faithful word which is in accordance with the teaching," the ability to exhort "in sound teaching," and the ability to "refute those who contradict." Verses 10-16 are focused on false teachers, stressing that they are "teaching things that they should not" (1:11), with the admonition to reprove severely the false teachers so that they may be "sound in the faith." In 2:1-10, the admonition is given to teach sound doctrine for all the groups of the church. This "sound doctrine" (2:1) is also referred to as that which is "sound in faith" *(hygiainontas tē pistei)* (2:2), "teaching what is good" (2:3), "purity in doctrine" (2:7), and "sound in speech" (2:8). Then 2:11-15 is an exhortation to conduct that recognizes salvation history. General exhortations are the gist of 3:1-7, with particular exhortations concerning heretics in 3:8-11, followed by a brief conclusion in 3:12-15.

This content overview provides some definite leads to pursue in these books, taken both individually and collectively. The primary contribution that it makes is to clarify the relationship of the parts to the whole; and once the various key terms and texts are isolated and examined, this will make it possible to keep them anchored solidly in context. One thing is crystal clear: All three letters are centrally concerned with Christian conduct, or holiness of life.

What is indicated in considering holiness as **sound doctrine** in the Pastoral Epistles is not so much sanctification as an individual or isolated experience but rather holiness and sanctification as a significant part of the theological wholeness of God's work of salvation. Sanctification is "wholeness," "completeness," "Christian perfection," or being "sound and healthy." In other words, it is a significant part of that which makes a life "whole," "healthy," and "strong." In the Pastoral Epistles all of this is incorporated within the concept of **sound doctrine.** This implicit understanding is made explicit by Martin Dibelius, who wrote: "The Pastoral Epistles designate with 'sound teaching' *(hygiainousa didaskalia)* or 'sound words' *(hygiainontēs logoi)* the loftiest and holiest things they know: the true faith, the true message about faith."[17]

J. N. D. Kelly comments: "The Apostle borrows the present metaphor from current philosophical jargon, in which 'wholesome' connoted 'sound' or 'reasonable,' and uses it here to designate the authentic Christian message as applied to conduct. It expresses his conviction that . . . a life based on the teaching of the gospel is clean and healthy."[18]

Theological Interpretation

The understanding of sanctification in the Pastoral Epistles may be viewed from several perspectives:

A. The first perspective is that of seeing sanctification as the work of God within humanity. This can be expressed by relating sanctification to the calling of God as well as in passages that emphasize that it is clearly God who is the active Agent in the sanctifying process.

In the Pastoral Epistles, there are only two passages that deal with the calling of God. The first is 1 Tim. 6:12, a passage that deals with the calling to eternal life but which has no direct connection to the concept of sanctification at all. The second is 2 Tim. 1:9, a passage that directly links holiness with the calling of God. In that text, God is said to have saved and called with a holy calling according to His own purpose and grace. There is no mention of God's calling in Titus.

God is clearly the Sanctifier in 1 Tim. 4:4-5, as is evident by the declaration that sanctification is accomplished by means of the Word of God. In 2 Tim. 1:9, it is stated that it is God who has saved and called with a holy calling; there can be no mistaking the fact that God is the Source of this holiness. Titus 2:11-14 strongly emphasizes the priority of the grace of God in bringing salvation in all of its dimensions to bear on His people, including their purification so that they may become the people of His possession.

B. Holiness can also be seen in the perspectives provided when sanctification is considered in relation to justification with both viewed as parts of the theological whole spoken of as salvation, including the eschatological dimension of salvation.

The Pastoral Epistles are teeming with salvation terminology. First Timothy has salvation language in 1:1, 15; 2:3, 4, 15; 4:10, and 16. Second Timothy has salvation language in 1:9, 10; 2:10; 3:15; and 4:18. Titus has salvation language in 1:3, 4; 2:10, 11, 13; 3:4, 5, and 6. With the terminology of holiness and sanctification located in 1 Tim. 2:15 and 4:4-5; 2 Tim. 2:19-22; and Titus 2:11-14, there is some definite overlap. In 1 Tim. 2:15, salvation is a holistic concept consisting of the components of faith, love, and sanctification. In Titus 2:11-14, salvation is also used in a comprehensive sense with the concept of purity a part of that whole. Throughout the Pauline corpus, salvation terminology tends to be broader and more inclusive while sanctification and holiness terminology tends to be a part of that all-encompassing concept. This relationship becomes more distinct when sanctification is considered in its relation to justification in the Pauline corpus.

In the Pastoral Epistles, there is one passage that directly relates justification language with the language of sanctification. Second Tim. 2:19-22 speaks of the one that has become a vessel for honor, sanctified and useful to the Master. Such a one is urged to pursue after righteousness.

There are also some hints at the relationship between the Parousia and sanctification in the Pastorals, although they are not very direct. In 1 Tim. 2:15, the implication is that if women (or possibly their children) will continue in faith, love, and holiness, they will be saved *(sōthēsetai);* however, the future tense in this context appears to refer to the immediate future as much as to the eschatological day of the Lord. Second Tim. 1:9 points to the holiness of the calling as that which was granted in Christ Jesus from all eternity, implying a past act with present implications, but it is affirmed in 1:12 that these implications will carry forward until that day. The implications in 2:19-26 are primarily present, with a view to their ongoing nature, and as 3:1 and 4:8 indicate, they will go on until that day. Titus 2:11-14 contains an absolutely unmistakable relationship of the present living out of the holy life with the hope of the appearance of the Lord in eschatological glory.

C. Another perspective is that of seeing sanctification as the response of humanity to God, the living out in love a life of holiness in response to God's sanctifying work within us. That leads inevitably to a consideration of sanctification and ethics.

In 1 Timothy, there are three passages that demonstrate a connection between love and sanctification. In 1:5, it is stated that the goal of the commands that have been given is love from a pure heart and a good conscience and a sincere faith. There is an obvious relationship here between a pure heart, a heart that has been purified, and the love that flows out from this kind of heart. The sanctifying and purifying work of God within the heart makes possible the dynamic activity of love flowing out from that heart. In 1 Tim. 2:15, love and sanctification are complementary concepts, paralleled side by side as elements within the salvation mentioned. In 4:12, Timothy is urged to show himself an example in his speech, conduct, love, faith, and purity. The concepts of love, faith, and purity are all present in this verse again just as they were in 1:5, but linked here also with speech and conduct, indicating an entire way of life. In 2 Timothy, the exhortation to flee from youthful lusts is balanced by the command to pursue after righteousness, faith, love, and peace with those who call on the Lord from a pure heart. The only mention of love in Titus (2:2) is not directly connected with any sanctification terminology. It can be concluded that the concept of love, linked as it is throughout the Pauline corpus both explicitly and implicitly with sanctification and the life of holiness that results therefrom, emphasizes the dynamic and relational dimensions of sanctification and aids in the prevention of a notion of sanctification that is rigid, static, and lifeless. A love relationship requires growth and nourishment to flourish, and a life lived in holiness as a response to God's sanctifying work within will be a dynamic, growing life as sanctification is put into practice day by day.

D. The concept of the life of sanctification as expressed in the image of the walk as a way of life, found frequently in the other Pauline Epistles, is not present in the Pastorals. There is, however, a close relationship between sanctification as a way of life and the ethical exhortations contained in the hortatory material in these letters. The clearest example of that relationship is found in 2 Timothy. Immediately after the distinction made between vessels created for honor and those created for dishonor (2:20), it is suggested (2:21) that those who cleanse themselves will be vessels for honor, sanctified *(hēgiasmenon)* and therefore useful to the Master, prepared for every good work. This is followed by further exhortations in 2:22-26 as that which is in keeping with this sanctification. When all the references to the life of holiness and sanctification found throughout the Pauline corpus within the concept of the "walk" are included with those in this additional hortatory material, it provides overwhelming suppport for the definite ethical implications of the life of sanctification that is to be lived out in holiness in response to the holy God.

Preaching Suggestions

In the light of the content analysis, terminology analysis, and theological analysis, the next step would be to carefully reread the text of the Pastoral Epistles, looking for particular passages that contain significant potential as resources for holiness preaching. In 1 Timothy, the first such text can be found in 1:3-11, with primary emphasis on 1:5. Highlighting the significant differences between those who teach strange doctrine and the sound doctrine of the Pauline gospel, the clearly stated aim and goal of Paul's instruction is "love from a pure heart and a good conscience and a sincere faith." The crux of this passage is the ability to "use the law lawfully," something that Paul considered himself most capable of doing. The entire second chapter of 1 Timothy could be considered an admonition to adopting a holy life-style, although most of the instructions found there are general, and the concept of holiness described therein tends to be more descriptive than prescriptive. The third chapter likewise tends to refer to general conduct for those who would be exemplary leaders within the churches, and links to sanctification would be indirect at best. Chapter 4 requires some significant investigation, for it contains direct reference to the sanctifying activity of God in 4:5 and the even more significant concept of godliness and the godly example throughout the chapter. Chapter 5 contains several specific admonitions, but the only possible concern for the understanding of holiness would be 5:17-25 as it relates to the relationship of sin with the Christian leaders. And 6:1-16 contains great potential for further examination under the theme "the doctrine conforming to godliness" stated in 6:3, a theme that dominates the whole passage.

In 2 Timothy there are also several texts that deserve close consideration for their potential as holiness passages. First, 1:6-14 details the holy calling of God with an admonition to "guard the treasure that has been entrusted to you" and the exhortation to "retain the standard of sound words." Then 2:14-26 is a passage that implores the "accurate handling of the word of truth," which is reinforced with the metaphor of the sanctified vessel prepared for the Master's use and followed by an exhortation to pursue righteousness from a pure heart. Also 3:10-17 sets forth the adequate equipment essential for the godly workman. And 4:1-8 sets "sound doctrine" in contrast with that which may appease and tickle the ears, and makes that "sound doctrine" the basis for fulfilling the ministry.

There are three passages in Titus that warrant closer scrutiny in the quest for discovering holiness texts. The first stretches from 1:5 to 2:5 and contrasts the true and the false under the now familiar designation of "sound doctrine." Then 2:6-14 continues the thrust of the previous passage with the specific focus on the example that Titus is to be to the people as a member of "a purified people for God's own possession." Last, 3:1-7 details the great contrast between what once we were and what now we have become through the "full salvation" of God's redemptive work wrought through Jesus Christ our Savior and through the Holy Spirit.

Endnotes

1. *Theology of the New Testament* (Grand Rapids: Wm. B. Eerdmans Publishing Co., 1975), 519.

2. Donald Guthrie, *The Pastoral Epistles,* in *Tyndale New Testament Commentaries,* ed. R. V. G. Tasker (Grand Rapids: Wm. B. Eerdmans Publishing Co., 1957), 74.

3. *Theology,* 477.

4. Karl Rengstorf, *"Didaskō,"* in *Theological Dictionary of the New Testament* (TDNT), ed. Gerhard Kittel (Grand Rapids: Wm B. Eerdmans Publishing Co., 1964), 2:135.

5. Klaus Wegenast, "Teach *(didaskō),"* in *The New International Dictionary of*

New Testament Theology (NIDNTT), ed. Colin Brown (Grand Rapids: Zondervan Publishing House, 1978), 3:760.

6. Ibid. Rengstorf, TDNT 2:137, is in agreement.

7. Rengstorf, TDNT 2:137.

8. Ibid.

9. Ibid., 153.

10. Wegenast, "Teach," 3:765.

11. Willard Taylor, "Doctrine," in *Beacon Dictionary of Theology*, Richard S. Taylor, ed. (Kansas City: Beacon Hill Press of Kansas City, 1983), 173.

12. Ulrich Luck, *"Hygiēs,"* in TDNT 8:308-9.

13. Dietrich Muller, "Heal *(hygiēs),"* in NIDNTT 2:169.

14. Luck, *"Hygiēs,"* 310; Muller, "Heal," 169.

15. Muller, "Heal," 170.

16. Luck, *"Hygiēs,"* 312.

17. Martin Dibelius, *The Pastoral Epistles,* Hermeneia Commentary Series (Philadelphia: Fortress Press, 1972), 24.

18. J. N. D. Kelly, *The Pastoral Epistles,* in *Harper's New Testament Commentaries* (San Francisco: Harper and Row, 1960), 50.

TOM FINDLAY

Holiness—the Goal of Ministry

Whereas the aim of our charge is love that issues from a pure heart and a good conscience and sincere faith (1 Tim. 1:5, RSV).

Many pastors have become so bogged down with administrative details, institutional promotions, or social activities that they have lost sight of the real purpose of their calling. Others have not lost sight of the vision, but other duties have so filled their hours and sapped their energies that they have been frustrated and disillusioned. No doubt both these situations contribute to a high incidence of ministerial burnout.

Every now and then it is helpful and liberating to delve into the Word for a fresh vision of the proper function of the ministerial office. Such an experience is needed occasionally by both clergyman and layman to avoid becoming preoccupied with secondary matters and getting off on dead-end streets.

Few places in Scripture provide resources for doing this as well as the letter from which our passage is chosen. This First Epistle of Paul to Timothy belongs to a group of letters, including Second Timothy and Titus, known as the Pastoral Epistles. They receive this name because they were written to men charged with the oversight of local churches—Timothy in Ephesus and Titus in Crete. Their author was the "senior pastor," Paul, and they were directed to two young men who were dealing with specific questions that arose in their local churches. They are, therefore, not only pastoral letters but also "people" letters, since they offer guidance for practical Christian living.

First Timothy is an immensely practical letter. It addresses such matters as prayer in public worship (2:1-8); a "dress code" for women in the church (2:9-10); the practical qualifications for pastors and deacons (3:1-13); personal spiritual discipline (4:1-16); pastoring "senior citizens" (5:1-16); and defending the faith against false teaching (6:3-16). No pastor could be more encouraged than by the theology found here, and no theologian could be more challenged to make his theology practical.

Exegetical Setting

The situation in the church at Ephesus when Paul wrote to Timothy was potentially explosive. Heretics were threatening the church with false teaching, which was leading to false living. When Paul had bade the Ephesian Christians farewell, he had foreseen the impending problems and attempted to warn the church in advance (Acts 20:20-30). But the situation arose exactly as he had feared, and now he was dealing with the reality of heresy, instead of just the potential.

Perhaps because he was so young, the authority of Timothy was being called into question, and there were a variety of practical issues that needed his attention. In this potentially divisive situation, Paul commanded Timothy to gain credibility by love and ethical living (see 4:12). The apostle does not accompany this letter with a copy of the Epistle to the Romans, his theological treatise, as an antidote to heresy. Nor does he, like Irenaeus, bishop of Lyons over a century later, compile a refutation of all heresies. His approach to the problem is a command to love.

Love, for Paul, was the sum of the commandments and the fulfillment of the law (Rom. 13:9-10), and he knew that it would only be by the way of love that there was any chance of these teachers who had gone astray being won back into the fellowship of Christ and His Church. Was it any wonder, then, that Paul should urge Timothy to combat heresy in the church by increasing love in it?

Notes on the Text

The specific passage before us has been translated in a variety of ways. To provide a point of departure for exegetical purposes, we have chosen to use the RSV.

Charge. This same word is used in v. 3 where Timothy is reminded how Paul had urged him to remain in Ephesus with the responsibility to **charge** certain people. This assumes that Paul had given Timothy authority to do this, thus introducing the central theme of 1 Timothy: the issue of the proper exercise of authority. Both here and in v. 3 the verb translated **charge** is *parangellō,* a common military term that gives the impression of a solemn mandate or admonition given by a superior to a junior.

It is used by Paul five times in 1 Timothy (1:3; 4:11; 5:7; 6:13 [the RSV inverts the passage for the sake of sense, and the verb occurs in v. 14; but in the Greek text it is in v. 13]; 6:17), and in each case it is an authoritative command. But how is this authority to be exercised? On what is it based? Authority may be exercised in a severe or in a kindly manner, be it a secular or a spiritual authority. It is to this issue that Paul responds in 1:5 by showing the purpose for which authority is to be exercised.

Aim. The word **aim** in the passage is a translation of the Greek word *telos* and reinforces the theme of ministry with a goal in view. The word, in this context, means the "goal" or "the true and intended end" or the "purpose." The **charge** that Paul gave Timothy (the noun is used here *[parangelia]* in place of the verb in v. 3) is not one that invests him with dictatorial powers. Its *intention* is to produce love, the central result of the abiding presence of God's Spirit in the lives of believers (cf. Gal. 5:22). Thus, v. 5 sets out God's intended purpose for those who are His ministers; and it is with this in view that their charge is to be exercised.

The **charge** is repeated in v. 18. The Greek word itself is used in 1 Thess. 4:2 as a synonym for "gospel," that is, the content of the apostolic preaching, and it is from the gospel that the authority invested in the preacher derives. According to George Milligan, the word in 1 Timothy "refers to the whole practical teaching of Christianity."[1] We may, therefore, paraphrase the opening words of this verse as "the intended goal of our preaching is practical Christianity expressed in love."

Love. This is a subject on which Paul already had had occasion to write to the Ephesians. Both the noun *(agapē)* and the verb *(agapaō)* occur 10 times in that letter, and his prayer for them is that they may be "rooted and grounded in love" (3:17). Now, writing to their overseer, the great goal of his ministry has not changed.

It is instructive to note that in Gal. 5:22-23, where Paul talks about the fruit of the Spirit, a singular noun and a singular verb are used: "The fruit of the Spirit is *love.*" All the other benefits of the Spirit's presence are but the expression of this divine nature within us (1 John 4:13-18).

Heart. According to Hebrew psychology, the heart is the source of man's moral, psychic, and volitional action.[2] In the OT, man thinks with his heart (Gen. 6:5), wills with his heart (Exod. 35:5), and feels with his heart (Judg. 19:5-6, 22; 2 Sam. 6:16); in short, his intellectual, volitional, and emotional life and its morals are determined by the condition of his heart. Thus, when a man's heart is cleansed, he is protected from sinning in the moral and volitional areas of his life (Gen. 20:5-7). Since God is holy in His nature and cannot tolerate sin in His presence (Ps. 5:4; Hab. 1:13), only those who are pure in heart may commune with Him (Ps. 24:4-5; Matt. 5:8). One who has sinned before God pleads that his *heart* may be cleansed, since it is there, at the seat of his volition, that the sin was conceived (Ps. 51:10).

The quality of love, which is the gift of God's Spirit and which Paul longs to see reproduced in the Ephesians, is only possible when it originates from a pure heart. As Kelly says: "If purity is lacking there [man] obviously cannot radiate Christian love."[3]

Good conscience. Paul further says that this love originates from **a good conscience.** In the NT, **conscience** is singularly, though not exclusively, a Pauline concept. In all NT writings the word is used only 30 times, and 20 of the 30 are found in the writings of Paul. Of the other examples, 2 are found on the lips of Paul in his speeches recorded in Acts (23:1 and 24:16). It denotes for Paul "man's inner awareness of the moral quality of his own actions."[4]

Paul is, however, aware that, by itself, conscience must be trained to develop standards of good and evil. He therefore speaks about a **good** conscience, implying, as the writer to the Hebrews explicitly states, that there may be such a thing as an evil conscience (10:22).

The phrases **a good conscience** and "a clear conscience" are found at other places in the First Epistle to Timothy (1:19; 3:9, respectively), and in each case (as in the present) they are linked to a proper understanding of the Christian faith. It is contrasted with the heretics with whom Timothy had to contend in Ephesus (and also Titus in Crete; see Titus 1:13-16, especially v. 15), whom Paul so vividly describes in 4:2 as having had their conscience seared or cauterized. They are dead and insensitive to any moral distinctions. Paul himself could testify to the Jewish council: "Brethren, I have lived before God in all good conscience up to this day" (Acts 23:1, RSV), and he is now encouraging Timothy to produce the same results among those at Ephesus.

Sincere faith. As we have already seen, Paul associates a good conscience with a firm hold of the Christian faith. In the present passage it is expressed as **sincere faith.**

The Greek word, which here is given a positive translation in the RSV (**sincere),** literally means "unhypocritical" faith. Exactly the same word is used in 2 Tim. 1:5 to describe Timothy's own faith—the result of two generations of pious example. He is here exhorted to reproduce this in the lives of his people. It is faith in which there is no pretense or playacting. It is genuine; it has the ring of truth about it; it will stand the test of reality.

A pure heart; a good conscience; a sincere faith; here indeed is a threefold cord that cannot easily be broken.

Theological Exegesis

On the assumption that 1 Tim. 1:5 is a holiness text, we have presented there a series of characteristics of the sanctified person. The heart of the matter is love. John Wesley insisted that this was the essence of Christian perfection, and virtually all his definitions touched on this subject. The threefold description of the nature of this love implies that love is more than an emotion, it is a behavior, an expressed attitude, a lived-out reality. Furthermore, the text demonstrates conclusively the ethical character of holiness. This truth is distinctly Pauline. His prayer for the Philippians (1:9-10) embodies these same qualities. His appeals to the Corinthians (see especially 1 Corinthians 13) emphasize the central role of love in genuine spirituality. The Pauline doctrine of sanctification is through and through ethical.

Sermonic Suggestions

One approach to this text might concern itself with "The Goal of the Gospel." The sermon may be introduced by explaining that the word **aim** in the passage means intention; and the word **charge** is sometimes an equivalent for the apostolic preaching (see exegesis). Paul is telling Timothy that the goal of the gospel is holiness of heart and life and defines what this means in a threefold analysis:

I. The first goal of the gospel is to *purify our motives.* This does not necessarily mean that all we do will turn out right. Even the best of motives may occasionally produce catastrophic results. But our intention, that which determines our culpability before God, will be untroubled.

II. The second goal of the gospel is to *educate the conscience.* Conscience is not naturally able to distinguish good from evil, any more than man himself is naturally good. It must be nurtured, weaned away from the standards of this world and imbued with God's standards as its natural measuring rod.

III. The third goal of the gospel is to *refine our faith.* A distinction is often made between appearance and reality. Unfortunately, not everything is really what it appears to be. This has no more tragic results than in the Christian Church. In 1892 J. P. Struthers, a minister in Greenock in Scotland, wrote to James Denny about a church member who reportedly swore at his work when in a passion: "A minister doesn't know what his people are through the week. On Sabbath he sees them *as they would like to be."* Struthers, a very saintly man, went on to confess, "It's true about myself." The work of the gospel is to refine our faith, to remove all hypocrisy and leave it true and genuine before the Lord, all characteristics of true holiness. The sermon may be concluded by appealing to the words of Charles Wesley:

> *Refining Fire, go through my heart;*
> *Illuminate my soul;*
> *Scatter Thy life through every part,*
> *And sanctify the whole.*

Another sermon possibility could develop the topic "Transformed by the Gospel." In this approach, one would need to both keep in mind and make clear in his message that "transformation" is a theological synonym for "sanctification." As John Wesley insisted, sanctification is a real change, and that involves both outward and inward transformation. Furthermore, the essence of holiness as Wesleyan theology conceives it may be defined as love, and this theme is elaborated in terms of those characteristics that would allow it to be interpreted as "perfect love."

Let us look at these traits individually. The message could be outlined and developed as follows:

I. *Paul says that the gospel will produce love.* In saying that, of course, he has said it all. Love is the magnificent summary of the gospel. Love is the origin, the expression, and the end of God's plan of redemption. But in the present context, it is given a specific application.

A. In the first place, Paul says love will see us through difficult times of life. The strong language of v. 3 suggests that the situation in Ephesus was so difficult that Timothy was considering leaving it. Timothy was a young man, perhaps somewhat timid in nature and overwhelmed by the task with which he was confronted. As a young man he had to exhort those older than himself (5:1), and he may have felt that it was all too much for him. The easiest way out was to leave.

But Paul reminds him that love will see him through. This is not some abstract theology. It is practical admonition for everyday life. Within our marriage relationship, for example, there are times when the situation is so strained that we think that leaving is the easiest way out. But love will see us through. Confronted with a problem in the fellowship of God's Church, pastors are often tempted to go to another church and simply leave the situation. Laymen, when the opportunity is present, may face the same temptation. But Paul's word applies here too. Love will see us through.

B. Again, Paul tells Timothy that love will not only win the argument but also win the person. It is remarkable that Paul's answer to the spread of heresy in the church is to counteract it with love. The danger in theological debate is that we can win the argument and lose the person. Paul encourages his young associates to "love them in." Two of the qualifications for the work of a pastor outlined by Paul in chap. 3 are that the pastor must be gentle and not quarrelsome, and it is difficult to achieve this in the heat of theological controversy. Not so, says Paul, where love is reigning in the heart; it dispels the *odium theologicum* and is an agent of reconciliation.

II. *The second point Paul makes is that the gospel will transform man at the seat of his motivation.* In scriptural language, this is the **heart.**

A. A pure heart will not keep us from the capability to sin; but it will save us from the culpability of unwitting sin. The magnificent words of Jesus from the Cross, "Father, forgive them; *for they know not what they do"* (Luke 23:34, RSV, italics added), pinpoints for us that the guilt and culpability for sin lie in the intention of the heart and not merely in the execution of the action. Paul echoes the same thought in 1 Cor. 2:8, when, speaking about the "hidden wisdom of God" (v. 7, i.e., God's plan of salvation in the death of Christ), he says: "None of the rulers of this age understood this; for if they had, *they would not have crucified the Lord of glory"* (RSV, italics added).

Purity of heart is a cleansing of the source of our moral motivation, and although we all may make many mistakes, we experience that glorious freedom from condemnation about which Paul speaks in Rom. 8:1-2.

B. But purity of heart goes beyond this. It also fits us for fellowhip with God.

There is in all of us a desire to know what God is like. The story is told of a child whose mother had just brought home a new baby from the hospital. He asked his mother where his little brother came from. The mother answered that he came from God. Later the child pushed his nose through the cradle and said to his newborn brother, "Tell me, before you forget, what is God like?" In the same vein, William Temple, archbishop of Canterbury, and one of the most brilliant Christian philosophers of the 20th century, said, "The wise question is not 'Is Christ divine?' but 'What is God like?'" Philosopher and child, sage and simple—they both express the same desire: to know God. Jesus said, "Blessed are the pure in heart, for they shall see God" (Matt. 5:8, RSV).

Purity of heart removes the barrier that prevents us from knowing God, and it creates the conditions for entry into His presence. The wrath of God is that instinct of self-preservation in the divine nature (that is holy) that must revolt against sin. Purity of heart removes the barrier and enables us to enter into His presence on the basis of what Christ has done for us (Heb. 10:11-22).

III. *Another aspect of the transforming power of the gospel is that it refines the conscience.* Paul speaks here about a *good* conscience. Conscience is not naturally God's instrument for determining right from wrong. Conscience may fall under the control of Satan and become evil and perverted. Paul knew this but promises that when submitted to the transforming power of the gospel, conscience will, by the grace of God, become the means whereby the Spirit develops moral judgment in the lives of God's children. In his treatment of the conscience in his writings, Paul tells us that there are three blessings of a good conscience:

A. To begin with, he says that a good conscience allows us to live with ourselves. In Rom. 9:1 Paul testifies that his conscience bears him witness in the Holy Spirit. Paul could live with himself, untroubled by personal, hidden guilt. The reason is, as he says, "The law of the Spirit of life in Christ Jesus has set me free from the law of sin and death" (Rom. 8:2, RSV).

B. Paul goes on to say that a good conscience allows us to live with others. It is one of the peculiarities of the Pauline teaching that he submits his own conscience to the judgment of others, and he allows the conscience of others to determine his action. His life in the service of the gospel was sufficiently transparent, that he could "commend [himself] to every man's conscience in the sight of God" (2 Cor. 4:2). At the same time, if the conscience of another passed judgment on an action of Paul, even although he may personally have felt no scruples in the performance of that act, then Paul could abstain, in order not to wound a weaker conscience (1 Cor. 8:12-13; 10:28-29). In this way, his good conscience permitted him to live at peace with his fellowmen in the harmony of the gospel.

C. The final point that Paul makes on the good conscience is that it enables us to live with God. In his witness before the Jewish council in Acts 23:1, Paul declares that he has "lived before God in all good conscience up to this day" (RSV). Here is the ultimate value of a good conscience: It makes us friends with God.

The deceitfulness of sin (Heb. 3:13) may lead us into deceiving ourselves, and the defense of our public image may lead us to deceive others; but we cannot deceive God. There is nothing hidden from Him. Secrecy is much more common than lying in the moral sphere. We can do almost anything without fear, although not without guilt, if no one discovers our actions. But God knows them. That was why the Psalmist prayed for cleansing from secret sins (Ps. 19:12); he confessed before the Lord, "Thou hast set our iniquities before thee, our *secret sins* in the light of thy countenance" (Ps. 90:8, RSV, italics added).

The conscience under the Lordship of Jesus Christ, refined and purified, enables us to live with God.

IV. *The fourth experience of the transformation of the gospel is that it cultivates our faith.* When Paul speaks here about sincere or unhypocritical faith, he does not mean, in the first instance, correct theology. This impression could be gained, since it is heresy that is referred to in the context. Paul, however, is talking about the personal convictions of our own lives and the life-styles we live before the world.

There is, in the very best of us, the tendency to give the impression that we are better than we are. We want people to see us in a certain light or to think about us in a certain way, so we behave toward them in ways that we believe will produce the desired effect. This is true even in our Christian walk. Paul tells the Galatians that Peter and his Jewish friends were guilty of hypocrisy, and that they were so convincing that even Barnabas was impressed (Gal. 2:13).

It need not be so. The dross and alloy of a contaminated walk with God can be removed, and we are able to walk before Him in an open and transparent relationship. Only then will we have experienced that "fulness of the blessing of the gospel of Christ" (Rom. 15:29, KJV); only then will the world be attracted to, and want to know, the God whom we serve.

Endnotes

1. George Milligan, *St. Paul's Epistles to the Thessalonians* (Old Tappan, N.J.: Fleming H. Revell Co., n.d.), 47.

2. See H. Wheeler Robinson, "Hebrew Psychology," in *The People and the Book* (Oxford: Clarendon Press, 1925), 362-64.

3. William Kelly, *An Exposition of the Two Epistles to Timothy,* 3rd ed. (London: C. A. Hammond, 1948), 46.

4. Ibid., 47.

ALEX VARUGHESE

Holiness and Pastoral Responsibility

For the grace of God has appeared, bringing salvation to all men, instructing us to deny ungodliness and worldly desires and to live sensibly, righteously and godly in the present age, looking for the blessed hope and the appearing of the glory of our great God and Savior, Christ Jesus; who gave Himself for us, that He might redeem us from every lawless deed and purify for Himself a people for His own possession, zealous for good deeds (Titus 2:11-14, NASB).

What is the task of the pastor? Much confusion exists in the contemporary church over this issue. Many see him as a business manager, or a public relations person, or even an errand boy for every conceivable whim of the parishioner. A healthy corrective to various misconceptions can be found in the Pauline letters known as the Pastoral Epistles: 1 and 2 Timothy and Titus.

Paul's charge to Titus in the letter to him clearly indicates that pastoral responsibility includes instruction not only in the doctrines of the church but also in godly living in accordance with the ethical demands of the gospel. Christians live today in a world that is profoundly influenced by public opinion on moral, social, and ethical issues confronting our society. Paul's letter to Titus warns the church to guard herself against this danger, and admonishes it to conduct herself according to the grace that has been received from God in salvation and in sanctification through Jesus Christ.

Exegetical Section

The Context. The opening statement of the Epistle (1:14)

makes the burden of the apostle clear. He has become a "bond-servant of God, and an apostle of Jesus Christ, for the faith of those chosen of God and the knowledge of the truth which is according to godliness, in the hope of eternal life" (vv. 1-2, NASB).[1] His injunctions throughout the letter reflect this consciousness of his call and commission as an apostle to instruct the believers to live a life based on "sound doctrine" (see 1:9, 13; 2:1-2, 10).

The text of this study (2:11-14) is closely connected to this apostolic concern. In chapter 1, Paul has asked Titus to appoint qualified men as elders in every town in Crete with the charge to exhort in sound doctrine and to refute those who contradict it (v. 9), and to silence those who are rebellious, empty talkers, and deceivers (v. 10). Titus' own speech must be sound in doctrine, and he must instruct men and women of all walks of life to live a godly life, exemplifying their faith in God (2:1-10). This emphasis is continued in 3:1-11, where Paul once again takes up the theme of godly Christian living based on sound doctrine.

Notes on the Text

For the grace of God has appeared (2:11). **For** is a connecting participle that introduces the theological basis for the Christian's duty to live a godly life. **The grace of God** that **has appeared** is the primary motivating factor for a believer to live such a life.

The concept of God's grace is a key theme in Paul's writings, particularly in his theology of salvation. Grace has been manifested historically on the cross of Christ, through which God offers salvation to all mankind (Rom. 3:23-24). It is possible to think that Paul understood grace as "the kindness and love of God" that "appeared" for the salvation of the unrighteous (see Titus 3:4-5).[2]

The expression **the grace of God has appeared** *(epephanē)* is found only here in the NT. This act **(appeared)** refers to a sudden intervention of God on the historical scene. Accounts of such appearances are numerous in the Bible. But here it has to do with the climactic divine entrance into history, the Christ event. Paul here summarizes all the historical events associated with the life of Christ as **the grace of God.**

The purpose of this gracious divine activity is evident in the phrase **bringing salvation to all men.** Salvation *(sōtērios)* is essentially freedom from the power of sin. It is a gift that God himself brings to us.[3]

The phrase **instructing us** (v. 12) conveys Paul's understanding of the educative power of the grace of God. Grace has the power not only to save sinful mankind but also to instruct those who respond favorably **to deny ungodliness and worldly desires and to live sensibly, righteously and godly in the present age.** The Greek word for **instructing** is a participle form of the verb *paideuein.* In 1 Cor. 11:32 and 2 Cor. 6:9, Paul uses the same verb to describe actions of discipline through judgment/punishment. The Septuagint uses this word most often in this sense. However, in 2 Tim. 2:25; 3:16; and here, Paul uses this verb to express the idea of educating the uneducated.

Furthermore, grace disciplines a believer to say no to the world (see NIV on v. 12) and yes to God. Paul conveys here both the negative and the positive results of the teaching ministry of grace. A Christian is instructed to deny **ungodliness and worldly desires.** First of all, there is the act of denial or renunciation. The Greek aorist participle used here *(arnēsamenoi)* leads us to think that the reference is to a particular time when the act of a complete break away from the past is accomplished. Though some commentators may see here a reference to the sacrament of baptism as a specific context for such renunciation, it is more likely that Paul has in mind the consecration of a believer, a theme well expressed in Rom. 6:12-19. **Ungodliness** (*asebeia,* often used by Paul as the opposite of *eusebeia,* which means godliness; see 1 Tim. 2:2; 4:7; 6:5, 11) is not only a lack of reverence for God (impiety) but also a lack of acknowledgment of God in one's thoughts and actions. It is the denial of the power of the true and living God. Elsewhere Paul describes ungodliness as the religious condition of the heathen (Rom. 1:18).

The educative power of grace also enables a believer to deny **worldly desires** *(kosmikas epithumias).* Paul uses this phrase here as a synonym of another favorite Pauline expression, "desires of the flesh" (see Eph. 2:3; Gal. 5:16-24). The world *(kosmos)* through its own wisdom does not acknowledge God, and therefore it is apart from God (1 Cor. 1:21). Consequently, its plans and actions are also evil (John 7:7).

Paul now turns to the positive effects of the teaching ministry of God's grace. Grace teaches a believer **to live sensibly, righteously**

and godly in the present age. A Christian's ideal behavior is expressed in these phrases. Paul has already instructed Titus to urge the church leaders, old men, old women, young women, and young men to live sensibly (or, to live a sober life, a life with "self-control," as in NIV). A Christian is taught by grace to exercise self-control in his thoughts and actions.

Grace also instructs a believer to live a righteous life *(dikaiōs)* or to behave in an upright manner. Uprightness is the right kind of behavior toward others. The idea of being conformed to the moral standards set forth by God is meant here.

A Christian also receives instruction on his relationship to God. He is called to live a "godly" *(eusebōs)* life, in total acknowledgment of God's power and authority over him, and in total consecration of his whole being to the service of his Creator and Redeemer. Moreover, a believer is instructed to live such a life of renunciation and consecration **in the present age.** Paul's use of **the present age** as the sphere of Christian life leads directly to the hope of life in another age that is yet to come.

Looking for the blessed hope. Paul expresses here an eagerness in his **looking,** for it does not refer to a casual peek at the future, rather to an active and eager expectation and diligent waiting. This **hope** *(elpida)* is further qualified with the adjective **blessed.** It is a blessed hope because it is centered around one's faith in Jesus Christ (see 1 Tim. 1:1). This hope is based on an assurance from God, and therefore, it is certain (see Rom. 8:18-25). Again, it is a blessed hope, for it contains the expectation of **the appearing of the glory of our great God and Savior, Christ Jesus.** Paul has already dealt with the **appearing** of the grace of God in v. 11. Here he uses again the same Greek word for appearing *(epiphaneian);* however, this time in reference to the *glory* of Jesus Christ. Paul is most likely thinking in terms of the second appearing *(parousia)* of Christ. Commentators notice here a similarity to the language of the accession of great monarchs in the ancient times. Paul is contemplating the majestic appearance of "the King of kings and Lord of lords" (1 Tim. 6:15).

The next phrase in the Greek text *(tou megalou theou kai sōtēros hēmōn)* may be literally rendered, "of the great God and our Saviour" (KJV). Another possible translation is **of our great God and Savior** (NASB, NIV, and RSV). The question that has been raised by this phrase is this: Does Paul speak here about the appearing of two Persons, that is, God and Jesus Christ, or one Person, that is, Jesus Christ? It is certain that Paul does not entertain here the thought of a great God and a little God (the Arian heresy). The context suggests that the emphasis here is on the second coming of Christ. Christ is not only our Savior but also our God.

Who gave Himself for us. These words summarize the redeeming and purifying ministry of the grace of God. The proper basis for a believer's hope in the Second Coming is laid for him in the work of Christ. A believer does not wait for the appearance of an unknown benefactor in his life, but the One "who gave himself" for him. This is both the uniqueness and the paradox of the Christian gospel. A heathen king or god would not surrender his life to save a nation. Such an idea is inconceivable. The good news of God's grace is that this great God gave up His life "as a ransom for all" (1 Tim. 2:6; cf. Mark 10:45). It is described as a willing and voluntary act, not a coerced one or something that was imposed upon Him. The purpose of His death makes His sacrifice the purest, the noblest, and the most desirable of all events in mankind's history.

Christ gave up His life **that He might redeem us from every lawless deed.** The Greek verb translated here as **redeem** *(lutroō)* includes the concept of freeing someone by paying a ransom. This meaning is illustrated in the practice of the Israelites paying half a shekel to the Lord as a ransom during the time of census (Exod. 30:12-15; see also 13:13; Lev. 25:47-55). The payment of a set amount is thus central to this concept. The language of this verse is reminiscent of Ps. 130:8: "And He will redeem Israel from all his iniquities" (NASB). Paul here deals with the redemptive work of Christ (Gal. 1:4; 1 Tim. 2:6). In Paul's theology, Christ's death is described as a representative act (Rom. 5:6-8). The Greek prepositional phrase *huper hēmōn* **(for us)** conveys the idea of "on behalf of" that brings out the representative character of Christ's death.[4]

Christ's death offers to a sinner total freedom from his **lawless deed** or "wickedness." Lawlessness *(anomias)* is breaking the law, and it is the essence of sin (1 John 3:4). It is also the evidence of a person's state of subjection to the power of sin.

Purify for Himself a people for His own [special] possession. ... Deliverance from the power of sin is followed by the purifying ministry of grace. Some commentators attempt to connect the phrase **purify** *(katharizō)* with "the washing" of regeneration in 3:5 and prefer to see here a reference to the sacrament of baptism.[5] It is more likely that Paul has in mind the sanctifying work of Christ, "since the act of purification is performed by Christ Himself."[6]

The language of purifying/cleansing is a familiar theme in the Bible. After the people of Israel made the covenant with God at Mount Sinai, Moses sprinkled the blood upon the people to consecrate them as a holy nation before God (Exod. 24:3-8). This act was in accordance with God's plan to make Israel His "own possession . . . a kingdom of priests and a holy nation" (19:5-6, NASB). Paul makes here a direct allusion to the prophetic statement of Ezekiel:

> They shall not defile themselves any more with their idols and their detestable things, or with any of their transgressions; but I will save them from all the backslidings in which they have sinned, and will cleanse them; and they shall be my people, and I will be their God *(37:23, RSV).*

The goal of this cleansing is to create **for Himself a people for His own possession. A people for His own possession** is a frequently used expression in the OT (cf. Exod. 19:5). This phrase indicates special property rights or ownership and the value of the property as a treasure. Paul here expresses the special relationship between the Redeemer and the redeemed. This becomes clear when we consider the ancient pagan practice of a conqueror king keeping for his special use a portion of the spoil before it was divided among his soldiers. In like manner Christ, the victorious King, who triumphed over the power of sin, is described here by Paul as choosing the redeemed for His special use. Once they were slaves to sin, now they are called to be servants **zealous for good deeds.** This is the proper response of the redeemed to the Redeemer (see also Eph. 2:10). Just as Israel was called in the OT to obey the law as a response to their deliverance from slavery, the Church is called to live out the gospel in its ethical life-style.

Theological Truths of the Text

Several theological truths come to expression in this passage:

The grace of God is an event that has happened in mankind's history **(the grace of God has appeared).** The incarnation of Jesus

Christ (see John 1:14), His life and ministry, and His sacrificial death make visible for us the appearance of grace in a personalized form. Paul elsewhere speaks of the time of this appearance as "the fulness of the time" (Gal. 4:4, NASB). This historical manifestation of God's grace is something that can be individually experienced (see Paul's words: "recognizing the grace that had been given to me," Gal. 2:9, NASB).

Grace is God's *unmerited favor and His free and good will* to all mankind. Paul's use of the word **grace** in the greeting section of all of his Epistles is an evidence of his joy and gladness at this divine favor that God bestowed upon the Church. Grace thus evokes gladness in a believer, because he is the recipient of the favor of God without his own merit.

Grace **appeared** to sinful mankind. *God comes to us in the context of our need.* Where there is bondage, where there is a cry of despair and hopelessness, God manifests himself as Yahweh, with the promise of His presence (see Exod. 3:7-8).

Grace enables an individual to receive salvation (**For the grace of God has appeared, bringing salvation**). Grace therefore may be spoken of as *prevenient,* or grace that goes before salvation. It is this grace that enables a sinner who is "dead in trespasses and sins" (Eph. 2:1, KJV) to awake and to hear the gospel of salvation. Grace further enables a believer to respond to the gospel call. This grace is bestowed upon *all* mankind.

Salvation is extended to all mankind. Grace shows no partiality to anyone. All who favorably respond to the gospel call become the recipients of salvation. God through Jesus Christ offers freedom from the power of sin impartially to all men, and He **desires all men to be saved and to come to the knowledge of the truth** (1 Tim. 2:4, NASB).

One who responds to the favor of God *receives instructions* from God *in the art of godly living.* It is the ministry of grace to educate a believer and to produce in him true Christian character. The Book of Proverbs refers to this activity as the function of **wisdom,** the source of which is God (see Proverbs chaps. 1—4).

Grace also enables a believer to renounce ungodliness and worldliness and to live a sober, righteous, and godly life. It is the *power of the grace of God* that is at work in the life of a believer that *brings him to the moment of his denial* of his former way of life *and to the consecration of his life* to God (Gal. 5:24).

The hope of a believer in Christ is *a solid assurance* of eternal life in Him. Therefore it is a blessed hope.

Jesus Christ is God. He alone is the true God and the Savior of mankind. His glory will be manifested at His second coming, and this glory will be the glory of God.

Christ alone is the Redeemer of sinners. Christ's death is a representative act to proclaim freedom to those under the captivity of sin. He died to redeem sinners not only from the guilt of sins committed but also from the power of sin.

Christ is also our Sanctifier. The goal of His death also includes the cleansing of the heart of a believer. Peter's remark that God made no distinction between Jews and Gentiles when He cleansed the Gentiles' heart by the Holy Spirit (Acts 15:9) is a testimony to this effect of the Atonement. Paul speaks of this ministry of Christ also in Eph. 5:25-27. In this passage, he describes the goal of Christ's work: "sanctify . . . [and] present to Himself the church . . . having no spot or wrinkle . . . that she should be holy and blameless" (NASB). It is clear that in this passage Paul has in mind an activity other than a ceremonial washing by water. The emphasis is on the need for an inner cleansing; that is, the cleansing of the heart that remains to be accomplished subsequent to the ministry of redemption from the power of sin.

The Church is the possession of Christ. Christ alone is her Savior and Lord. A believer is consequently called to be *zealously* involved in living out the character of her Lord.

Preaching Ideas on the Text

Topic: **Possibilities of Grace**

Introduction: "Master the Possibilities" is a challenge we have heard from a particular credit card system. The resources and possibilities of this card are, however, severely limited. Christ offers to us unlimited resources and possibilities of His grace and invites us to accept His offer of an abundant life.

A. *The Enabling Grace of God* (v. 11). Grace that enables us to come to Christ is: (1) reality that continues to make its appearance even today; and (2) impartial and extends itself to all mankind.

B. *The Educating Grace of God* (v. 12) comes to us and instructs us

(1) to renounce ungodliness and worldly desires, and (2) to live a self-controlled, upright, and godly life.

C. *The Redeeming and Sanctifying Grace of God* (v. 14) is at work in (1) the redemptive ministry of Christ through His death, and (2) the cleansing ministry through which Christ sets apart a special people to do good work for Him.

Topic: **"Sound Doctrine"**

Introduction: Paul uses this phrase frequently in his letter to Titus to emphasize our Christian duty to commit ourselves to the knowledge of the doctrines of the Church. Some of these are:

A. *The Universal Scope of Christ's Redemption* (v. 11) that includes (1) the atonement of Christ for all mankind, and (2) man's inability to exercise faith in the atonement of Christ without the prevenient grace of God.

B. *Christ the Redeemer and the Sanctifier of the Church* (v. 14) is the One who (1) paid His life as the price for our redemption; (2) sanctifies us to be a people unto himself.

C. *The Christian Hope in the Second Coming* (v. 13) is (1) a blessed hope, and (2) a solemn assurance given to the Church by the Redeemer God.

Sermon on the Text
The Call to Live a Godly Life

Text: **Titus 2:11-14**

Introduction: All of the three Synoptic Gospel writers tell us the story of a young man who was concerned about his eternal relationship with God. He was an extremely rich man. He was also a very religious individual who carefully kept all the rules of his faith. However, he found himself lacking in something, and living a religious life with no assurance of eternal life. He came to Jesus with his religious dilemma. In his conversation with Jesus, he recognized what was lacking in his religious life. Though he zealously kept the moral demands of the law, he tragically failed in keeping its religious demands. He understood godly living primarily in terms of his relationship to others. When Jesus challenged him in terms of his relation to God, he went away with regret. We are told that his unwillingness to give up all his wealth, thus putting God first, prevented him from finding satisfaction in his religious life.

A Christian's call to godly living demands from him not only his knowledge and experience of the doctrines of the Church but also his commitment to fulfill the ethical demands of the gospel of Jesus Christ. Overemphasis of the doctrines at the expense of the ethical response, or vice versa, is detrimental, and the result will be an unbalanced religious life.

The apostle Paul was convinced that true Christian faith must produce its ethical results. He was also convinced that the task of his apostolic ministry included both instruction in the doctrines of the Church and training the believers in living a life based on doctrine (see 1 Tim. 1:1-3). This latter concern is reflected in his letter to Titus.

In the letter to Titus, Paul gives charge to Titus, his "true child in a common faith" (1:4, NASB), who was appointed to the ministry at Crete, to instruct men and women of all walks of life to live a godly life. Specific mention is made in his letter concerning elders or bishops, older men, older women, young men, young women, and Christian slaves (1:5—2:10). All of these people, regardless of their ecclesiastical, social, age, or sex differences, have a Christian's obligation to live a godly life. No one is given exemption or special treatment. Such an appeal is made not as a personal wish of the apostle but rather as the demand of the gospel that comes to every Christian.

The text of this sermon (2:11-14) is thematically connected to the preceding and the following sections of this Epistle. Here Paul outlines the theological reasons for godly living. These reasons may be grouped into the following four categories:

1. *All Christians are recipients of God's grace* (v. 11). It is God's grace that enables a sinner to respond to the call of the gospel and to accept the salvation that God offers to all mankind. All Christians are thus beneficiaries of the enabling grace (prevenient grace). This grace is an unmerited favor, the display of the love and kindness of God, that God grants to all mankind in spite of man's unworthiness.

   a. Grace appears to man in the context of his need for salvation. "All have sinned and fall short of the glory of God" (Rom. 3:23). This universal need for salvation is explicit in Paul's description of the human condition as "helpless" (Rom. 5:6), and "dead in . . . trespasses and sin" (Eph. 2:1, both NASB). Regardless of one's present place in the social structure, all believers once shared this same need for salvation.

   b. Grace shows no partiality. Grace enables all men to come to God's salvation. No one is given any special recognition because of his social or economic condition.

2. *All Christians are students under the teaching ministry of grace* (v. 12). All Christians are in need of instruction in proper Christian living. The Greek word for **instruct** *(paideuein)* conveys the ignorant condition of an individual at the time of his response to God's grace. At the moment of his response to the gospel call, he becomes a pupil in the art of godly living. The teaching ministry of grace is intended to accomplish the following objectives:

   a. Grace trains us to **deny** ["renounce," RSV] **ungodliness and worldly desires** (v. 12).

   Ungodliness and worldly desires are characteristics of unsaved individuals. Ungodliness is not only a lack of reverence for God but also a mind-set that includes a total rejection of God's power and authority. It is characteristic of a heathen who favors falsehood instead of truth. It is a perverted religious understanding. Grace also instructs all believers to renounce their desires for the things of this world, "things we could not show to God" (Barclay). Such desires are characteristics of the carnal mind. Worldly desires are symptomatic of a believer's continued tendency toward the wisdom and passions of this age.

   Grace teaches a believer to bid farewell to these characteristics of his former way of life once and for all, in an act of complete breakaway from the past. The Greek verb used here *(arnēsamenoi)* indicates that such renunciation must take place at a particular moment, as an act of a final decision. Such a decision is a crucial act, and that moment of decision is therefore decisive in the life of a believer. This is indeed a crisis moment that cannot be faced with our human resources, but solely by the enabling and instructing ministry of grace. The call here is to "crucify" (JB) our "flesh with its passions and desires" (Gal. 5:24, NASB).

b. The teaching ministry of God's grace also includes a curriculum in living **sensibly, righteously and godly in the present age** (v. 12).

At the critical moment of our renunciation of ungodliness and worldly desires begins the educative ministry of grace in the art of living a sober, righteous, and godly life. Sobriety is one's duty to himself. It is his commitment to exercise self-control. Righteousness is one's duty to others. It is his commitment to behave in an upright manner. Godliness is one's duty to God. It is his commitment to respond to God's authority over his life. Again, it is the ministry of grace that enables all believers to maintain a balanced relationship with themselves, others, and God.

3. *All Christians are heirs to the glorious hope in Jesus Christ* (v. 13). The ultimate purpose of the teaching ministry of grace is to establish believers in their hope in Jesus Christ. A Christian who submits himself to the instructions of grace receives a solid hope in the appearing of Christ in His glory. Grace instructs a believer to wait in anticipation for the fulfillment of his hope in Christ. **Looking** indicates an active and eager expectation for a glorious day. There is no place for impatience, passivity, or coolness in this expectant waiting.

a. The Christian hope in the Second Coming is not a wishful thinking. It is described here as a **blessed hope,** a solid assurance, and a guaranteed promise. The work that Christ has already performed on behalf of a sinner to redeem and purify him (see v. 14) is the foundation upon which this assurance is given.

A Christian has, therefore, reason to live. He has a grand hope in his Savior God who will come in all of His glory. He lives with this hope in the midst of hopelessness in this world. This hope gives him joy in the midst of his sorrow, peace in the midst of his anxiety, and an abundant life in a world that cries out in agony and despair.

4. *All Christians are beneficiaries of the redemptive and purifying ministry of Jesus Christ* (v. 14).

a. He is the Redeemer and the Sanctifier of all believers. "All of us like sheep have gone astray, each of us has turned to his own way" (Isa. 53:6, NASB). He paid His own life as a price (Mark 10:45) for the freedom of mankind from their bondage to the power of sin. His death alone is the basis for a believer's freedom from lawlessness. After redemption from the power of sin follows the purifying work of Christ in the life of a believer. It is a cleansing ministry that Christ himself will accomplish through His Holy Spirit. The cleansing here does not refer to a ceremonial cleansing with water, rather a cleansing of the heart, just as it happened on the Day of Pentecost (see Acts 2; 15:9; Eph. 5:25-27).

b. The redeemed and the sanctified are a special possession of Jesus Christ, with a mission to carry out (v. 14). They are holy and blameless to Him (Eph. 5:27). Christ values them as a special treasure. This is the attitude of the Redeemer to the redeemed. His special possession, the Church, is called to live a life with zealousness for doing good deeds. The call here is to find joy in service, and excitement in doing even little things for Jesus. This is the ethical demand of the gospel of Jesus Christ.

Conclusion: Paul's admonition to Titus to instruct believers to live a life based on sound doctrine is a direct challenge to believers in all walks of life today. Such a challenge comes to us on the basis of the ministry of grace in salvation and in sanctification. A balanced Christian life and our growth in Christian maturity depend on our understanding and experience of the basic beliefs of the Christian Church as well as on our commitment to live a godly life in this world by following the ethical demands of the gospel of Jesus Christ. This is the most appropriate response to God's grace that comes to us through Jesus Christ.

Endnotes

1. Most Scripture quotations are taken from the *New American Standard Bible.*
2. In the following is a list of some other key references to his use of the word "grace" in his Epistles. We are called to enter into grace by participating in the historical event of grace through being crucified with Christ (Gal. 2:20; Rom. 5:2). We are justified by the grace of God (2 Tim. 1:9; Titus 3:7). Though we possess grace, it remains to be a free gift. Therefore, no one can boast about it (1 Cor. 1:20; 2 Cor. 12:1-5). This grace is now at work in the life of believers, the power of which not only overcomes sin in the historical scene (Rom. 5:20), and in the lives of individuals (1 Tim. 1:14), but also provides support and comfort to a believer in distress or weakness (2 Cor. 12:9). On the one hand, self-effort to continue in grace will lead to a believer's fall from it (Gal. 5:4); on the other hand, one must grow strong in grace (2 Tim. 2:1), guarding through the Holy Spirit this treasure that has been entrusted to him (2 Tim. 1:14).
3. Although the KJV reading, "For the grace of God that bringeth salvation hath appeared to all men," is possible, it is more likely and theologically appropriate to add "to all men" to the noun "salvation" as in NASB and RSV, rather than to the

verb "appeared." The KJV reading suggests the universality of the manifestation of God's grace. The text here emphasizes the universal scope of Christ's death and atonement, and not universalism. See Donald Guthrie, *The Pastoral Epistles,* in *The Tyndale New Testament Commentaries* (Grand Rapids: Wm. B. Eerdmans Publishing Co., 1957), 198.

4. See H. Orton Wiley, *Christian Theology,* 3 vols. (Kansas City: Beacon Hill Press, 1941), 2:246; W. T. Purkiser, Richard S. Taylor, and Willard H. Taylor, *God, Man, and Salvation* (Kansas City: Beacon Hill Press of Kansas City, 1977), 385-87; H. Ray Dunning, *Grace, Faith, and Holiness: A Wesleyan Systematic Theology* (Kansas City: Beacon Hill Press of Kansas City, 1988), 378-79.

5. Newport J. D. White, *The Expositor's Greek New Testament: The Epistle to Titus* (reprint, Grand Rapids: Wm. B. Eerdmans Publishing Co., 1974), 196.

6. Guthrie, *Pastoral Epistles,* 201.

—**8**—

HOLINESS
AS GOD'S
PROVISION

JOHN M. NIELSON

Holiness—an Atonement Provision

And so Jesus also suffered outside the city gate to make the people holy through his own blood (Heb. 13:12).

Introduction

I've seen the bumper sticker frequently. It bothers me a little—like a lot of other bumper stickers I see. It says, "Christians aren't perfect—just forgiven." To the degree that this statement means that Christians have not yet reached absolute perfection, I could agree. But to the degree that it implies that the death of Christ does not radically change us but only changes the way that God perceives us; to the degree that it states that we are offered only perpetual forgiveness for continuing to be rebellious sinners; to the degree that it claims that we are not changed, regenerated, cleansed, or sanctified but are "just forgiven"—to that degree we must vigorously deny the statement. God does not call us to be forgiven sinners. He calls us to be saints—holy ones. Forgiveness is but one aspect of God's overall plan that includes His intention to make us holy.

The Bible has many significant statements pertaining to the purpose of the coming and death of our Savior. Some of them come from Jesus himself: "I have come that they may have life, and have it to the full" (John 10:10). "For the Son of Man came to seek and to save what was lost" (Luke 19:10). The apostle Paul wrote, "Christ Jesus came into the world to save sinners—of whom I am the worst" (1 Tim. 1:15).

In this text, the author of the Epistle to the Hebrews gives us

353

one of the clearest statements in Scripture of the purpose of Christ's death. He came and died to **make the people holy**. This declaration is particularly relevant in a day when so much evangelical preaching seems to offer cheap grace: forgiveness without regeneration, new birth without a new life, religion without responsibility, imputed righteousness without imparted righteousness, the gospel of success without the call to the holy life and the pure heart.

Exegesis

The Setting. The Epistle to the Hebrews is one of the books of the NT about which there is much confusion when it comes to matters of authorship, date, and so on. Probably the safest position, after listening to all of the arguments, is to assume that the author is unknown and that he probably penned his letter to Jewish Christians shortly after the middle of the first century. Whether he originally wrote in Hebrew or Greek is also a matter that remains up in the air.

What *is* clear is that his audience has a deep understanding of the old covenant and its sacrificial system. Throughout the book, the old and new covenants are compared and contrasted. In every case, the sacrifice of Christ, our High Priest, is shown to be superior to the old system that has been made obsolete by Christ.

It is probable that the book was written to counter the efforts of the Judaizers who sought to keep Christianity wedded to Judaism with its forms and legalism. It was thus designed "to confirm the Jewish Christians in their faith and to guard them against an apostasy to Judaism."[1] It may also have been intended to evangelize Jews by convincing them that Christ was the fulfillment of all that was prefigured in the old covenant and that the gospel was in every way superior to the religion of the law.

Immediate Context. The text we are considering comes at the conclusion of a carefully developed argument. What will be considered in our discussion here as the primary phrase—**to make the people holy through his own blood**—is almost a parenthesis in the flow of this argument. Yet, since it is such a clear statement of purpose, it can hardly be ignored. Before examining the language of the text, it is important that we examine its immediate context.

In his warning about being carried away by strange teachings, the author specifically mentions "ceremonial foods" (v. 9). There is no agreement among scholars as to the practice to which he is referring. To explain what is wrong with this teaching, he, in typical fashion, finds a contrasting parallel in OT imagery.

Leviticus 4 outlines the requirements for the various sin offerings. In each case, the guilty person is to lay his hands upon the sacrifice (an animal without defect), thus apparently transferring guilt. The priest is to slay the animal, sprinkle the blood within the sanctuary, and then burn the fat upon the altar of burnt sacrifices. If the blood is taken into the holy place to make atonement (Lev. 6:30), then the remainder of the carcass was to be taken outside the camp to be burned. If the blood was not taken into the holy place, then the priests were allowed to eat the meat (vv. 26, 29).

The author of Hebrews notes that those who follow Christ have an altar that supersedes the one that put ceremonial food on the priestly table. Since Christ suffered outside the gate, His blood having been taken into the holy place (9:12), there is no ceremonial food provided by His sacrifice. Rather, the value to us is mediated by His grace (13:9). It is thus that the "strange teachings" about ceremonial foods are refuted.

Throughout the Epistle, the author draws on the symbolism of the OT sacrificial system to explain and interpret the ministry of Christ. In this text, the author establishes one additional detail of the sacrifice of Christ that can be compared and contrasted with the OT system in that the location of Jesus' crucifixion occurs outside the city just as in the OT sacrifice for sin. Thus even the place of His death is seen as part of the cosmic drama that is prefigured in the sacrificial system. Wiley notes that a full study of this symbolism is too large for his 395-page volume. (One preaching from this text could delve more deeply into this aspect of the Epistle and of this text than can be done in this brief chapter.)

So while it is clear that the immediate context of our text deals with the eating of ceremonial foods, that does not mean that to focus on the more parenthetical statement as a proclamation of God's intention to make us holy is to take the verse out of context.

In the first place, many of the great truths of Scripture are similar asides—phrases dropped like gold nuggets in the middle of other discussions. A prime example of this occurs in Paul's treatise on family relationships in Ephesians where he suddenly inserts a statement that bears a close relationship to our text: "Christ loved the church and gave himself up for her to make her holy, cleansing her by the washing with water through the word, and to present her to himself as a radiant church, without stain or wrinkle or any other blemish, but holy and blameless" (5:25-27).

Second, our understanding of this verse is consistent with the immediate context. The author is clearly comparing and contrasting the purpose of the sacrifice of Christ with the sin offerings of the former dispensation. To ignore the importance of this key phrase would be to make its insertion by the author meaningless.

Third, the broader context (that is, the entire chapter and for that matter the whole Epistle) clearly deals with the theme of holiness. Note some of the key Hebrews verses that illustrate this point.

> Both the one who makes men holy and those who are made holy are of the same family *(2:11)*.
>
> He did not enter by means of the blood of goats and calves; but he entered the Most Holy Place once for all by his own blood, having obtained eternal redemption. The blood of goats and bulls and the ashes of a heifer sprinkled on those who are ceremonially unclean sanctify them so that they are outwardly clean. How much more, then, will the blood of Christ, who through the eternal Spirit offered himself unblemished to God, cleanse our consciences from acts that lead to death, so that we may serve the living God! *(9:12-14)*.
>
> And by that will, we have been made holy through the sacrifice of the body of Jesus Christ once for all *(10:10)*.
>
> Because by one sacrifice he has made perfect forever those who are being made holy *(10:14)*.
>
> But God disciplines us for our good, that we may share in his holiness *(12:10)*.
>
> Make every effort to live in peace with all men and to be holy; without holiness no one will see the Lord *(12:14)*. [And who did Jesus say were the ones who would see God? "Blessed are the pure in heart, for they will see God" (Matt. 5:8).]
>
> You have come to God, the judge of all men, to the spirits of righteous men made perfect *(12:23)*.

Key Words. In seeking to understand our passage, it is important that we examine some of the words of the text more carefully.

So *(dio)*, also translated as "wherefore" (KJV) and "therefore" (NASB). It is no doubt dangerous to try to make this word a hinge on which the entire Epistle turns. That is, the antecedent of *dio* is not the first 12½ chapters but is rather v. 11. Because the bodies from the sin offerings were disposed of outside the camp, "therefore" Jesus' death took place outside the city of Jerusalem. Or, as the Phillips paraphrase puts it, "That is why Jesus, when he sanctified men by the shedding of his own blood, suffered and died outside the city gates."

To *(hina),* also translated "that" (KJV, NASB) or "in order to" (RSV). The word literally means "in order that,"[2] so the RSV is the most direct translation. The word clearly introduces a statement of purpose.

Through his own blood *(dia tou idiou haimatos).* There is comparison in this phrase—comparison to the fact that in both the old covenant and the new, cleansing from sin requires the shedding of blood. There is contrast in this phrase—contrast between the old covenant, where the blood is that of a lamb offered repeatedly, and the new covenant, where the blood is that of Christ himself, offered once. This emphasis on Christ's own blood is made in other sections of the Epistle, such as 9:12-14; 10:19-20; and 13:20.

The people *(ton laon).* This phrase and its variations is used in the OT as a designation for Israel and in the NT is extended to cover those who under the new covenant are the "true Israel."[3] Kistemaker notes that this is the 13th and last use of the phrase in the Epistle and that each time it refers to God's people.[4] It should be noted, however, that the word in its broader context denotes the masses. It is by the blood of Christ that "the masses" become "God's People." *Laon* is the word from which we derive our term *laity.*

Make the people holy *(hagiasē)* is translated "sanctify" (NASB, KJV). This is the primary word we need to understand in the text. Most translations use either the phrase "make holy" or "sanctify" except the *New English Bible* that uses the weaker term "consecrate." Our English word "sanctify" comes from the Latin words *sanctus* (holy) and *ficare* (to make).

Wiley, in noting that the word occurs in the first aorist active subjunctive, states that it "can mean only the act of sanctification —that supreme redemptive act by which Christ with His own blood makes His people holy in heart and life."[5] Kistemaker believes that its use "has been occasioned by *ta hagia"* (the most holy place) in the preceding verse. He also underscores the fact that it "stands in a purpose clause."[6]

Robinson lists the first meaning of *hagiazō* as "to make clean, to cleanse." He notes that it is used in a moral sense, and he refers specifically to this text. Its second meaning is listed as "to make sacred or holy, to consecrate, to set apart from a common to a sacred use."[7] Liddell and Scott indicate that in relation to persons, it denotes purity.

In the Book of Hebrews, the contrast is between ceremonial and ethical sanctification. The rituals of sacrifice and so on effected a ritualistic holiness, which was inadequate. The writer of Hebrews is claiming that Jesus' sacrifice is better because it provides for a real, ethical holiness. Thus even though the book uses ceremonial language, as is appropriate for its symbolism, we must interpret it in ethical terms.

Historically, many theologians have understood the word in a positional rather than an ethical sense; that is, they have interpreted the word to mean that we are viewed by God as if we are holy, rather than that we are made ethically pure by the power of God in our lives. They have emphasized the secondary meaning of "setting apart" (which is used particularly of things) rather than the primary meaning of purity and cleansing. On the basis of this viewpoint, the Wesleyan understanding of holiness and entire sanctification has frequently been attacked. Some would excuse sin in the life of the Christian and postpone any imparted sanctity until the hereafter. We must always be careful not to let our theological preconceptions dictate the meaning of the biblical word and thus our interpretation of Scripture. Instead, the meaning of the term should dictate the interpretation of Scripture and thus the formulation of theology. So it is important that we properly understand the meaning of *hagiasē*. It is unfortunate that so often this word is interpreted only in the sense of consecration, separation, or imputed righteousness.

In this regard, Wiley comments on the
> perverted but popular theory of imputation. This is a perverted view that is untrue both to the Scriptures and to human experience; popular, because it is a plea for sin remaining in the heart. This theory holds that holiness is not imparted to us by the Spirit, but is merely imputed to us, so that by our "standing" we are accounted holy, but as to our "state" or condition we are still in sin.[8]

If the sacrifice of Christ is once for all and final, and we are to be freed from repetitive sacrifice, then His death must deliver from the present practice and dominion of sin, not just assuage the guilt of past transgressions.

Wiley analyzes a number of occurrences of the word in the Epistle, such as 2:11-13; 10:10; 10:14; and 12:14. He consistently underscores this ethical rather than positional emphasis. He also distinguished between the objective aspect of sanctification (that is, the work that Christ has completed for us by the shedding of His blood) and the subjective aspect (that is, the work of the Holy Spirit in our lives).[9]

Theology of the Passage

In the light of the above, therefore, it becomes evident that to ignore the moral and ethical meanings of *hagiasē* is to make a mockery of the commands of Jesus ("Go, and sin no more," John 8:11; see 5:14, KJV), the teachings of the apostles ("I write this to you so that you will not sin," 1 John 2:1), and the basic message of the Epistle to the Hebrews itself, where the author repeatedly underscores the theme of holiness in ways that are empty of real meaning if we only understand the word ceremonially or positionally.

Key Phrase. There is far from unanimous agreement among biblical scholars as to the importance of what is considered here as the primary phrase of the text—**To make the people holy through his own blood.** Many commentators ignore the phrase altogether, focusing instead on either the question of ceremonial foods or the meaning of **outside the city gate** in conjunction with v. 14.[10]

Holiness preachers have often ignored the phrase as well. In the 14 volumes of Wesley's works, there is no record of his ever using this verse as a text. Richard S. Taylor's *Preaching Holiness Today* gives it only a passing mention.

Other authors come a bit closer to a fuller understanding, but not much closer.[11] A few authors approach a more complete viewpoint. Kistemaker notes that the author

> compares the implied purpose of the sacrifices made on the Day of Atonement to the suffering Jesus experienced on the cross. As he explains in earlier parts of his epistle, Jesus' sacrifice is once for all and incomparably superior. . . . The comparison in general points to Jesus' work to make his people holy. . . . Through the shedding of his blood, Jesus removed the sin of his people and made them holy. That is, by fulfilling the stipulations con-

cerning the removal of sin on the Day of Atonement (Lev. 16:26-28), Jesus cleansed his people and sanctified them. The author of Hebrews briefly summarizes the purpose of Jesus' suffering: to make the people holy through his own blood." In many places he has explained this point and therefore has no need to elaborate on it now (see 2:11; 10:10, 14; 12:14).[12]

Perhaps the clearest statement is one by Wiley: "We have now reached the climax of the entire Epistle, that is, the high and sacred purpose of Jesus to sanctify the people with His own blood. For this He suffered without the gate."[13] But even here, the discussion is not all that could be desired. Wiley turns immediately to a lengthy discussion of entire sanctification through the work of the Holy Spirit that is not developed from an exposition of his passage in Hebrews.

Some Wesleyans (Wiley, for example) find here an emphasis on the secondness of entire sanctification in this passage. They do so on the basis that they view the Epistle as being addressed to those who are already Christians rather than to those who are still in their sins, and in that the imagery deals not with the Passover but with the period of the wanderings.[14] While such a view may be correct, it is not the primary meaning of this passage. There are much stronger scriptures on which to build the case for entire sanctification as a second definite work of grace. To find that view here is to overlook a truth that is far more encompassing.

This text makes one of the strongest cases in Scripture for a theology of holiness in the broad sense. Fully understood, holiness is not an equivalent of "entire sanctification," although it includes it. Nor is holiness an add-on to the rest of our theology of salvation. It is rather the way we understand *all* of the Atonement. It is the environment—the very air—that suffuses and envelops all of the plan of redemption. Jesus didn't die primarily to forgive us, to get us out of hell and into heaven, to placate an angry God, to make us church members, or to make us candidates for baptism. He died to make us holy. Any lesser concept is defective.

Holiness, then, is the whole purpose behind all of redemption. The purpose behind conviction is to show us our own unholiness and to call us toward His holiness. The purpose behind forgiveness and regeneration is to cleanse us from acquired depravity and guilt, from the practice of sin, and to initiate holiness in us. The purpose behind entire sanctification is to cleanse the inner nature and bring about holiness in the heart. The purpose of progressive sanctification is to increasingly develop holiness in the life-style and personality. The purpose of glorification is to remove the deficiencies of our mortality and usher us into the paradise of a holy God.

This verse does not necessarily speak to the issue of the secondness of entire sanctification as much as it defines the purpose God is seeking to accomplish through the atoning work of Christ and through the various works of grace as they are appropriated into our lives. If we deny the possibility of holiness in this life; if we refuse the sanctifying work of God in our hearts; if we refuse to accept the personal, purifying, ethical implications of sanctification, then we frustrate the clearly stated purpose of God in Christ.

This sanctification is obtained at no small cost. It is accomplished through the precious blood of Christ (see also 1 Pet. 1:19). In addition, it cost Him the reproach of man (vv. 12-13) and separation from the Father (Matt. 27:46).

It is significant to note that while the sacrifice of the OT is offered by the priest, the sacrifice of Christ is the offering of himself. He is not the direct object of the verb but its subject. His death is volitional. Our response is also volitional (we must "go to him"), but it is not optional. Not only are the commands to holy living directed to those who claim to be entirely sanctified, but they are God's call to every Christian—actually to every man and woman whom He has created.

Sermon Suggestions

There are numerous ways in which the preacher can approach this text and its context. The concepts below may be developed individually, or various elements may be combined to suit the need of the hour. Some of the outlines could even become a series of sermons if developed fully.

God's Ultimate Plan
1. The Purpose of Christ
   To make the people holy
2. The Provision of Christ
   Through his own blood

3. The Priorities for Christians
   Let us join Him (v. 13)
   Let us praise Him (v. 15)
   Let us live like Him (vv. 16 ff.)
Or the same concept could be covered as:
Holiness—
   It Is God's Purpose
   It Is Christ's Provision
   It Is Our Potential

To Make the People Holy

Four Phases of the Sanctification Christ Died to Provide
   1. Initial Sanctification
      He forgives the past.
   2. Entire Sanctification
      He purifies a heart.
   3. Progressive Sanctification
      He corrects the life.
   4. Final Sanctification
      He glorifies the body.

   One could also use the same four points but build on the theme "Holiness Lost—Holiness Regained," using Gen. 2:8—3:24 and Heb. 13:12.

The Nature of Holiness

(Based on the meanings of the word found in this text)
   1. Holiness Is Purity
   2. Holiness Is Consecration
   3. Holiness Is Separation
      a. From sin
      b. From the law
      c. To God

Holy Sacrifices
   1. Theirs was an animal sacrifice
      —offered repeatedly
      —for themselves (v. 11)

2. His was His own blood
   —offered once
   —for others (v. 12)
3. Ours is of praise and goodness
   —offered continually
   —for Him (vv. 15-16)

Four Facts of Holiness
1. The Persons (v. 12)
2. The Purpose (v. 12)
3. The Price (v. 12)
4. The Prize (v. 14)
   —W. T. Purkiser, BBE

The Way of Sanctification
1. The Person Who Sanctifies
   a. Who Christ is
      (see 1:1-6 et al.)
   b. It is His work, not ours
2. The Place of Sanctification
   a. Outside the gate
   b. His reproach
   c. Therefore our reproach and self-denial
3. The Plan for Sanctification
   a. Voluntary, not optional
   b. Sharing His shame
   c. Separation from sin
   d. Identification with Christ
4. The Purchase of Sanctification
   a. His blood
   b. His separation
   c. Purity
      (1) at divine expense
      (2) for human benefit

The Enduring Covenant

1. A Holy Consecration (**The disgrace he bore,** v. 13)
   a. Surrender vs. self-centeredness
   b. Shouldering the cross of humility
   c. Accepting my disgrace
2. A Holy Sacrifice (**Through his own blood,** v. 12)
   a. Blood of bulls vs. blood of Christ
   Law vs. grace
   b. Trusting the power of His blood
   c. Accepting Christ's disgrace
3. A Holy People (**make the people holy,** v. 12)
   a. Imparted vs. imputed righteousness
   Is holiness a cover-up or actual deliverance?
   b. Fashioned in His likeness
   c. Accepting the holiness of God
4. A Holy Hope (**The city that is to come,** v. 14)
   a. Jerusalem vs. the Holy City
   Ended covenant vs. enduring covenant
   b. Waiting for the enduring city
   c. Accepting my place in the kingdom of God

—William B. Nielson

Four Great Truths of Redemption

1. Sanctification (v. 12)
2. Separation (v. 13)
3. Seeking Eternity (v. 14)
4. Sacrifice (vv. 15-16)
   a. of praise
   b. of service

—Adapted from Charles Carter (WBC, 181)

It is also possible to preach from the broader context of this passage. One sermon could focus on the **Hallmarks of the Holy Life** that Christ died to obtain for us. This topic seems to be the theme of the 13th chapter of Hebrews that contains many exhortations to practical holiness.

1. Show Brotherly Love (v. 1)
2. Show Hospitality (v. 2)
3. Remember Prisoners (v. 3)
4. Remember Those Mistreated (v. 3)
5. Preserve Sexual Purity (v. 4)
6. Avoid Materialism (v. 5)
7. Honor and Follow Leaders (v. 7)
8. Avoid Strange Teachings (v. 9)
9. Bear Christ's Disgrace (v. 13)
10. Praise (v. 15)
11. Share (v. 16)
12. Obey (v. 17)
13. Pray (v. 18)
14. Do God's Will (v. 21)

Any sermon on this passage could well close with the holiness-impregnated words with which the author closed his Epistle.

> May the God of peace, who through the blood of the eternal covenant brought back from the dead our Lord Jesus, that great Shepherd of the sheep, equip you with everything good for doing his will, and may he work in us what is pleasing to him, through Jesus Christ, to whom be glory for ever and ever. Amen *(13:20-21).*

Hymns and Poems

There Is a Green Hill Far Away

There is a green hill far away,
Without a city wall,
Where the dear Lord was crucified,
Who died to save us all.

We may not know, we cannot tell
What pains He had to bear;
But we believe it was for us
He hung and suffered there.

He died that we might be forgiv'n,
He died to make us good,
That we might go at last to heav'n,
Saved by His precious blood.

There was no other good enough
To pay the price of sin;
He only could unlock the gate
Of heav'n and let us in.
Oh, dearly, dearly has He loved,
And we must love Him, too;
And trust in His redeeming blood,
And try His works to do.
——C. F. ALEXANDER

Forever Here My Rest Shall Be (v. 2)

My dying Savior, and my God,
Fountain for guilt and sin,
Sprinkle me ever with Thy blood,
And cleanse, and keep me clean.
——CHARLES WESLEY

Battle Hymn of the Republic (v. 4)

In the beauty of the lilies
Christ was born across the sea,
With a glory in His bosom
That transfigures you and me.
As He died to make men holy,
Let us die to make men free,
While God is marching on.
——J. W. HOWE

A Heart like Thine (v. 3)

Open mine eyes that I may see;
Show me the cross of Calvary;
There may I go and not repine.
Give me a heart like Thine.
Come to my soul, blessed Jesus.
Hear me, O Savior divine!
Open the fountain and cleanse me;
Give me a heart like Thine.
——J. W. VAN DEVENTER

Poem

Thou who taught the thronging people
By blue Galilee:
Speak to us, Thy erring children,
Teach us purity.

Thou whose touch could heal the leper,
Make the blind to see:
Touch our hearts and turn the sinning
Into purity.

Thou whose word could still the tempest,
Calm the raging sea:
Hush the storm of human passion,
Give us purity.

Thou who sinless met the tempter:
Grant, O Christ, that we
May o'ercome the bent to evil
By Thy purity.

—HENRY S. MINDE

The Sermon

Holiness Lost, Holiness Regained

Text: **Heb. 13:12**

Purpose: To unfold the plan of salvation as it relates to holiness and to help people find where they are in God's plan for their spiritual development.

Proposition: The purpose behind God's plan of redemption is to make us holy persons. His work in us is not complete until that purpose is accomplished.

Introduction: In the early chapters of Genesis we learn about humanity's fall from their original relationship to God into sin. It is the story of holiness lost. All of the rest of Scripture is the story of God's efforts to re-create holiness in mankind and to bring us into an eternal paradise.

The text describes God's all-encompassing purpose in the atonement of Christ as being **to make the people holy.** If the provision for that cost the blood of Christ, then it is imperative that we understand the fullness of that plan and that it find fruition in our lives.

1. *Initial Sanctification.* One of the concomitants of conversion is initial sanctification. In order to maintain the importance of entire sanctification as a second definite work of grace, it is not necessary to undervalue what God does for us in regeneration. Not only are we treated as forgiven (justified), but also we are made new persons in Christ. The old life of sin has passed away (2 Cor. 5:17). This first phase of God's holiness in us deals with acquired depravity and includes *(a)* cleansing from sin's guilt and *(b)* cleansing from sin's practice. This cleansing is not reserved until the second crisis. It must be found in every child of God. It is thus that Paul is able to address all Christians as "saints"—"holy ones."

2. *Entire Sanctification.* Dr. Sydney Martin tells of a Scotsman who testified after his conversion, "When God saved me, it was as if He took down the shutters from the windows of my heart, and the light of God came pouring in. That light did two things: It dispelled the darkness, and it showed up the dirt." He was recognizing what God's Word and the experience of God's people (of all theological persuasions) find to be true. The human heart needs more than cleansing from the accumulation of guilt and sinful practices. God desires also to deal with the sin principle—the predisposition to sin—with which we were born and which got us into trouble in the first place. Christ died outside the city gate to make us holy "through and through" (1 Thess. 5:23). Unless we allow God to cleanse our nature from this sinful disposition, we will find that our Christian lives are far from victorious. The carnal nature will soon get us back into the sin business.

This second cleansing can occur only when we recognize the need for it and are willing to commit *everything* to God. He can cleanse only as much as we give Him. The second phase of God's holiness in us deals with inherited depravity and includes *(a)* cleansing from the principle of sin and *(b)* cleansing from the power of sin.

3. *Progressive Sanctification.* Holiness is more than two experiences. It is a dynamic way of life—a vital relationship with Christ through the Holy Spirit. The work that God has wrought in the heart must be brought to maturity in the life-style.

The apostle Peter, after he had been reinstated by Christ, after he had experienced Pentecost, after his anointed preaching and leadership and persecution, still held some unchristian prejudices. They were not automatically cleansed at his sanctification. They were only dealt with as he walked in the new light that God gave him on a rooftop in Joppa (Acts 10—11). Even then, he had to struggle with the issue (Gal. 2:11). Perhaps that is why Paul told Timothy to train himself to be godly (1 Tim. 4:7), why he said that he sought to make his body his slave (1 Cor. 9:27), and why Peter himself underscores the fact that if we are to endure, we must grow (2 Pet. 3:18).

This progressive sanctification (or "growth in grace") is a process that both precedes and follows entire sanctification. It is the means by which the Holy Spirit remolds us into the image of Christ. It is an ongoing relationship with God that includes *(a)* cleansing of the flaws in our personalities and *(b)* cleansing of the failures caused by our humanness.

Our testimony to the experience of entire sanctification must never become a cover-up for things in our lives that are not like Christ, nor should our humanity ever become an excuse for tolerating our failures. They also need the cleansing for which Christ died.

4. *Final Sanctification.* As long as I live and walk with God, He will be making me more like His Son—making me more holy in my life-style. But even then, God is not finished with me. The time is coming when "this mortal [shall] put on immortality" (1 Cor. 15:53, KJV), and we shall once again have access to "the tree of life . . . in the paradise of God" (Rev. 2:7). Then sanctification will be complete. Then we will be truly holy. Then the purpose for which Christ died will be accomplished, and holiness will be regained. Final sanctification will include *(a)* cleansing from the deficiencies of my humanity and *(b)* cleansing from the dominion of an evil environment.

Conclusion

This overview of God's plan of redemption—His plan to make us holy—should prompt us to praise Him for the completeness of the work of Christ on Calvary. He does not forgive us and then leave us in our sin. He actually makes us holy. He keeps working in us until we die—and then some. But this text should also drive us to introspection. Where do you find yourself on your spiritual jour-

370 / Biblical Resources for Holiness Preaching

ney? Are you frustrating the purpose of God in Christ? Do you need to allow God to accomplish His purpose for you in some new area of your life? He offers to you now the holiness you do desperately need if you are going to live victoriously and someday be among the pure in heart who see God.

Endnotes

1. H. Orton Wiley, *The Epistle to the Hebrews,* ed. Morris A. Weigelt, rev. ed. (Kansas City: Beacon Hill Press of Kansas City, 1984), 19.
2. Liddell and Scott, *A Greek-English Lexicon* (Oxford: Clarendon Press, 1961).
3. Marvin R. Vincent, *Word Studies in the New Testament* (Grand Rapids: Wm. B. Eerdmans Publishing Co., 1946), 4:569.
4. Simon J. Kistemaker, *New Testament Commentary* (Grand Rapids: Baker Book House, 1984), 425.
5. Wiley, *Hebrews,* 371-72.
6. *New Testament Commentary,* 425.
7. Edward Robinson, *Greek and English Lexicon of the New Testament* (New York: Harper and Brothers, 1882).
8. Wiley, *Hebrews,* 373.
9. Ibid., 84.
10. For example, see *Broadman Bible Commentary, The Interpreter's Bible, The Communicator's Commentary,* and James Moffatt, where the phrase is ignored; and the *Critical and Exegetical Handbook,* Adam Clarke, and Vincent's word studies, where the emphasis is on other phrases.
11. Dods and Carter make passing references but do not develop the theme.
12. *New Testament Commentary,* 420-21.
13. Wiley, *Hebrews,* 370.
14. Ibid., 13, 20-21.

WILBUR BRANNON

Holiness—a Resurrection Possibility

Now get up and stand on your feet. I have appeared to you to appoint you as a servant and as a witness of what you have seen of me and what I will show you. I will rescue you from your own people and from the Gentiles. I am sending you to them to open their eyes and turn them from darkness to light, and from the power of Satan to God, so that they may receive forgiveness of sins and a place among those who are sanctified by faith in me (Acts 26:16-18).

Holiness is a recurring theme among contemporary religious leaders. Charles Colson, Luis Palau, and Anthony Campolo are outside the traditional holiness movement and yet represent an impressive number of evangelical voices who are speaking out forcefully on Christian holiness.[1]

This emphasis reflects the renewed sense of the importance of the doctrine of sanctification in Christian teaching. As holiness people we should be in the forefront of such a movement. Our message is that the quality of life required in these times is specially gifted to **those who are sanctified by faith.**

The prevalence of abortion, drug abuse, sexual immorality, and divorce calls attention to the low moral tone of our time. Concern has arisen over the impact of this cultural situation on the church, and many leaders are lamenting the widespread absence of any significant difference between the church and the world. This is one factor that has given rise to the emphasis on holiness as a life-style that is distinguishable from our pagan culture.

Wesleyans see holiness, however, as more than (but including) a life-style change. It involves a divine activity within the person effecting an ethical transformation. In this event, mutually decisive action is involved on the part of both God and the person. On the human side faith acts by consecrating what God has already saved. On the divine side the Holy Spirit sanctifies by filling the heart with divine love. This love brings all our desires into a unifying supreme preference for the will of God.

We must announce in clear, unapologetic terms God's claim to make persons holy. He sets us apart to be His alone, His to obey! It is God's grace working within us (Phil. 2:13), purifying all desires and filling us with His love (Rom. 5:5; 2 Cor. 5:14). As Oswald Chambers puts it: "Christ will put His worker . . . through . . . spring-cleaning until there is only one purpose left—I am here for God to send me where He will."[2]

Such a proclamation appears in the message of Paul that the risen Christ directed him to preach to all people. It is succinctly embodied in our text.

Exegetical Section

Some of the most dramatic passages in Scripture are Luke's descriptions of Paul's appearances before Felix, Festus, and Agrippa. Acts 26:16-18 is a climax in this series of Paul's witnesses to the gospel of Christ before imperial representatives. The overarching issue for Paul in these apologies was the "promise made by God to our fathers" (v. 6, NASB). This promise, he is convinced, has been fulfilled in Jesus of Nazareth, who appeared to him on the Damascus road and gave him a commission to proclaim this Good News to both Jew and Gentile.[3] The benefits of this fulfillment when acknowledged and accepted are enumerated in our text.

One remarkable thing about this passage is the way commentators have ignored it. Many have tended to be preoccupied with the historical and political dimensions of Paul's defense before the various authorities. It is true that one of Luke's major purposes is to demonstrate with this whole series of events that Christianity is not politically dangerous, that Paul is not a troublemaker. Nonetheless there is a significant theological structure to the apology. Our research has found few interpreters who have attempted to work with this.

Although our study focuses on this brief segment of Paul's speech (26:16-18) because the word **sanctified** appears there, it includes a number of other desired outcomes of the apostolic preaching: (1) **to open their eyes;** (2) **turn them from darkness to light;** (3) turn them **from the power of Satan to God;** (4) they will **receive forgiveness of sins;** and (5) **receive . . . a place among those who are sanctified by faith in me** (Jesus).

It is questionable that Paul is self-consciously detailing the stages in the order of salvation, but there is, nevertheless, a close correlation between this listing and the traditional Wesleyan view of the *ordo salutis.* It begins in awakening and consummates in sanctification.

These five aspects of salvation blessing can also be seen as the series of occurrences that marked Paul's own conversion. His eyes were opened (both physically and spiritually) in the Damascus road/Straight Street complex of events. This resulted in his emerging from the darkness of ignorance about who Jesus was to the light of a new understanding (see 2 Cor. 5:16). In the new perception of the work of Christ that occurred, he was now able to experience the forgiveness of sins, a reality he had never been able to earn by his Pharisaism (cf. Gal. 2:16-21; Phil. 3:3-7). Closely related to this is his recognition that attempting to be justified by the law only intensified the power of Satan over him, Satan actually using the law as a weapon. This phrase further reflects his understanding of how the work of Christ effectively broke Satan's perceived dominion in this present age and set his captives free (see Col. 2:11-17). If it is understood broadly enough, and not simply as a second stage in the process of his conversion, we may see the visit of Ananias as the occasion of Paul's inclusion into the company of those who are **sanctified by faith.** He was baptized, received the Spirit, and by those realities became a part of the Body of Christ.

This last point is made in the light of the fact that it is not possible to identify the connotation of *hēgiasmenois* (sanctified) in our text by either a word or textual analysis alone. For Paul at this point the words would have come to denote all the implications that he had come to understand them to include. In the years following his initial encounter with the risen Christ, his faith had matured, his theology had flowered, and at this time most of his letters had been written. Hence it is fair to say that he would have understood by **sanctified** all the concepts included in his mature theology as expressed in the Epistles; that is, it is a holistic reference.

Let us now turn to the pivotal issue in the whole apology that is the point of controversy between himself and his opponents: God's promise to the fathers.

Herein lies a major problem for anyone who would make such a claim as Paul preached, namely, that God's promise had been fulfilled in Jesus of Nazareth. The problem is to convince his fellow Jews that Jesus was the Messiah (see references to his synagogue preaching above). It was contrary to all the Jewish expectation to claim that a man who was rejected by the religious establishment and died on a cross (a death that put Him under the curse of the law, according to Deut. 21:23) could be the Messiah (Christ). His synagogue preaching took the form of "reasoning" with his audience that this was *not* contrary to the Scripture as they thought, but that it was "according to the Scriptures" (cf. 1 Cor. 15:1-3). This issue was compounded by Paul's preaching to the Gentiles, and the waters were truly muddied. Verses 20-23 reflect this controversial situation.

The apostle's most decisive evidence for the truth of his claims was the resurrection of Jesus from the dead. This explains why he refers to the logical consistency of the Resurrection with the beliefs of both the Jews (Pharisees) and Agrippa.

It may be that some of his defense involved the implicit testimony that he too was convinced by the Resurrection. Look at some of the central phrases:

"I too was convinced" (v. 9). Saul had been so convinced that this new movement was a threat to Judaism that he was driven to destroy "the name of Jesus of Nazareth." He admitted putting "saints in prison" and approving their death (v. 10).

Nothing short of a cataclysmic intervention could have turned this man around. A direct confrontation with the living Christ was the only revelation that could convince this disbeliever to become a "follower of the Way" (cf. 22:4).

"It is hard for you to kick against the goads" (v. 14). Saul began to fully realize he was fighting a losing battle. So consumed was he with carrying out his persecutions that it seems he was trying to drown out the voice of his own doubts. Perhaps subconsciously he was trying to erase from his memory "the wisdom and the Spirit" he saw in Stephen at his stoning (6:10, NASB; 22:20).

He may not have realized how much within himself he was

resisting. But "the voice" on the road reminded him that it always hurts to "kick against the goads" (the bar behind the ox's heels studded with wooden spikes). He was making it difficult on himself by resisting the truth!

"Who are you, Lord?" (v. 15). He who had been arresting those in "the Way" was now being arrested on the way. Saul's initial response was a respectful answer ("Lord" here carries the connotation of "sir"), as he had not yet learned the source of the voice. When he heard, "I am Jesus, whom you are persecuting," the understanding of his mission suddenly shifted. He realized his persecution of Christians had been directed against Jesus, the living Christ, himself. Jesus was present, personal, a living reality. The conversion was total and radical.

It certainly cannot be the case that Paul is on trial for believing in the general resurrection of the dead. As he points out, this is the official belief of the sect of the Pharisees, of which he was a member. The problem was not with this belief but with applying it to a particular case, that of Jesus.

Not only was the validity of Paul's message dependent on the truth of Jesus' resurrection, but also the possibility of all the benefits of Christ's work likewise hinged on its reality. In 1 Corinthians 15 the apostle insisted on the pivotal character of the Resurrection. If Christ is not raised, we have no hope, and we are yet in our sins (vv. 14-19). Hence all the promises listed in Jesus' commission to Paul are possible *because He lives:* awakening, deliverance from darkness, liberation from bondage, forgiveness of sins, and sanctification (see 1 Cor. 1:30).

It is at this point that the phrase **faith in me** becomes critical. The resurrection of Christ is a "covered promise" (Wesley's term) that the same power that raised up Jesus from the dead shall work within us to effect a preliminary transformation here and a final transformation in the eschaton (cf. Phil. 3:10-11).

What is included in the **place among those who are sanctified by faith?** The word translated **place** or "inheritance" (KJV) *(klēron)* is the same word used by the Septuagint to refer to the distribution of the inheritance of Canaan, the Promised Land, among the tribes of Israel. Thus the implication of a place among the people of God who are called to be His holy people is clear. It seems feasible to suggest that it includes initial sanctification (cf. 1 Cor. 1:2; 6:9-11), entire ("through and through") sanctification (1 Thess. 5:23), progressive transformation into the image of Christ (2 Cor. 3:18), and the final perfecting in the presence of God. We know that all is possible because of the resurrection of Jesus Christ from the dead.

Sermon Suggestions

Topic: **The Glorious Hope**

Samuel Medley (1738-99) penned the lines, "Oh, glorious hope of perfect love! . . ." These words capture the import of our text in the light of the major issue of Paul's defense before Agrippa. Validated by the resurrection of Christ, we have the glorious hope of:

A. Coming to a Knowledge of the Truth
B. Knowing the Forgiveness of Sins
C. Experiencing a Deliverance from the Slavery of Sin
D. Becoming a Part of the Holy People of God

> *Oh, glorious hope of perfect love!*
> *It lifts me up to things above;*
> *It bears on eagles' wings.*
> *It gives my ravished soul a taste,*
> *And makes me for some moments feast*
> *With Jesus' priests and kings.*
>
> *Rejoicing now in earnest hope,*
> *I stand, and from the mountaintop*
> *See all the land below.*
> *Rivers of milk and honey rise,*
> *And all the fruits of paradise*
> *In endless plenty grow.*
>
> *A land of corn, and wine, and oil;*
> *Favored with God's peculiar smile,*
> *With ev'ry blessing blest;*
> *There dwells the Lord, our Righteousness,*
> *And keeps His own in perfect peace,*
> *And everlasting rest.*

Oh, that I might at once go up,
No more on this side Jordan stop,
But now the land possess;
This moment end my legal years,
Sorrows and sins, and doubts and fears,
A howling wilderness.

Topic: **Holiness: Possibility and Provision**

Based on the assumption that **sanctification** in the text is a holistic reference, the following suggestion for a sermon draws on certain facets of the Spirit's sanctifying work that appear in the Book of Acts. It begins with what the exegesis identifies as the major motif of the larger context.

A. Sanctification Grounded in the Resurrection

Our salvation has its ultimate ground in the resurrection of Jesus (1 Cor. 15:14). We are redeemed and reconciled to God through "the blood of His cross" (Col. 1:20, NASB; cf. Eph. 1:7); but the Cross is given validity by the Resurrection. If Jesus had not been raised, our preaching of initial salvation (regeneration), intermediate salvation (sanctification), and final salvation (glorification) would be, at best, problematic. Jesus' story would be only that of a courageous martyr who had lived a life of self-denial. It would have been an interesting replay of other noble characters who have graced the stage of history. But the unique qualities required of a Savior would have been absent.

The distinctive that sets Jesus of Nazareth apart from all other world-class figures is the miracle of His resurrection. That singular event should inspire universal reflection. In faith it lifts Him as the Object of worship, so that we may join Thomas in his great confession, "My Lord and my God!" (John 20:28).

Jesus promised the coming of the Holy Spirit on the Day of Pentecost as the public confirmation of His resurrection (John 15:26; 16:8, 10).

B. Sanctification and Empowerment

The Spirit's effusion was to be understood in terms of an empowerment. This requires the prerequisite of a spiritual resurrection experienced in regeneration. Thus the disciples at Pentecost were able to bear witness convincingly (Acts 1:8) and charge: "You, with the help of wicked men, put him to death . . .

But God raised him from the dead" (2:23-24). They were unin-
timidated by threats. A reality had seized them.

Saul depended on this empowerment to declare to both
Jews and Gentiles the benefits of being forgiven and sanctified.
Only those who turn to look into the light, choose the authority
of God, and receive forgiveness have a right to be among those
who are sanctified by faith in Christ. John Wesley states that
pardon, holiness, and glory are all received through faith.

C. Sanctification and Cleansing

The Holy Spirit not only energized them but also purified
them by a personalized faith (Acts 15:9). As witnesses they were
persuasive because they were unimpeachable. That is to say, the
Spirit is convincing through sanctified witnesses (John 16:8-11).

Without doubt Jesus expected Saul to be a witness qualified
and equipped the same as His disciples were at Pentecost. Thus
Saul discovered (1) the Lordship of Jesus, which in turn helped
him recognize his servant role (Acts 26:15; cf. 9:5 ff.); and (2) the
"sanctifying work of the Spirit" (2 Thess. 2:13), enabling him to
be an effective witness (Acts 1:8; 9:17-18, 22; 26:18).

Saul's eyes were opened by the power of the Holy Spirit in
order that he might **open their eyes and turn them from darkness
to light** (Acts 26:18).

D. Sanctification and Regeneration

Sanctification is begun in regeneration. Wesleyan theology
calls it "initial sanctification." The forgiven sinner begins
enjoying the freedom of a new life that is different. Holiness is
that difference.

Then our responsibility and privilege is to consecrate what
Christ has saved. That makes the Holy Spirit's action "subsequent to regeneration." We are flooded with divine love as our
controlling motive and choose God's will as our supreme preference. Thus we are purified by faith, willing only one thing—the
will of God!

Another sermon suggestion draws on the implication of the
exegesis that Paul's description of the benefits of Christ's work
listed in the text reflects his own experience.

Topic: **Holiness and Resurrection Power**

Introduction: The relationship between power and sanctification
has been dealt with in various ways. This passage offers a unique

approach by focusing on Resurrection power, one of the gospel's fundamental claims. Remember, Pentecost was the confirmation and consequence of Jesus' resurrection and ascension. The disciples were so caught up in that reality it did not matter what the world thought. They knew who Jesus was and would rather die than deny His resurrected life. To develop the idea of the promise of power to the sanctified, we propose to look at Paul's experience in the light of Acts 1:8:

1. He Staggers Under the Power of Revelation
    Convinced that the reports of Jesus' resurrection were preposterous, he zealously opposed the name of Jesus. It was a convicting light that revealed the corruption of his self-righteousness (2 Cor. 4:6).

2. He Stands in the Power of the Resurrection
    "Get up and stand" brought a response of obedience. This empowerment motivated and sustained him in all of life's circumstances (2 Cor. 4:8-10), including his defense before Agrippa. He demonstrated the resurrected life of Jesus by Resurrection power in his own life. This power is sanctifying power. We would have nothing to preach if Jesus had not been raised (1 Cor. 15:14).

3. He Is Sent by the Power of the Resurrection
    When the resurrected Christ lays hold of our lives, He empowers us to go! He sends us precisely because we are His (John 17:17-19). He empowers us to "stand," so that we will not collapse under the pressure of our paganized society and capitulate to their moral standards or lack of them. The disciples were persuasive because they were unimpeachable. Sanctification involves a commitment to fidelity and purity (1 Cor. 6:18-20). The temple of the body is not to be desecrated by any kind of immorality but consecrated alive and holy to God as our "spiritual service of worship" (Rom. 12:1, NASB).

Sermon on the Text

The following sermon develops the Pauline experience that is embodied in the apology, emphasizing the first phrase of the text.

Topic: **Open Mine Eyes**

Text: **Acts 26:18**

Introduction: Jesus called a blind man. His blindness was caused not by impaired eyes but by the religious prejudice formed by an education in rabbinic theology. Born in Tarsus, young Saul moved to Jerusalem to go to seminary when quite young. He grew up to be a typical orthodox Jew regulated by the strict religious rules of the Pharisees.

He was an unlikely candidate to become a follower of Jesus, much less a world missionary. He was completely blinded to the legitimacy of Christ's way. What would turn him around?

There was only one thing to do. Make Saul blind to everything else but Jesus! Saul believed in the general resurrection, but his blindness kept him from believing in Jesus' resurrection. For Saul, Jesus had been dead for about three years, a memory that he intended to blot out.

The blazing light, brighter than the sun, sent him staggering to the ground, blinded! With the light came a voice, and with the voice the recognition of Jesus. Nothing less than a dynamic experience was necessary. It took a cataclysmic intervention. His eyes had to be opened.

Having opened his eyes, Jesus now commissions Saul to turn other people from darkness to light. Like him before the Damascus encounter, they could not see the light, therefore they did not recognize that they were under the rule of Satan. In like manner, the 20th-century American admits belief in God and then concludes that is enough, not recognizing the need for divine deliverance.

It is possible to have blind faith in traditions and practices. It is easy to rely on good works or have an institutional faith. Through the work of the Holy Spirit the eyes of the blind may be opened and like Paul be . . .

A. Startled by a Radiant Person

The words Paul heard, "I am Jesus" (Acts 26:15), could not have been more startling. "It can't be. He is dead." But this was not all: "Why do you persecute me?" (v. 14). "I have been persecuting not just Christians but You!" Here is more than believing a doctrine about Jesus, it is encountering Him in a living way.

Paul's religious prejudice had convinced him that this new

movement that had sprung up around Jesus of Nazareth was a threat to Judaism. The only option he saw was to destroy the name of Jesus and the followers of "the Way" (9:2).

In pursuing this driving passion, no doubt Paul experienced many a flashback on "the wisdom and the Spirit" of Stephen (Acts 6:10, NASB; 22:20). The difference in this martyr was unforgettable. Saul saw a "love, which comes from a pure heart" (1 Tim. 1:5). Now he himself had caught a vision of the same Jesus Stephen had professed to see as he fell under the impact of the stones. Paul now learned the truth: "You're only hurting yourself by kicking against the goads" (Acts 26:14, Beck), by fighting against the resurrected Jesus.

B. Transformed by Resurrection Power

At the appearance of the risen Christ, Saul came alive. A new faith was born in him by the confirming evidence of Jesus' resurrection. He was released from the grave of dead works (religious futility) to serve "the living God" (see Matt. 16:16). He was turned from "the power of Satan to God."

He was arrested (apprehended) on the Damascus road. As he said in Phil. 3:12, "Christ Jesus took hold of me"! He was confirmed on Straight Street. Filled with the Holy Spirit, he was *energized* and began at once to witness to his newfound faith.

Empowered by the sanctifying Spirit, his witnessing was convincing and *persuasive* (Acts 9:20-22). All of Paul's ministry was lived out in the power of the Resurrection, and the trail of Christian congregations he left behind him testifies to the effectiveness of his work. Now he stands before Agrippa and gives the same witness he had been giving throughout Asia Minor, Macedonia, and Achaia, and he is sustained by the same power.

C. Set on a Resolved Purpose

The commission given to Paul is the same one Jesus would give to us today: **To appoint you as a servant and as a witness ... sending you** (Acts 26:16-17). Jesus' message to him was that others experience the reality that Saul experienced (v. 18). He was sanctified for a mission, and so are we. But his mission took place through conflict, and ours will, too. If we are in God's will, however, conflict is not crushing (2 Cor. 4:7). When one is fully consecrated to God, there is no place to give up or give in. The power of the Resurrection is at work within us to make it so.

Following his commission faithfully in all circumstances brought Paul to the end with a triumphant testimony (2 Tim. 4:6-8).

Conclusion: We need our eyes open to the will of God. But our blindness can be overcome only by the glorious light of His resurrected Son. The sanctifying work of the Spirit that purifies the heart also overcomes the powers of evil that would destroy us, because sanctification is the appropriation of Resurrection power.

To have a **place among those who are sanctified by faith in** Him is something we can't afford to miss; it is the great heritage made available to us in the completed work of Jesus Christ.

Endnotes

1. In addition to these popular writers, see William Hordern's *Introduction* in a series titled *New Directions in Theology Today,* chapter titled "Sanctification Rediscovered" (Philadelphia: Westminster Press, 1966). For a full discussion see Paul Hessert, *Christian Life,* vol. 5 of *New Directions in Theology Today* (Philadelphia: Westminster Press, 1967).

2. Oswald Chambers, *My Utmost for His Highest* (New York: Dodd, Mead, and Co., 1935), 269.

3. This truth is clearly seen by making a survey of Paul's preaching as Luke records it in Acts 13:32-33; 17:1-4; 18:4-6.

C. S. COWLES

Holiness as Freedom
from Sin

*My little children, I am writing these things to you that you may
not sin. And if anyone sins, we have an Advocate with the Father,
Jesus Christ the righteous; and He Himself is the propitiation for
our sins; and not for ours only, but also for those of the whole world.
And by this we know that we have come to know Him, if we keep His
commandments. The one who says, "I have come to know Him,"
and does not keep His commandments, is a liar, and the truth is not
in him; but whoever keeps His word, in him the love of God has truly
been perfected. By this we know that we are in Him: the one who
says he abides in Him ought himself to walk in the same manner as
He walked. Beloved, I am not writing a new commandment to you,
but an old commandment which you have had from the beginning;
the old commandment is the word which you have heard. On the
other hand, I am writing a new commandment to you, which is true
in Him and in you, because the darkness is passing away, and the
true light is already shining. The one who says he is in the light and
yet hates his brother is in the darkness until now. The one who loves
his brother abides in the light and there is no cause for stumbling in
him. But the one who hates his brother is in the darkness and walks
in the darkness, and does not know where he is going because the
darkness has blinded his eyes. I am writing to you, little children,
because your sins are forgiven you for His name's sake. I am writing
to you, fathers, because you know Him who has been from the
beginning. I am writing to you, young men, because you have
overcome the evil one. I have written to you, children, because you
know the Father. I have written to you, fathers, because you know
Him who has been from the beginning. I have written to you, young*

men, because you are strong, and the word of God abides in you, and you have overcome the evil one (1 John 2:1-14, NASB).[1]

It was my first pastorate. Gary was one of my first converts. He was so excited about his new relationship to Christ that he brought his divorcée girlfriend to see me. Guilt-ridden over an earlier abortion, she found forgiveness and release in Christ. Together they became enthusiastic worshipers.

As I began to disciple them, however, I discovered that they were living together without the benefit of marriage. Further, he was married and was doing nothing to support his wife or three children. Gently I opened the Word. I began to share with them God's requirements for a holy life. They became very defensive. I never saw them again.

Warren and his wife were early converts in that same church. They showed every indication of responsible commitment to Christ. Hence I did not hesitate to cosign a loan to help him get started in a small business. He made one payment and left town in the middle of the night with no forwarding address. It took two years for me to pay back that obligation.

Oh, how good those solid Christian laymen began to look to me as I struggled with new converts in trying to get them grounded in the disciplines of the Christian life. So naturally, I began to lean heavily upon Jerry, a gifted young leader who had been born and raised in the church and was a Christian college graduate. That is, until I noticed his increasingly judgmental attitude. When I confronted him about his critical spirit, he began to weep. He confessed to being a practicing homosexual. Although he repented at the altar with bitter tears, he failed to change his life-style and had to be removed from all leadership roles.

With a jolt I was confronted, as a young pastor, by the urgency of following up on one's profession of religion with ethical behavior. I began to understand John's great concern for his **little children** in the Lord, that they would demonstrate their "love for God" by *not sinning* and by a positive life of holy obedience to the revealed will of God. The burden of this passage—that believers' walk would match their talk—is relevant to the needs of the Church in every age.

Exegesis of the Text

John's high call to holiness flows out of a passionate heart that beats with love for his **little children** (2:1, 12-13). In the Greek these words are diminutives "which are used, as it were, with a caress."[2] John's great overarching concern is that they **may not sin** (2:1*a*). Yet his pastoral heart, fully cognizant of the pull of the world and the weakness of the flesh (2:15-17), is quick to affirm that **if anyone sins, we have ... Jesus** (2:1*b*). John's development of this triumphant, victorious, and yet responsible Christian life gathers around four fundamental ideas.

I. *Grace* (2:1-2)

Two key words highlight the way in which Jesus helps us to **not sin**. The first is *paraclētos,* **Advocate,** "helper," or as Barclay renders it, "one who will plead our cause to the Father."[3] He is supremely able to intercede for us, in that (1) as *Jesus,* born of woman, He is able to fully sympathize with our humanity (Heb. 2:17-18; 4:15-16); (2) as *Christ,* God's anointed Son, He is able to deliver us from the tyranny of sin's power (2:23; 4:2-3, 14-15); and (3) as the *righteous One,* He alone is able to offer up a perfect sacrifice to atone for, and cleanse us from, all sin (2:2; 4:10).

Hilasmos is the second key word used by John. It is drawn from the OT sacrificial cultus and may be translated as **propitiation** (KJV, NASB) or "expiation" (RSV), depending on one's theological perspective. *Hilasmos* refers to the sacrifice that sinful man makes to a holy God to effect forgiveness and release from guilt. The striking difference in John's usage is that it is "used for God's divine action in relation to us and on our behalf," and not as a human act to appease God.[4] This "radical reversal" from the pagan view of sacrifice means that Christ died, not to change God's mind about men but to change men's mind about God. Christ offered up himself as a sacrifice, not to placate the wrath of an angry God but to demonstrate the love of a gracious God.

Hilasmos is broader than forgiveness for acts of sin. It offers "a means of sterilizing human weakness ... a radical removal of the taint of sin."[5] By His one sacrifice, the problem of sin has been dealt with so fully and finally that it becomes possible for those who **know Him** and **abide in Him** (2:3-6) to not sin (cf. 3:5-10)!

II. *Obedience* (2:3-6)

We are released *from* bondage to sin in order that we may be free *for* the practice of righteousness (3:7). God's gracious action on our behalf calls us to the obedience of faith wherein we seek to do the will of God as revealed in **His commandments.**

This obedience is specifically indicated to be the consequence of "knowing" God. Four times in these four verses, *ginōskō* **(know)** appears. "To know" was a highly coveted attribute in the Greek world. To "know God" was the highest quest of the religious soul. The philosophers sought to "know God" by way of the intellect, while the mystery religions offered a way of "knowing" by means of mystical union with the divine.[6]

But the biblical meaning of "knowing" transcends both of these. It is characterized by the quality of personal relation, involving trust, obedience, respect, worship, and love. As Otto Piper points out, "According to John, knowledge does not lead to a gradual merger of the knower's mind with that of God, but rather to a harmony of their wills in which God remains distinctly the authority to be recognized."[7] With this understanding it is clear how John can insist that knowledge of God, if genuine, results in obedience. It could be no other way.

Thus, "knowing Him" must result in a life of holy obedience to the revealed will of God that, in the final analysis, enables us to truly love one another with integrity. Failure to be faithful to the moral demands of the law involves us in duplicity and deception. Our faith is rendered meaningless.

No doubt John is responding to a claim of his opponents "to know God," as he had done in chap. 1 to some of their other claims. Their understanding was that sin did not create a barrier to fellowship with God (Johannine synonym of "knowing God"), but John's emphasis reflects the central biblical understanding that "to know God . . . involves knowledge of his character and requirements and obedience to these requirements."[8]

The major purpose of 1 John is to identify ways by which we may know that we have eternal life (5:13). Here is one of the characteristics, that we "walk as Jesus did" (v. 6). A major theological issue needs to be addressed here. The apostle is not suggesting that certain conditions have to be fulfilled before a person can come to know God; rather, obedience is the expression of the knowledge of God.

A major holiness motif comes to light in this context when, in v. 5, the apostle says, **Whoever keeps His word, in him the love of God has truly been perfected.** "Made complete (or perfected) means that the Christian's love is entire and mature."[9] This was one of John Wesley's favorite texts for his teaching of "perfect love" as the mark of the mature Christian or the entirely sanctified one. Wesley also used as a synonym for "Christian perfection" (by which is meant perfect love) the phrase in v. 6; it is to "walk as Jesus walked."

III. *Love* (2:7-11)

Specifically, the obedience to which John refers in vv. 3-6 is now indicated to be the commandment to love, which he declares to be both a **new** and **old** commandment. He spells it out with the same simplicity and power as did Jesus: "And this is His commandment, that we ... love one another, just as He commanded us" (3:23, NASB; cf. John 13:34-35; 15:12, 17). It is an **old commandment** in that love for God is the highest purpose of the OT Shema (Deut. 6:5), and love for our neighbor is the "bottom line" commandment in the realm of human relations (Lev. 19:18). Jesus, however, poured "new wine" into the "old wineskins" of the great love commandments in at least three ways: (1) in Jesus, love reaches beyond those who are righteous to the sinner, the outcast, and the unworthy; (2) in Jesus, love extends beyond the neighbor (i.e., the fellow Jew) to embrace the stranger (i.e., the Gentile); (3) in Jesus is personified "the breadth and length and height and depth" (Eph. 3:18, NASB) of God's self-giving *agapē* love, which does not depend upon reciprocity for its motivation. "But God demonstrates His own love toward us, in that while we were yet sinners, Christ died for us" (Rom. 5:8, NASB). Or as John puts it, "In this is love, not that we loved God, but that He loved us and sent His Son" (4:10, NASB).

Holiness is both negative and positive. It involves the absence of sin and the presence of love. Both are described in this passage (vv. 1-6).

IV. *Maturity*

The final section of this passage has puzzled commentators;

but many concur with John Wesley that it describes stages of spiritual maturity, although few would say that "father" is equivalent to those who are entirely sanctified, as Wesley did.

The other designations reflect the "earlier" phases of the spiritual pilgrimage. However, Wesley certainly did not consider the **children** and **young men** as second-class citizens but simply as pilgrims on the path toward their divinely intended destiny of being renewed in the image of God.

Theological Implications of the Passage

John's exposition of freedom from sin provides two important insights for our understanding of holiness. *First, right behavior is an expression of a right relationship.* John puts it bluntly: **The one who says, "I have come to know Him," and does not keep His commandments, is a liar** (2:4). Later he defines sin in terms of intentionality. "Sin is lawlessness" (3:4, both NASB). In other words, John would define sin subjectively according to the intention of the heart, which manifests itself in disobedience. Only by such a qualification can the holiness claim of "freedom from sin" be established. Nonetheless, this does not make possible the ignoring of the objective standard of the law of God in the name of good intentions. This corrective is needed to avoid a drift into antinomianism. Whatever violates the principles of God's created order, whatever distorts the reflection of His will and purposes, whatever damages people must be regarded—and dealt with—as sin.

Second, love takes precedence over law. This speaks to the opposite extreme of reducing the commandments to a set of rules and taboos, hence, legalism. John affirms, as does Jesus, that all the commandments find their *telos,* realization, fulfillment, summation, in the one "old" and yet "new" commandment, namely, that we "love one another" (3:23). It is a total distortion of the intent and spirit of God's commandments to turn them against people by way of criticism, judgmentalism, and condemnation. He who treats his brother "hatefully," even if it is in the defense of holiness standards, is guilty of murder (3:15)! As Mildred Bangs Wynkoop puts it:

No more important message can be spoken than that personal sanctification should be expressed in terms of personal relationships. This takes *precedence* over methodology and understands *the person-to-person reality central* in all aspects of Christian experience *(italics added).*[10]

Preaching Ideas

[In these suggestions, the message focuses on the text, but the content is drawn from a wide-ranging appropriation of material from the context.—Ed.]

Topic: **Whole People in a Broken World**

It was a perfect day as we stood on Mount Whitney's lofty summit. We could see for hundreds of miles in every direction. Dean gave the Frisbee a mighty toss, and we watched it sail off into the canyon. Dwayne was feeding some birds. Debbie began to sing softly "How Great Thou Art!" We joined her in singing, and then in prayers of thanksgiving. One week later, a freak August blizzard dumped over a foot of snow on that same summit. Two climbers were trapped and died of hypothermia.

That is a parable of our world as the apostle John saw it: perfection and destruction, beauty and ugliness, wholeness and brokenness. In our passage (2:1-14), he not only describes the two faces of humanity but also shows us how we can be restored to our original design and purpose.

I. *God's Purpose:* WHOLENESS (**that you may not sin,** 2:1)

From the Anglo-Saxon root word *hal* comes a family of English words, including *holy, whole, hale, heal,* and *health.* God's intention for man is that he be complete, coherent, and in perfect communion with Him and his fellowman. He has purposed this by way of (1) *predestination* (Eph. 1:4), (2) *creation* (Gen. 1:26-27), (3) *redemption* (1 John 3:5-8), and (4) *ultimate destiny* (vv. 2-3).

II. *Man's Predicament:* BROKENNESS (1:8-10)

We have (1) walked in *darkness* (1:6; 2:8-10), (2) broken His *commandments* (2:3-5), (3) been *unchristlike* (3:6), and (4) failed in *love* (2:7-11). Therefore, as A. W. Tozer observes:

Since God's first concern for his universe is its moral health, that is, its holiness, whatever is contrary to this is necessarily under his eternal displeasure. To preserve his creation God must destroy whatever would destroy it. . . . God's wrath is his utter intolerance of whatever degrades and destroys.[11]

III. *Christ's Provision:* HEALING (**if we sin,** 2:1)
(1) We are *healed by His death* (1:7-9; 2:2). (2) We are *helped by His life* (2:1). (3) We are healed and helped in order to be *helpers in forgiving* and *helpers in loving* one another. Mildred Bangs Wynkoop has a powerful paragraph on the healing power of forgiveness:

> God in Christ tells us what this love is; it is forgiveness. Forgiveness is taking all the *hurt* given by an "enemy" (even in the form of our friends) without demanding reparations. The cost is all on the one who offers the forgiveness. It is accepting the one who has delivered the blow, or the injustice, as if he had never transgressed against us. Reconciliation costs the reconciler more than it can ever cost the one to whom reconciliation is offered. . . . It lifts the "sinner" to his feet and treats him like a person worth loving.[12]

Irenaeus, the great second-century church father, summed up John's message well when he declared, "The Son of God became a son of man in order that sons of men might become sons of God!"

Topic: **Called to Flesh Out Jesus in the World**
Text: 1 John 2:6

"Johnny, what are you drawing?" asked the first grade teacher.
"I am drawing a picture of God."
"But nobody has ever seen God. Nobody knows what He looks like."
"After I'm finished, they will know!"
Even as God has revealed himself to us through Jesus (1:1-2), so Jesus makes himself known through us to our world (1:3; 2:6).

I. *Jesus Makes Himself Known "To Us"*
. . . by way of (1) *revelation* through the gospel (1:1-2), by (2) *incorporation* into the fellowship of believers (1:3), and by (3) *transformation* through the forgiveness of, and cleansing from, sin (1:9; 2:1-2).

II. *Jesus Discloses Himself "In Us"*
. . . as we (1) walk in the *light* (1:5-7), as we (2) live a *holy life* (2:1), and as we (3) obey His *Word* (2:3-5).

III. *Jesus Exhibits Himself "Through Us"*
. . . in our (1) *walking* as He walked (2:6), in our (2) *loving* as He loved and commanded (2:7-11; 4:7-21), and in our (3) *overcoming* by His "abiding in us" (2:13-14; 4:4; 5:4-5).

Steve, a talented young convert, waged a fearsome battle with alcohol even after first receiving Christ. Our people would not give up on him, in spite of his many relapses. On more than one occasion, he stood up to sing on a Sunday morning while under the influence. A year ago, in a mighty second work of grace, God delivered him from his slavish craving. He hasn't touched a drop since.

Recently he wrote a letter to me that I shall treasure all my life. In it he said, "Thank you, Pastor, for accepting me even when there was liquor on my breath. You have been Jesus to me." No greater compliment can ever be received than that!

Sermon on the Text

Free at Last

Text: **My little children, I am writing these things to you that you may not sin** (2:1).

It was a simple yet audacious plan. Armed only with a backpack of provisions and equipment, Alexander Jourjine, a 26-year-old Russian physicist, headed for his country's northwestern border. He could no longer tolerate the suffocating oppression of Communism. His goal: Sweden. His escape was barred by a heavily wired Soviet fence, keen-eyed border patrols, and some of the toughest terrain in Europe. Yet he succeeded after a 23-day trek that was a test of endurance and stretched his nerves to the breaking point.

After making it to safety by an eyelash margin as his pursuers were closing in on him, he wrote a friend: "The sense of freedom exhilarates me constantly in my new life!"[13] So it was for the apostle John. So it is for all who enter into "exhilarating" freedom from sin through Christ. Let us rejoice in this great *emancipation declaration* that is the "good news" for all God's children in our passage (2:1-14).

A. *We Are Born to Be Free*

The artist Matisse tells how he discovered his vocation. He stumbled upon a Bohemian painter at work beside the sea one day when he was about 12. He stood for hours, lost in wonder, as a beautiful seascape gradually emerged from the blank canvas. Said he, "All of a sudden I was 'born again' to the fascinating world of color. It was as if my eyes had been skinned, and for the first time I could really see."

As we gaze upon the incredible portrait of spiritual freedom from the inspired pen of the aged apostle John, we too will find our eyes skinned to see what God has planned for us. Like a great golden eagle released from its chains, our spirits will begin to soar. And our hearts will sing the song of "Glorious Freedom"!

It is God's gracious design that we be (1) free *from* sin (2:1; 3:5-10), (2) free *for* righteousness (2:3-7), (3) free *in* Jesus (2:6, 24, 27-28; 3:24; 4:12-16), free *to* become who we are ("children of God," 3:1-3), and free *within* the promise of eternal life (5:11-13).

It is lunch hour. Teams are being chosen on the school ground for a game of baseball. As each choice is made, our attention is drawn, in this comic strip, to one little fellow whose sorrowful countenance elicits our sympathy. It looks like another day is going by when nobody will want him on their side. It comes down to the final selection. There resounds across the baseball diamond the greatest name that this little boy could ever hear: "Charlie Brown!" The caption under the last frame, which shows him leaping and skipping down the third-base line, is: "Happiness is being chosen to play on the team!"

Happiness, says the apostle John, is to discover through the revelation of the gospel that God has chosen to set us free from sin and has destined us for fellowship with Him forever.

B. *We Have Been Born into Sin*

Unfortunately, as sons of Adam we are actually born under the shadow of the Fall and infected with the virus of sin (1:8-10). The symptoms are (1) *lawlessness* (2:4; 3:4; 5:17), (2) *deviousness* (2:4), (3) *worldliness* (2:15-16), (4) *ungodliness* (3:8), and (5) *lovelessness* (2:9; 3:15; 4:20).

Two boys were playing catch. The ball sailed over the outstretched mitt and broke a window. Nobody saw it except one boy's younger brother. The guilty boy promised his brother that if he wouldn't tell, he would give him a candy bar. The younger brother refused the deal.

"I'll give you candy and my baseball as well."

"Nope."

"I'll even give you my brand-new glove."

"Nope."

"Well, what do you want?"

"I wanna tell!" replied the little brother.

Sin not only alienates us from God but also sets us against one another, until we cry out, "O wretched man that I am! who shall deliver me from the body of this death?" (Rom. 7:24, KJV).

C. We May Be Born Again into Freedom from Sin

1. Jesus is the One who stands alongside us as our *paraclētos* and pleads our cause to the Father (2:1).

Just before Paderewski was to come out on stage, a five-year-old boy got away from his mother, ran up on the platform, sat down at the piano, and began to pick out with one finger "Twinkle, Twinkle, Little Star." Before the embarrassed mother could retrieve him, the great pianist came out, sat beside the boy, reached one arm around him, and began to play variations as the boy continued to pound out the melody. Immediately the lad's simple tune was transformed into a concerto that filled the auditorium with such power and grace that it brought the audience to its feet in enthusiastic applause.

So it is that Jesus comes alongside us, takes our humble efforts, and translates them into spiritual artistry that fills even the heart of God with joy.

2. Jesus is the One who offered up His life as our *hilasmos,* sacrifice, in order that we might be released from the *guilt* of our sins (forgiveness), and be set free from the *compulsion* to sin (cleansing) (1:7-9; 2:2; 4:10).

In the chaos on Normandy's beach on D day, 1945, a burning ammunition truck with the driver dead at the wheel careened toward a company of pinned-down soldiers. An unknown GI leaped into the cab and steered the smoldering vehicle into the sea. He was killed instantly when it exploded.[14] "I came . . . to give my life as a ransom for many" (Mark 10:45).

3. Jesus is the One whose abiding presence gives us the power to continually *overcome the world* (2:13-14; 4:4; 5:4, 18), and to enjoy a life of *freedom from condemnation* (3:19-22; Rom. 8:1).

Bob Benson, Sr., told how he let himself in by the kitchen door late one night. On a crude cardboard sign taped to a chair was this message: "Dad, I really blew it today. I'm sorry. Please forgive me. Curt." Immediately he went to his son's bedroom, aroused him, put his arms around him, and told him that he was forgiven. It was all OK.

When I heard Mr. Benson tell this story, I found myself asking, "What in the world did Curt do that was so bad?" Sensing this very question in all of our minds, Bob continued, "I suppose you are curious as to what it was that my son did." We nodded our response.

"Well, I don't know," he said. "I never asked him, because there is nothing in the whole wide world that my son could ever do that is beyond my willingness to forgive!"

That is God's kind of love—love that sets us free!

It was the Fourth of July, 1965. Over 100,000 people jammed Washington Park, facing the Lincoln Memorial. It was a scorching, humid day. Yet the crowd didn't notice as they stood enthralled by one of the most eloquent and memorable speeches of this century. Rising on a soaring wave of electrifying emotion, Martin Luther King, Jr., concluded his impassioned oration in this manner:

"I have a dream! I have a dream that someday all of God's children will come home. I have a dream that all of them—rich and poor, young and old, black and white—will be able to say:

"Free at last!

"I'm free at last!

"Bless God Almighty, I'm free at last!"

Another Sermon

A Picture of a Johannine Church

Exposition

It was in the middle of the third century. The Church was suffering persecution from without and schism from within. Cyprian, who was later martyred for his faith, wrote a letter to a friend in which he said:

> It is a bad world, Donatus, an incredibly bad world. But I have discovered in the midst of it a quiet and holy people who have learned a great secret. They have found a joy that is a thousand times better than any pleasure of our sinful life. They are despised and persecuted, but they care not. They have overcome the world. These people, Donatus, are the Christians—and I am one of them.[15]

Cyprian describes the kind of church that John envisioned, particularly in our passage: a community of Christians who were making a real effort to walk . . . as He walked (2:6). There are at least three dimensions of this "fellowship" of believers (1:3) that stand out clearly in these verses (2:1-14).

A Holy People

Mahatma Gandhi lived in South Africa during the most formative period of his life. It was there he became exposed to the gospel and developed a lifelong fascination with Jesus Christ. It was also there, however, that he encountered blatant discrimination in that ostensibly Christian society. He was thrown off trains, excluded from hotels and restaurants, and treated shabbily by Christians. For instance, having heard so much about a preacher named C. F. Andrews, whom some of his Indian Christian friends had nicknamed "Christ's Faithful Apostle," he went to a church to hear him speak. He was met at the entrance by burly ushers who refused to let him in—his skin color was not white!

E. Stanley Jones, longtime missionary to India and friend of Gandhi, sadly observed, "Racialism has many sins to bear, but perhaps its worst sin was the obscuring of Christ in an hour when one of the greatest souls born of a woman was making his decision."[16]

That is why there is such a deep and passionate concern in both Testaments for God's people to "be holy; for I am holy" (Lev. 11:44, NASB; cf. Matt. 5:48; 1 Pet. 1:15-16; Col. 1:21-23). And this is why John is almost strident in his insistence that those who profess to know Him and abide . . . in Him must exhibit godliness; such should not sin, keep His commandments, and walk in the same manner as He walked; and such a one . . . loves his brother (1 John 2:1, 3, 6, 10). Anything less corrupts the gospel, distorts the image of Christ, and repels hungry hearts like those of Gandhi.

"God is light" (1:5). Yet the only means He has of illuminating the darkened souls of lost humanity is when we, His people, "walk in the light" (1:7; cf. 2:9-10). Jesus Christ the righteous (2:1) has ascended to the right hand of the Father. The only way people are going to see Jesus "fleshed out" is when they observe that we walk in the same manner as He walked (2:6).

A Healing Fellowship

A. W. Tozer writes, "The moral shock suffered . . . through our mighty break with the high will of heaven has left us all with a permanent trauma affecting every part of our nature."[17] It has left us depraved in our hearts, diseased in our environment, and divided in our churches. "If we say that we have no sin . . . [or] have not sinned, . . . we are deceiving ourselves . . . [and] we make Him a liar" (1:8, 10, NASB).

However, the cleansing, healing, and reconciling blood of Jesus penetrates deeper than the stain has gone (1:7). God's provision for man's moral sickness was worked out fully and finally when Christ offered up himself as a sacrifice **for our sins; and not for ours only, but also for those of the whole world** (2:2; cf. 4:10).

During the height of India's civil war between the Hindus and Muslims following its independence from Great Britain in 1948, a Hindu gave shelter to a Muslim friend. This infuriated his Hindu neighbors who demanded the head of his friend. The Hindu would not surrender him. So the mob attacked his house, broke down the door, and hacked them both to death, literally in each other's arms.[18] That is God's kind of love! And that is, literally, what Jesus did for us. He wrapped His arms of love around us, and "died to sin, once for all," in order that we too might consider ourselves "to be dead to sin, but alive to God in Christ Jesus" (Rom. 6:10-11, NASB).

A Helping Community

God has not called out a people just so they can sequester themselves far from the corruption and pollution of this world's life where they can endlessly devote themselves to polishing their "holiness image." The God who is light calls His people to plunge into a darkened world where they can radiate **the true light,** which is **already shining** (2:8). They are to carry out this mission by the integrity of their lives (2:1, 3-5), by the Christlikeness of their walk (2:6), and by the quality of their love (3:7-11).

I opened this message with a negative illustration out of South Africa. Now for a positive one. A black schoolteacher saw a white man respectfully tip his hat to a black woman, who just happened to be the teacher's mother. The white man was an Anglican priest by the name of Trevor Huddleston, later a bishop. A friendship developed between the schoolteacher and the priest. When the Black developed tuberculosis, Huddleston visited him *every day* for the 20 months he was in the hospital. Profoundly impressed, he followed his friend into the Anglican ministry. Few people have heard of Bishop Huddleston, but nearly every person around the civilized world recognizes the name of his convert—Bishop Desmond Tutu.

Endnotes

1. Most Scripture references are taken from the *New American Standard Bible.*

· 2. William Barclay, *The Letters of John and Jude,* in *The Daily Study Bible Series* (Philadelphia: Westminster Press, 1960), 40.

3. Ibid.

4. Friedrick Buchsel, "Hilasmos," in *Theological Dictionary of the New Testament,* ed. Gerhard Kittel and Gerhard Friedrich, abr. in 1. vol. by Geoffrey W. Bromiley (Grand Rapids: Wm. B. Eerdmans Publishing Co., 1985), 364.

5. C. H. Dodd, *The Johannine Epistles,* in *Moffatt New Testament Commentary* (New York: Harper Bros., 1946), 28-29.

6. Barclay, 48-50.

7. Otto Piper, "Knowledge," in *Interpreter's Dictionary of the Bible,* ed. George A. Buttrick, 4 vols. (New York: Abingdon Press, 1962), vol. 3.

8. I. Howard Marshall, *The Epistles of John,* in *The New International Commentary on the New Testament* (Grand Rapids: Wm. B. Eerdmans Publishing Co., 1978), 122.

9. Ibid., 125.

10. Mildred Bangs Wynkoop, *A Theology of Love: The Dynamic of Wesleyanism* (Kansas City: Beacon Hill Press of Kansas City, 1972), 165.

11 A. W. Tozer, "Knowing God in Justice, Love, and Holiness," *Christianity Today,* Jan. 18, 1985, 38; taken from "The Holiness of God," in *Knowledge of the Holy: The Attributes of God: Their Meaning in the Christian Life* (New York: Harper and Brothers, Publishers, 1961).

12. Wynkoop, *Theology of Love,* 34-35.

13. George Feifer, "Escape from Russia on Foot," *Reader's Digest,* Feb. 1985, 178-210 (quote from 210).

14. *Time,* May 28, 1984, 29.

15. George E. Sweazey, *Preaching the Good News* (Englewood Cliffs, N.J.: Prentice-Hall, 1976), 258.

16. Philip Yancey, "Gandhi and Christianity," *Christianity Today,* Apr. 8, 1983, 37.

17. Tozer, "Knowing God," 37.

18. Louis Fischer, *Gandhi* (New York: A Mentor Book from New American Library, Times Mirror, 1954), 161-62.

—9—

THE HOLY SPIRIT—AGENT OF SANCTIFICATION

———

Editor's Introduction to
A Johannine Theology of the Holy Spirit

W. F. Lofthouse has argued that the experiences of the Holy Spirit in Acts are informed by the understanding of the Spirit found in John 14—16.[1] This is an important consideration on two grounds: (1) The experiences of the Spirit recorded throughout Scripture are diverse in character, although the language is the same (clearly the instances of being "filled with the Spirit" recorded in the early Lukan passages have a different meaning from Pentecostal and post-Pentecostal references using the same terminology). (2) There is need for some other criteria than the language of Acts to determine its theological and experiential significance.[2] For these reasons it is important to consider the Johannine teaching as a background for exegeting Acts passages.

It is helpful in understanding their larger significance to place the Paraclete passages from the following essay in the larger context of the Johannine teaching about the Spirit. John contains an interesting structure that, if not by design, certainly lends itself to illustrating essential truths concerning the NT doctrine of the Spirit.

There are 12 passages divided equally into two groups of 6 each. The first group of passages deal with the Spirit's relation to Jesus, whereas the second group refer to the Spirit's work in relation to believers.[3] It is obvious that the first group of references provide the foundation for the second. If the distinctiveness of the NT understanding of the Spirit is His embodiment in Jesus, then His indwelling in believers is to produce Christ's character in them. If this is true, then the experiences of the Spirit recorded in Acts are Christ-centered experiences. The reader should note particularly, in the essay that follows, the way in which the Paraclete is related to Jesus, thus paving the way for the recognition that the Holy Spirit at work in Acts is the Spirit of Jesus (see 16:7).

Endnotes

1. W. F. Lofthouse, "The Holy Spirit in the Acts and the Fourth Gospel," *Expository Times* 52, no. 9 (1940-41): 334-36.

2. It will be noted in the exegesis of Acts passages that follow that the writers appeal to sources outside of the actual language to provide their interpretation of the texts. In particular, there is widespread reference to the transformation that occurred in the life of the apostles after the Pentecostal outpouring with the assumption that these changes resulted from their having been filled with the Spirit. Our point here is that this is both necessary and legitimate.

3. See Dale Moody, *Spirit of the Living God* (Philadelphia: Westminster Press, 1968), 34-37.

ARNOLD AIRHART

A Johannine Theology of the Holy Spirit

The Paraclete Sayings

1. The Meaning of "Paraclete"

The distinctive Greek term for the Holy Spirit in John is transliterated as "Paraclete." Although this word occurs only five times in Scripture and only in the writings of John (John 14:16, 26; 15:26; 16:7; 1 John 2:1), it is a word of great importance. When one notes the struggles of translators with it, it becomes obvious that it is also a difficult word. William Barclay concludes that it "is really untranslatable."[1]

In theological discourse, the transliterated word, "paraclete," is commonly used in order to avoid the translation problems. The verb is *parakaleō* (*para*, "by the side of," and *kaleō*, "to call") and thus by derivation, "to call to one's side, summon." Of course, it is the purpose for which the *paraclētos* is called that gives the word its intensive richness.

This richness of meaning makes impossible an adequate translation by a single English word. In translating Jesus' sayings about the Paraclete, the KJV has "Comforter," the RSV as well as NIV has "Counselor," the NEB has "Advocate," and the NASB "Helper." J. B. Phillips uses "someone to stand by you," and Ronald Knox "he who is to befriend you." Translators are generally agreed that for the fifth occurrence in 1 John 2:1, where the reference is not to the Holy Spirit but to our Lord's intercession in the presence of the Father, the proper word is "Advocate."

With reference to translations Barclay observes,

> The English translation *comforter* goes all the way back to Wiclif; but it must be noted that Wiclif was using the word

comforter with a width of meaning which in modern English it does not possess . . . in Wiclif's time it was much more closely connected with its root, the Latin word *fortis,* which means *brave, strong, courageous* . . . So . . . Wiclif . . . was meaning that the function of the Holy Spirit was to fill a man with that Spirit of power and courage which would make him able triumphantly to cope with life.[2]

J. Behm, after noting the occurrence in 1 John 2:1, adds,

More richly developed, and difficult to define, is the idea in John of a Paraclete working in and for the disciples. . . . This work is similar to that of the OT advocate and links up with descriptions of the Spirit's ministry elsewhere in the NT (Rom. 8:26-27; Mk. 13:11; Lk. 13:6 ff.). The Greek term may well go back to the term used by Jesus himself in his mother tongue. In translation the many secondary senses rule out any single equivalent. If we are to avoid "Paraclete," the basic thought is that of "Advocate" but the more general "Supporter" or "Helper" is perhaps the best rendering.[3]

Ralph Earle quotes Behm approvingly: "Thus the history of the term in the whole sphere of known Greek and Hellenistic usage outside the NT yields the clear picture of a legal advisor or helper or advocate in the relevant court." Earle comments: "We have always felt that the only word that takes in all the work of the Holy Spirit for us as the Paraclete is 'Helper.' . . . This is all-inclusive."[4]

It is useful to examine the cognate words. In the NT the verb *parakaleō* occurs 103 times and appears to carry most frequently the meaning of exhorting, appealing, urging, imploring, requesting (cf. Acts 8:31; 9:38). Almost as frequently it is translated as encouraging, heartening, consoling (cf. 20:12; 2 Cor. 1:4-6).

The noun *paraklēsis,* "a summons," "a calling alongside," occurs 29 times and usually refers to strength, encouragement, consolation, comfort. Neither of these cognate words appears in John's writings.

After citing examples of verbal usage found in earlier Greek literature and later Christian writings, William Barclay sums up:

Parakalein not infrequently means to *exhort* or to *urge* . . . But above all *parakalein* is used of exhorting troops who are about to go into battle . . . Again and again we find that *parakalein* is the word of the rallying-call . . . It is the word used of words which send fearful and timorous and hesitant soldiers and sailors courageously into battle . . . A *paraklētos* is therefore an encourager, one who puts courage into the fainthearted . . . one who makes a very ordinary man cope gallantly with a perilous and dangerous situation.[5]

2. Trinitarian Implications in the Paraclete Sayings

The Paraclete sayings make a significant contribution to the biblical raw materials that were developed into Trinitarian dogma in the early centuries of Christian theologizing. In fact "they carry us a degree farther than any other writing in the development of the New Testament doctrine of the Godhead."[6]

The personhood of the Paraclete, the Holy Spirit (14:26), is clearly identified. *"To Pneuma* (a neuter noun) [is identified] as *ho Paraklētos* (a masculine noun; 14:26; cf. also 14:15-16; 15:26-27; 16:7-11). Notice also the use of the masculine pronouns in 14:26; 15:26; 16:7-8, 13-14 (*ekeinos* and *autos*). These can in no way be interpreted as signifying a [mere] tendency or influence."[7]

In these passages the parallels between the Paraclete and Jesus himself are striking. Commentators sometimes describe the Paraclete as Jesus' alter ego (other self), and some even mean by this that the glorified Christ and the Holy Spirit are one and the same. But this is to confuse a certain oneness in operation or function with essential unity or identity. (Cf. the interchange of persons in Paul's discussion in Rom. 8:9-11 and the near identification in 2 Cor. 3:18.) Jesus spoke of the Paraclete as "another Paraclete" (14:16, "another" of the same kind), another who would continue Jesus' work. As Jesus came in the Father's name, so the Paraclete will come in Jesus' name.

In the Upper Room sayings the Paraclete is inseparably related to the person of Jesus Christ. The central idea is that the Paraclete is known Christologically.

(1) The coming of the Paraclete is dependent upon Jesus' going away (16:7; cf. 7:37-39 and Acts 2:33). (2) Jesus' designation of the Paraclete (14:16) implies His continuation of Jesus' work. (3) The reception of the Paraclete is dependent on a prior knowledge of Jesus (14:17). (4) The coming of the Paraclete is identified with Jesus' personal, abiding presence. The Spirit is not a substitute for Jesus' absence but rather the One who accomplishes the presence of Jesus. As already noted, in the NT the *operations* of the risen, glorified Christ and those of the Spirit are not differentiated. (5)

The Paraclete's work is Christ-centered (14:26; 15:26; 16:13-14).[8]

It is clear that to have the gift of the Paraclete is to have the indwelling of Christ, indeed, to have the Father and the Son (cf. 14:23). The Son makes known the Father, and the Spirit makes known the Son.

B. F. Westcott points out the progression within the sayings relative to what theologians call "the procession" of the Holy Spirit. "Procession" is derived from the verb "proceeds," which translates *ekporeuetai* (15:26). The verb means "to go out," "to flow out," "to emerge." This supports the position of the Western church that the Spirit proceeds from both the Father *and* the Son.[9]

In 14:16 Jesus "will ask the Father, and He will give you another Helper." In 14:26 "the Father will send [the Holy Spirit] in [Jesus'] name." In 15:26 Jesus "will send [the Helper] to you from the Father, that is the Spirit of truth, who proceeds from the Father." In 16:7 Jesus "will send [the Holy Spirit] to you" (all NASB).[10]

The essential oneness along with the personal distinctions of Father, Son, and Holy Spirit are implied especially in 15:26 when compared with 14:16, 18, 26; 16:7, 13-15; and 20:22. The tenses of 15:26 are noteworthy: The Son "will send" (future tense) the Holy Spirit, "who proceeds" (present tense, suggesting a permanent relation?) from the Father (NASB). In 16:15, closing the last of the sayings, there is a remarkable intimation of the complete intercommunion of Father, Son, and Holy Spirit, their essential unity, the personal distinctions, and the subordination relative to office or function (not essence, cf. 14:28). In the NT there are no more important texts than these for Trinitarian theology.

3. The Paraclete as the Promise of the Father

In this study at least four biblical contexts should be considered. They are: (1) the OT promise of the Spirit fulfilled under the new covenant. (2) The NT doctrine of the Holy Spirit in the light of the Paraclete sayings. (We can deal with this here only in part, and in connection with the study of each of the sayings.) (3) The Johannine teachings on the Holy Spirit other than the farewell discourses. (4) The farewell discourses and the prayer following (John 13:31—17:26). Now we turn to the first of these.

The Promised Spirit

Luke records Jesus' command to the disciples to wait for "the promise of My Father" (Luke 24:49), and "for what the Father had promised" (Acts 1:4). Preaching at Pentecost, Peter said, "The promise is for you and your children" (2:38-39). In another context we will take note of the "promise" language of v. 33. These expressions also point back to the Paraclete sayings, for Jesus said of the promise, "which you heard of from Me" (1:4, all NASB).

Paul argues that "in Christ Jesus the blessing of Abraham [has] come to the Gentiles, so that we might receive the promise of the Spirit through faith" (Gal. 3:14). He identifies the covenant blessings promised to Abraham and his seed with the dispensation of the Spirit. In Eph. 1:13 "the Holy Spirit of promise" (the promise here refers to OT prophecy) is the One who seals believers in Christ, the metaphor denoting total possession (both NASB).

It is clear that the language of the OT concerning a new covenant with the people of God, that includes the pouring out of the Spirit on all God's people and the putting of God's Spirit within them, is fleshed out and made explicit by Jesus in the Paraclete sayings. Covenant language is retained, inasmuch as "to receive" the Paraclete involves a choice and the full consent of a covenant relationship. However, covenant language yields to the intimate and personal relationship language of the Paraclete passages. The new covenant involves the Church; personal plural language is used. In Wesley's expression, the Bible knows no holiness but social holiness.

The agelong quest of God, through the Spirit, to restore the creation-designed fellowship with man that sin had shattered, had, in the fullness of time, neared its goal when "the Word became flesh, and dwelt among us" (John 1:14). Although the realization of the promise in its ultimate dimension awaits our final redemption, with the consequence that we live with certain "not-yet" limitations, the promise was fulfilled on the Day of Pentecost. In Jesus' words, God has, in answer to our Lord's intercession for us, given us "another Helper, that He may be with [us] forever" (14:16, both NASB). The abiding presence of the seeking God re-creates for us and restores to us the forfeited fellowship.

The giving of the Spirit also ushered the kingdom of God into human experience. Laurence W. Wood observes that Luke's writings show that "Jesus' understanding of the restored kingdom was radically different from the popular notion. The true Kingdom which was brought about by the Pentecostal event means that the exalted Christ reigns in the life of believers through the indwelling Spirit. In this respect, it is of symbolic significance that 'the promise of the Father' which brought about the inauguration of this spiritual Kingdom occurred in Jerusalem, the capital city of the Promised Land (Acts 1:3-4)."[11]

Some of the prophetic passages are: Isa. 44:3, where the Spirit is symbolized by water in abundance; Jer. 31:31-34, where the inward truth-teaching relationship within the new covenant is stressed (cf. Hebrews 8); Ezek. 36:25-27, outlining the cleansing, transforming, abiding ministry of the Holy Spirit; and the familiar promise from Joel 2:28-29, remembered in Peter's Pentecost sermon.

Various NT passages that refer to the fulfillment of the promise should be noted. These include Rom. 7:6 and 8:1-4; 2 Cor. 3:1-18; Gal. 5:16-25; Heb. 11:13, 39-40.

4. The Paraclete Sayings and the Other Johannine Writings

On the teaching about the Holy Spirit John represents an advance upon the Synoptics. Charles Carter says, "The Gospel According to John, more than any other book of the New Testament, except perhaps the book of Acts, has influenced the thinking of scholars and laymen alike on their understanding of the Holy Spirit."[12] Barclay calls the Fourth Gospel the "high-water mark" of NT teachings concerning the Holy Spirit.[13]

The Gospel contains, in addition to the Paraclete sayings, concepts about the Holy Spirit that give structural support to the Paraclete teaching. In the First Epistle doctrinal and devotional statements reflect the Paraclete passages and appear in the context of the Church's life a generation after Jesus uttered the sayings. Without discussing critical matters related to comparison with the Synoptics, we here take note of some salient Johannine references so as to enhance understanding concerning the Paraclete.

John 1:32-34. In this passage, Jesus is the prototype of all those in the age of the Spirit in whom the Paraclete would dwell permanently: "and He remained upon Him" (cf. 14:16-17). Here also are the two major relationships, seen in the Gospels, between Jesus and the Spirit: The One who is the Bearer of the Spirit is also especially the Giver of the Spirit: this is the one who baptizes in the Holy

Spirit" (both NASB; cf. 15:26; 16:7). The Holy Spirit is our Lord's Great Bequest, and this is the distinguishing characteristic of the Church age.

John 3:5-8. Unless God breathes life into us from above, we remain inexorably trapped in the confines of the world of darkness "below," spiritually dead in our sins. The life that God imparts is His own shared life, something so transforming that it is "a new creation" (2 Cor. 5:17; cf. Gen. 1:27; 2:7), a "new birth" (1 Pet. 1:3). In this shared life it is the Spirit who is the Sharer; indeed everything God does for us and in us is the Spirit's doing. The Spirit "produces and maintains the vital connection" between God and us.[14]

The work of the Spirit is essential, it is unseen to natural eyes, and it cannot be manipulated by human effort. The relationship with the Spirit is on the level of faith. It is God's gift of himself—to us (cf. 14:17).

John 3:34. "For He gives the Spirit without measure" (NASB). Probably the meaning is that the Father gives the Spirit to Jesus, not by measure. The principle, which would apply to the gift of the Spirit to believers, is that this Gift is qualitative, not quantitative. God's gift of himself is "poured out" (Acts 2:33). It is "the fullness of God" (Eph. 3:19) freely offered to "us men, and for our salvation" (Nicene Creed).

John 4:23-24. The contrast here is not between two styles or modes of worship, but between two levels of life. One is mere human existence and endeavor; the other is the realm of fellowship with God. The higher reaches down to us and is apprehended through the person of the Holy Spirit. Worship will be "in truth" because of the love and knowledge of God and the witness to Christ that will be imparted to worshipers by the Paraclete (4:24; cf. 14:16-17, 26; 15:26; 16:13). Worship confined to race and place and book will yield to the new reality of life in God.

John 6:63. Jesus' words about himself will not make sense on the solely intellectual, unspiritual level (cf. v. 60). The ability to appropriate in faith the teaching of Jesus is the Spirit's interior work. Without the Spirit of Truth (14:17) the death of Christ (v. 51) will be to us a mere historical event. "It is the Spirit who gives life" (NASB).

John 7:37-39. The apostle adds in v. 39 the interpretation of this great proclamation and promise. This anticipates the Paraclete sayings, and especially Pentecost. The promise is free and universal to those who qualify: those who thirst after God, those who consciously respond, those who are believers in Christ (cf. 14:17). The Spirit's effective operation in the world is to be launched from the "innermost being," the core of personality, the control center of those in whom He makes His residence. The promise assures the success of Christ's mission to the world through those who believe in Him.

The figurative language of the continuous outflowing illustrates continuing dynamic freshness, cleansing, adequacy, and service orientation in the Spirit's ministry in the relationship we know as the Spirit-filled life (cf. 15:27; 16:14).

"The Spirit was not yet given" in the sense of the promise of the Father, of the Paraclete sayings, and of Pentecost. This cannot come except through the provisions of the Cross and must await the exaltation of the Son to the Father's right hand: "because Jesus was not yet glorified" (NASB; cf. 16:7; Acts 2:33).

John 20:21-22. It is a mistake to confuse this event with the fulfilling of Jesus' promises about the Paraclete's coming. That took place at Pentecost. George Eldon Ladd has called this symbolic act of Jesus "an acted parable"[15] (cf. Gen. 2:7). It was a reinforcement of the promise of the Paraclete. (See later comments on "to receive" the Holy Spirit relative to 14:17.)

Here the gift of the Spirit is again coupled with the mission to the world (cf. 16:7-11; Acts 1:8). The "acted parable" suggests, by comparison with the Genesis creation account, a new creation indwelt by the Spirit of God at a new level of relationship with God through faith and moral choice. This heralds a new beginning, even a "new race" of redeemed men and women.

We now move to the First Epistle. Here the most prominent references to the Holy Spirit throw light upon facets of the Paraclete as Truth, as Witness, and as Bringer of assurance.

1 John 2:20-21. The "anointing from the Holy One" refers to the gift of the Spirit. The result is that "you all know." (Cf. statements about Spirit of Truth in the sayings.) This is salvation knowledge, without reference to nonsalvation matters. Christians who "abide in the Son and in the Father" (v. 24, all NASB) have a deeper witness to the person of Christ (cf. John 15:26-27) and need not rely solely or primarily on rational argument. The Spirit is the Guard at the door of the heart against lies and heresies.

1 John 3:23-24. Here the promise is of assurance, the inner witness of the Spirit to an "abiding" relationship with Christ based on reliance on Him wholly and on voluntary obedience to His will. We demonstrate our love for God by loving one another and practicing truth and righteousness. Our own spirits witness to whether or not we are doing this. But there is a deeper witness or knowledge, the inner voice of the Spirit.

John Wesley admonishes: "Let none ever presume to rest in any supposed testimony of the Spirit which is separate from the fruit of it"; and again, "let none rest in any supposed fruit of the Spirit without the witness."[16]

1 John 4:1-3. John writes against the backdrop of denial of the truth of Jesus as the God-man. At stake is the doctrine of the Incarnation, and consequently the true doctrines of the Resurrection and the Atonement. The Spirit of God illuminates the person of Christ as being true man and true God, the God-man, the sufficient Savior (cf. John 16:14-15).

1 John 4:12-13. The Spirit witnesses to us that we abide in God and God abides in us. This is parallel to 3:24. The internal witness illuminates our understanding of Jesus, who, in His person, tells us all that we need to know about God (cf. John 16:13-15). The work of God in us is love, and God intends to bring His love in us to fulfillment, that is, to perfect love. Thus, the abiding of the Spirit produces both assurance and perfection in love.

1 John 5:6-8. Again it is affirmed that the Holy Spirit bears essential witness to the truth and gives assurance with regard to our faith in Christ. The crucial issues are Jesus' life as the God-man, His real death, and His bodily resurrection. The other two witnesses, the water and the blood, are attestations of the facts of Jesus' life among us, and of His vicarious death as the God-man. To this established twofold evidence the Holy Spirit bears the clinching witness. Note, "the Spirit is the truth."

Rev. 21:1-7. Especially v. 3. The revelator sees the ultimate fulfillment of the eschatological promise that God's dwelling place will be among and in men. He sees the age to come as having begun. In Christ the Omega has been written. In the vision, God's gracious, yearning purpose for His creation has been realized in the consummation of human history.

Although Spirit-filled believers live in the present age (not yet in the age to come), nevertheless, under the provisions of the Cross, and in the experience of the indwelling Spirit, the spiritual blessings of the age to come have already been invested in this present time (cf. Romans 8). The age to come has overlapped this present age, so that we live in "the time between the times," the Church age, having already tasted "the powers of the age to come" (Heb. 6:5, NASB). This eschatological situation is at work in the Paraclete sayings.

Rev. 22:17. To the very end the mission of the Spirit and the mission of the Church (the Bride) are one mission. The voices that invite all who will to come are really one voice: the voice of the Spirit indwelling the Church and the voice of the Church inspired by the Spirit, united in confessing, witnessing to, and exalting Jesus Christ (cf. John 15:26-27; 16:7-15).

5. The Paraclete Sayings and the Upper Room Discourses

John 13 through 17 breathes the atmosphere of Jesus' imminent death and the wrenching bereavement that the disciples will suffer. A spirit of tenderness pervades events and teachings. Even so, the emphasis is not focally on the severed ties, but rather upon a transition—an anticipated, decisive transition in relationship. Contrast between the *now* and the *afterward* is continuous (cf. 13:3, 7, 36). In chapters 14, 15, 16, and 17 this theme is a thread binding together various subject matters. We should keep in mind both the disciples' difficulty in understanding and the limitations that this imposed on Jesus' desire to instruct them (16:12).

Westcott writes, "The book of Acts—'the Gospel of the Holy Spirit'—is in part a commentary upon these last words. At the same time it is most important to observe that the ideas are not made definite by exact limitations. The teaching gains its full meaning from the later history, but the facts of the later history have not modified it . . . At first [the promises and warnings] could not have been intelligible in their full bearing."[17]

Carl F. H. Henry observes: "It is this transition which carries the message of the Fourth Gospel beyond that of the earlier Gospels, and foresees Pentecost in the Acts of the Apostles, where the Risen Christ participates in the life of His radiant Church."[18]

The seven conversational exchanges that take place between Jesus and the Eleven in the Upper Room (and possibly elsewhere subsequently) point up the frailties, the fears, the mistaken concepts of these men. It is plain from this that they are ordinary folk. The great mission upon which they will embark in no way rests upon their own courage or special gifts. The gospel could not have had its origin in them. Only their relationship with Christ, to be perfected in the coming of the Paraclete, comprises the secret.

The language about "abiding" (also "going away," "coming again," "abiding-places") highlights the emphasis on transition. This is intertwined with the union of the Father and the Son: "In that day you shall know that I am in My Father, and you in Me, and I in you" (14:20, NASB). The ethical nature of this abiding is underscored by references to strengthening the disciples' love for Jesus, a love demonstrated only by keeping His words, words that are His Father's in whose love He abides (14:23-24; 15:10). The will, rather than merely the emotions, is involved. In the figure of the Vine He further expounds this reciprocal abiding and lifts up its vital and ethical nature (15:1-10).

The permanent relationship that will be theirs afterward is discussed in terms that can mean nothing less than a free, uncoerced, moral, and personal relationship with Christ through the Paraclete. To "abide" is obviously no once-for-all decision but a continuing choice (cf. 15:6, 14). This is not contradicted by Jesus' reminder, "You did not choose Me, but I chose you" (15:16, NASB). J. H. Mayfield comments: "The basis of this friend relationship is not of man's merit or working. . . . This is not to deny man his free moral agency, but it is to affirm that apart from Christ man is impotent (15:1). . . . The self-appointed man is doomed to dismal defeat when he tries apart from Christ to produce the fruit that abides."[19]

The legacy of relationship through the Paraclete will include power in prayer, success in fruit bearing, victory over the world, peace, and joy, besides the bequests within the sayings themselves.

At chap. 17 Jesus moves from teaching to praying. The hallowed memory of our Lord's intercessory prayer gave the Eleven sacred insights into His love for them, His desire that they be with Him, and that He be with them in their mission in the world. His closing prayer-words that the Father's love be in them they would understand in the light of the fulfillment of the promise of the Paraclete. His pleading "that they may all be one; even as Thou, Father, art in Me, and I in Thee, that they also may be in Us; that the world may believe that Thou didst send Me" (17:21, NASB), they would see as the holy fellowship between God and man that is God's agelong quest, the realization made possible by the Paraclete.

But at the center of His concern for their relationship with Him and with the Father was His essential petition: "Sanctify them in the truth; Thy word is truth" (17:17, NASB). This they would come to see as the very heart of the ministry of the Paraclete.

6. The Paraclete as the Gift of the Father and the Son

The Father gave the Son to be the Savior of the world (1 John 4:14). Now, Jesus announces, the Father and the Son will give the Holy Spirit to those who have received the Son.

We will consider the teachings about the Gift somewhat in the order in which they occur, an order that may or may not be best suited to preaching. The Paraclete as the Gift of truth and teaching will be considered separately.

There are conditions that restrict eligibility to receive the Gift. Relationship with Christ is the key. Satisfactory relationship hinges upon loving Him and keeping His commandments (14:15). This is made more emphatic in vv. 21-24. In this context "loving" means oneness of will and purpose. Obedience is more than ritual observance; it is a new level of living, by a standard based on inwardness and attitude. And for this, "personal companionship with Christ is the first requirement."[20]

The world cannot qualify for the Gift (14:17). It has neither vision nor experience to enable it "to take" the Gift (cf. 1 Cor. 2:14-15). "The world" is characterized by self-centeredness and love of the world itself (cf. 1 John 2:15-17). Temple adds that God's love in the Son "had to come first . . . because this is what calls forth the new response from our hearts, or (to put it from the other side) breaks through the hard shell of selfishness and self-complacency so that the Comforter may enter."[21]

William Barclay illustrates:

> An astronomer will see far more in the sky than an ordinary man. . . . Always what we see and experience depends on what we bring to the sight and the experience. . . . and we cannot receive the Holy Spirit unless we wait in expectation and in prayer . . . The Holy Spirit gate-crashes no man's heart; He waits to be received.[22]

The disciples, however, do qualify for the Gift: "but you know Him because He abides with you, and will be in you" (14:17,

NASB). What did Jesus mean by the terms "with" and "in"? These are spatial terms, obviously used figuratively to describe nonspatial realities. What is the qualifying "with you"? It is unlikely (although not impossible) that Jesus meant that He himself was abiding "with" them as the Paraclete, as distinct from the coming of the Holy Spirit. MacGregor, somewhat modifying this view, states, "The Spirit was present in Christ for his contemporaries just as for us Christ is present in his Spirit," thus denoting a dispensational distinction.[23]

The disciples had some awareness of the Holy Spirit himself "with" them. Some commentators suggest that this awareness reflected the Spirit's work within their company collectively and contrasted with His future indwelling individually. According to Richard S. Taylor, we can say, "The believer knows [the Spirit] relationally, through Jesus, though without full understanding . . . Clearly one may have the Spirit as a Christian without having been baptized with the Spirit or without being filled with the Spirit."[24] Charles W. Carter likewise sees the distinction as being made between the Spirit in regeneration and the subsequent deeper work of the Spirit.[25]

Significantly, William Temple, agreeing with the interpretation of "with" as a collective awareness versus "in" as individual experience, suggests that the "two stages are marked ritually [within some liturgical communions] by Baptism and Confirmation." He writes, "This individual experience of the Spirit is normally subsequent to, and consequent upon, our experience of [the Spirit's] activity in the Church or Christian fellowship."[26] It appears that he means entrance into the church's fellowship. The two ritual stages correspond, at least structurally, to the crises of regeneration and entire sanctification when interpreted as being filled with the Spirit.

The word translated "receive" (14:17) is *lambanō*. The ordinary, basic sense of the word is "to take," "to take to oneself." The recipient has an active role in the reception. It is not the picture of receiving the Gift unawares or without intent.

A facet of the Gift is permanence: "that He may be with you forever" (14:16; cf. 23, "make Our abode with him," both NASB). It is this uninterrupted presence that makes possible the abiding in the Vine (cf. 15:1-11). This is the NT realization, in this "time between the times," of God's yearning to tabernacle with His people.

It is the true Shekinah (cf. Exod. 25:22; 33:11). Christ is present with His people through the Spirit. The fulfillment of 14:18 began at the Resurrection but was completed with power after the Ascension at Pentecost.

The Paraclete is himself the Gift of strength and steadfastness in the face of the world's hatred (read 15:26-27 in the context of the preceding vv. 17-25). He is the Gift of joy in place of sorrow (16:6-7, 20-22). Indeed, 16:17-33 implies a feast of Pentecostal blessings through the Spirit.

The Paraclete is the incomparable Gift (16:7). What could possibly be better than the physical presence of Jesus? Wonderful as that was, the implication is that the dispensation of the Spirit is higher than that of the Son, as that of the Son is higher than the time before the Son's advent. The visible, external presence of Jesus, intermittent and not universal, was exchanged for the permanent presence of the Spirit as the very Breath of believers. The outworking is seen in the disastrous conduct of the disciples before Pentecost in contrast with their courage afterward. The apparent greatest calamity is turned into the supreme blessing.

The Paraclete is the incomparably costly Gift. Jesus' going away, as the condition of the Paraclete's coming, thrice repeated in 16:7, is clearly stated in 7:39: Jesus must first be glorified. And now, concluding His teaching, Jesus prays, "Father, the hour has come; glorify Thy Son, that the Son may glorify Thee" (17:1). The glory was by way of the Cross, the Resurrection, and the Ascension to the Father. Peter, on the Day of Pentecost, probes to the heart of the matter: "Therefore having been exalted to the right hand of God, and having received from the Father the promise of the Holy Spirit, He has poured forth this which you both see and hear" (Acts 2:33, both NASB).

Our Lord, in His glorified humanity, representing us who believe on His name, received vicariously the promised Gift, which He "poured forth" upon His people. The language connotes abundance. The first Adam represented us badly, and by way of him the holy relationship with God was lost. Jesus, the "last Adam," has represented us gloriously, and by Him and in Him the Gift is restored (cf. 1 Cor. 15:22, 45). Thus, the redemptive purpose is realized.

What is truly a gift cannot be earned but only gratefully received. To knowingly refuse a gift is to offer insult to the giver (cf. Luke 11:13).

7. The Paraclete as the Spirit of Truth, and Teacher

This subject appears to be the one most prominent in the Paraclete sayings. Note the clauses that relate to it: "the Spirit of truth"; "He will teach you all things, and bring to your remembrance all that I said to you"; "He will bear witness of Me"; "And He, when He comes, will convict the world"; "He will guide you into all the truth; . . . He will disclose to you what is to come"; "He shall take of Mine, and shall disclose it to you" (14:16, 26; 15:26; 16:8, 13, 14, all NASB).

Notice the related verbs: "teach," "bring to your remembrance," "bear witness," "convict," "guide," "disclose." A study of the six Greek words would be profitable. We will examine "convict" in the next section.

God is truth. Wayne E. Caldwell writes, "Absolute truth is God, and truth apprehended is the knowledge of God. He is both the Key and the Core of truth, and all lesser truths relate to Him and flow from Him."[27]

Jesus said, "I am . . . the truth" (14:6). In Jesus we see the truth revealed, and the Spirit discloses to us the truth that is in Jesus. The Paraclete internalizes truth in our hearts both by witnessing to reality in Jesus and by creating in us the longing and willingness for this reality. He is the Spirit of truthfulness (cf. Isa. 11:2; John 17:17; Eph. 1:17).

Truth, *"alếtheia* is 'authenticity,' 'divine reality,' 'revelation,' especially in John, where this reality, as a possibility of human existence, is out of reach through the fall but is granted to faith through revelation by the word (cf. Jn. 8:44; 1 Jn 1:8; 2:4)."[28]

The world cannot receive the Paraclete and therefore also the truth brought by the Spirit partly because, by the world's method, this truth is unavailable. Truth is differentiated from the empirical knowledge of facts. The Spirit rescues man from "a wilderness of relativity, religiously, ethically, and in every other manner."[29] There may be a mere worldly worship of truth. But, as William Temple observes, "Those who follow truth without finding it incarnate in the historical Jesus of Nazareth cannot claim to be led by that Spirit to whom reference is here made [referring to 14:17]."[30] This should,

I think, be tempered by the observation that wherever truth is actually perceived, there, in prevenient grace, the Spirit of truth is at work.

The teaching, witnessing, guiding ministry of the Paraclete is essential to the Church's preservation. He is the Conservator and Guarantor of true doctrine.

> The Spirit's subjective, dynamic, and unhindered work in believers (vital Christian experience) is the only final safeguard against the encroachment of false authorities such as tradition (churchly authority) or biblicism (a merely intellectual and legal use of Scripture). The *testimonium Spiritus Sancti* reconciles reason and revelation, and points to Christ the Eternal Word, who is Lord of both Scripture and inward experience (1 Cor. 2:10-12, 14; 2 Cor. 3:6, 14-17; cf. Luke 24:27, 32).[31]

"He will teach you all things" (14:26, all NASB). Not, certainly, encyclopedic or infallible knowledge. "The coming of the Spirit means the realization, on the part of the new Christian community, of the full and true meaning of the life, teaching, death, and exaltation of Jesus."[32]

". . . and bring to your remembrance all that I said to you" (14:26). Here, the authority of the apostles as witnesses (evidenced in the NT writings) is safeguarded. Theirs is not some new thing beyond what is revealed in Christ. And yet, it is "more than a reminiscence of the *ipsissima verba* [the very words] of the Son of God: it is a living representation of all that He had once spoken to His disciples, a creative exposition of the gospel."[33]

"The Spirit of truth . . . will bear witness of Me" (15:26). "The primary concern of the Spirit of truth is to bear witness concerning Jesus Christ. For He is the very truth of God, the Eternal Word or self-utterance of the Father."[34] Marcus Dods writes, "Our Lord assures them that together with their witness-bearing there will be an all-powerful witness—'the Spirit of truth'—; one who could find access to the hearts and minds to which they addressed themselves and carry truth home to conviction."[35] (Cf. notes on "the witness" in 1 John.)

"He will guide you into all the truth" (16:13). Jesus could not be the disciples' final teacher (v. 12). "The Spirit would lead his disciples . . . into the full revelation of the mind of God in redemption."[36] This would include the meaning of the acts and events culminating in the Ascension.

This guidance is far more than an intellectual exercise. The Paraclete is the Guide along the way, and Jesus is the Way; the Guide into the truth, and Jesus is the Truth (14:6). His guidance is transforming in its effects. "This He did first of all by shaping the teachings of the Apostolic Church, and through that Church producing the New Testament as the written Word. . . . Whether being preached by the apostles or being read in the twentieth century, the Holy Spirit takes the words which are already His and uses them as His instrument in sanctification"[37] (cf. John 17:17; 2 Thess. 2:13).

"He will disclose to you what is to come" (16:13). The events of the end-time, including the eternal purpose of God for the future, were disclosed to the apostles in the form that we have them in the NT. Special guidance was given in the formation of the Church (cf. Acts 15:28).

"He shall glorify Me; for He shall take of Mine, and shall disclose it to you" (16:14). (For preachable material here read especially chap. 5, "The Traced-Over Blueprint," in Donald Joy's excellent book.)[38] In Isa. 53:1-4 the prophet pictures the suffering Savior as without "beauty or majesty," with "nothing in his appearance that we should desire him." Christ is glorified by the manifestation of the truth about Him and about His work. Joseph Parker preached that as the rising sun glorifies the darkened earth, revealing its splendid colors and beautiful landscapes, so the Spirit glorifies Christ. "The Christian religion is a *witness* to the person and redemptive work of Jesus Christ. Anything less than this is not Christian."[39]

The Spirit's sole aim as Teacher is to lift up and make known Jesus. Not the Spirit himself but Christ is in the spotlight of truth. Wilson T. Hogue makes use of the story of Abraham's self-effacing servant, putting forward the merits of Isaac, for whom he was seeking a bride, as an illustration of this text (cf. Gen. 24:31-38).[40] All pretended revelations that would add to or supersede Christ's finished work are excluded.

8. The Paraclete's Ministry to the World

"And He, when He comes, will convict the world" (see 16:8-11, all NASB). The verb *elengchō*, "convict," carries more meaning than can be easily compressed into one English word. The RSV has "convince," NEB "confute," TEV "prove." Ralph Earle, quoting

TDNT (Kittel), says that it means (in NT): "to show someone his sin and to summon him to repentance." . . . "The word *does not mean only* 'to blame' or 'to reprove,' nor 'to convince' in the sense of proof, nor 'to reveal' or 'expose,' but 'to set right,' namely, 'to point away from sin to repentance'" (italics mine).[41] The many facets are suggested in other references. See the word's use in Eph. 5:11, "expose"; Heb. 11:1, noun form, "conviction"; Rev. 3:19, "reprove"; 1 Cor. 14:24-25, "convicted," and note the synonyms (all NASB).

Using the language of the lawcourt, MacGregor speaks of the Paraclete as the Accuser of the world. The result is a conviction in a double sense: "The world reaches the 'conviction' that Christ is the truth, and it is 'convicted' of the crime of rejecting the truth." There are three counts of "guilty" in the verdict: on the question of sin, the question of righteousness, and the question of judgment.[42]

Barclay, using a similar paradigm, writes of the Spirit's action as cross-examination, in which a man is both convicted of a crime committed, and convinced of the wrongness of his defense.[43]

For an excellent homiletical treatment of the issues of this passage read Donald Joy under his chapter "What's Going On Here?" He points up the three indictments, "Pinpointing Sin," "Upholding Righteousness," and "Proclaiming Deliverance."[44]

Any treatment of the Spirit's convicting work must take into account the relationship between faith and reason. It is enough here to simply note some guidelines. True faith requires evidence; the evidence is available; it is sufficient, but it is not overwhelming in the sense of being coercive. Doubt is possible because not every possible question will be answered, and so faith is a choice, or decision, based on sufficient evidence. Faith is a doing word. The Paraclete's work is compatible with these truths of experience.

The interior work of the Spirit is indispensable if evangelism is to succeed. Truth is essential, witnessed to and taught by the Spirit-filled Christians. But truth alone is not enough. Donald Joy quotes Charles Malik in "A Civilization at Bay": "How can the Christian remnant recover an apostolic initiative in witnessing to the world? Not by magic; not by a clever trick; . . . not by . . . methods and techniques . . . not by mass organization simply. But especially by ardent prayer for the Holy Spirit to come mightily into the hearts of men."[45] (For a homiletical emphasis on the Spirit's power versus human failure see Daniel Steele.)[46] The NT gives eloquent historical assurance of this power (Rom. 15:18-19; 1 Cor. 2:4-5; 1 Thess. 1:5; 1 Pet. 1:12).

The Spirit's method in His work in the world is Christologically oriented. Note the references in 16:9 and 10 and the implication in 11. Verses 14 and 15 also relate to truth as it is in Jesus. The light from heaven is focused with burning intensity within the hearts of unbelievers by the Spirit, and the Light that is thus focused is Jesus Christ. Attempts to place anyone else in the spotlight, even the Spirit himself, fall short of the Johannine understanding of the Holy Spirit.

The Paraclete will convict the world "concerning sin, because they do not believe in Me" (16:9). This was vividly fulfilled on the Day of Pentecost (cf. Acts 2:37 and note the emphasis of vv. 22-36). The revelation of sin is more than of guilt and wrongness; it uncovers the condition that underlies the actions.

"The rejection of Jesus Christ is the central appearance of all the sins of all the world."[47] The Paraclete speaks to the sleeping or deluded conscience, unmasks the true nature of the unbelief that rejects Christ, that crucified Christ, and shows it to be, at root, willful. The Spirit tears away the facade behind which the unbelief masquerades, a proud, flawed intellectualism that parades unbelief as a veritable virtue. Those who crucified Jesus claimed (believed) they were doing God's service. How deceitful is sin! The Paraclete will make unbelief to be seen for what it is, "the selfishness which sets itself up apart from and so against God. It is not defined by any limited rule, but expresses a general spirit. To believe in Him, is to adopt the principle of self-surrender to God. Not to believe in Him, is to cleave to the legal view of duty and service which involves a complete misunderstanding of the essence of sin."[48]

Temple writes, "So the world's failure to believe on Christ is the proof that the world is wrong in its conception of what sin is . . . We try to cure our symptoms—our habits of lying, or cheating, or resentment, or envy . . . But the disease is that we are self-centered, not God-centered . . . if we knew our sickness we should know our need of the physician"[49] (cf. John 8:24; 9:40-41).

Concluding an eloquent description of conviction for sin, Marcus Dods wrote: "This is ever the damning sin—to be in the presence of goodness and not to love it, to see Christ and to see Him with unmoved and unloving hearts, to hear His call without response, to recognize the beauty of holiness and yet turn away to lust and self and the world."[50]

The Paraclete will convict the world "concerning righteousness, because I go to the Father, and you no longer behold Me" (16:10). The righteousness referred to is, first of all, the incomparable purity, goodness, and holiness of Jesus. By His exaltation in Resurrection triumph to the Father's right hand, God vindicated Him. His scandalous death as a criminal had to be reinterpreted. The Cross, a stumbling block to the Jews and folly to the Gentiles, was thenceforth transformed into a profound symbol of God's hatred of sin and His everlasting mercy. But it is just this immense truth that lifts us up, as sinners, by the Spirit's help, to glimpse in hope and awe a righteousness that can now be ours by faith in that atoning death. This is the insight of the apostle Paul (Rom. 3:21-26); Christ is revealed as the Source of salvation.

William Temple points out that here again the Paraclete convicts the world of its wrong view of righteousness. The world approves honor and success, "but real sacrifice for higher than material or patriotic causes it regards with anxiety and alarm. . . . We do not believe in any radical self-sacrifice enough to recommend it to our friends, even when we might follow that cause ourselves."[51] A radical commitment to righteousness, the view that this issue should have supremacy over our lives, is to be obtained at Calvary, and the world without the Paraclete's ministry regards it as fanaticism.

The Paraclete's conviction is also of the possibility of righteousness. "For each of us it is of the utmost importance to have a fixed and intelligent persuasion that righteousness is what we are made for . . . Righteousness has been attained . . . There has lived One . . . putting Himself as a perfect instrument into God's hand ready at all cost to Himself to do the Father's will . . . who not only approved . . . of a life of holiness and sacrifice, but actually lived it."[52]

The Paraclete will convict the world "concerning judgment, because the ruler of this world has been judged" (16:11).

> In the background of all God's direct dealings with men is the shadow of a cosmic struggle between God and Satan. In a very real sense, man himself is the prize in this struggle, in sav-

ing man, God defeats His enemy. . . . It is this hideous power aiding and abetting man's willful sinning that has made human history not only corrupt but so strangely and irrationally demonic. . . . Satan and the demons constitute a kingdom of evil (Matt. 12:26) that is highly organized, maliciously anti-God, and therefore anti-Christ (Eph. 6:12). For some reason they have been permitted to claim this planet as their special domain, and likewise have been permitted to involve themselves with evil intent in the affairs of men.[53]

Speaking of Christ's work, Paul says, "And then, having drawn the sting of all the powers and authorities ranged against us, he exposed them, shattered, empty and defeated, in his own triumphant victory!" (Col. 2:15, Phillips).

Lange puts it: "The judgment executed upon the devil through the death and resurrection of Christ, is the central appearance of all God's judgments in the history of the world, until the end of the world."[54]

In two different senses the already accomplished judgment on "the ruler of this world" is pungently pressed home to the hearts of sinners by the Holy Spirit. First, moral distinctions are clarified. The whole deceptive system of worldly morality has been exposed and condemned. It is not a question of some good and a bit less evil, with the good hopefully outweighing the evil. It is rather a question of "renouncing the devil and all his works" and aligning oneself with the holiness of God.

Second, the present possibilities of grace and holiness through the triumph of Jesus mean that men and women are under judgment *now*. Choice must be made between the kingdom of this world and the Kingdom of righteousness, and not in some future time, because the door to righteousness is now open. The question is, Am I now living in the domain of the doomed and the damned, or in the light and power of the Victor, Jesus Christ? (Cf. John 9:39; 12:31-33; 1 John 4:17.)

As to the future, the triumph of Christ has certified the final day of judgment. "To adhere to worldly motives and ways and ambitions is to cling to a sinking ship, to throw [oneself] away on a justly doomed cause. The world may trick itself out in what delusive splendours it may . . . [and] men who are deluded by it . . . destroy themselves and lose the future."[55]

Endnotes

1. William Barclay, *The Gospel of John, Vol. 2*, rev. ed., in *The Daily Study Bible Series* (Philadelphia: Westminster Press, 1975), 166.
2. William Barclay, *New Testament Words* (London: SCM Press, 1964), 216-17.
3. J. Behm, "paráklētos," *Theological Dictionary of the New Testament* (TDNT), ed. Kittel and Friedrich, trans. and abr. in 1 vol. by Geoffrey W. Bromiley (Wm. B. Eerdmans Publishing Co., 1985), 783-84.
4. Ralph Earle, *Word Meanings in the New Testament* (Kansas City: Beacon Hill Press of Kansas City, 1986), 92-93.
5. *New Testament Words*, 220-21.
6. George Johnston, "Spirit," in *A Theological Wordbook of the Bible*, ed. Alan Richardson (New York: Macmillan Co., 1950), 80, quoting W. F. Howard, *Christianity According to St. John*.
7. W. T. Purkiser, Richard S. Taylor, and Willard H. Taylor, *God, Man, and Salvation: A Biblical Theology* (Kansas City: Beacon Hill Press of Kansas City, 1977), 241.
8. H. Ray Dunning, *Grace, Faith, and Holiness: A Wesleyan Systematic Theology* (Kansas City: Beacon Hill Press of Kansas City, 1988), 415-17.
9. This issue divided the Eastern and Western churches in 1054.
10. B. F. Westcott, *The Gospel According to St. John* (1881; reprint, Grand Rapids: Wm. B. Eerdmans Publishing Co., 1964), lxv.
11. Laurence W. Wood, "Dispensation of the Spirit," in *Beacon Dictionary of Theology*, ed. Richard S. Taylor (Kansas City: Beacon Hill Press of Kansas City, 1983), 167.
12. Charles W. Carter, *The Person and Ministry of the Holy Spirit* (Grand Rapids: Baker Book House, 1974), 115.
13. William Barclay, *The Promise of the Spirit* (London: Epworth Press, 1960), 30.
14. Edwin Lewis, "The Ministry of the Holy Spirit," in *The Revival Pulpit* (Nashville: Tidings, The Methodist Church, 1944), 31.
15. George Eldon Ladd, *A Theology of the New Testament* (Grand Rapids: Wm. B. Eerdmans Publishing Co., 1974), 289.
16. *The Works of John Wesley*, 3rd ed. (Kansas City: Beacon Hill Press of Kansas City, 1978), 5:133.
17. Westcott, *Gospel According to St. John*, lxiv.
18. Carl F. H. Henry, "John," in *The Biblical Expositor*, ed. Carl F. H. Henry (Philadelphia: A. J. Holman Co., 1960), 179.
19. J. H. Mayfield, "The Gospel According to John," in *Beacon Bible Commentary* (Kansas City: Beacon Hill Press, 1965), 7:176-77.
20. William Temple, *Readings in St. John's Gospel* (London: Macmillan and Co., 1963), 230.
21. Ibid.
22. *Gospel of John, Vol. 2*, 167-68.
23. G. H. C. MacGregor, "The Gospel of John," in *The Moffatt New Testament Commentary* (London: Hodder and Stoughton, 1928), 309.
24. *God, Man, and Salvation*, 488.
25. Carter, *Holy Spirit*, 134.
26. Temple, *Readings*, 233.
27. Wayne E. Caldwell, "Truth," in *Beacon Dictionary of Theology*, 532.
28. TDNT, 39.

29. Carter, *Holy Spirit*, 133.
30. *Readings*, 232.
31. Arnold E. Airhart, "Holy Spirit," in *Beacon Dictionary of Theology*, 264.
32. Mayfield, "John," 171.
33. Ibid., quoting Hoskyns, *The Fourth Gospel*, ed. Davey.
34. Temple, *Readings*, 265.
35. Marcus Dods, "The Gospel of St. John," in *An Exposition of the Bible* (Hartford, Conn.: S. S. Scranton Co., 1907), 5:240.
36. Ladd, *Theology*, 296.
37. *God, Man, and Salvation*, 492.
38. Donald M. Joy, *The Holy Spirit and You*, rev. ed. (Kansas City: Beacon Hill Press of Kansas City, 1978), 67-76.
39. Carter, *Holy Spirit*, 135.
40. Wilson T. Hogue, *The Holy Spirit* (Chicago: Free Methodist Publishing House, 1916), 235.
41. Earle, *Word Meanings*, 93.
42. MacGregor, "John," 297.
43. *Gospel of John, Vol. 2*, 192.
44. Joy, *Holy Spirit*, 17-28.
45. Ibid., 17.
46. Daniel Steele, *The Gospel of the Comforter*, abr. Ross E. Price (Kansas City: Beacon Hill Press, 1960), 26-44.
47. John Peter Lange, "The Gospel According to St. John," *A Commentary on the Holy Scriptures: Critical, Doctrinal, and Homiletical*, ed. Philip Schaff, trans. Edward D. Yeomans and Evelina Moore (New York: Charles Scribner's Sons, 1884), 475.
48. Mayfield, "John," 183, quoting Westcott.
49. Temple, *Readings*, 272-73.
50. Dods, "John," 243.
51. Temple, *Readings*, 273.
52. Dods, "John," 243.
53. *God, Man, and Salvation*, 666-67.
54. Lange, "St. John," 477.
55. Dods, "John," 244.

NEIL B. WISEMAN

Holiness, Power, and the Great Commission

You will receive power when the Holy Spirit comes on you; and you will be my witnesses in Jerusalem, and in all Judea and Samaria, and to the ends of the earth (Acts 1:8).

The word *power* causes strong feelings in many modern minds. Civic and industrial leaders, preoccupied with organizational power, want more. Educators write and read books about their power in modern society. Masses of people grasp for power to improve their living standards because they feel outmaneuvered by social systems. Angry, disenfranchised voices demand Black power, Hispanic power, and woman power. And social scientists believe contemporary families are fractured by power struggles between men and women.

On another level, people feel powerless because everything seems too big, too complicated, or too evil. Psychologist Rollo May, commenting about this frustration, says people feel "they are powerless to do anything effective about their lives or the world they live in."[1] Modern technology encourages this idea in a thousand subtle ways. Thus, large segments of the world population live with a continuous sense of desperate helplessness or powerlessness.

Lust for political power provokes revolutions and wars. Attempts to balance nuclear weapons and fighting forces keep the world on edge and nearly bankrupt international monetary systems. And voters' ideas about political power determine elections. Obviously, the power of government affects every human being on this planet.

Our modern vocabulary is filled with countless power words

426 / Biblical Resources for Holiness Preaching

like *horsepower, manpower, hydroelectric power, solar power, atomic power, thermonuclear power, jet power,* and *rocket power.* Everyone seems caught up in a whirlwind of power issues because power is such an essential ingredient for getting things done.

Many people are either frustrated or fascinated by power. But Jesus put these issues in proper perspective with His announcement in this text. Though His plan impresses the mighty with His omnipotence, it also enables ordinary Christians to do His work well.

This message of the passage is clear: God enables powerless people for holy living and effective service. Though the disciples were overwhelmed by the immense assignment Jesus gave them, divine power was promised. Far from denying human abilities, this scripture simply states an obvious fact: Evangelizing the world requires infinitely more moral, physical, and emotional resources than human beings naturally possess. But the Helper is promised for every need and assignment.

This promise connects God and the believer in an effective enabling partnership. Such an enduement resources the missionary who is overwhelmed by pressing needs. It anoints the preacher to speak a life-changing word for God. It energizes a compassionate believer to deal with crushing poverty and injustice. This power gives supernatural unction to the evangelist weighed down by the wickedness of a church, city, or nation. It provides courage and strategy for the Christian business person who has to meet competition in an environment of bribes and dishonesty. This enablement gives healing talent to the godly physician disheartened by his patient's pervasive cancer. And this power helps the witness accomplish impossible achievements for God. Much more than physical energy, this power provides divine enablement to be holy as the Father is holy, to love as He loves, and to achieve as He wills.

Present-day Christians want to know more about this power. And this passage helps the Christian preacher tell them for Him.

Exegetical Notes and Exposition of Text

Since Acts 1:8 records the last words of Jesus before His ascension, this verse contains important instructions for the development of His kingdom.

Luke, commonly believed to be the author of Acts, reports to Theophilus the Early Church's incredible progress. Luke viewed the Gospel that bears his name as a historical record "about all that Jesus began to do and to teach until the day he was taken up to heaven" (Acts 1:1-2). But his writings in Acts summarize the endless rippling effect of worldwide evangelization that God continued through the disciples. Volume 1, the Gospel of Luke, records the ministry of Jesus; but volume 2, the Acts of the Apostles, gives the results accomplished by these empowered Upper Room folks.

Bible authorities view Acts 1:8 variously as a commission, command, prediction, or promise. Perhaps it is all of these wrapped up in one sentence. As a mind-boggling missionary commission to His followers, Jesus charged them to take the gospel to every person everywhere. To accomplish the command, Jesus promised to help them be and do what was needed. As always, His enablement and His expectations exactly match.

But this passage is also an accurate prediction of what disciples do who have been "baptized with the Holy Spirit" (Acts 1:5)—they evangelize because of the pressing needs of the world. Their own discovery must be shared. Their response shows how holiness is intertwined with the missionary imperative of the NT.

Acts 1:6-8 is usually treated in one of two ways: (1) as a part of the preface to the Book of Acts, or (2) as an introduction to the Ascension section. Actually it provides a table of contents for the Book of Acts.

Chapters 1—7: *Witnessing in Jerusalem.* These chapters report near-home evangelism to relatives, neighbors, and longtime friends in a place where one is well known and sometimes suspected. Peter and Stephen are the main characters. And their prospects' religious background was Judaism.

Chapters 8—12: *Witnessing in Judea and Samaria* provides reports of home mission and church planting expansion. Peter, Philip, and Barnabas are the main leaders. And their prospects came from a confused mixture of religious and cultural backgrounds.

Chapters 13—28: *Witnessing to the World* provides a record of step-by-step missionary activity throughout the Roman Empire from Caesarea to Rome. The apostle Paul, the prominent personality of this section, evangelizes both Jew and Gentile. For him, the

428 / Biblical Resources for Holiness Preaching

missionary vision of Acts 1:8, **to the ends of the earth,** must have seemed nearly fulfilled when his witness bore fruit in Rome, the seat of civic authority. But it continues to this day.

Thus within a brief span of years, this small band of Spirit-filled followers of Christ spilled out of the Upper Room to carry the gospel all the way to corrupt Rome—the world center of political control, intellectual life, and artistic achievement. And those same witnesses impacted most places between Jerusalem and Rome. Their ministry was so effective that Maclaren suggests Acts should be titled "Acts of Jesus Through His Servants."[2] Their empowered effort made enormous expansion a common occurrence in the Early Church.

"It is not for you to know the times or dates . . . But" (vv. 7-8). Note the disciples' spiritual ignorance as their heady ambitions for high place in a political theocracy showed up again (cf. Mark 9:33-34; 10:35-41; and Luke 22:24). After their recent experience of Christ's miraculous resurrection, they hoped again for an earthly kingdom established by catastrophic intervention. They wanted to be powerful political leaders in this new scheme.

But Jesus shocked the disciples as He set an entirely different priority before them. He reminded them that because God controlled the future, useless speculation about the future should stop, and global evangelism must begin. They were to continue His ministry in the world in place of political ambitions and curiosity about the future.

Without reprimand, Jesus turns speculation to service and moved their attention from future to present. These instructions clarified their perspective. Until this time they were not ready for this assignment because they could not envision the worldwide mission of Christ.

You will receive power when the Holy Spirit comes on you (v. 8). Though this promised power is God's strength at work through human beings, it is also the enabling grace for holy living and perfect love. It is enablement to achieve God's purposes through ordinary people.

Power *(dynamis)* is the word from which we get *dynamite, dynamic,* and *dynamo.*[3] Carter says it is divine energy.[4] It is a "complete and adequate equipment of mind and spirit for the great future task."[5] This enablement is supernatural power of "the quality revealed in Jesus' own life."[6] The apostle Paul speaks often of this power from God: "Strengthened with might by his Spirit in the inner man" (Eph. 3:16, KJV); "My strength is made perfect in weakness. Most gladly therefore will I rather glory in my infirmities, that the power of Christ may rest upon me" (2 Cor. 12:9, KJV); "I can do all things through Christ who strengthens me" (Phil. 4:13, NKJV).

This promised power provides supernatural strength and personal readiness for world evangelization. Only the Holy Spirit could cleanse their hearts, equip them with the ability to witness, provide insights into the needs of people they met, and give them understanding for leading the infant Church.

Then and now a pure heart provides a strong foundation for effective witness. Because being always comes before doing in spiritual matters, Spirit-empowered service begins with a clean heart. The power of the Holy Spirit cleanses from inner pollution, strengthens for service, and provides a holy love for God and one's fellows. Reader Harris says the apostles "needed the sin and fear burnt out, and the love and power burnt in."[7] A. M. Hills explains, "This is what makes weak, ineffective Christians become giants. This is the blessing that enables ordinary people to do exploits and bring things to pass for God."[8] Personal holiness commits believers to Christ's mission in the world, and holy love motivates them to joyful, effective service.

C. W. Ruth explained the relationship of empowerment and purity:

> Sanctification negatively stated is the entire devotement and setting apart of our all to God, and the destruction of inbred sin—the sin nature which we inherited—thus purifying the heart; but the positive side of sanctification is the infilling with the Holy Ghost, accompanied by the enduement of power. . . . Seeking power for service is almost the equivalent to asking for the Holy Spirit, in order that we might use Him; instead, we should be so utterly and completely abandoned to Him that He might use us.[9]

In insightful language, Jowett summarizes the issues: "He can send His holy power into human speech, and the words can wake the dead. He can send His virtue into the human will, and its strength can shake the thrones of iniquity. He can send His love into the human heart, and the power of its affection can capture the bitterest foe."[10]

You will be my witnesses (v. 8). The concept of witness is so prominent in Acts (the word appears 39 times in its various forms) that everything else in the Book of Acts could be organized around it.

The words *martyr* and *witness* come from the same Greek word. Witnessing can be risky business. Thus Jesus was accurately realistic about witnessing; frontline soldiers must be prepared to pay the supreme sacrifice for the cause of Christ.

But notice the change in His followers after their Upper Room experience. After Pentecost, persons who could not stand the pressure of the judgment hall or the agony of Gethsemane now spoke boldly in the face of threats and danger. Though they did not know it at this time, the Early Church would soon experience Stephen's stoning, civic ridicule, and threats from Saul of Tarsus. But Christ's call to witness pushed them in spite of their worst fears to full surrender to His great cause.

Until now, the disciples did not possess either the inclination or the ability to fulfill the Great Commission. Before Pentecost, they did so little to bear witness to Christ, and their spiritual instability embarrassed the cause. But in the Upper Room Someone changed them, so that they became steadfast in prayer, happy in association, and deeply loyal to Christ. Now they had something important to say, supported by holy conduct and Christlike character.

Since the content of this witnessing is to be "all that Jesus began to do and to teach" (Acts 1:1), the work is always unfinished. That sounds a lot like the promise of John 14:12-13: "I tell you the truth, anyone who has faith in me *will do what I have been doing. He will do even greater things than these,* because I am going to the Father. And I will do whatever you ask in my name, so that the Son may bring glory to the Father" (italics added). Acts 1:8 seems to anticipate the fulfillment of Luke 24:49, "I am going to send you what my Father has promised; but stay in the city until you have been clothed with power from on high." Even now the work continues through present-day witnesses.

My witnesses is a testimony of intimate relationship, "royal words of magnificent and Divine assurance."[11] The idea is beautiful intimacy between Christ and His witnesses, "My witnesses—called by me, to witness for me, about me."[12] The witness is called to close relationship to his Lord.

Their witness was to tell what they personally knew of Christ's life and work; their telling always grew out of their own experiences of Christ. Their assignment was the actual accomplishment of the Great Commission: "Go and make disciples of all nations, baptizing them in the name of the Father and of the Son and of the Holy Spirit, and teaching them to obey everything I have commanded you" (Matt. 28:19-20).

But the issue of their own self-sovereignty had to be faced. Calling the signals had to be turned over to God. Did they really want Someone else to control their lives? But the future hope of the Church depended on their commitment to be filled with the Holy Spirit and to follow Him *all* the way into *all* the world.

A witness in a lawcourt must be examined to be sure he is trustworthy. He must also be questioned to be sure he has personal knowledge of the events in question. Thus, a firsthand witness for Christ sounds like 1 John 1:1-3: "That which was from the beginning, which we have heard, which we have seen with our eyes, which we have looked at and our hands have touched—this we proclaim concerning the Word of life. The life appeared; we have seen it and testify to it, and we proclaim to you the eternal life, which was with the Father and has appeared to us. *We proclaim to you what we have seen and heard"* (italics added, also next par.). The trustworthy witness always sounds like Peter and John before the Sanhedrin, "We cannot help speaking about *what we have seen and heard"* (Acts 4:20). The authentic witness says without equivocation, "I was there, I saw, I heard."

These Early Church witnesses literally changed their world. When Paul went to preach at Thessalonica, he was greeted by rioters who reported their accomplishments: "These that have turned the world upside down are come hither also" (Acts 17:6, KJV). In an account probably written within 30 years of Acts 1:8, Paul says to the Romans, "Your faith is being reported *all over the world"* (1:8). And in the Colossian letter, Paul reports, *"All over the world* this gospel is bearing fruit and growing, just as it has been doing among you since the day you heard it and understood God's grace in all its truth" (1:6). E. Stanley Jones said of their achievements, "The early Christians did not say in dismay, 'Look at what the world has come to,' but in delight, 'Look who has come into the world!' "

The NT record supports Ogilvie's conclusion, "There are very few examples in two thousand years of Christian history of people becoming Christians with no direct or indirect influence from witnesses in whom the Savior communicated His love."[13]

My witnesses in Jerusalem (v. 8). The order of the commission can be considered chronological, geographical, or ethnic. But it is a universal challenge to take the gospel to everyone, everywhere until the return of Jesus. Evidently the disciples were to start at Jerusalem, their home, a place of embarrassing earlier failure. Jerusalem was a tough place to begin because the Resurrection so thoroughly offended the Pharisees and Sanhedrin. But the gospel, then and now, possesses power to impact incredibly difficult places.

For the disciples, Jerusalem held hallowed Upper Room memories. There Jesus told them to tarry in Jerusalem, and they did. A deepening unity of purpose, begun in the Upper Room, produced a network of community and fellowship that strengthened all their future service for Christ. They remembered and used these inner resources for years to come.

Thus, the waiting followed by witnessing at Jerusalem did much more than establish a headquarters church. Rather it resulted in a sacred memory of a time and a place where they had failed, prayed, waited, and then succeeded. It was God's special preparation for years of effective future service.

Their kinfolks and neighbors believed their message because it was authenticated by the quality of their holy lives.

My witnesses . . . in all Judea and Samaria (v. 8). This is a broad hint that rigid exclusiveness was over for the Church because the Samaritans were racial hybrids whom most Jews hated with intense prejudice. But Christians were forced to desert Jerusalem when persecution came. Then Philip, one of the seven lay leaders (Acts 6), fled for his life to Samaria. There he could not keep from speaking the things about Jesus he had heard and seen, and a genuine revival resulted among the natives of Samaria (Acts 8). But when Peter and John arrived, "They prayed for them that they might receive the Holy Spirit, because the Holy Spirit had not yet come upon any of them; they had simply been baptized into the name of the Lord Jesus" (vv. 15-16). And God answered their prayers as "Peter and John placed their hands on them, and they received the Holy Spirit" (v. 17). Note, Samaritan believers sought and received the fullness of the Holy Spirit as a second crisis.

My witnesses . . . to the ends of the earth (v. 8). This part of the plan declared that the whole world was to be their goal for evangelism. According to Christ, the barriers were down, and the Church was ordered to go to the ends of the earth to preach the gospel to every people, race, tribe, color, nationality, and culture. Thus, from this starting point, every believer in every generation is called to be a global Christian.

Since this commission involved everyone, the apostles had to include the Romans in their new way of thinking. Think how threatened they must have felt when they considered the authority Rome had over them. But after Pentecost fear no longer gripped them. So the record says, "For two whole years Paul stayed there in his own rented house and welcomed all who came to see him. *Boldly and without hindrance he preached the kingdom of God* and taught about the Lord Jesus Christ" (Acts 28:30-31, italics added).

With the promise of Jesus, they went in His power to the ends of the earth. William Barclay explains the effect of the Holy Spirit at work in the Church: "Acts begins with the account of the coming of the Spirit and goes on to show us a church dominated by the Spirit."[14] History records the incredible results.

Though global expansion is needed in every generation, the commission also includes those neglected nearby areas of society and life that have been largely unclaimed for Christ.

Application of Text

There are several ways this passage speaks to modern folks:

1. Witnessing is required and empowerment promised for all believers.

2. A holy life must authenticate our witness.

3. The Holy Spirit calls believers to global evangelism.

4. Power, purity, and presence are results of Pentecost.

5. Empowerment makes possible Christ-centered living and useful service.

6. The empowered Christian continues the work of Jesus in the world.

7. Intimacy with Christ intensifies as the believer witnesses.

8. World evangelism is done by ordinary folks.

9. The result of our witness is beyond our comprehension.

Preaching Ideas on the Text

Several sermon ideas flow from this passage.

THE LAST WORDS OF JESUS (Acts 1:8). (1) The Divine Commission, "Ye shall be witnesses unto me"; (2) The Divine Enablement, "Ye shall receive power"; (3) The Divine Mandate, "Jerusalem, . . . Judaea, . . . Samaria, and unto the uttermost part of the earth" (KJV).

THE PROMISE OF PENTECOST (Acts 1:8). (1) A Person, (2) A Power, (3) A Program.[15]

THE POWER OF PENTECOST (Acts 1:8). (1) Adequate Power, (2) Personal Power, (3) Perpetual Power.[16]

THE WITNESS FOR CHRIST IS (Acts 1:8): (1) Accountable, (2) Approachable, (3) Adaptable.[17]

THE EMPOWERED GREAT COMMISSION (Acts 1:8 and Matt. 28:18-20). Develop the command of Jesus and the promised power in both passages. Those ideas might be applied to the purpose of Jesus as found in John 3:16.

THE MANDATE FOR WORLD EVANGELISM (Acts 1:8). (1) The Parameters—everywhere; (2) The Person—Christ, witnesses of Me; (3) The Power—enablement will be received when the Holy Spirit comes upon you.

CONTRASTS OF PENTECOST (Acts 1:8). Develop a sermon on the contrasts in the life of Peter or John before and after Pentecost.

PURPOSE OF PENTECOST (Acts 1:8). (1) The Promise of Pentecost—ye shall receive power; (2) The Persons of Pentecost—the Holy Spirit and the believer; (3) The Purpose of Pentecost—ye shall be witnesses; (4) The Plan of Pentecost—Jerusalem, Judea, Samaria, the ends of the earth.

CHURCH GROWTH MENTALITY (Acts 1:8). (1) Next Town Mentality, (2) Sending Mentality, (3) Other Sheep Mentality, (4) All People Mentality (Bill M. Sullivan).

THE POWERFUL CHRISTIAN (Acts 1:8). Check all the references to power as enablement in the Scripture and build a sermon on three or four of the main passages. It will produce an effective message of God's promise to provide enablement for every demand He makes.

CHRIST'S WITNESSES (Acts 1:8). (1) Called by Him, (2) Witnesses for Him, (3) Witnesses About Him.[18]

FULLY QUALIFIED TO WITNESS (Acts 1:8). (1) Power of a Holy Life—witnesses who have been with Christ; (2) Power of Anointed Lips—tell them for Me; (3) Power of Global Vision—the ends of the world.

Sermon on Text

Power to Accomplish the Great Commission
Acts 1:1-11; Text: v. 8

In this power-hungry age, we face interesting questions about scientific power, youth power, gray power, social power, civic power, and ecclesiastical power. The world seeks power to control; God gives power to achieve spiritual exploits through dedicated service. In God's plan to change character, culture, and civilization, He begins with human helplessness. Our weakness provides the starting point for His enabling adequacy.

I. THE POWER TO SPEAK—The witness of our lips authenticated by a holy life provides an effective evangelistic tool for God to use. Who can fully comprehend the effect of an empowered word spoken at the right time for the right reason authenticated by a Christ-centered life? Often our speaking grows out of a compulsion to tell what we have experienced of Christ. Thus, we witness from an inner drive for the same reason that compelled Peter and John: "For we cannot but speak the things which we have seen and heard" (Acts 4:20, KJV).

II. THE POWER TO SERVE—As Jesus promised the Holy Spirit, He predicted, "I tell you the truth, anyone who has faith in me will do what I have been doing. He will do even greater things than these, because I am going to the Father" (John 14:12). The text promises power for effective service everywhere all the time.

The action side of faith is expressed as service for God to our fellow human beings. A servant's actions done in the name of Jesus and motivated by perfect love provide a powerful force, so that the world can conclude, "What you do speaks so loudly that I gladly hear what you say."

III. THE POWER TO SEE—Until believers began to witness with the promised power, racial prejudice and cultural provincialism nearly strangled the Early Church. But the Holy Spirit's coming broadened their vision, so that they saw people as Jesus does.

In Acts 8, Philip took the gospel to Samaria. When the news reached headquarters at Jerusalem, the leaders sent Peter and John to check on the revival. These inspectors, impressed by such genuine conversions by the Samaritans, prayed and preached that the Samaritans might receive the Holy Spirit. And they did. Later in the same chapter, Philip was sent to witness to an Ethiopian in a desert place. So in one chapter of Holy Scripture these newly empowered witnesses reached a new nationality, the Samaritans; plus the Ethiopian, a member of another race, was baptized.

Acts 8, a microcosm of global conquest, illustrates how public and personal evangelism mesh to win the world.

A global vision often accompanies the coming of the Holy Spirit. It is a fulfillment of Joel's prophecy that Peter preached in Acts 2:17, "Your sons and daughters will prophesy, your young men will see visions, your old men will dream dreams." God wants to open believers' eyes to evangelistic opportunities next door, down the freeway, and around the world.

IV. THE POWER TO SHAPE—Everyone knows of some situation that seems too difficult for the gospel witness. But in OT times when people feared Goliath, God already had David, His shepherd boy, ready to slay the giant. When England faced revolution, God had a boy named John being spiritually shaped in the parsonage at Epworth. When the Church of the Nazarene needed a voice to call her back to a viable ministry in the cities, God was molding a young pastor named Tom Nees to speak a quiet, prophetic word that rearranged Nazarene mission priorities. Acts 1:8 calls us to shape our church and change our world for God. It is to be done by ordinary folks like us who have been empowered by divine resources and motivated by holy love.

CONCLUSION—The Great Commission (Matt. 28:18-20) and Acts 1:8 belong together. We feel incredibly weak and small before the pressing worldwide demand of Scripture. But Jesus makes this bold promise in the Great Commission, "All authority in heaven and on earth has been given to me," and "Surely I am with you always, to the very end of the age."

Is that enough for you? Of course, the divine provision is all we need and more. Note the superlatives—"all power," "alway," "even unto the end of the age" (all KJV). But the greatest assurance of all is the promise, "I am with you"!

Down almost 2,000 years of Christian history, our Lord's commission keeps ringing in our hearts and ears, "As the Father has sent me, I am sending you. . . . Receive the Holy Spirit" (John 20:21-22).

Endnotes

1. Wayne Oates, *The Struggle to Be Free* (Philadelphia: Westminster Press, 1983), 113.

2. Alexander Maclaren, *The Acts,* in *Exposition of Holy Scripture* (Grand Rapids: Baker Book House, 1978), 2.

3. Ralph Earle, *Word Meanings in the New Testament* (Kansas City: Beacon Hill Press of Kansas City, 1982), 2:63.

4. Charles W. Carter, *The Acts,* in *Evangelical Commentary* (Grand Rapids: Zondervan Publishing House, 1956), 9.

5. R. C. H. Lenski, *Interpretation of the Acts of the Apostles* (Columbus, Ohio: Lutheran Book Concern, 1934), 31.

6. Lloyd Ogilvie, *Acts,* in *The Communicator's Commentary* (Waco, Tex.: Word Books, 1983), 40.

7. Reader Harris, *Power for Service,* 23, as quoted in Jack Ford, *What the Holiness People Believe* (Birkenheade, Cheshire, England: Emmanuel Bible College, n.d.), 27.

8. A. M. Hills, *Holiness and Power* (Cincinnati: Revivalist Office, 1897), 49.

9. C. W. Ruth, *Entire Sanctification Explained* (Chicago: Christian Witness, 1903), 53-54.

10. John Henry Jowett, *My Daily Meditations* (LaVerne, Calif.: El Camino Press, 1975), 59.

11. Furneaux, quoted in A. T. Robertson, *Word Pictures in the New Testament* (Nashville: Broadman Press, 1930), 10.

12. Lenski, *Acts,* 32.

13. Ogilvie, *Acts,* 41.

14. William Barclay, *The Promise of the Spirit* (Philadelphia: Westminster Press, 1960), 55.

15. Richard Longenecker, "Acts of the Apostles," in *Expositor's Bible Commentary* (Grand Rapids: Zondervan Publishing Co., 1981), 9:256.

16. Earle, *Word Meanings,* 62.

17. Ogilvie, *Acts,* 42.

18. Lenski, *Acts,* 32.

HAL PERKINS

Jesus' Baptism with the Holy Spirit

I baptize you with water for repentance. But after me will come one who is more powerful than I, whose sandals I am not fit to carry. He will baptize you with the Holy Spirit and with fire. His winnowing fork is in his hand, and he will clear his threshing floor, gathering his wheat into the barn and burning up the chaff with unquenchable fire (Matt. 3:11-12).

As Jesus looks at His Bride, the Church, surely He aches over the gap between what she could and should be, and what she is. He knows that the best of strategies, the best of facilities, the best of programs are all bound to futility until a genuine revival of the biblical baptism with the Holy Spirit and fire replaces the self-centered, carnal condition of a terribly high percentage of believers. For this reason alone, John's promise that Jesus would baptize His followers with the Holy Spirit and with fire needs to be thoughtfully yet convincingly modeled and trumpeted. When believers are actually baptized with the Holy Spirit and fire, they grow rapidly in hunger for God's Word, in faith that God will accomplish His Word, and in absolute yielding of all their energies, time, and resources to the accomplishment of His work. They grow in Christlikeness. They bear fruit that remains. Bonded together in the church, a core of Spirit-baptized believers becomes a powerful force for God.

In the light of the present situation in the Church, Matt. 3:11-12 needs to be grappled with and presented clearly because it raises several fundamental issues about which there is either great confusion or terrible lethargy. Clarity and commitment with respect to repentance, the baptism with the Spirit, and judgment can transform lives, families, churches, and communities.

439

Exegetical Section

Setting: The appearance of John the Baptist was a significant moment in the history of God's saving work in the world. For centuries, the devout Israelite had looked for the coming of the rule of God but was always frustrated. By the time John came preaching, many, if not most, had given up the possibility that the age of salvation would ever come until history had been brought to an end. But the Baptist proclaims the startling announcement that "the kingdom of heaven is near" (Matt. 3:2).

When John spoke of the Coming One, and a baptism with the Spirit, he was drawing on a deep well of tradition about the anticipated new age. Doubtless all his listeners would have identified the significance of his words. They would have known that there were two strands of biblical prophecy concerning the coming of the Spirit in the age of salvation. One was that the Spirit would endow all God's people for the task of being His witnesses (see Joel 2:28-29), and the other was that the Spirit's outpouring would bring moral renewal or sanctification (see Ps. 51:11; Isa. 63:10-11; Ezek. 36:26 ff.). In addition the OT suggested that the Coming One would be both the Bearer (cf. Isa. 11:2) and the Bestower of the Spirit; and as one rabbinic source said, "The evil impulse would be taken out of Israel's heart in the age to come, and the Spirit, as a power for moral renewal, would rest upon her."[1] With this background, it seems clear that they would have heard the Baptist announcing a baptism for both power and purity.

Notes on the Text

I baptize you with water for repentance. The word translated **baptize** (*baptizō,* first person singular, present active indicative, progressive) is from the Greek *baptō,* meaning to dip repeatedly, to dip under. It came to be used of dyeing a cloth or garment or the drawing of water by dipping a vessel into another. When cloth was dipped into dye, it came under the control or influence of the dye, and thus "baptized" came to mean coming under the dominant influence of, or to be brought under the control of, a superior power or influence.

Repentance (*metanoian,* accusative, singular feminine) is from the Greek words *meta* (change) and *noia* (mind). It means literally to change the mind, to reconsider, to change opinion or attitude. The word does not necessarily connote emotion or sorrow, although "Godly sorrow brings repentance" (2 Cor. 7:10). The convictions of past error or sin often lead to sorrow, but regret or remorse is not to be confused with repentance. Nor is repentance to be confused with life change, or else forgiveness would be conditioned on a changed life (Acts 2:38), and we would be into legalism. However, repentance (change of mind) inevitably leads to good works, fruit, change of life (Matt. 3:8).

Because some of the listeners had repented and honestly confessed their sins (Matt. 3:6, changed their minds and agreed with God), John was baptizing them as a validation of their mind-set to return to and come under the dominant influence of God and His Kingly authority. John is saying in v. 11*a*, in effect, "I have participated with you in securing your commitment to an outside, objective influence and government, the government of God."

But after me will come one who is more powerful than I, whose sandals I am not fit to carry. He will baptize you with the Holy Spirit and with fire. Matthew is here reporting John's witness to the greatness, even supernatural powers, of the Coming One; and John's relation to Him is one of such humility that John is not worthy to do what even the most unworthy servants do for their masters.

He will baptize you with the Holy Spirit. He (Jesus) will participate with you in enabling you to come fully under the influence of the Holy Spirit. He will enable you to be dipped in, colored by, dominated by, and controlled by the Holy Spirit of God. John is saying an amazing thing to these people: "I participated with you in securing your commitment to an outside, objective influence and government, the government of God. But the One who is coming will make possible your being brought internally, subjectively under the coloring, influencing, controlling power of the Holy Spirit. He will make it possible for the Holy Spirit of God to actually penetrate into and through your entire being to transform you from the inside out. It will be more than just your personal resolve; He will engulf you and be with you and be in you to make possible your transformation."

And with fire. What could John have meant or his hearers have understood about the alliance of the baptism with the Holy Spirit and fire? What is a baptism of fire?

1. The linkage to the Holy Spirit requires a primary conclusion that the baptism with the Spirit includes a fiery baptism. The Spirit will have an influence like fire as He penetrates the heart and mind of the recipient, warming the heart, enlightening the mind, purifying the will.

2. When the Spirit was poured out on Pentecost, one of the symbols was tongues of fire. Perhaps John was prophetically enabled to link fire with the baptism of the Holy Spirit.

3. The context (Matt. 3:10-12) so deeply involves judgment that it is probably right to assume that John's use of fire had a dual aspect to it; if the Spirit is not allowed to effect His enlightening, warming, and purging ministry to eliminate sin in persons, then ultimately the fire must fall and purge the sinner from God's kingdom in ultimate judgment (Joel 2:30-31; 2 Pet. 3:7-12; Mal. 3:2; etc.). Fire does often symbolize wrath and judgment (Heb. 10:27; 2 Pet. 3:7; Rev. 14:10-11; etc.), but it also symbolizes grace and cleansing (Isa. 6:6-7; Zech. 13:9; Mal. 3:3; 1 Pet. 1:7). Therefore, the dual meaning is quite feasible: The baptism with the Spirit is a baptism of fire to "burn away" sin: either to purge sin from persons, or if not allowed to do so, to purge sinners (and thus sin) from God's kingdom.

His winnowing fork is in his hand, and he will clear his threshing floor. John's hearers understood this word picture. A threshing floor was a natural or artificially created flat place exposed to the wind. Grain was laid on the floor, and oxen pulled a sled with cleats or barbs on the bottom over the grain to separate the grain from the stalk. This was threshing. The remainder of the kernel's hard coat, the dust, the dirt, and the straw was called chaff. The chaff is what still clung to the kernel after the threshing process. Winnowing is the process whereby the threshed grain is picked up with a pitchfork and thrown up into the air. The wind blows the lighter chaff away, while the heavier kernels fall down to the floor.

Gathering his wheat into the barn and burning up the chaff with unquenchable fire. The barn is the place where valued things are kept or stored. The wheat is stored here. The chaff, having been separated from the wheat, is collected and burned.

What is John meaning to say? John has just told his hearers of One who is coming to baptize them with the Holy Spirit and fire, and next he says this One has a pitchfork in hand to separate the good from bad.

The same ambiguity attaches to this phrase as to the phrase **and with fire.** Does it refer to cleaning or judgment? Perhaps, as with **and with fire,** it includes both. Both are legitimate, and thus we cannot arbitrarily exclude either.

If cleaning is the focus, it refers to the purging out of the dross of the "old nature" or inward sin so as to result in a pure heart. This is clearly in line with the anticipated work of the Coming One in relation to the gift of the Spirit (see above). The chaff is removed and the solid, good residue is preserved. If judgment is emphasized, it means that those who do reject the ministry of the Spirit and remain sinners shall be cleansed from the fellowship of God and His people. They shall be cast into the unquenchable fires of hell prepared for Satan and his angels (Matt. 25:41). The eternality of their torment is affirmed in Mark 9:48; Dan. 12:2; Jude 6-7; Rev. 14:9-11; 19:3; 20:10.

Note: Fire may mean physical fire, but the **fire** is prepared for the devil and his angels, who are not hurt by physical fire. Since fire is often a symbol of God's wrath (see earlier notes), the meaning here could refer to existing in the perpetual state of God's wrath, apart from His love and family. Whatever heaven is, it is impossible to picture its goodness; and whatever hell is, it is impossible to picture the extent of its evilness.

Application

Having attempted to understand what the original hearers were intended to understand, what is God's message to us today from Matt. 3:11-12?

1. *Jesus wants the requirement of repentance to be preached today.* One of the greatest reasons for an unholy church is the misguided assumption that something less than authentic repentance ushers one into God's family. Some assume that baptism and Communion do it. Some assume that avoidance of some sin (stealing, murder, adultery, etc.) does it. Some assume that doing some good (church attendance, giving, altruism) does it. Some assume that

merely believing that Jesus died in history (cheap grace, faith in faith) will do it. But not so. Jesus said, "Repent" (Matt. 4:17)! God's wrath remains on those who do not repent (Rom. 2:5)! Those who don't repent will perish (2 Pet. 3:9)! Without repentance there is no forgiveness (Luke 24:47; Acts 2:38)! Repentance must be understood and preached! It is not simply remorse (feeling guilty, bad, or sorry). It is not merely a change of life (salvation by self-righteousness). It is a change of mind *(metanoia)*, an honest determination to let God be God, a faith in Jesus that results in seeking to do what He says (to not obey is to be either a rebel against Him or to have no faith in Him). The world and church both need to know that God requires repentance for salvation. God does not require what we cannot do (keep the law, atone for our sins), but we can commit to His Lordship, and this He requires.

2. *Jesus wants to baptize believers with the Holy Spirit today.* What John announced Jesus would do has been done and documented in the pages of the NT and the history of the church. It was not just for those listening; the baptism with the Holy Spirit has been and continues to be for all believers, then and today! A study of Acts 1:5 and 2:4 reveals that the baptism with the Holy Spirit results in believers being filled with the Spirit. Eph. 5:18 was and remains a command for all believers to be filled with God's Spirit. Jesus today wills for His Church to be so baptized (colored, influenced, dominated) with His Spirit that the world sees *agapē* in believers' homes and businesses, peace and joy in their hearts, patience and kindness, goodness and gentleness, faithfulness and self-control in all aspects of their lives. Jesus wants to baptize His Church today with His Spirit so that she might be pure, radiant, holy, entirely sanctified, and godly. The fire from heaven that purified and empowered the Early Church is the norm. Believers are to be an electric force in the world, loving, witnessing, leading—all because they are fully under the control of the Holy Spirit. If this is not the case, something is abnormal, unhealthy, and wrong. Jesus wants believers to be authentically baptized with His Spirit.

If we understand what John meant in Matt. 3:11-12, and we agree that his message is God's Word for today, how shall we respond?

First, we need to analyze where we are. Could it be that a terribly small percentage of a typical congregation is actually entirely sanctified? Could it be that if a significant percentage of a congregation were entirely sanctified, then the world would be attracted to Jesus in His Body, Judgment Day realities and authentic repentance would be effectively preached, and authentic conversions and explosive growth would occur? Could it be that there exists such indifference to or confusion about the baptism with the Holy Spirit, entire sanctification, heart holiness, and being filled with God's Spirit that the very solution we need (to be entirely sanctified) is extensively absent from our midst? If the answer to the above questions is, in part or in whole, yes, then one of our great needs is to live and teach a biblical understanding of being baptized with the Holy Spirit and being entirely sanctified.

How can the intent of the baptism with the Holy Spirit be accomplished? The answer to this question is the sermon found at the end of this chapter.

Preaching Ideas

Topic: **Jesus' Desire for His Church**

Introduction: Jesus is pleading with His Church to be His Body

I. Jesus wants the requirement of repentance to be preached today (Matt. 3:1, 11; 4:17).
   A. What is repentance? (meaning of *metanoia*)
   B. Why is repentance absolutely necessary? (Rom. 2:4-5; 2 Pet. 3:9; Acts 2:38; Luke 24:47)

II. Jesus wants to baptize believers with His Spirit today (Matt. 3:11).
   A. He has made baptism with His Spirit possible (Luke 11:13; Acts 2; Rom. 8:9-16).
   B. We must make baptism with His Spirit actual (James 4:8; 2 Cor. 7:1; Rom. 6:13, 19; 12:1-2; etc.).

III. Jesus wants to warn the world of judgment today (Matt. 3:12).
   A. Let us demonstrate an attractive quality of life (Matt. 5:16; John 13:35).
   B. Let us demonstrate love for our neighbors (Luke 10:25-37).
   C. Let us demonstrate love that warns (Acts 20:20-21).

Conclusion: The key to being useful for God in the world is actualizing the baptism with the Spirit in our lives.

Topic: **The Baptism with the Holy Spirit**

Introduction: Jesus wills that we be baptized with His Spirit.

I. What is the baptism with the Holy Spirit?
   A. Meaning of baptism
   B. Meaning of baptism with Holy Spirit
II. Why is being baptized with the Holy Spirit so important?
   A. Church is to have abundant life (John 10:10).
   B. Church is God's instrument to redeem the world (2 Cor. 5:18-21; Matt. 28:19-20).
III. What must be done to be baptized with the Holy Spirit?
   A. Repent and believe in the Lord Jesus (Acts 2:38).
   B. Respond to the Spirit's purging work (Rom. 6:13, 19; Luke 14:27).
   C. Remain clean and filled with the Spirit (John 15:1-8; Eph. 5:18).

   Conclusion: If God has convicted of sin at the heart, confess, repent, and offer all to God.

Topic: **Preparation for Judgment**

Note: This suggestion adopts one of the alternative interpretations of the text.

Introduction: Judgment is the great certainty for which we must all be prepared.

I. The Certainty of Judgment
   A. Jesus' winnowing fork is in His hand (Matt. 3:12*a*—describe).
   B. Jesus will clear His threshing floor (Matt. 3:12*b*—describe).
   C. Jesus will gather His wheat into the barn (Matt. 3:12*c*—Ps. 116:15; Luke 16:22; 23:43; Phil. 1:21-23; 2 Cor. 5:8; John 11:11; 14:2-3; 2 Pet. 3:13; Rev. 21:1-5).
   D. Jesus will burn up the chaff with unquenchable fire (Matt. 3:12*d*—Matt. 25:41; Mark 9:48).
II. The Preparation for Judgment
   A. Non-Christians: repent (2 Pet. 3:9; Acts 2:38).
   B. Unsanctified believers: for own and others' sake, let baptism with the Spirit be completed.

1. Initiated in initial sanctification (Acts 2:38; Rom. 8:9-16)
2. Actualized in entire sanctification
    a. Entirely dead to the idolatrous self
    b. Entirely alive to the indwelling Spirit
C. Sanctified believer: Examine effectiveness with a goal of maximizing our potential.
Conclusion: God convicting anyone of need to change anything?

Sermon on the Text
The Holy Spirit's Thorough Work

The baptism with the Holy Spirit is a matter of great importance for many people. Some think it occurs in the new birth. Some think it is a special outpouring of God's Spirit evidenced by speaking in tongues. Others understand it to be a special empowerment for service. Others believe it to be the moment of entire sanctification.

It is my deep belief that the baptism with the Holy Spirit, properly understood and responded to, is the great thing God wants to do in and through us. Let us listen to the reading of Matt. 3:11-12. Time prohibits dealing with the total context. We shall focus entirely on understanding the baptism with the Holy Spirit.

What is the importance of this baptism John said Jesus would bestow? Why should we be open to the baptism with the Holy Spirit? Four reasons: (1) the baptism with the Holy Spirit enables God's family to be free from the corrupting sin (self-idolatry) that disintegrates individuals, families, and society; (2) the baptism with the Holy Spirit enables believers to experience the joyous, fulfilling, abundant life God intends for His family; (3) the baptism with the Holy Spirit enables God to powerfully work through His Body, the Church, His holy temple; (4) the baptism with the Holy Spirit will maximize the glory of God and reconciliation of the lost to God. For these reasons, we must maximize the possibilities of the Church being baptized with God's Spirit.

What exactly is the baptism with the Holy Spirit? We see an explanation by comparing Acts 1:5 with 2:4. In 1:5, Jesus tells the disciples that in a few days they will be baptized with the Holy Spirit. In a few days Pentecost occurs, and Luke notes that the believers were filled with the Spirit (2:4). We can conclude that being baptized with the Spirit results in being filled with the Spirit. But exactly what is the meaning of being baptized with the Spirit?

A study of the Greek word for baptism helps. In the Greek, *baptizō* means "to be dipped," or "brought under," or "brought under the influence of," or "controlled by." The street usage occurred in describing the activity of taking cloth and dipping it into a dye to change the color of the cloth. The cloth was baptized with the dye. It was dipped, brought under the influence of, controlled by the dye. This is the word picture that John, Jesus, Peter, and others use in describing the baptism with the Spirit. It seems fair to conclude, then, that the baptism with the Holy Spirit results in being filled with the Spirit (Acts 1:5 and 2:4) and has the effect on the one baptized of being dipped in, brought under, influenced by, dominated and controlled by, colored by, the Holy Spirit.

How does this occur? How are we to be baptized with the Holy Spirit? We shall discuss the answers under the following three topics: (1) The Birth of the Spirit; (2) The Communication by the Spirit; (3) The Filling with the Spirit.

I. *The Birth of the Spirit.* The Holy Spirit is vibrantly at work all around the world (John 16:8-11). He convicts persons of sin, enabling repentance. As a person changes his mind and receives Jesus as his Lord (repents), he is forgiven and receives the gift of the Spirit (Acts 2:38; cf. John 3:5-8; Rom. 8:9-16). Through this reception of the Spirit, a believer is brought under the influence of the Spirit. To receive the Spirit is to be the recipient of His ministry of counsel (John 14:16), truth (16:13), teaching and reminding (14:26). It is to come under His influence and power. Reaching the goal of the baptism with the Spirit (Spirit fullness and full control) is begun, but certainly not accomplished, at new birth. D day has occurred; V day is yet to come.

II. *The Communication by the Spirit.* At new birth, a believer has received the Spirit, but experience and Scripture testify that the Spirit does not fully have the believer, though the believer rightly intends and assumes that He has. After new birth, the believer is brought under the Spirit's communicating influence. His counsel (John 14:16), truth (v. 17), teaching and reminding (v. 26) become a sanctifying force in the believer. His communication impacts the believer. He is speaking, correcting, and guiding with all the impact needed to enable change. He does not overpower the believer or coerce response, for that would violate our God-ordained freedom as persons. He reinforces the good while confronting the behavior that is ungodly. He illumines and convicts the believer of sin in the heart, the essence of which is self-worship, the self focused on itself as the object of devotion and dependence (carnal mindedness). The Spirit's fire of convicting truth enables the dross to be smelted from the gold, the idolatrous self to be removed from the God-intended throne. He confronts habits and values that the believer has come to hold dear, and in that confrontation He meets clear-cut resistance. The believer is not fully dominated and controlled by the Spirit at new birth.

Let me illustrate. We've all dyed Easter eggs. If I dip the egg into the dye and immediately take it out, does the egg come out the color of the dye? No. Why? It is because the egg is hard, and the dye does not easily permeate the shell. To be transformed into the color of the dye, the egg needs longer exposure to the dye. If the egg is left in the dye, the greater impact and influence of the dye enables the egg to come under the control of the dye. But the hard egg requires time to be controlled by the dye. By contrast, a handkerchief dipped in the dye is quickly transformed. The nature of the object being impacted determines the observable effect of the impact.

The Spirit communicates to the believer, counseling, giving light, revealing truth, convicting. Most believers are more like hard-boiled eggs than handkerchiefs and need significant impact by the Spirit before fully yielding to Him. As long as the believer relies on himself or lives for himself, he impedes the Spirit, remains carnal, prohibits the desired control by the Spirit, and minimizes his Kingdom usefulness and personal joy. Further, he dangerously risks not walking in the light. The Spirit's conviction of sin at the heart (self-enthronement) cannot be blatantly ignored without resulting eventually in backsliding and darkness. Though D day has occurred, the resistance is strong, and V day is yet to be achieved. The Spirit is actively involved in cleaning house in order to actually fill His temple, the believer.

I grew up in a town near the Continental Divide in the Rocky Mountains. It was determined to replace the horrendously old and dangerous road that snaked its way up to the summit. Dynamite was exploded in the right place to break up the rock. Huge steam shovels then loaded the debris into giant earthmovers. Little by little that mountain was impacted and cleaned out until finally an adequate pass was created on which a road could be built over which cars could safely and swiftly travel. The mountain was so impacted and influenced by the dynamite and shovels and trucks that finally it came under their control to the point that it was being used the way the engineers and workers intended it to be used. The mountain was impacted for some time before it was finally controlled. The rock and dirt had to be cleaned out, and then just the right materials had to be built in place to create a useful road. Much the same occurs in believers. A believer receives the Holy Spirit at new birth. The Spirit goes to work with dynamite (communicating the truth) to explode the rock that needs to be removed, thus making it possible to haul it away. He enables the character of Christ to be formed in our lives to make us useful. We are not to the point God intends us to be until we are cleansed of all heart debris and resistance to the Spirit and actively cooperating with the Spirit's full control.

In a carnal Christian, much of the work of the Spirit is being dissipated *in* him, instead of being channeled *through* him. The Spirit's power and effect is in getting the vessel ready rather than using the vessel. The Spirit says, "Change your style on the job. Don't cheat the boss by wasting time; the pictures in the shack have got to go; and the immoral stories you tell the group must stop." The Spirit is dynamiting ungodly behavior and soon will dynamite the ungodly nature. As He speaks, we are enabled to respond—to be sure, in different ways by different persons, depending on their sensitivity and maturity. The carnal Christian, plagued with self-idolatry, consciously or unconsciously battles with the presence of a Rival to the throne of his life and needs to be cleansed of this idolatry before the Spirit is genuinely free to work through him.

The Spirit dwells in the carnal Christian (Rom. 8:9), but His intended effect, the "coloring," the controlling is not accomplished until the fiery work of the Spirit has effected a cleansing of all idols, and He is fully sovereign in our hearts. At spiritual birth, the believer is brought under the full *impact* of the Holy Spirit. At Spirit fullness, the believer is brought under the full *control* of the Holy Spirit. A spiritual impacting—a dynamiting—begins occurring at the time of new birth and continues until the believer is actually cleansed of heart sin and filled with the Spirit.

III. *The Filling with the Spirit.* The ultimate issue, the critical battle, occurs when the Spirit moves from dealing with the fruit (unchristlike behavior) to the root (the heart, self-idolatry)—me serving me, me relying on me. This is the core and cause of ungodliness and must be cleansed. The Spirit, when the believer is ready, makes it plain. "My child, you have other gods in your heart. In fact, you are serving yourself to a great degree. You do not love God with all your heart, soul, mind, and strength. God wants and needs your total love and service. What will you do?" The believer is faced with either dying to self in a full and loving consecration of himself to God (Matt. 22:37; Rom. 6:13, 19; 12:1-2; 2 Cor. 5:14-15; John 12:24-25; James 4:8) or failing to walk in the light and thereby grieving the Spirit. The Spirit says, "Your focus is on your ability or lack of it. You are patting yourself on the back for a small thing, and I enabled you to do even that. You have no significant mission or vision because you focus on your weakness instead of God's ability. You don't trust God with all your heart. Your faith is based on your ability. What will you do?" The believer is faced with dying to himself as the object of faith and establishing faith in God for all things (Rom. 14:23; Prov. 3:5; Heb. 11:6; 2 Cor. 7:1; 1 John 3:3).

The believer is at a *critical* crisis at this stage of his spiritual pilgrimage. Will he not only have the Spirit but fully yield himself so that the Spirit has him? Will he let the Spirit move from Resident to President? More is involved than just the passive acknowledgment of the carnal condition with confidence placed in God to cleanse. Also involved is the active, purposeful dethronement of self and total enthronement of Christ with all the implications of full reliance on Him, active communion with Him, and service for Him as the absolute Sovereign over every detail of life. As a believer is *emptied* of self and consequently filled with God's Spirit (a relationship of pure faith in and love for God that must be established and maintained), the promised baptism with the Spirit is actualized. The believer is cleansed of the carnal nature (self-idolatry, self-worship) and set apart entirely for God. The meaning of the baptism with the Holy Spirit is that the Spirit now has the believer, so that He can work not only upon him but primarily through him. When the believer fully responds to the Spirit, he is purged of the carnal self, so that Christ reigns supreme. Now, as never before, the Spirit is able to make the life holy because the heart has been sanctified (made holy, cleansed, freed from sin, set apart for God). The believer now increasingly becomes a useful instrument of God; free from his own ungodliness, he enjoys the abundant life of love, peace, and joy. This is the purpose God intends for His children.

The burning question for us today is this: Is it possible that we are being impacted by the Spirit but not controlled? Is it possible that the Spirit of God who works in us is not able to work through us because of all the dross that remains in our lives? Is it possible that we claim to be entirely sanctified, baptized and filled with God's Spirit, and yet we are serving ourselves instead of serving God with all our heart, soul, mind, and strength? Have we come to believe that God will fully work through us without our dying to everything but Him and living entirely for Him? Is it possible that we see time and money as ours to use as we want when we've claimed to have died to self and to have offered everything to Christ? Do we claim to be pure in heart and yet do virtually nothing for fear of failure? Is it possible that the Spirit has revealed the divided Lordship of our lives, but we are rationalizing our self-idolatry and sin?

The reason more Christians are not entirely sanctified is not the failure on God's part to do that which needs to be done, but the unwillingness of believers to do that which God enables and asks, which is to die to self-government and offer themselves fully and entirely as living sacrifices to God (Rom. 12:1-3). Carnal believers are dramatically more able to do this when they see the fully consecrated life modeled in pastors, parents, and lay leaders (2 Cor. 5:14-15; 1 Pet. 2:21). I plead with all of us: Allow the Spirit to sanctify and fill and accomplish the intent of Spirit baptism by emptying yourselves of self-government and consecrating yourself —every thought, word, act; every minute and every dime; every problem, every fear, every hope—to God for His safekeeping and use. I invite you to respond fully to the word the Spirit is speaking to you now.

Endnote

1. Cf. H. Ray Dunning, *Grace, Faith, and Holiness: A Wesleyan Systematic Theology* (Kansas City: Beacon Hill Press of Kansas City, 1988), 403-4.

J. KENNETH GRIDER

The Holy Spirit's Baptism

*F*or John baptized with water, but in a few days you will be baptized with the Holy Spirit (Acts 1:5).

This text of Scripture cries out to be preached. Its subject, the baptism with the Holy Spirit, is like a story in a novelist's mind waiting to be told. One of its main advantages is its concreteness. Entire sanctification, the most appropriate name for the second work of grace, is probably the favorite term for it in the holiness movement.[1] Yet that term is abstract, whereas "baptism" in "the baptism with the Holy Spirit" is concrete. It is like the difference between a drawing of water and water.

Christ's baptism with the Holy Spirit referred to in this text occasioned changes in the lives of His early disciples that are needed by people today. Before the apostle John's Pentecost, he wanted a favored place at Jesus' side; after his Pentecost, jail was good enough for him (Acts 4:3). Exile on a barren Patmos Island was so acceptable that he wrote the Book of Revelation there (Rev. 1:9-11). Peter had denied Christ three times before Pentecost (John 18:17, 25, 27), even to such persons as an innocuous maid (vv. 16-17); but after his Pentecost he put his life on the line in preaching Christ to the powerful Sanhedrin (Acts 4:8-12). And jail kindled a fire in his bones to herald Christ when people of power told him to shut up.

The entire sanctification received by Christ's baptism with the Holy Spirit will enable people today to put Christ first, over advancement at the workplace. It will give people power (Acts 1:8) to witness for Christ. It will give people the needed cleansing from

453

Adamic sin (Ezek. 36:25-27; Mal. 3:1-3; John 7:37-39; 17:17; Acts 15:8-9).

This text needs to be preached because, when believers receive their baptismal cleansing, they are eager to witness about Christ (Acts 1:8; 11:19-21). Today Christ wants followers who are not only decent but dynamic; and the power of their Pentecost will impact them with that dynamic.

This text sometimes leaps out at the preacher, clamoring to receive attention, because the believer's Pentecost means purity of heart (Acts 15:9; Matt. 5:8), and that purity is needed today. If purity of heart means "to will one thing," as Søren Kierkegaard said, such is surely needed today. Many people are "double minded," and it makes them "unstable" in all their ways (James 1:8, KJV). With television, sports events, and recreation areas vying for our time and energy, and the widespread disregard of morals, believers need as perhaps never before the purity and the power that will help them to will one thing: God's will.

This text needs to be preached in the holiness movement today because the fastest-growing division of Protestantism emphasizes this baptism (as holiness people do) but do so in error, not understanding that it purifies from Adamic sin, understanding instead that it will be evidenced by speaking in unintelligible syllables. If Babel was a curse in OT times (Gen. 11:1-5), it would be strange that unintelligible syllables would be a sign of blessing today. Since the Holy Spirit interpreted dreams and visions to the prophets in OT times, helped people to write down the Scriptures, and guides into all truth, it is strange that He would today do the opposite, that is, occasion unintelligibilities—which then many well-intentioned people believe God helps them interpret in plain words.

Exegetical Section

Notes on the text and context. "Over a period of forty days" (v. 3). This is the only place in the NT where the length of Christ's postresurrection ministry is given. It was long enough for Him to meet with them numerous times for going-away instructions. Like most of us, they needed to be told things over and over. It was not a ghost but a really resurrected Jesus, whose resurrection was real enough for Thomas (John 20:28), who actually "appeared to them" (v. 3) and was "eating with them" (v. 4).

"While he was eating with them" (v. 4). It was while they were eating together that the disciples were given the important message about waiting for their Pentecost. Only Luke, here and in his Gospel (24:41-43), tells us that Christ ate food after the Resurrection. As Christ did eat, He gave His followers an exceedingly important message about Pentecost. It often happens that we receive important insights when we are going about something as ordinary as eating with friends.

"Do not leave Jerusalem" (v. 4). Their homes were up north in Galilee, and they were no doubt inclined to return there. Especially would this have been so after they had seen Jesus' ascension into heaven (v. 9). Jesus knew He had to impress this upon them because He wanted them to be Spirit-baptized when Jerusalem would have in it twice as many people as was usual. Then, news of the event would be spread far and wide. It was a needed strategy in a time when so few means of communication were available.

"My Father promised" (v. 4). This was promised in Joel 2:28 and in Matt. 3:11-12 (the same being referred to in Ezek. 36:25-27, in Mal. 3:1-3, in John 7:37-39, etc.). Paul refers to this when he says, "Having believed [the first work of grace], you were marked in him with a seal, the promised Holy Spirit" (Eph. 1:13).

"Which you have heard me speak about" (v. 4). (Luke 24:40-53 refers to the same event, and see Acts 11:16.) John 14—17 is a lengthy passage recording what Jesus had earlier said about the Spirit's being sent.

"The gift" (v. 4). In the Greek, no word for "gift" appears here (although "gift" in the NIV gives the sense). NASB and RSV do not include "gift." Yet in Acts 2:38 and 11:17 the actual word for "gift" appears in the Greek *(dōrean,* from *dōrea),* where the Spirit baptism is called a "gift." Peter says, "Repent and be baptized, every one of you, in the name of Jesus Christ for the forgiveness of your sins. And you will receive the gift of the Holy Spirit" (2:38). After the first work of forgiving grace, they would be baptized in water (sometimes that baptism occurred after Spirit baptism, as in 22:16). Then they would receive what the multitudes had seen the 120 disciples receive: the baptism with the Holy Spirit. And it is here called a gift. The singular "gift" is the baptism and to be distinguished from the "gifts" where basically different Greek words are used (e.g., in 1 Cor. 12:4, where "gifts" is from *charismatōn*).

John (v. 5). Several men named John figure significantly in Scripture. This is not the John who wrote the Gospel and so much else, the apostle who is so daring according to the early chapters of Acts. Rather it is John the Baptist, forerunner and baptizer of Jesus. He emphasized water baptism so much that that fact got put into his name, so that Mark calls him *ho baptidzōn,* "the one who baptizes" (Mark 1:4; 6:14).

Baptized (v. 5). This word is from the Greek *baptidzō,* which, according to the Arndt and Gingrich *Lexicon,* means to "dip, immerse . . . dip oneself, wash."

John baptized with water (v. 5). This was a significant baptism. If people were not repenting, John was not baptizing (Luke 3:7-9). If the people did not mean to turn to God believing on Christ (see Acts 19:4-6), John was not baptizing. But many people in that "generation of vipers" (Matt. 3:7; 12:34; 23:33; Luke 3:7, all KJV) did repent. And they were baptized in water. This was to symbolize the cleansing of regeneration (Titus 3:5) and to assert to all and sundry the changed life they were embarking upon.

In a few days (v. 5). This was about 10 days. It was 40 days after the Resurrection, which happened on Passover weekend, that it was said. And Pentecost, as a Jewish feast, was always held 50 days after Passover.

It is not known whether the disciples waited those 10 days in anything like constant prayer. We know that they took care of the matter of replacing Judas with Matthias (vv. 15-26). Perhaps Jesus knew that these ambitious disciples (see Matt. 20:20-28), who had all been vacillating at the Crucifixion time, needed to do some extended preparation for their Pentecost.

You will be baptized (v. 5). This baptism of Christ with the Holy Spirit instead of water as the agent is called a baptism for various reasons. One is because a cleansing from Adamic sin occurs through it (Rom. 5:12-21; Matt. 3:11-12; John 17:17; Acts 15:8-9). Another basis for its being described as a baptism is because that figure indicates that it is received instantaneously even as regeneration is.

"Lord, are you . . . going to restore the kingdom . . . ?" (v. 6). The disciples' interest was misplaced. They were interested in Jesus' reestablishing the Jewish kingdom, freeing them from rule by Rome. The risen Christ had just told them to stay in "Jerusalem" and "wait for the gift" of the Spirit (v. 4). Yet their mundane interest in having their own earthly king prevented them from actually hearing what Jesus had just told them. It prevented them from actually hearing what He had told them on other occasions.

Theological Exegesis

This passage speaks of two baptisms, John's kind with water, to symbolize the cleansing of regeneration, and Jesus' baptism with the Holy Spirit, to effect the cleansing of Adamic depravity. The special reason why the one baptism of Christ with the Holy Spirit does not occasion both works of grace, justification ..nd sanctification, is because entire sanctification, wrought by this baptism, is received only by believers, subsequent to justification. The figure of baptism is occasionally used in the NT other than to refer to water baptism or Spirit baptism. A different usage occurs, for example, when the apostles James and John are asked if they were willing to die as Christ was and thus to be "baptized" with, or to experience, Christ's sufferings (Matt. 20:22, KJV; Mark 10:38). Yet Jesus' baptism with the Spirit is never used to symbolize, occasion, or refer to justification or other grace-helps besides the second work of grace.

In the holiness movement, we need to take care that we do not simply guide people through a technique to receive entire sanctification. Wesley set people to a steady preparation for entire sanctification, whereas Phoebe Palmer gave a three-step "altar" technique; and in this, Wesley (and Acts) is surely to be preferred. Often there is a slower pace in receiving the second work of grace than in receiving the first. This is partly because the carnal mind is deceptive (Rom. 7:11), and that condition, personified by Paul, might occasion the believer's understanding that he is fully consecrated when that is not so. It is partly because to repent, as preparation for justification, is more clear-cut than is the positive yielding needful to receive by faith Christ's baptism with the Spirit (Matt. 3:11-12; Acts 15:8-9).

Sometimes the gift of the Holy Spirit, occasioning the sealing, empowerment, and heart purity of entire sanctification, has been oversold by its friends. It does accomplish much that will be discussed below, but the crisis experience results in a basic cleansing of Adamic depravity and a pervasive indwelling of the Holy Spirit, who begins to help us correct life aberrations.

Practical Applications

After the Spirit-gift, we might still need to counsel with a professional on marriage or occupational or other problems even though the love of God gets "shed abroad" (KJV) or "poured out . . . into our hearts by the Holy Spirit" who has been given to us (Rom. 5:5).

And although the Holy Spirit, not now hampered by carnality, will help us in all the areas of life, aberrations that are environmental, that occur during this life, and that therefore are not a part of the birth package of Adamic depravity do not necessarily become corrected when Adamic depravity is cleansed away. For example, although an only child who has been pampered all his life receives the gift of the Holy Spirit, it will likely be through growth in grace that adequate regard for the wishes of others will be learned.

Or suppose a person has become an alcoholic and is then regenerated and receives the gift of the Holy Spirit. The acquired tendency to drink may be cleansed away in "the washing of regeneration" (Titus 3:5, KJV), and the person given enablement not to drink. But it might take many years of growing in grace before an alcoholic would have as little interest in and desire for alcohol as the Christian who had never become addicted.

Or take the various prejudices: educational, geographical, and especially the racial type. They all occur during this life. They are learned. They are environmental. We can therefore have the Adamic birth-depravity cleansed and still experience prejudices. In the racial area, Peter was still prejudiced against Gentiles well after his entire sanctification at Pentecost. It took three visions and various other helps before Peter could overcome his prejudice against Gentiles and minister to Gentile Cornelius (Acts 10:9 ff.).

Also, some have taught that such matters as nervousness, impatience, and anger will be corrected by the gift of the Spirit. Yet all of these might be consistent with the life of entire sanctification in a given person. A mother of several children might have a proneness to nervousness, might become quite impatient with a disobedient child, and might more readily become angry over something. A man of age 55 might be angry over a younger person's being given his job due mainly to the age factor. Those who live in the pervading fullness of the Spirit's indwelling presence will be helped peculiarly in crisis times, but it is probably too much to expect that entire sanctification will give them complete control over their emotions. Such control will be attained as Christian growth takes place all through the Christian life following the gift of the Spirit.

The gift of the Holy Spirit in its proper light does accomplish much:

1. It provides that the aversion to God, the inclination to sin, the propensity to sin, the tendency to choose our own way instead of God's way, with which we are born, is expelled. It is only human to emulate another person. It is carnal to have a "me first" attitude toward another person.

2. The gift of the Spirit means that we are empowered to witness for Christ. Christ said, "But you will receive power when the Holy Spirit comes on you; and you will be my witnesses" (Acts 1:8). This does not mean that each believer thus filled with the Spirit will be enabled to witness the way another believer is enabled to witness. Each will be empowered to witness for Christ in his own way. With some it is by preaching or singing to large audiences. With others, it is by less public and more small-scale, but equally needful, ways.

3. The gift of the Spirit will occasion a stepped-up establishment in God's redeeming grace. Pentecost meant such establishment for the various apostles who had all previously followed Christ from afar. According to Acts, vacillating persons such as Peter and John, after Pentecost and due to it, became valiant promoters of Christ's Church. It is to be noted also that when Paul powerfully rebuked "Elymas the sorcerer" and put a temporary blindness (Acts 13:8, 11) upon him, he was "filled with the Holy Spirit" (v. 9). And Paul tells believers in whose faith something needs to be made "perfect" (1 Thess. 3:10, KJV) or that he can "supply" (NIV, RSV) or "may complete" (NASB), according to v. 13: "so that He may establish your hearts unblamable in holiness before our God" (NASB).

4. The gift of the Spirit means that we are truly owned and approved by God. This gift is called a sealing (Eph. 1:13; 4:30; 1 Cor. 1:21-22), and sealing signified ownership or approval. The Romans sealed Christ's tomb to signify their ownership there. Seals are today put onto letters to signify ownership, and on diplomas and degrees to signify approval. And when we consecrate ourselves to God for His use, to receive entire sanctification (Rom. 12:1-2), that indicates that we are content with His ownership of us. And when He then, in response to our faith, sanctifies us wholly by the gift of the Spirit, He is able to approve our lives because Adamic depravity is then expelled.

5. The gift of the Holy Spirit also means that we become true-believer Christians, who belong to Christ without reservation. This is the happiness of a marriage partner who is not still looking around. It is the happiness of a person who is so completely settled in the matter of a career that he would pay for the privilege of going to the workplace. It is the happiness of a parent who has legally adopted a loved child. It is the happiness of an Olympic gold medalist who, in order to win, has sacrificed many lesser pleasures.

6. The gift of the Holy Spirit will mean that the fruit of the Spirit will be produced in one's life. Paul lists "the fruit of the Spirit" as "love, joy, peace, patience, kindness, goodness, faithfulness, gentleness and self-control" (Gal. 5:22-23). On its topmost branch, the tree bears love on it—a "you-first" attitude toward others expressed in word and deed. Next to it is joy, a below-the-surface pleasure in being doubly righted with God through forgiveness and Adamic-depravity expulsion. Peace as a fruit, in addition to the "peace of God" of justification (Rom. 5:1), results from the cessation of the corrupt Adamic hostility to God (see Rom. 8:7-8; Gal. 5:17; Eph. 2:3). Patience includes a willingness to accept God's time schedules, since one is now yielded to God totally. Kindness, goodness, faithfulness, gentleness, and self-control are also fruits of the gift of the Spirit, resulting from the kind of experience that this gift of the Spirit is: a cleansing from Adamic depravity and a pervasive indwelling of the Holy Spirit.

Preaching Ideas

A sermon could be preached from Acts 1:5 titled "Our Two Baptisms." The two are the kind John the Baptist administered, and the kind administered by Christ (see Matt. 3:11-12). The sermon could be structured around three points.

A. Both are cleansings. Titus 3:5 and Eph. 5:25-27 show that in regeneration there is a cleansing from acquired depravity, the tendency to sin that is built up by repeating various sins such as telling lies, stealing, adultery, whatever. Cleansing from inherited depravity occurs through the baptism with the Holy Spirit (Matt. 3:11-12; John 17:17; Acts 15:8-9).

B. Both are received instantaneously. This since the figure of baptism is used as related to both.

C. Both are prepared for. Repentance was and is prior to justifying faith (Luke 3:8; Acts 2:38). A waiting yieldedness is prior to sanctifying faith (Acts 1:4; 15:9; 26:18).

A sermon on "The Good News of Our Personal Pentecost" could be developed from Acts 1:4-5:

A. Who? The Father (Acts 1:4)

B. Where? In a group (1:4; 19:1-7), in a family setting (10:44), one-to-one (9:17)

C. When? After waiting yieldedly (1:4) and after exercising faith (15:9; 26:18)

D. How? Through the baptism with or the pervasive filling of the Holy Spirit (1:5; 2:4; Rom. 5:5)

E. Why? To empower (Acts 1:8) and to purify the heart (15:9)

A Sermon

Our Gift of the Holy Spirit

You and I have received gifts that have been most special. A doll or bicycle? A car at 16? A wedding ring? Such gifts are significant. Yet surely God's redemption gifts are the most significant of all gifts. How important is the gift of salvation, whereby we receive forgiveness of all our sins! Of comparable importance is the gift of the Holy Spirit. Today, let's center in especially on Acts 1:4-5 as we consider together "Our Gift of the Holy Spirit."

The word "gift" in the NIV of this passage, "the gift my Father promised," is not in the Greek. That is why it does not appear in the

NASB or in the RSV. Yet the Greek implies the word "gift" here. Besides, the Greek has a word for "gift" in Acts 2:38, where Peter speaks of "the gift of the Holy Spirit," referring also to Pentecost. And the Spirit baptism is called a "gift" in the Greek of Acts 11:17.

Christ's baptism with the Holy Spirit is indeed a gift, whether this is only implied, or stated, in the Greek NT. We do not simply do good works to receive it, and do not deserve it—as is so with justification, the first work of grace.

Let us study this passage of Scripture from the standpoint of (1) its promise, (2) its preparation, and (3) its purpose. First, then, think with me about *its promise.*

A. The Promise of the Spirit Baptism

1. Its Source. The source of this most special promise of the gift of the Holy Spirit is God the Father. That is what our text says: "the gift my Father promised" (Acts 1:4). In Joel the prophet, God the Father says: "I am the Lord your God" (2:27) and promises: "And afterward, I will pour out my Spirit on all people" (v. 28). This is clearly a promise by God the Father of the gift of the Spirit received at Pentecost. Peter at Pentecost declared the same to all and sundry. Addressing the curious "crowd," he said, "These men are not drunk . . . No, this is what was spoken by the prophet Joel: 'In the last days, God says, I will pour out my Spirit on all people'" (Acts 2:14-17). Notice that "God says" this. That's a pretty good source, isn't it, for such a gift?

2. Its Universality. Besides the Source of this promise (see Eph. 1:13), let us note its universality. This is a gift for everyone. It is for both men and women, young and old, preachers and lay ministers, free people and "servants." Thus we read in Joel: "Your sons and daughters will prophesy, your old men will dream dreams, your young men will see visions. Even on my servants, both men and women, I will pour out my Spirit in those days" (2:28-29).

And Peter at Pentecost quoted all this, about the inclusiveness of this gift of the Spirit (see Acts 2:17-18). At Pentecost itself, 120 believers received this outpoured gift. This included apostles, "along with the women and Mary the mother of Jesus, and with his brothers" (1:14). Luke tells us that there were "about a hundred and twenty" (v. 15).

That must be telling us that any of us in our time may receive this gift. Isn't that right? It seems to be for us short ones and tall ones, those of us who are wrinkled like raisins and those of us who look like grapes just picked. It is for all, as many as will prepare properly to receive the gift.

B. The Preparation for the Spirit Baptism

The 120 followers of Jesus needed to prepare for receiving the gift of the Holy Spirit, even as we need to do today. God was and is gracious to do what He has promised, but He does not pour out the Holy Spirit in baptismal fullness upon persons who are unprepared. It is for everyone, but we need to meet the conditions God sets for receiving this Spirit-baptism gift.

1. To Be Believers. It is a prerequisite for this gift that the recipients be believers. Of the Holy Spirit to be poured out at Pentecost, Jesus said, "I will ask the Father, and He will give you another Helper, . . . the Spirit of truth, whom the world cannot receive, . . . but . . . He abides with you, and will be in you" (John 14:16-17, NASB).

And Luke tells us that the "group numbering about a hundred and twenty" were 'believers" (Acts 1:15); and Peter addressed the group as "Brothers" (v. 16). Thus they had already repented of their sins and had become justified and regenerated. Of some of them it was already said, "They are not of the world, even as I [Jesus] am not of it" (John 17:16). The 120 believers were among the people who had already received eternal life (3:36). Mary of Magdala might have been one of "the women" (Acts 1:14), her life had certainly been transformed, and she had announced Christ's resurrection (John 20:17-18). Thomas is named as being among them (Acts 1:13), and he had already declared to the resurrected Christ, "My Lord and my God!" (John 20:28). The fields had "been already white for harvesting," and these and others had been harvested (4:35-39, Williams).

So one of the ways of being prepared to receive the gift of or the baptism with the Holy Spirit is to enjoy regenerating grace already.

2. To Wait Yieldedly. Another step in preparing to receive the gift of the Spirit is to wait for it yieldedly. To the "apostles" (Acts 1:2), while "eating with them," Jesus "gave . . . this command: 'Do not leave Jerusalem, but wait for the gift my Father promised, which you have heard me speak about. For John baptized with water, but in a few days you will be baptized with the Holy Spirit'" (vv. 4-5).

It was a "command," then, and the disciples had obediently stayed in Jerusalem and were waiting for what was promised. They "went upstairs," in Jerusalem, "to the room where they were staying" (Acts 1:13). This time of prayer and waiting was 10 days, since Pentecost fell 50 days after the Passover-time Crucifixion, and it was 40 days from the Resurrection when Christ told them to do this waiting. They were in prayer, and no doubt they yielded themselves up to God in consecration—as we do today, based on such passages as Rom. 6:13 and 12:1-2.

3. To Exercise Faith. The word "faith" does not appear in Luke's first account of Pentecost. Yet it does appear, in describing Pentecost, when Peter tells about the event. At the Council of Jerusalem, later, when Peter is discussing what happened at Pentecost and at Cornelius' house, he said: "God, who knows the heart, showed that he accepted them by giving the Holy Spirit to them, just as he did to us. He made no distinction between us and them, for he purified their hearts by faith" (Acts 15:8-9). Here it is, their preparation that included faith (see also 26:18).

Their preparation for their Pentecost, then, as for us also, included (1) to be believers, (2) to yield themselves obediently to God, and (3) to exercise the faith that procures the Gift.

But besides the *promise* of the gift of the Holy Spirit, here, and besides the *preparation* for it, let us consider the gift's *purpose*.

C. The Purpose of the Spirit Baptism

The purpose of the gift of the Holy Spirit is at least twofold: for purity and power.

1. Purity. One of the purposes of their Pentecost, then, and of ours, has to do with purity—that is, heart purity, heart cleansing.

We know that some kind of cleansing was involved because it was a "baptism" with the Holy Spirit, for baptism, whether with water or with the Spirit, symbolizes purification or cleansing or washing. John's baptism with water symbolized the cleansing, following repentance, of regeneration—the "laver" (ASV, margin) or the "washing" of regeneration spoken of in Titus 3:5. And Christ's baptism "with the Holy Spirit" (Matt. 3:11-12) also signifies cleansing. That is why John the Baptist said, "I baptize you with water for repentance. [This is the first work of grace.] But after me will come one who is more powerful than I . . . He will baptize you with the

Holy Spirit and with fire" (v. 11). It is to be noted that this baptism is to be "with fire." Sometimes in Scripture, as here, fire signifies both judgment and cleansing. This fire signifies cleansing and judgment because the next words read: "His winnowing fork is in his hand, and he will clear his threshing floor, gathering his wheat into the barn and burning up the chaff with unquenchable fire." Judgment, yet, with "unquenchable fire." The NASB says here that "He will thoroughly clear His threshing floor," gathering the wheat, those redeemed, but burning up the unredeemed, who refuse even John's baptism to repentance, "with unquenchable fire" in hell. But positively, and especially, it signified cleansing.

The cleansing of this baptism is also signified by the fact that the fire mentioned in Matt. 3:11 is referred to in its fulfillment at Pentecost when people "saw what seemed to be tongues of fire that separated and came to rest on each of them" (Acts 2:3). Also, when Peter later described that first Pentecost and the Pentecost of Cornelius, he said it "purified their hearts" (15:9). Moreover, the reference in Joel 2:28 to the Spirit's being poured out denotes purification. Also, as Ezekiel foretells Pentecost, cleansing is singled out. "I will put my Spirit in you," God says through the prophet (36:27). As He had already said, "I will sprinkle clean water on you, and you will be clean; I will cleanse you from all your impurities and from all your idols. I will give you a new heart and put a new spirit in you" (vv. 25-26)

Malachi seems to see this cleansing also. He speaks of a "messenger," John the Baptist, "who will prepare the way." Then "the Lord," Christ, "will come" (3:1). And he adds, "For he will be like a refiner's fire or a launderer's soap. He will sit as a refiner and purifier of silver" (3:2-3). This no doubt refers to the cleansing of initial sanctification at regeneration and also the cleansing through Christ's baptism with the Holy Spirit.

And John 7 refers to this Pentecostal cleansing. There Jesus says, "Whoever believes in me, . . . streams of living water will flow from within him" (John 7:38). Then John comments, "By this he meant the Spirit, whom those who believed in him were later to receive. Up to that time the Spirit had not been given" (v. 39). It is to be noted that only "those who" had already "believed" could receive the Spirit in the way He would be poured out at Pentecost. And it is to be noted that receiving the Spirit would constitute a cleansing, for "living water" would "flow from within" such a person.

Cleansing from sin, heart purity, is also indicated from John 17:17. There Jesus prays for persons who had already believed in Him, "Sanctify them by the truth; your word is truth." As Asa Mahan and many other holiness writers have said, "sanctify," here, cannot mean "set apart for God's use" as it often does, because the Twelve had already been set aside for ministry. The other meaning, to cleanse, to purify from sin, seems to have been meant by Jesus. Assuming that the prayer was answered at Pentecost, the apostles would have been sanctified in this sense at that time.

2. Power. Besides purity, a second important purpose of the gift of the Holy Spirit is to give empowerment. "But you will receive power," the departing Jesus said, "when the Holy Spirit comes on you; and you will be my witnesses" (Acts 1:8). This power is somewhat for living the holy life, for now the Holy Spirit indwells a person pervasively, for one help after another. Contextually, though, the power is for witnessing. And the remainder of Acts shows that indeed such power was given. Peter and John had it, as did Philip and Stephen, and Paul and others.

The gift of the Holy Spirit has been received already by many of us. For us, this study has perhaps helped to give us further joy in better understanding our faith. For those believers here who have not as yet received this gift, please realize that you may. It is a sure promise of God the Father. It needs to be prepared for. And it has the important purpose of both purity and power.

Endnote

1. See this treated in the chapter "The Nomenclature of Wesleyanism," in J. Kenneth Grider, *Entire Sanctification: The Distinctive Doctrine of Wesleyanism* (Kansas City: Beacon Hill Press of Kansas City, 1980).